The Epicenter of Crisis

A Washington Quarterly Reader

The Epicenter of Crisis

The New Middle East

Edited by

Alexander T. J. Lennon

The contents of this book were first published in *The Washington Quarterly* (ISSN 0163-660X), a publication of The MIT Press under the sponsorship of The Center for Strategic and International Studies (CSIS).

Rachel Bronson, "Rethinking Religion: The Legacy of the U.S.-Saudi Relationship," *TWQ* 28, no. 4 (Autumn 2005); John R. Bradley, "Al Qaeda and the House of Saud: Eternal Enemies or Secret Bedfellows?" *TWQ* 28, no. 4 (Autumn 2005); Gwenn Okruhlik, "The Irony of *Islah* (Reform)," *TWQ* 28, no. 4 (Autumn 2005); Eyal Zisser, "Bashar Al-Assad: In or Out of the New World Order?" *TWQ* 28, no. 3 (Summer 2005); Dennis Ross, "U.S. Policy toward a Weak Assad," *TWQ* 28, no. 3 (Summer 2005); Daniel Byman, "Confronting Syrian-Backed Terrorism," *TWQ* 28, no. 3 (Summer 2005); Emile el-Hokayem, "Hizballah and Syria: Outgrowing the Proxy Relationship," *TWQ* 30, no. 2 (Spring 2007); Carlos Pascual and Kenneth M. Pollack, "The Critical Battles: Political Reconciliation and Reconstruction in Iraq," *TWQ* 30, no. 3 (Summer 2007); Michael O'Hanlon and Nina Kamp, "Is the Media Being Fair in Iraq?" *TWQ* 29, no. 4 (Autumn 2006); Brian Fishman, "After Zarqawi: The Dilemmas and Future of Al Qaeda in Iraq," *TWQ* 29, no. 4 (Autumn 2006); Michael McFaul, Abbas Milani and Larry Diamond, "A Win-Win U.S. Strategy for Dealing with Iran," *TWQ* 30, no. 1 (Winter 2007); Graham E. Fuller, "The Hizballah-Iran Connection: Model for Sunni Resistance," *TWQ* 30, no. 1 (Winter 2007); Elliot Hen-Tov, "Understanding Iran's New Authoritarianism," *TWQ* 30, no. 1 (Winter 2007); Karim Sadjadpour, "How Relevant Is the Iranian Street?" *TWQ* 30, no. 1 (Winter 2007); Peter van Ham and Jorritt Kamminga, "Poppies for Peace: Reforming Afghanistan's Opium Industry," *TWQ* 30, no. 1 (Winter 2007); Vanda Felbab-Brown, "Afghanistan: When Counternarcotics Undermines Counterterrorism," *TWQ* 28, no. 4 (Autumn 2005); Craig Cohen and Derek Chollet, "When $10 Billion Is Not Enough: Rethinking U.S. Strategy toward Pakistan," *TWQ* 30, no. 2 (Spring 2007); Ashley Tellis, "U.S. Strategy: Assisting Pakistan's Transformation," *TWQ* 28, no. 1 (Winter 2005); C. Raja Mohan, "What If Pakistan Fails? India Isn't Worried ... Yet," *TWQ* 28, no. 1 (Winter 2005); Husain Haqqani, "The Role of Islam in Pakistan's Future," *TWQ* 28, no. 1 (Winter 2005).

Library of Congress Cataloging-in-Publication Data

The epicenter of crisis : the new Middle East / edited by Alexander T.J. Lennon.
p. cm. — (A Washington quarterly reader)
Text first published in the Washington quarterly.
Includes bibliographical references.
ISBN 978-0-262-62216-5 (pbk. : alk. paper)
1. Middle East—Politics and government—21st century. 2. Islam and Politics—Middle East. I. Lennon, Alexander T. II. Washington quarterly.

JQ1758.A58E65 2008
956.05'4—dc22

10 9 8 7 6 5 4 3 2 1

CONTENTS

tential radical changes in Pakistani state and society, even though few decisionmakers in New Delhi are convinced that Pakistani state failure is imminent. Finally, addressing the future of the Pakistani state itself, Husain Haqqani warns that unless Islamabad's objectives are redefined to focus on economic prosperity and popular participation in governance, the state will continue to turn to Islam as a national unifier and Pakistan will remain a major center of radical Islamist ideas and groups.

By gathering detailed examinations of these six countries, *The Epicenter of Crisis* seeks to put some of the challenges of the Middle East in a slightly untraditional geographic context. While extending the reader's vision eastward, this volume addresses the changing role of Islam and the risks of ethnic conflict, civil war, failed states, rogue states, proliferation and terrorism. Taken together, the goal of these chapters is to stimulate you, as a reader, to learn from the authors' insights, challenge their thoughts, and most importantly, continue the debates to reshape your own ideas as well as the ideas of others about arguably the most dynamic and dangerous region in the world today.

Alexander T. J. Lennon

Introduction: The Epicenter of Crisis

European analysts, among others, refer to a global "arc of crisis" stretching from the Balkans through the Middle East into Southeast Asia. This global cauldron of potential ethnic conflict, civil war, failed states, rogue states, proliferation, and terrorism contains many of the security challenges that accelerated globalization presents today.

Traditionally, analysts envision the center of this arc, the Middle East region, as the area from Turkey south to Yemen and from Egypt east to Iran. Yet this vision excludes the countries on Iran's eastern border: Afghanistan and Pakistan, the two states most fundamentally transformed, along with the United States itself, by the September 11 attacks. Refocus your vision slightly to the east and six contiguous states—Saudi Arabia, Syria, Iraq, Iran, Afghanistan, and Pakistan—form what might be called the epicenter of the arc of crisis, where Islam and the way it influences the world has been most dramatically changing since al Qaeda's September 11 attacks.

The Epicenter of Crisis: the New Middle East challenges readers to reconceptualize the boundaries of the Middle East, and the changing role Islam is playing in arguably the most geopolitically dynamic and challenging part of the world. Although any definition of the Middle East and its security challenges certainly includes Israel and its relations with its neighbors, this book focuses on these other six critical states—the

Alexander T. J. Lennon is editor-in-chief of the *Washington Quarterly* and a research fellow in international security policy at the Center for Strategic and International Studies (CSIS). He is also an adjunct professor in security studies at Georgetown University.

epicenter of crisis—to better understand the way they are changing, and the evolving threats of state failure, rogue states, proliferation and terrorism so prominent since September 11.

Saudi Arabia, the westernmost of the six states, is home to Mecca, the birthplace of Muhammad and the holiest city in Islam, as well as the Wahhabi branch of Sunni Islam and 15 of the 19 September 11 hijackers. Rachel Bronson, author of the book *Thicker Than Oil: The United States and Saudi Arabia—A History*, explains that although Saudi Arabia's religiosity was historically an asset to the United States, it has since become a political liability and must be addressed as part of a strategic reformulation of the bilateral relationship. John R. Bradley, reporter and author of *Saudi Arabia Exposed: Inside a Kingdom in Crisis*, then examines the contemporary relationship between the al-Saud regime and al Qaeda, concluding that the regime is both part of the problem and indispensable to any solution to terrorism. Finally, in the irony of *Islah*, or reform, Gwenn Okruhlik argues that the regime has implemented meaningful social reforms but has carefully choreographed political reforms by capitalizing on the fear of jihad and al Qaeda to consolidate the ruling family's centrality.

To the north, Syria, ruled by Bashar al-Assad, is also under continuing international pressure to reform after the war in Iraq and ongoing changes in Lebanon, according to Tel Aviv University professor Ayal Zisser. What does that mean for U.S. policy? Former U.S. Special Middle East Coordinator Dennis Ross advises that Washington should not launch a major new policy initiative toward Damascus, but should focus on Lebanon and engage Syria's neighbors to deal with the possible consequences of Syrian instability. Daniel Byman, director of Georgetown's security studies program and author of the book *Deadly Connections: States that Sponsor Terrorism*, prescribes continued pressure through U.S. leadership and multilateral, particularly Arab, action to help push the Syrian regime to reduce its support for terrorism. In the chapter, he contends that Syria has aided a daunting array of terrorist groups over the years, but it seldom has been an ardent supporter and is therefore able to be influenced by continuing pressure. The final chapter of this part takes an in-depth look at Hizballah, the terrorist organization most commonly associated with Syria. According to the Stimson Center's Emile el-Hokayem, Hizballah has actually gained leverage over Syria and greater independence from its former patron, reducing Damascus' ability to control the organization.

To Syria's eastern border, the threats presented by Iraq have, of course, been transformed from those of a rogue state under Saddam Hussein to a potential failed state today. The Brookings Institution's Carlos Pascual and Kenneth M. Pollack outline a U.S. reconstruction and reconciliation strategy to try to achieve a sustainable peace and set in motion processes to begin to rebuild Iraq's capacities for self-governance and economic regulation, the essential components for stability. Michael O'Hanlon and Nina Kamp then address the charge that the U.S. media has been exaggerating the bad news and chaos out of Iraq. They use original data to systematically assess individual outlets and the media overall, concluding that broad criticism of the U.S. media is often badly overstated. Finally, Brian Fishman, an associate in the Combating Terrorism Center and an instructor from the Military Academy at West Point, assesses the terrorist threat from the group "al Qaeda in Iraq" by assessing its internal security dilemmas, external penetration, and the lingering doctrinal impasse with al Qaeda proper after Abu Musab al-Zarqawi's death.

With the threats from Iraq fundamentally transformed, Iran is now viewed as the principal rogue state threat from the Middle East. Stanford's Michael McFaul, Abbas Milani, and Larry Diamond prescribe a bold and fundamentally different "win-win" U.S. strategy to simultaneously engage the Iranian regime and people on two tracks, enabling U.S. diplomats to pursue arms control and democratization at the same time. Former vice chair of the National Intelligence Council and author of *The Future of Political Islam*, Graham Fuller, then delves into the terrorism threat by taking issue with those who believe Iran has been responsible for the growing power of Hizballah as part of the rise of the "Shi'a axis." Rather, he concludes that Hizballah's rise actually reflects a broader intensification of resistance to the status quo throughout the region which Iran seeks to capitalize upon. The final two chapters of this section look inside Iran. Princeton's Elliot Hen-Tov argues that a new generation in Tehran, strengthened by the surprising stability of its political economy, is beginning to shift from the existing clerical theocracy toward a more conventional authoritarian regime. Karim Sadjadpour concludes by assessing evidence about popular discontent among the Iranian public, distinguishing the currently deep seated and widespread support for political, economic, and social reform from popular attention to foreign policy.

Whereas most volumes on the Middle East stop there, this one extends to Iran's eastern neighbors: Afghanistan and Pakistan. Both countries have been transformed after the September 11 attacks; shape the external environment within which the rest of the Middle East, particularly Iran, operate; and face many of the same challenges from radical interpretations of Islam as well as the risks of state failure, ethnic strife, proliferation and terrorism. In Afghanistan, the drug trade remains an intractable problem for development and reconstruction of the country while simultaneously providing a source of revenue for terrorist operations. Peter van Ham and Jorritt Kamminga propose that the international community establish a pilot project and investigate a licensing scheme to legalize the production of medicines such as morphine and codeine from poppy crops to help prevent Afghanistan from further descending into chaos. Vanda Felbab-Brown also argues that traditional counternarcotics efforts frequently paradoxically complicate counterterrorism and counterinsurgency and can even undermine democratization efforts. Instead, she argues that counternarcotics strategy should be transformed to concentrate on strengthening the Afghan state's capacity.

Concluding in Pakistan, Craig Cohen and Derek Chollet contend that the United States needs to rethink its strategy as its post-9/11 engagement with Islamabad is highly militarized and centralized, with very little assistance reaching the vast majority of Pakistanis. Staying on U.S. policy, Ashley Tellis advocates that Washington should concentrate its assistance on safeguarding Pakistan's nuclear estate and restoring democracy as part of a grand bargain with Islamabad. Although India historically has been bitter adversaries with Pakistan, Indian strategic thinker and author C. Raja Mohan recommends that New Delhi should consider five elements for a contingency strategy to account for po-

Part I:
Saudi Arabia

Rachel Bronson

Rethinking Religion: The Legacy of the U.S.-Saudi Relationship

At a January 2005 counterterrorism conference in Riyadh, Frances Fragos Townsend, assistant to the president and homeland security adviser, stressed that "the world cannot defeat terrorism without Saudi Arabia defeating terrorism on its own grounds."[1] Saudi Arabia's brand of religion, Wahhabi Islam, and its reputation for intense proselytizing have landed it in the global hot seat. Home to 15 of the 19 hijackers in the September 11 attacks, a disproportionate number of Arab fighters cycling through Al Qaeda training camps during the 1990s, and Osama bin Laden himself, the kingdom has become a central focus in the war on terrorism.[2]

Saudi Arabia's religiosity, which the White House once considered an asset, has become a political liability. For nearly a half-century, the kingdom's religious fervor kept the oil-rich country in the U.S. political camp, helped inoculate future generations against Communist expansion, and aided U.S. causes from Central America to Central Asia. As early as 1954, historian Bernard Lewis wrote that "pious Muslims—and most Muslims are pious—will not long tolerate an atheist creed."[3] True to these words, Saudi Arabia stood steadfastly against the spread of communism and was a useful Cold War partner to the United States. Yet,

Rachel Bronson is a senior fellow and director of Middle East studies at the Council on Foreign Relations. She is the author of *Thicker Than Oil: The United States and Saudi Arabia—A History* (Oxford University Press, forthcoming winter 2006).

The Washington Quarterly • 28:4 pp. 121–137.

when the Berlin Wall came down and the Soviet Union collapsed, Saudi Arabia's policies did not change. In this new global political order, the religious zealots spawned by Saudi funding and U.S. complicity turned their wrath from Moscow toward Washington, Riyadh, and other capitals. The existence of radical Islamic groups is in part a legacy of political decisions made in another era to address a different set of security concerns.

The role of religion in the U.S.-Saudi relationship has to date garnered far too little attention. Although oil and security remain enduring features, the utility of Saudi religious proselytizing has changed dramatically, and the United States has grown increasingly wary of how Saudi Arabia uses its religious power in international politics. In the past, Saudi leaders did not have to choose between religious and political ends, yet since the September 11 attacks, the international spotlight has focused on Saudi Arabia's willingness and ability to rein in Islamic extremism, both at home and abroad. Funding radical religious inculcation no longer serves U.S. or global interests. The Saudi leadership must now determine whether such activities still serve its own.

The Rise of Religious Extremism

The basic political bargain that underpins Saudi Arabia's current power structure was made in 1744, in a small town outside Riyadh. Muhammad ibn Abd al-Wahhab, then an itinerant religious scholar preaching an austere form of Islam, agreed to provide religious legitimacy to a local potentate, Muhammad ibn Saud, the patriarch of today's Saudi royal family. Drawing on this history, many conclude that hostile religious proselytizing is endemic to the Saudi state, making change and reform unlikely if not impossible.

The determinism of this political/religious bargain, however, can be overstated. Although it is true that all Saudi kings have paid deference to the religious establishment and relied heavily on the *ulema* (the guardians of legal and scholarly traditions) to legitimize controversial decisions, over time Saudi leaders have calibrated their religious message according to the circumstances at hand. Whereas the first Saudi state (1745–1818) fell because unrestrained religious fighters antagonized the Ottoman Empire, the leaders of the second Saudi state (1843–1891) restrained their religious warriors to avoid their predecessor's fate. In the early 1900s, during the formation of the third Saudi state, Saudi Arabia's founder, King Abdel Aziz bin Abdel Rahman al-Faisal al-Saud (ibn Saud), organized and encouraged religious fighters to settle the population and provide foot soldiers for territorial aggrandizement. Known as *ikhwahn*, these fighters emerged as an important force to conquer Mecca and Medina, in particular. By 1929, however, Aziz destroyed his religious fighting force after it had served its original purpose and was no longer politically useful.

During the Cold War, Saudi Arabia, whose leaders wielded considerable international religious influence because of their ability to speak for Mecca and Medina, became a useful U.S. partner. Realizing that religion could be a tool to staunch the expansion of godless communism, U.S. policymakers sought to partner with religious believers. As far back as the 1950s, the Eisenhower administration had hoped to make King Saud (1953–1964) into a globally recognized Islamic leader and transform him into "the senior partner of the Arab team."[4] Later, Saudi Arabia's value was augmented by its oil wealth, which provided ample resources to fund anti-Soviet operations. Yet, such funding was often accompanied by religious proselytizing.

The Soviet Union supported revolutionary Arab nationalists to undercut Washington's more conservative partners, such as Saudi Arabia; Jordan; and, after 1973, Egypt. In response, the United States tacitly supported the politicization of Islam and those states and domestic groups that rejected godless communism, even though they did not and were never expected to embrace liberal democracy. This U.S. policy coincided with the Saudi royal family's desire to align religious and political interests in the kingdom. From the mid-1950s until 1967, for example, Saudi Arabia was engaged in a bitter conflict with Soviet-backed Egypt. King Saud welcomed members of the Muslim Brotherhood (a grassroots Islamist organization) to Saudi Arabia as a way to challenge Egypt, from which the Brotherhood was fleeing.

Similarly, Crown Prince Faisal, who became king and ruled from 1964 to 1975, was a determined anti-Communist. He created a host of domestic and international Islamic institutions that had both political and religious purposes. Faisal helped establish the Islamic University of Medina in 1961 to spread Saudi-inspired Wahhabi Islam and, more instrumentally, to compete ideologically with Cairo's prestigious al-Azhar University. The Islamic University eventually became a well-known recruiting ground for jihadi fighters. In 1962, Faisal helped found the Muslim World League, a worldwide charity to which the Saudi royal family has reportedly since donated more than a billion dollars.[5] In December 1965, Faisal embarked on a nine-nation tour through Muslim countries to establish "Islamic solidarity" and check Gamal Abdul Nasser's continued regional appeal.

In 1967, after Saudi Arabia triumphed over Egypt at the Khartoum summit, which put an end to the Egyptian-Saudi proxy war in Yemen and left Egypt dependent on Saudi aid, Faisal did not disband these Islamic institutions or halt the creation of more. Unlike his successor, however, Faisal worked to ensure that the most radical clerics did not assume society's most powerful religious posts. He tried to block extremist clerics from gaining dominion over key religious institutions, such as the Council of Senior Ulema, the kingdom's highest religious body, and from rising to high religious positions such as grand mufti, a politically recognized senior expert charged with maintaining the whole system of Islamic law.[6] Still, at least some of the king's advisers warned early on that, once religious zealots were encouraged, they would come back to haunt the kingdom.[7] Faisal, who was assassinated in 1975, was ultimately unable to control the future direction of the institutions he created. These Saudi-based institutions became increasingly radicalized over the 1980s and 1990s.

In response to the dramatic events of 1979—the Iranian revolution, religious extremists' seizure of the Grand Mosque of Mecca, and the Soviet invasion of Afghanistan—King Khaled, who reigned from 1975 to 1982, and Crown Prince Fahd, who ruled the kingdom from 1982 to 2005, allowed the unconstrained radicalization of Saudi Arabia's elaborate religious machinery. For two decades, it produced severe anti-Soviet and ultimately anti-U.S., anti-Zionist, and anti-regime opponents who were willing to die for their beliefs. Harsh laws were imposed on women, and the king appeared in public with the most rabid preachers. One astute Saudi political observer recalls that, after 1979, "society was given an overdose of religion."[8]

In the decade that followed, the confluence of U.S.-Saudi anti-Communist interests was most obvious in Afghanistan. The United States and Saudi Arabia each spent no less then $3 billion, channeling assistance to armed, anti-U.S. Islamic fundamentalists. Their shared vitriol for communism spawned proselytizing that stretched from Somalia to Sudan, Chad, Pakistan, and beyond—the same areas where today the Islamist threat is particularly vexing.

Saudi Arabia after 9/11

In the tradition of their predecessors, some members of Saudi Arabia's royal family have sought to subordinate the religious establishment since the September 11 attacks. Shortly after the attacks on New York and Washington, Turki al-Faisal, King Faisal's son and the retired longtime director of Saudi Arabia's General Intelligence Department and recently appointed ambassador to the United States, directly challenged Sheikh Abdullah al-Turki, secretary general of the World Muslim League and a member of the Council of Senior Ulema. In a widely read newspaper article, the prince argued that "those responsible for affairs of state are the rulers," whereas religious scholars "only act in an advisory capacity."[9] Prince Talal bin Abdel Aziz, the king's half-brother, similarly challenged the "potentially very confusing" claim that rulers and religious scholars should jointly decide affairs of state.[10] In June 2004, in a well-publicized op-ed piece published in the Saudi newspaper *Al-Watan*, Saudi Arabia's then-ambassador to the United States, Prince Bandar bin Sultan, argued in Arabic that religious fighters operating inside the kingdom should be "vanquished" the way "King Abdul Aziz did at the Battle of Al-Sabla [in 1929]."[11] At least some elements of the royal family clearly are deeply engaged in the running ideological battle and are making some headway against religious extremism.

Reining In Religious Extremism

Today's political landscape provides some reason to be optimistic about the royal family's ability to stem the radical religious tide. May 2003 marked a turning point in Saudi Arabia's willingness to confront the worst excesses of religious radicalism directly and fight Al Qaeda and *takfireen* (those willing to define other Muslims as apostates). On May 12, 2003, homegrown suicide bombers simultaneously attacked three housing complexes in Riyadh. The Saudi leadership defined the attacks as a "wake-up call" and "our September 11" and began to take political, security, and economic action against local terrorists and their support base.[12]

In June 2003, then–Crown Prince Abdullah instituted an important "national dialogue," a broad-based series that has given Saudis a forum to engage on highly sensitive topics such as intolerance, the role of women, and socioeconomic challenges. It emboldened moderates within society who now use the sessions' findings to build their case for reform, including most recently a renewed push in support of a women's right to drive automobiles. Today, newspapers are increasingly able to publish articles that question fundamental religious principles. As several Saudi journalists and diplomats have recently pointed out, for the first time in recent history, Saudis can examine the works of ibn Taymiyya, a central figure in Saudi religious thought who emphasized a literalist interpretation of the Koran and supported the practice of declaring other Muslims as apostates.[13] Although this progress is not without its obstacles—one daring journalist recently reported that three of his articles on ibn Taymiyya were rejected, non-Muslims continue to be rounded up for privately practicing their religion, and the imprisonment of three human rights activists has dampened enthusiasm for reform—the evolving openness does appear designed to address some of society's grievances and to question the most radical interpretation of Islam.

From the spring of 2003 until today, a steady stream of reports describe Saudi security forces' efforts to hunt down militants, disband Al Qaeda cells, and seize weapons caches. By late summer of 2004, the forces had successfully foiled a number of potential attacks, rounded up hundreds of suspects, and killed dozens of militants. By the spring of 2005, Saudi forces had either killed or incarcerated 24 out of 26 individuals on the kingdom's most wanted list and issued a new list of 36 men. Radical clerics were warned to tone down their fiery sermons; more than 2,000 of them were either banned from preaching or underwent "reeducation" programs. After the May 2003 attacks, the Saudi government also became more serious about reducing the flow of funds feathering the bank accounts of known terrorists. In July 2004, the Financial Action Task Force, an Organization for Economic Cooperation and Development group devoted to combating money laundering and terrorist financing, judged that the kingdom was "compliant or largely compliant" with international standards in almost every indicator of effectiveness.[14] Although the report also identified three areas in which Saudi Arabia was not in compliance with established standards, progress has clearly been made.[15]

Over a two-year period, Saudi officials shut down the al-Haramain Islamic Foundation, the Riyadh-based charity responsible for disbursing $40–50 million annually with ties to Al Qaeda's funding stream, although recent reports suggest that some of its offices may still be operational or operating under a different name.[16] The Saudi government implemented a series of laws making it much more difficult for its citizens to move money internationally, putting charities under the watchful eye of state regulators and eliminating the practice of placing charitable collection boxes in malls and other places in order to increase accountability. Abdullah urged Saudis to keep charitable support within their communities. Accordingly, Saudi citizens are now contributing more money to local causes than to those further afield. In 2004, Saudi domestic giving increased by approximately 300 percent as charitable monies were redirected home from foreign countries.[17] This shift necessarily reduces the financial flows to terrorists and radical extremists abroad.

The royal family appears committed to crushing Al Qaeda elements operating from its territory. Saudi Arabia's determination to diffuse the spiritual context that nurtures radical and violent groups, however, has been more difficult to assess, especially as a new generation of Islamic leaders increasingly vie for power and influence. Yet, how the House of Saud resists and co-opts its religious opposition, as well as how it manages the kingdom's growing socioeconomic problems and imminent political transitions, will in large part determine Saudi Arabia's direction in the future.

A New Generation of Radical Clerics

Although Saudi Arabia appears to have turned a corner in its fight against violent jihadis, it was much easier to galvanize Saudi religious leaders for the battle against communism than it is against radical Islam, which is less powerful but more difficult politically to combat. The legitimacy of the Saudi regime has always been based in part on the country's religiosity, which the royal family has used purposefully to secure geopolitical ends. Even if the royal family is inspired to check religious extremism, undoing the decades of political patronage that served yesterday's global realities will be an extremely difficult and dangerous task. It is hard to imagine fiery imams conferring their support on a government policy that targets Islamic extremists with the same conviction that moved them to support their government's anti-Communist policies during the 1980s.

Moreover, the regime has become entangled in a delicate and dangerous dance with a group of non-establishment ulema, often referred to as the *sahwa*, or "awakening clerics."[18] Led by men such as Safer al-Hawali and Salman al-Awda, this new generation of Islamic leaders came of age during the late 1970s and 1980s, when Saudi Arabia was reaping the first benefits of its dizzying oil wealth and calls for jihad permeated society. These clerics became highly visible in 1990 when they ardently protested the king's decision and ulema's fatwa to allow the United States and other non-Muslim governments to defend the kingdom and eject Iraqi forces from Kuwait. These young, intense men, many of whom spent the 1990s in and out of prison, represent a generational shift in Saudi Arabia's religious hierarchy. Their preachings inspired bin Laden and his followers. The sahwa, who are vehemently opposed to the United States, relentlessly criticize the traditional ulema's fawning passivity and call for greater influence over all aspects of Saudi society, including foreign policy.

Since Abdullah released them from prison in 1999 as a goodwill gesture, the sahwa have mellowed somewhat. For the most part, they seem more intent on working with, rather than undermining, the Saudi government. Some clerics have even tried to help the ruling family identify and capture Saudi Arabia's hard-core dissidents in return for limited amnesty.

Others have participated in reconciliation efforts between the Sunnis and Shi'a. In May 2003, the sahwa denounced the bombings inside the kingdom and publicly questioned the religious justification claimed by those who had carried out the attacks.

Still, the sahwa are virulently opposed to the United States and continue to provide succor to radical elements of society.[19] In November 2004, prominent sahwa members signed an open letter to the Iraqi people, urging a jihad against the United States. In a public scandal, Salman al-Awda's son was intercepted on his way to Iraq, following what he reportedly believed to be his father's exhortations to fight. The royal family faces difficult choices when confronting the sahwa. Working with these popular clerics offers some benefits, and by slowly engaging them, the government can point to real gains in co-opting and controlling their message. Nevertheless, the sahwa's anti-Americanism and the toxic environment they have helped to create is profoundly troubling. The growing number of Saudis going to Iraq—some 2,500, according to one Saudi researcher[20]—is a disturbing indication that the context inside the kingdom has not changed as much as many had hoped. This poses challenges to the futures of the United States and Saudi Arabia, as battle-hardened radicals return home trained in the latest urban warfare techniques. Clearly, the Saudi leadership still has a way to go to undo the radicalism that was encouraged over the last decades.

Recommendations for U.S. Policy

The question remains, can the United States actually do anything to help interested Saudi government members reduce the influence of the radical extremists? After the September 11 attacks, President George W. Bush defined the transformation of the Middle East as one of his administration's foremost foreign policy priorities. He concluded from the attacks that "decades of excusing and accommodating tyranny, in the pursuit of stability, have only led to injustice and instability and tragedy."[21] The attention that high-level U.S. officials are giving to reform is a welcome departure from traditional practices of engaging Middle Eastern governments and only focusing on external security challenges. If not pursued deftly, however, increased attention from the U.S. government runs the risk of steamrolling local reform efforts and undermining the very people and projects Washington hopes to promote. For the last half of the twentieth century, the United States was willing not only to coexist with tyranny, as Bush suggested, but to overlook the politicization of religion. U.S. policies that help encourage opportunities outside or alongside religious pursuits would be a useful palliative to yesterday's complacent policies.

Certainly, some immediate joint counterterrorism efforts need bilateral attention, particularly those that seek to end terrorist financing. Having largely succeeded in shutting down illicit wire transfers of money, Saudi leaders must now turn equally aggressive attention to cash couriers who move easily throughout the kingdom. This task will be difficult in a country with a deeply ingrained cash culture. Saudi Arabia has recognized this problem but has been slow to address it. Nevertheless, as part of a long-term approach to depoliticizing religious extremism in Saudi Arabia, Washington should develop a comprehensive social, economic, and political reform strategy that supports local efforts.

Social Reform

The United States should make a commitment to assist in the development of human capital in Saudi Arabia and, more broadly, in the region. Higher oil prices will not solve all or even most of Saudi Arabia's looming social problems. Saudi Arabia has one of the world's fastest-growing populations, and nearly 40 percent is below the age of 15.[22] Similar to many of its neighbors, the kingdom has a young population and suffers from an exceedingly high rate of unemployment. Between 15 and 30 percent of Saudi men and approximately 95 percent of women are jobless.

The kingdom is in desperate need of technical training and educational reform to provide employment for its growing population as well as opportunities outside the religious realm. Unfortunately, between 1993 and 2003 the number of U.S. Department of State–sponsored exchange programs, which help top students acquire necessary skills, fell by 21 percent in Saudi Arabia, Egypt, and Yemen.[23] A recent survey found that 29 percent of U.S. colleges and universities polled registered a decrease in Saudi student enrollment.[24] After the September 11 attacks, Saudi student visa applications fell 80 percent and have yet to recover.[25] The dramatic decrease in the number of Saudi students studying in the United States over the last few years follows a general decline in Saudi students studying abroad since the 1980s. According to the *Statistical Yearbooks of Saudi Arabia*, the number of Saudis studying abroad reached a peak of more than 12,500 in the mid-1980s but then dropped to 3,554 in 1990 and to only slightly more than 3,400 in 1996.[26] Over time, the Saudi government has offered less funding for its students to travel abroad. This reduction is partly the result of the Saudi government's desire to promote its own local universities but also of a lack of available resources.

Today, with oil revenues once again increasing, renewed attention should be paid to promoting educational and cultural exchanges between the United States and Saudi Arabia. To facilitate these exchanges, the U.S. government needs to streamline visa and entry procedures. Bush administration officials deserve credit for fixing a number of the problems that originally stalled many visa applications after the September 11 attacks.[27] Providing more opportunities for young Saudis to pursue outside or alongside religious study is one way to slowly "drain the swamps" of terrorism. Still, there are far too many stories of reformers and moderates who opt not to come to the United States because of the difficulties and harassment that others have experienced.

Bush and Abdullah made significant headway in addressing such issues during their spring 2005 meeting in Crawford, Texas. In a joint statement, the two leaders announced a commitment to increase the number of Saudi students studying in the United States, expand military exchange programs that provide education to Saudi officers, and facilitate travel to the kingdom by U.S. citizens. In addition to making such proposals a reality, Saudi leaders must now also commit to real educational reform inside the kingdom. This is important not only to the United States but also to Saudi Arabia's future.

A good model for U.S. assistance to the long-term development of human capital in Saudi Arabia is a small ($100,000) U.S. Agency for International Development grant to Effat College, a relatively new Saudi women's college based in Jeddah, which will enter into a partnership with

Duke University to establish an engineering program and provide desirable employment skills for new graduates. The Bush administration deserves considerable credit for this initiative, a public diplomacy coup that is reaping dividends far beyond its cost. Until recently, it was almost impossible to get U.S. foreign aid into the kingdom, an oil-rich country that few understandably believed worthy of aid. Yet, if the United States does not support its potential friends, it is now clear that few others will. Committing to broadening human capital will help wean some away from radical religious pursuit and, just as importantly, is a cause many moderates and reformers actively support.

Economic Reform

Given its rapidly increasing population and the fact that, when controlled for inflation, oil prices are nowhere near as high as they were in the late 1970s, Saudi Arabia's oil money does not go as far as it once did. The kingdom's per capita revenue from oil exports during the early 1980s was $22,174. In January 2005, with oil prices hovering around $50 per barrel, that figure settled at a mere $4,511.[28]

In 2000, Condoleezza Rice wrote on a related topic that, "although some argue that the way to support human rights is to refuse trade with China, this punishes precisely those who are most likely to change the system. ... [T]rade in general can open up the Chinese economy and, ultimately, its politics too."[29] The same logic applies to Saudi Arabia's entry into the World Trade Organization (WTO), which would benefit those within the kingdom who promote transparency and accountability. Joining the WTO would also provide cover for Abdullah, allowing him to make some very difficult and potentially explosive decisions at home, such as restricting corrupt practices among royal princes.

After a slow start, Washington has been more active in engaging Saudi Arabia on WTO accession since September 11, 2001. Over the last few years, Saudi Arabia has also become more serious about the process, changing the composition of its negotiating team and working to meet imposed membership requirements. By making the high-level political commitment to Saudi Arabia's entry, Washington and

Riyadh can overcome the remaining obstacles. The United States will need to prioritize its economic concerns and demonstrate some leniency. Because Saudi Arabia's membership in the WTO will support the kingdom's more Western-oriented business elite and reformers attempting to introduce controversial policies, such prioritization and leniency are well worth the potential costs. A congressional petition circulated in May 2005 calling Saudi Arabia's WTO accession "premature" is shortsighted.[30]

Economic reform will help absorb the waves of young Saudis entering the market. Increased transparency and accountability will also reduce existing corruption, a chief complaint among the population and the regime's opposition. It will also expand Saudi Arabia's business class, which has a direct stake in economic stability and domestic security.

Political Reform and Domestic Challenges

Washington should continue to pressure Riyadh to gradually open its domestic political arena to ensure that violence is not the only available form of political expression. In particular, the harsh sentencing in May 2005 of three nonviolent political activists—Ali al-Domaini, Matruk al-Falih, and Abdullah al-Hamid—has cast a pall over local reform efforts and should draw high-level attention from the United States. They, along with 10 others, were arrested in March 2004 for circulating a petition advocating a constitutional monarchy for the kingdom. The situation provides the United States a perfect opportunity to defend freedom and increase political participation by regularly calling for the release of political prisoners and would also put the United States squarely on the side of supporters of political reform inside the kingdom.[31]

Another looming domestic political challenge stems from the Saudi government's persistence in defining major Islamic organizations such as the World Association of Muslim Youth, the Muslim World League, and the International Islamic Relief Organization as international nongovernmental organizations (NGOs) rather than charities,[32] rendering the new laws centralizing and monitoring charitable organizations less effective. When pressed by one U.S. representative about the distinction before her trip to the kingdom in early 2005, Bandar likened Saudi control over NGOs to U.S. control over the United Nations. He pointed out that, just as the United States could not control the UN, which operates on U.S. soil, neither can Saudi Arabia fully control Islamic NGOs. What Bandar failed to acknowledge is that Congress is constantly battling the United Nations, threatening or actually withholding funds for activities related to policies conflicting with perceived U.S. interests.

Saudi Arabia has not made a similar public effort to rein in Islamic NGOs that operate on its territory—organizations that receive significant support from Saudi benefactors and whose leadership is often chosen by the royal family.[33] Steven Emerson, an analyst who closely tracks Islamic radicalism in the United States, testified before the Senate Committee on Governmental Affairs in July 2003 that "in March 1997, Secretary General [of the Muslim World League] Abdullah al-Obaid thanked King Fahd for his continued support, noting that the Saudi government had officially provided more than $1.33 billion in financial aid to the [Muslim World League] since 1962."[34] Until all Islamic NGOs operating on Saudi territory are strictly audited and monitored, outsiders will have good reason to suspect that money continues to flow to unsavory people and places. Insisting on such monitoring should be a top priority for the United States when engaging in talks with Saudi officials.

Washington should also explore ways to engage the winners of Saudi Arabia's first municipal elections in more than 40 years, which occurred between February and April 2005. Although voter turnout was thin and women were excluded, the precedent set by the election is significant, especially as Fahd had previously declared Islam and voting to be incompatible. Perhaps through a multilateral effort, Washington could support regional training programs for newly elected political officials. Introducing them to their regional counterparts and providing political training would acknowledge the importance of the election, help institutionalize the results, and encourage the Saudi royal family to take this new political group seriously. By reaching out to the winners, Washington could also avoid the charge that it is cherry-picking supporters and thus unintentionally discrediting them.

Beyond Oil and Security

Developing constructive policies that help local reformers steadily chip away at past decades of political decay is a subtle and painstaking exercise. This generational task requires sustained U.S. attention and instruments of power beyond the U.S. military. In today's battle of ideas in the Middle East, technical training, rational visa policies, and educational assistance are equally if not more important than assault rifles and fighter jets. Such sustained support cannot include gratuitous, counterproductive, and unwarranted anti-Saudi measures such as Representative Anthony D. Weiner's (D-N.Y.) June 2005 amendment that no funds be "obligated or expended to finance any assistance to Saudi Arabia," which specifically targets a paltry $25,000 International Military Education and Training grant for Saudi military training.[35] Although politically popular, such measures are strategically counterproductive and impede the ability of the United States to assist indigenous Saudi reform efforts, which are already fighting an uphill struggle slanted against liberalism and religious diversity.

Oil and security have consistently been defining features of the U.S.-Saudi relationship; religion has figured less prominently in even the most sophisticated analyses. Yet, Saudi Arabia's religiosity, whatever its specific teachings, had served a useful political purpose for the United States for half a century, making the kingdom a reliable Cold War partner and providing its leaders with a perception of global threats similar to the one held by the United States. Now, however, Saudi Arabia's proselytizing activities have contributed to today's dangerous religious environment.

In such a dramatically different global political context, can Saudi Arabia play a productive role in altering the course of religious radicalism? History suggests yes. Saudi leaders have repeatedly reined in religiously excessive spokesmen and calibrated messages to accord with varying political contexts. Today, Saudi Arabia's abilities are difficult to assess. Although the leadership is going after hard-core religious fighters, the extent to which the spiritual context is changing is less clear. The sahwa are still active, popular, and anti-American and have spawned an even younger and more radical group of extremists with which the sahwa are themselves engaging in an ideological battle. Such groups present real challenges to moving quickly toward altering Saudi Arabia's social and cultural milieu.

Riyadh clearly has the public confidence and support of the current U.S. administration. In his 2004 congressional testimony, Ambassador J. Cofer Black, then the State Department coordinator for counterterrorism, concluded that Saudi Arabia showed "clear evidence of the seriousness of purpose and the commitment of the leadership of the kingdom to this fight [against terrorism]."[36] In his acceptance speech at the Republican National Convention in August 2004, Bush himself mentioned Saudi Arabia explicitly, stating that "four years ago ... Saudi Arabia was fertile ground for terrorist fundraising" but now "Saudi Arabia is making raids and arrests."[37] Unfortunately, if Saudi Arabia is effectively to reduce the influence of radical Islam, the process will take time. To assist those in Saudi Arabia interested in this long-term reform struggle, the time has finally come to reformulate the U.S.-Saudi relationship.

The recent meeting between Bush and Abdullah in Crawford provides the basis for a more strategic recasting of the relationship. Both leaders committed to establishing "a high-level joint committee ... headed by the Saudi Foreign Minister and the U.S. Secretary of State that will deal with strategic issues of vital importance to the two countries."[38] Although profoundly uncomfortable, religion must be part of that discussion; it is the strategic issue confounding both sides and must be tackled head-on. The way that each country understands, manages, and engages today's religious trends will help shape the future of Wahabbi Islam in Saudi Arabia and subsequently the Islamic landscape throughout the Middle East and beyond. It is the core of the so-called battle for hearts and minds.

Notes

1. Ali Khalil, "Saudi Conference Focuses on Fighting Terrorism," *Arab News*, February 7, 2005.
2. "The 9/11 Commission Report: Final Report of the National Commission on Terrorist Attacks Upon the United States," 2004, p. 232, http://www.9-11commission.gov/report/911Report.pdf; Marc Sageman, *Understanding Terror Networks* (Philadelphia: University of Pennsylvania Press, 2004), p. 71; Peter L. Bergen,

Holy War, Inc.: Inside the Secret World of Osama Bin Laden (New York: Free Press, 2001), p. 90 (citing an article by Rahimullah Yusufzai in *The News* [Pakistan], December 8, 1995); unnamed officials, interviews with author, June 2005.

3. Bernard Lewis, "Communism and Islam," *International Affairs* 30, no. 1 (January 1954): 1–12. See Helen Lackner, *A House Built on Sand: A Political Economy of Saudi Arabia* (London: Ithaca Press, 1978), chap. 6.
4. "Discussion at the 310th Meeting of the National Security Council, Thursday, January 24, 1957," *Eisenhower: Papers, 1953–1961* (Ann Whitman Files), Eisenhower Library.
5. Steven Emerson, "Terrorism Financing: Origination, Organization, and Prevention: Saudi Arabia, Terrorist Financing, and the War on Terror," testimony before the U.S. Senate Committee on Governmental Affairs, July 31, 2003, http://hsgac.senate.gov/_files/073103emerson.pdf.
6. Mordechai Abir, *Saudi Arabia in the Oil Era: Regime and Elites: Conflict and Collaboration* (London: Croom Helm, 1988). For Faisal's role in creating these institutions and the domestic struggle over them, see Joshua Teitelbaum, *Holier Than Thou: Saudi Arabia's Islamic Opposition* (Washington, D.C.: Washington Institute for Near East Policy, 2000).
7. Michel Ameen, interview with author, Houston, January 25, 2005.
8. Saudi national, interview with author, Riyadh, February 2005.
9. Jamal Khashoggi, "Saudi Religious Establishment Has Its Wings Clipped," *Daily Star*, July 1, 2002.
10. Ibid.
11. "A Diplomat's Call for War," *Washington Post*, June 6, 2004, p. B1 (English translation of original Arabic article).
12. "Saudi-U.S. Cooperation in War on Terror Sharply Up: Official," Reuters, October 25, 2003. See Saudi-U.S. Relations Information Service, "Crisis and Opportunities in U.S.-Saudi Relations: Ambassador Robert Jordan Interview," September 7, 2004, http://www.saudi-us-relations.org/newsletter2004/saudi-relations-interest-09-07.pdf; Hussein Shobokshi, "Our September 11," *Arab News*, May 20, 2003.
13. Unnamed Saudi journalists and diplomats, interviews with author, Riyadh and Jeddah, February 2005.
14. Financial Action Task Force on Money Laundering, "Annual Report 2003–2004," July 2, 2004, annex C, http://www.fatf-gafi.org/dataoecd/12/44/33622501.PDF.
15. J. Cofer Black, "Saudi Arabia and the Fight Against Terrorist Financing," testimony before the U.S. House Committee on International Relations, Subcommittee on the Middle East and Central Asia, March 24, 2004, www.saudi-us-relations.org/newsletter2004/saudi-relations-interest-03-29a.html.
16. See, for example, Victor Comras, "Following Terrorists' Money," *Washington Post*, June 4, 2005, p. A17. In September 2004, the U.S. Department of the Treasury

designated the U.S. branch of al-Haramain as a source of terrorist financing. Office of Public Affairs, Department of the Treasury, "U.S.-Based Branch of Al Haramain Foundation Linked to Terror; Treasury Designates U.S. Branch, Director," JS-1895, September 9, 2004, http://www.ustreas.gov/press/releases/js1895.htm.

17. U.S. Department of State official, interview with author, Washington, D.C., September 2004.

18. See Teitelbaum, *Holier Than Thou*; R. Hrair Dekmejian "The Rise of Political Islamism in Saudi Arabia," *Middle East Journal* 52, no. 2 (Autumn 1999): 204–218; Madawi al-Rasheed, "Saudi Arabia's Islamic Opposition," *Current History* 95, no. 597 (January 1996): 16–22; Toby Craig Jones, "The Clerics, the Sahwa and the Saudi State," *Strategic Insights* 4, no. 3 (March 2005), http://www.ccc.nps.navy.mil/si/2005/Mar/jonesMar05.pdf; International Crisis Group, "Saudi Arabia Backgrounder: Who Are the Islamists?" *ICG Middle East Report*, no. 31 (September 21, 2004), http://www.crisisgroup.org/library/documents/middle_east___north_africa/iraq_iran_gulf/31_saudi_arabia_backgrounder.pdf; Gilles Kepel, *The War for Muslim Minds: Islam and the West* (Cambridge: Harvard University Press, 2005), pp. 177–195; Stephane Lacroix, "Between Islamists and Liberals: Saudi Arabia's New 'Islamo-Liberal' Reformists," *Middle East Journal* 58, no. 3. (Summer 2004): 345–365; Gwenn Okruhlik, "Networks of Dissent: Islamism and Reform in Saudi Arabia," *Current History* 101, no. 165 (January 2002): 22–28.

19. See Jones, "Clerics, the Sahwa and the Saudi State."

20. ABC News Investigative Unit, "Saudi Jihadists in Iraq," ABC News, May 9, 2005, http://abcnews.go.com/International/story?id=741525&page=1 (citing the Arabic language newspaper *al-Hayat*).

21. Office of the Press Secretary, The White House, "President Discusses War on Terror," Fort Lesley McNair, March 8, 2005, http://www.whitehouse.gov/news/releases/2005/03/20050308-3.html.

22. Central Intelligence Agency, "The World Fact Book: Saudi Arabia," June 14, 2005, http://www.cia.gov/cia/publications/factbook/geos/sa.html.

23. Peter G. Peterson et al., "Finding America's Voice: A Strategy for Reinvigorating U.S. Public Diplomacy," 2003, p. 47, http://www.cfr.org/pdf/public_diplomacy.pdf. For a more global look at this disturbing trend, see Joseph S. Nye Jr., "You Can't Get Here From There," *New York Times*, November 30, 2004, p. A21.

24. Institute of International Education, "Fall 2003 Survey: The State of International Education Exchange—International Students," November 3, 2003, p. 10, http://opendoors.iienetwork.org/file_depot/0-10000000/0-10000/3390/folder/28491/IIE+Online+Survey+Fall+2003.doc.

25. Unnamed source, interview with author, Riyadh, February 2005.

26. Ministry of Higher Education, Kingdom of Saudi Arabia, *Statistical Yearbooks of Saudi Arabia, 1979–1994*, http://www.mohe.gov.sa.

27. Maura Harty, "U.S. Visa Policy: Security Borders and Opening Doors," *The Washington Quarterly* 28, no. 2 (Spring 2005): 23–34; unnamed sources, interviews with author, Washington, D.C., January 2005; unnamed sources, interviews with author, Riyadh, February 2005.
28. Energy Information Administration, Department of Energy, "Country Brief: Saudi Arabia," January 2005, http://www.eia.doe.gov/emeu/cabs/saudi.html.
29. Condoleezza Rice, "Promoting the National Interest," *Foreign Affairs* 79, no. 1 (January/February 2000): 56.
30. Draft congressional letter to United States Trade Representative Robert J. Portman, May 2005.
31. See Condoleezza Rice, "Remarks at the American University in Cairo," Cairo, June 20, 2005, http://www.state.gov/secretary/rm/2005/48328.htm; "Joint Press Availability With Saudi Foreign Minister Saud Al-Faisal," Riyadh, June 20, 2005, http://www.state.gov/secretary/rm/2005/48390.htm.
32. Senior Saudi official, interview with author, Washington, D.C., June 2004.
33. See for example, Simon Henderson, "Institutionalized Islam: Saudi Arabia's Islamic Policies and the Threat They Pose," testimony before the U.S. Senate Committee on the Judiciary, Subcommittee on Terrorism, Technology, and Homeland Security, September 10, 2003, http://judiciary.senate.gov/testimony.cfm?id=910&wit_id=2573. See also David B. Ottaway "U.S. Eyes Money Trails of Saudi-Backed Charities," *Washington Post*, August 19, 2004, p. A1.
34. Emerson, "Terrorism Financing."
35. Office of Representative Anthony D. Weiner, "Congress Finally Cracks Down on Saudis; Weiner Amendment Prohibits U.S. Aid to Saudi Arabia," July 16, 2004, http://www.house.gov/apps/list/press/ny09_weiner/saudicrackdown041607.html. See Alfred B. Prados, "Saudi Arabia: Current Issues and U.S. Relations," *CRS Issue Brief for Congress*, IB93113, March 21, 2005, http://fpc.state.gov/documents/organization/46414.pdf.
36. Black, "Saudi Arabia and the Fight Against Terrorist Financing."
37. Office of the Press Secretary, The White House, "President's Remarks at the 2004 Republican National Convention," New York, September 2, 2004, http://www.whitehouse.gov/news/releases/2004/09/20040902-2.html.
38. Office of the Press Secretary, The White House, "Joint Statement of President Bush and Saudi Crown Prince Abdullah," Crawford, Texas, April 25, 2005, http://www.whitehouse.gov/news/releases/2005/04/20050425-8.html.

John R. Bradley

Al Qaeda and the House of Saud: Eternal Enemies or Secret Bedfellows?

In February 2005, less than two years after suicide attacks on Western residential compounds in Riyadh killed 34 people, including nine Americans, and ushered in an unprecedented wave of terrorist violence across the kingdom, the Saudi capital hosted a three-day international counterterrorism conference. During the short period between the bombings and the terrorism conference in Riyadh, Saudi Arabia's image had transformed from an oasis of relative calm in an often volatile region into the place held responsible in many ways for Al Qaeda's birth and growth and where the triumph or demise of this international terrorist organization would ultimately be determined. Underlining President George W. Bush's wish to work publicly as closely as possible with the al-Saud in the ongoing fight against Al Qaeda, its affiliates, and its sympathizers in Saudi Arabia and elsewhere, U.S. homeland security adviser Frances Fragos Townsend emerged from the conference declaring that Washington "stands squarely" with the kingdom's rulers. She emphasized that the conference was proof positive of a "commitment to the elimination of terrorism" on the part of the al-Saud ruling family.[1]

John R. Bradley is author of *Saudi Arabia Exposed: Inside a Kingdom in Crisis* (New York: Palgrave Macmillan, 2005). A former managing editor of the Jeddah-based *Arab News*, he has reported extensively from Saudi Arabia and the wider Middle East for the *Economist*, *New Republic*, *Salon*, *London Sunday Times*, *Washington Times*, *London Telegraph*, *Independent*, and *Prospect*. He writes a weekly column on the Middle East for the *Straits Times*.

The Washington Quarterly • 28:4 pp. 139–152.

Yet, not all observers were quite so bowled over by the stage-managed proceedings in Riyadh.[2] The delegates from numerous international organizations, the United States, and 50 Arab, Asian, and European countries, with the exclusion of Israel, which predictably was not among the invitees, sat listening to senior Saudi princes, routinely accused of at the very least failing to prevent the funneling of money from Saudi-based Islamic charities to terrorist organizations, give speeches condemning terrorism. As recently as July 2005, the U.S. government suggested that wealthy Saudi individuals remain "a significant source" of funds for Islamic terrorists around the world, despite widely publicized efforts to shut down these channels.[3] On top of such accusations, it is widely recognized that the royal family has empowered a hard-line Wahhabi religious establishment that propagates an extremist interpretation of Islam, which critics argue acts as a guide and inspiration to terrorists such as Saudi dissident Osama bin Laden and his followers, giving it ideological and day-to-day control over the kingdom's mosques, judiciary, schools, media, and religious police.

There were thus two polarized reactions to the conference, reflecting the diametrically opposed views among Saudi observers in the West when it comes to the question of the kingdom's role in the war on terrorism. On one side are those such as Townsend who, believing Saudi Arabia to be a crucial ally, focused on the conference's powerful symbolism. They stressed that one of its important objectives was to dispel persisting doubts in the West about the Saudi royal family's commitment to combating terrorism. On the other side are those who see duplicity in every al-Saud statement[4] and were especially critical of the conference's high symbolism, as it allowed the regime to showcase its purported counterterrorism successes without having to engage in substantive debate on broader, more controversial issues.

Both interpretations contain elements of truth. When it comes to the issue of fighting Al Qaeda, the al-Saud regime has been and continues to be part of the problem in fundamental ways. Yet, it is equally undeniable that, considering the absolute nature of the al-Saud family's rule and the dearth of acceptable alternatives, at least in Western eyes, the regime is indispensable to any solution to terrorism. Townsend implicitly acknowledged in Riyadh that, if bin Laden's goal is to overthrow the House of Saud and subsequently to gain the prestige that would come from the custodianship of Islam's two holy mosques and control of one-quarter of the world's known oil reserves, then the main U.S. policy objective in response must be to guarantee the royal family's survival.

Al Qaeda Stakes Its Claim

Oddly, it would appear that bin Laden shares Townsend's view that the endgame of the global jihad preached by Al Qaeda will be played out in Saudi Arabia. Having failed to topple regimes or establish permanent Islamic governments in Algeria, Egypt, Sudan, Yemen, and Afghanistan and with failure imminent in Iraq as well, bin Laden's birthplace remains his last gasp opportunity. If he fails there, he will ultimately have failed in his broader strategy. Despite their evident willingness to conduct smaller-scale terrorist operations, Al Qaeda cells in Saudi Arabia appear to be holding off from a direct attack on an oil installation or pipeline or against the Saudi royal family itself.

In his two direct addresses to the Saudi regime in August 1995 and December 2004, even bin Laden himself called for internal reform within the Saudi government rather than revolution from below. Self-appointed Al Qaeda spokesmen regularly post on Web sites that the organization is waiting to launch a full-scale assault against the al-Saud and its economic lifeline because a direct threat to their rule will cause the princes' "separate fingers to become an iron fist." A major attack would almost certainly result in the imposition of a state of emergency, restricting terrorists' mobility. It is better, the spokesmen argue, to let the royal family squabble among themselves about reforms as resentment grows over intensifying economic problems. An increasingly unstable Saudi Arabia would remain a fertile recruiting ground for arms, money, and volunteers.

All this, critics claim, is well understood by the al-Saud ruling family, who, it has long been argued, paid off Al Qaeda in the 1990s to ensure there would be no direct attacks launched against their regime.[5] It is indeed strange, considering the often trumpeted line that Al Qaeda wants to "overthrow the Saudi ruling family and replace it with a Taliban-style regime," that no Saudi princes have been assassinated, despite the many thousands of them, most of whom are more vulnerable to such targeting than Westerners who live in heavily guarded residential compounds. Could it be, therefore, that bin Laden recognizes that, in the official Wahhabi religious establishment he officially despises, because they legitimize the al-Saud regime's rule by, as the favorite Islamist taunt goes, "issuing fatwas for money," he nevertheless sees his closest ideological ally in a world where he is hunted and increasingly marginalized?

Promoting a Solution ...?

The House of Saud's role as part of the solution is the easiest to assess because it is trumpeted, rather than deliberately obscured, by the regime's officials and the state-controlled media. The Saudi government's counterterrorism framework included an amnesty offer for militants who turn themselves in, that they will not face the death penalty and will only be prosecuted if they committed acts that hurt others;[6] a massive anti-extremism campaign in the Saudi media and on billboards throughout the main cities, given a boost by the high number of Saudis and other fellow Muslims among the November 2003 bombing casualties;[7] the reeducation of extremist clerics by the Saudi royal family, although the details remained vague and there was never any independent verification that this retraining ever actually took place;[8] and unprecedented cooperation between the Central Intelligence Agency and Saudi security forces, which includes sophisticated command centers in Jeddah and Riyadh.[9]

The May 2003 bombings served as a wake-up call for the Saudi royal family, leading it to construct the above framework, and it has since been locked in an endless cycle of violent confrontation with militants. Between May 2003 and June 2005, more than 30 major terrorism-related incidents occurred in the kingdom. At least 91 foreign nationals and Saudi civilians have been killed and 510 wounded, according to former intelligence chief Prince Turki al-Faisal. Al-Faisal has also stated that 41 security force members have been killed and 218 wounded, while 112 militants have been killed and 25 wounded.[10] Included among these: a November 2003 attack on another Riyadh compound killed 17 people, but this time the dead were mostly Muslims. This attack, however, seems to have been an isolated incident, as all other attacks have targeted the regime, or Western people, buildings, and businesses.

In May 2004, gunmen attacked the offices of the Houston-based company ABB Lummus Global, in the Red Sea port city of Yanbu, killing six Westerners and a Saudi. One month later, oil company compounds in the Eastern Province city of al-Khobar were the target; hostages were taken at the Oasis residential building, and at least 30 people were killed. In December 2004, the U.S. consulate in Jeddah was attacked. Militants breached its heavily fortified defenses and, before being killed, managed to pull down the U.S. flag. A group calling itself Al Qaeda on the Arabian Peninsula claimed responsibility for most of these large-scale attacks. In the meantime, Al Qaeda–affiliated cells in Riyadh and Jeddah have periodically singled out Westerners for execution. Most infamously, U.S. contractor Paul Johnson was kidnapped in Riyadh in June 2004 and beheaded, the ghastly crime recorded on video and immediately posted on Islamist Web sites.

In the face of such atrocities, no one now seriously doubts the Saudi regime's commitment to hunt down and kill individual militants who have carried out or are believed to be planning terrorist attacks inside the kingdom. The denial of the existence of homegrown extremists, evident in Interior Minister Prince Naif's refusal for six months after the September 11 attacks to acknowledge that 15 of the 19 hijackers were Saudi nationals, is today a distant memory. In fact, Prince Naif's internal security force has born the brunt of the casualties, losing more men battling suspected Al Qaeda cells than any other security force in the Arab world. In April 2005, it was an Interior Ministry announcement that reported how residents of the tiny provincial capital of Sakaka in Saudi Arabia's northernmost province, al-Jouf, had witnessed a grisly scene in the main public square: the corpses of three convicted and beheaded militants had been tied to poles, on top of which were placed their severed heads. The three, who had returned to the kingdom after fighting in Afghanistan, were executed by the central government after being convicted of murdering the region's deputy governor, a top religious court judge, and a police chief. They had also killed a Saudi soldier and kidnapped a foreign national, long before such kidnappings became "fashionable" among Islamist groups in the Middle East.

At its height in 2003, the unrest in al-Jouf, a power base of the al-Sudairi branch of the ruling family, which included King Fahd, Defense Minister Prince Sultan, and Riyadh governor Prince Salman, represented in microcosm the kingdom-wide tensions that threatened to spill over into a general uprising.[11] The rebellion's end in April 2005, with the crudely symbolic public display of its leaders' heads, marked the moment that the al-Saud triumphed over the most extreme of its homegrown enemies, at least for the time being. From a list of the 26 most wanted terrorists issued after the May 2003 bombings, only two remain at large; the others have been killed or captured or have surrendered. Just hours after Riyadh issued a new list of 36 most wanted terrorists in July 2005, the Moroccan terrorist at the top, Younis Mohammed Ibrahim al-Hayari, was killed in a shoot-out with Saudi security forces.[12]

... Or Fueling the Problem?

The other role of the House of Saud—its part in the problem—is much more difficult to document and explain, as the Saudi regime does not want the world to know about it. What is clear, however, is the broad context: Riyadh's fight against terrorism since May 2003 and related calls for national unity have provided a façade for behind-the-scenes moves to strengthen the role of the Wahhabi religious establishment, with whom the al-Saud rules in effective partnership.[13] Such moves are bad news for the war on terrorism in Saudi Arabia and elsewhere. The Saudi royal family certainly cracked down hard on Al Qaeda in the wake of the September 11 attacks and the subsequent Islamist campaign of violence inside the kingdom. To shore up support among its core constituents, however, whom the crackdown risked alienating, it also reached out not only to the masses through advertising campaigns, but also to the hard-line religious establishment whose support legitimizes the royal family. The regime claimed to endorse a "truer" version of Islam than that of the terrorist organizations. Yet, the line between that "truer" Islam and Al Qaeda's proclaimed ideology is becoming increasingly blurred.

Saudi leaders, in their eagerness to prove their Islamist credentials in the face of charges of being U.S. puppets,[14] have empowered a number of clerics who, although not overtly critical of the regime, are also not overtly critical of the terrorists—indeed, on occasion, quite the reverse. The words and actions of these clerics challenge the official, antiterrorism narrative fine-tuned at the Riyadh conference, heavily promoted by the state-controlled media as well as Saudi embassies abroad, and tied to reality by the frequent clashes between the security forces and suspected militants. In this counternarrative, the al-Saud, despite its effort to hunt down those who directly threaten its own rule, is less serious about tackling the deeper issues related to the funding of, ideological legitimization of, and recruitment for Al Qaeda in the kingdom.

Particularly alarming was Riyadh's announcement, just days after the counterterrorism conference and one day before a first round of partial municipal elections got underway, that Abdullah al-Obeid, a former head of an Islamic charity, had been appointed as the kingdom's new education minister. Described by the *Wall Street Journal* as "an official enmeshed in a terror financing controversy," he is a former director of the Muslim World League (WML), the parent organization of the International Islamic Relief Organization, which the U.S. Department of the Treasury claims may have had financial ties to Islamist terrorist groups. Al-Obeid was head of the WML from 1995 to 2002, during which time the charity spent tens of millions of dollars to finance the spread of Wahhabism. The *Wall Street Journal* quoted an essay by al-Obeid from 2002 in which he blamed "some mass media centers that are managed and run by Jews in the West" for reports linking terrorism and Islam.[15] He also reportedly organized symposia to explain that Palestinian suicide attacks on Israelis "are conducted in self-defense" and "are lawful and approved by all religious standards, international treaties, norms, and announcements."[16]

On the basis of such evidence, al-Obeid, who replaced as education minister the secular, progressive-minded Muhammad al-Rasheed, a man hated by the hard-line Wahhabis,[17] is not an individual the West should trust to delete anti-Semitic and anti-Christian passages from the Saudi school curriculum, let alone its pro-jihadi rhetoric, all widely blamed as providing ideological justification for attacks on non-Muslims by terrorist groups such as Al Qaeda. Nor, for that matter, is there much cause for confidence in the Saudi chief justice, Saleh bin Muhammad al-Luhaidan, who also holds the rank of government minister. Al-Luhaidan has been accused of instructing Saudis on how to fight U.S. and Iraqi troops in Iraq in the name of Allah. An October 2004 recording obtained and distributed by a Washington-based Saudi dissident group has al-Luhaideen making remarks at a mosque in Riyadh in response to questions from a group of Saudis who wanted to join terrorist organizations in Iraq.[18] He is heard advising that those who still want to join the fight must be careful when entering the country because U.S. planes and satellite surveillance equipment may be monitoring the borders. He adds that those Saudis who do manage to enter Iraq will not be punished by the Saudi security forces and insists that money raised for the jihad must go directly to those who will launch attacks.

Two of the kingdom's most extremist, anti-Western clerics, Safar al-Hawali and Salman al-Auda, known as "awakening sheikhs" because of their powerful influence on young Arab Muslims in the early 1990s in the aftermath of the Persian Gulf War when they were imprisoned by the al-Saud, have also returned to the mainstream, even acting as intermediaries between the government and suspected terrorists.[19] Al-Hawali, who reportedly recently suffered a heart attack, is secretary general of the Global Anti-Aggression Campaign, a militant, anti-American entity established by more than 225 radical figures from across the Islamic world as a response to the U.S. invasion of Iraq. The group's initial statement condemned "the Zionists and the American administration led by right-wing extremists that are working to expand their control over nations and peoples, loot their resources, destroy their will, and to change their educational curricula and social system."[20] In November 2004, al-Hawali and al-Auda were among 26 Saudi clerics, most of whom receive their salaries from the Saudi royal family, who published a religious statement urging Muslims to wage holy war in Iraq. "Jihad against the occupiers is a must," said the statement. "It is not only a legitimate right, but a religious duty."[21] The fact that both of these men remain in their jobs speaks volumes.

The al-Saud's secret strategy is to put out the message that it is okay to attack "infidels" in Iraq, but not in Saudi Arabia. Critics of the regime refer to this when they point out alleged "Saudi duplicity." According to a recent study, some 60 percent of suicide bombers in Iraq are Saudi nationals,[22] and even a Saudi-based analyst concedes that as many as 2,500 Saudis have crossed over to Iraq to join the insurgency.[23] Saudi observer and Gulf expert Simon Henderson has written in a more general context:

> Worried about their own necks, the Saudi royal family tolerates a political fudge, hoping that it can reduce support for Al Qaeda from among its citizens and win the battle for Islamic legitimacy. Al Qaeda recognizes the basic rules, targeting foreigners. Hence, no direct attacks on members of the House of Saud itself. ... Before 9/11, Western officials say that senior princes were paying off bin Laden to avoid targeting the kingdom altogether. That changed when Western pressure stopped the payments. For the West, this means more terrorism and high oil prices.[24]

The new strategy of tacitly encouraging Saudi terrorists to blow themselves up in Iraq or at least not disciplining those who openly encourage such action is a continuation of this game. It represents yet another attempt by the al-Saud to postpone a final showdown with bin Laden and his followers. The al-Saud have certainly done little, if anything, to stop young Saudis from traveling to Iraq. The failure of the regime to challenge more rigorously the jihadi culture in its schools and mosques, beyond the confines of glossy advertising campaigns, as the remarks by the education minister and chief justice clearly demonstrate, compound the long-term risk of blowback from such appeasement.[25]

The al-Saud regime further muddies the water with its campaigns of outright misinformation. The hunt for Paul Johnson's corpse is a good example of this. Only hours after his murder, Saudi security forces gunned down a man believed to be Al Qaeda's leader in Saudi Arabia, Abdul Aziz al-Muqrin, in an ambush at a petrol station in the capital. He and several followers were caught, the Saudi authorities said, attempting to dispose of Johnson's corpse. Yet, the next day it became known that Johnson's corpse had not been found. Still today, it has yet to be located, and the U.S. Embassy in Riyadh has called off the search. In fact, despite the attempts to link al-Muqrin to the abduction and although al-Muqrin had a long and bloody history from fighting in Chechnya to apparently planning the May 2003 attacks, this is probably the one atrocity of which he was innocent. Saudi spokesmen had mournfully repeated in Riyadh and Washington that the authorities had launched a massive manhunt for Johnson that had narrowly missed saving him but had at least brought rough justice to his abductors shortly after the deed. But this story turned out to be another example of rhetoric replacing reality. Instead, the indications are that al-Muqrin was lured into a trap independent of and planned well ahead of the Johnson case and that it was another terrorist leader, Saleh al-Oufi, later named as al-Muqrin's successor, who had carried out the abduction. When Johnson's head was recovered a month later, it was in the freezer of a safe house used by al-Oufi.[26]

Dangerous Liaisons: Al Qaeda and the House of Saud

Al Qaeda's infiltration of the Saudi security forces, the widespread sympathy in those forces' rank and file for the terrorist organization's goals, and the intelligence leaks that result have had multiple negative consequences, the most profound being the assassination of senior officers and the collaboration between lower ranks of the security forces and terrorists during attacks. Members of the state security apparatus, whose job now ostensibly amounts to keeping the al-Saud in power in the face of growing domestic opposition, find themselves directly in the radicals' firing line. A radical Saudi Islamist group affiliated with Al Qaeda claimed they blew up a car in December 2003 in Riyadh belonging to Lieutenant Colonel Ibrahim al-Dhaleh, a senior Saudi security officer who escaped by the skin of his teeth. The group, the Brigade of the Two Holy Mosques, also said it had tried to kill Major General Abdel-Aziz al-Huweirini, the number three official in the Saudi interior ministry, who was shot in Riyadh the same month. The statement warned Dhaleh "and those like him" against pursuing their war against Islamists in Saudi Arabia.[27] These were not empty threats.

In April 2004, a suicide attacker driving a truck blew up the headquarters of the counterterrorism unit in Riyadh, destroying much of the building and killing five people. In December of the same year, militants attacked the Interior Ministry in Riyadh itself, although damage was minimal and claims that Prince Naif was the target were viewed skeptically because he was on an official trip to Tunisia at the time of the blast. Also, in June 2005, Mubarak al-Sowat, head of the police investigations department in Mecca and a leading proponent of launching preemptive strikes against suspected extremists, was shot nine times outside of his home and then hacked to pieces with an axe.[28] Giving a rare insight into the paranoia and fear with which senior security officials now have to live in Saudi Arabia, al-Sowat's wife told local media that her husband had received many death threats on his cell phone and by e-mail in the weeks and months leading up to his assassination and was "always distracted and nervous." He had become "constantly anxious and fearful" after he returned from Riyadh earlier in the year.[29]

Obviously, those singling out such individuals for attack must have excellent intelligence, likely provided by insiders. They know who to target, as well as their victims' exact movements and when best to strike. There is also ample evidence of collaboration between the terrorists and security forces in the execution of terrorist attacks or, at the very least, of an unwillingness to respond swiftly on some occasions. In the attacks on the compounds in Yanbu and Al Khobar in May 2004, at least 90 minutes passed before security forces responded. In Al Khobar, the attackers were actually allowed to go free to fight another day when security forces turned a blind eye, despite the fact that the compound in which they were holed up had been completely surrounded.[30] The attacks in Riyadh in May 2003 depended on a significant level of insider information about the three compounds targeted, almost certainly provided by those "defending" them. The suicide bombers detonated their vehicle right inside the main housing block in the Vinell compound, which took them less than a minute to reach from the gate. As they drove at breakneck speed with a bomb weighing nearly 200 kilograms to the most densely populated part of the complex, they had to know where the switches were to operate the gates after attacking the guards and exactly where the main housing block was located.[31]

The Final Showdown?

In his December 2004 address to the Saudi ruling family, bin Laden issued an unprecedented call for attacks that would sabotage the oil industries of the Gulf, including Saudi Arabia.[32] Al Qaeda elements in Saudi Arabia immediately endorsed attacks on their own oil industry. "We call on all the [mujahideen] in the Arabian Peninsula to unite ... and target the oil supplies that do not serve the Islamic nation, but the enemies of this nation," said an Internet statement.[33] Bin Laden's new tack is a shift in Al Qaeda tactics, reversing his and others' edicts from the 1990s that made oil facilities in the Muslim world off-limits to attack. Because the hoped-for Islamic empire that he and others had announced in Sudan in 1993 would need oil revenues to thrive, the oil facilities had to be preserved for the glory of Islam.[34] In Saudi Arabia, these pipelines have become the obvious new targets for the Saudi jihadis. They could be sabotaged by an amateur with no military training, and a successful attack would have a huge psychological impact.

Government officials in Riyadh dismiss talk of attacks on the oil pipelines as a scare tactic, arguing that, because Saudi security forces have killed or arrested dozens of Al Qaeda operatives, bin Laden's ability to influence events inside the kingdom has diminished. That may be true, and there is no denying the Saudi government's multiple counterterrorism successes. Yet, although attacks on the heavily guarded oil-pumping facilities are indeed unlikely, smaller incidents remain possible along the kingdom's more than 10,000-mile pipeline network. In his message to Saudi militants, bin Laden's main aim did not appear to be the destruction of major installations, which would rob the Saudi people of their primary means of financial income and turn them completely against him and his cause, but rather acts of sabotage that would increase oil prices, which he said should be $100 a barrel. Saudi Arabia has more than a quarter of the world's known oil reserves, and even an abortive attack on the Saudi petroleum network would raise oil prices. It also would dramatically increase concerns in Washington about the al-Saud family's ability to maintain stability.

Adding to concerns about the impact of bin Laden's tape is the knowledge that the thousands of Saudi jihadis who have snuck over to Iraq are likely to return to the kingdom once Iraq stabilizes. They will have been trained in urban warfare, including instruction on how to sabotage oil pipelines. As was the case after the fall of the Taliban in Afghanistan, these Saudis are going to bring their terrorism back home with them. A confidential Interior Ministry document obtained by a London-based Saudi dissident group apparently acknowledges that 200 Saudis may have already returned to the kingdom in the wake of bin Laden's call.[35] What happens next will largely determine Al Qaeda's future in Saudi Arabia. "We expect the worst from those who went to Iraq," Prince Naif said in remarks published in July. "They will be worse [than those who have already launched attacks], and we will be ready for them."[36]

There are troubling signs; the tactics employed by the Iraqi insurgents are evident in the attacks on Westerners in Saudi Arabia. Copycat incidents include the dragging of Westerners' bodies from the back of cars, the use of assassinations to sabotage the vital oil sector, and kidnappings. The ideological bonds that bind the insurgents in Iraq and Saudi Arabia were made explicit by those who beheaded Johnson in Riyadh when they signed their claim of responsibility "the Fallujah Brigade."[37] In an attack in which six Westerners and a Saudi were killed in Yanbu, militants dragged the body of one of the victims into a local school playground and forced students to watch. "Come join your brothers in Fallujah," they shouted, in reference to the city where four U.S. contractors had been similarly slain.[38] The Al Qaeda cell that attacked foreigners in Al Khobar also dragged the body of a Westerner through the streets from a car. The leader of the group said on an Islamic Web site afterward that a subsidiary of Halliburton had been singled out for attack because "it has a role in Iraq."[39]

The flow of Saudi jihadis to Iraq benefits the al-Saud regime in the short term, at least in the sense that, if they are blowing themselves up in Baghdad, they will not be doing so in Riyadh. Yet, there is potential for long-term blowback, just as there was when the "Afghan Arabs" returned from Afghanistan in the 1990s. The other main, related problem is that the al-Saud is increasingly following a domestic agenda focused solely on counterterrorism. Riyadh's relentless fight against militants and repeated calls for national unity have conveniently provided a façade behind which the monarchy can abandon the few reform initiatives previously in place and reverse any movement, at least in the short term, toward democratic change.

By remaining complicit with the regime, particularly at a time when Saudi citizens remain oppressed, unemployed, and in some cases even impoverished, Washington is essentially allowing the kingdom to become a recruiting ground for Al Qaeda. The United States is dependent on Saudi oil, but the Saudi regime is dependent on the United States for its survival. Current U.S. policy toward the kingdom should use that leverage to call for genuine reform, rather than just supporting the royal family in the belief that it will keep terrorists at bay. If the United States does not look beyond the short-term benefits of stability resulting from its relationship with the Saudi regime, it will face far more severe, long-term consequences.

Notes

1. Mohammed Rasooldeen "U.S. Says Saudi Victory Crucial to Defeating Global Terror," *Arab News*, February 8, 2005, http://arabnews.com?page=1§ion=0&article=58688&d=8&m=2&y=2005.
2. See, for example, Simon Henderson, "Lights, Camera, Inaction? Saudi Arabia's Counterterrorism Conference," *PolicyWatch*, no. 956, February 11, 2005, http://www.washingtoninstitute.org/templateC05.php?CID=2254.
3. "U.S. Calls Saudis 'Significant Source' of Terror Funding," Agence France Press, July 14, 2005.
4. Robert Spencer, "Ending the Saudi Double Game," *FrontpageMagazine.com*, June 23, 2005, http://www.frontpagemag.com/Articles/ReadArticle.asp?ID=18520.
5. Nick Fielding, "Saudis Paid Bin Laden 200 Million Pounds," *Sunday Times*, August 25, 2002, http://www.timesonline.co.uk/article/0,,2089-393584,00.html.
6. "Saudis Offer Amnesty to Militants," Associated Press, June 23, 2004.
7. "Saudi Attacks Blamed on Al-Qaeda," Associated Press, November 9, 2003.
8. "Retraining for 1,000 Saudi Preachers," Reuters, June 25, 2003.
9. Douglas Frantz, "Once Indifferent, Saudis Allied With U.S. in Fighting Al-Qaeda," *Los Angeles Times*, August 8, 2004.
10. Dominic Evans, "Saudi Arabia Says Ready to Beat Militants from Iraq," Reuters, July 10, 2005.
11. John R. Bradley, "Smoldering Rebellion Against Saudi Rule Threatens to Set Country Ablaze," *Independent*, January 28, 2004.

12. Abdullah Al Shihri, "Saudis Kill Top Militant in Gun Battle in Capital," Associated Press, July 4, 2005.
13. John R. Bradley, "The House of Saud Re-Embraces Fundamentalism," *Asia Times*, April 12, 2005.
14. Bin Laden makes this accusation, at some length, in both his August 1995 and December 2004 addresses to the Saudi royal family.
15. Glenn Simpson, "New Saudi Aide Is in Terror-Fund Probe," *Wall Street Journal*, February 9, 2005.
16. For more details about al-Obeid's appointment, see Henderson, "Lights, Camera, Inaction?"
17. "Saudi Islamic Doctrine Hard to Control," Associated Press, April 20, 2004.
18. See "Saudi Minister Supports War Against Iraq: Report," *Saudi Institute*, April 26, 2005. Al-Luhaidan admitted to NBC News that the voice on the recording was his and that they were his words but claimed, rather unconvincingly, that he had not intended to express those opinions. See Lisa Myers and the NBC Investigative Unit, "More Evidence of Saudi Double Talk?" April 26, 2005, http://www.msnbc.msn.com/id/7645118/. Since he was exposed, however, al-Luhaidan has made a clear statement calling for Saudis not to enter Iraq. See "Saudi Official Warns Youths Against Fighting in Iraq," *Deutsche Presse-Agentur*, July 6, 2005.
19. Erick Stakelbeck, "The Saudi Hate Machine," *National Interest* 2, no. 49 (December 2003), http://www.inthenationalinterest.com/Articles/Vol2Issue49/Vol2Issue49 Stakelbeck.html.
20. Ibid.
21. Ibid.
22. Stephen Schwartz, "The Foreign Face of Iraqi Terrorism," *Weekly Standard*, March 8, 2005.
23. Mahen Abedin, "Al-Qaeda: In Decline or Preparing for the Next Attack? An Interview with Dr Saad Al-Faqih," *Jamestown Foundation* 3, no. 5 (June 15, 2005), http://jamestown.org/terrorism/news/article.php?articleid=2369721 (hereinafter Jamestown interview).
24. Simon Henderson, "Bin Laden Increases His Challenge to the House of Saud," *London Times*, May 31, 2004.
25. John R. Bradley, "Saudis Jihadis Aping Iraq Rebels," *Washington Times*, June 23, 2004.
26. Michael Scott Doran, "Two Deaths and a Dissembling in Riyadh," *Daily Star*, August 27, 2004.
27. Faiza Saleh Ambah, "Saudi Bomb: A Shift in Al-Qaeda Tactics," *Christian Science Monitor*, April 22, 2004.
28. "Mecca: One Security Officer Assassinated," *Arabic News*, June 20, 2005.

29. "Slain Saudi Policeman Was Under Threat," United Press International, June 20, 2005.
30. "Saudi Security Forces 'Agreed to Let Al-Qaeda Killers Escape,'" *London Telegraph*, June 1, 2004.
31. Robin Gedye and John R. Bradley, "Bomber Moles in Saudi Security Forces," *London Telegraph*, May 16, 2003.
32. John R. Bradley, "Terror Comes to Saudis," *Washington Times*, January 19, 2004.
33. Ibid.
34. Amir Taheri, "What 'Fueled' the Saudi Raid," *New York Post*, December 6, 2004.
35. Jamestown interview.
36. Evans, "Saudi Arabia Says Ready to Beat Militants from Iraq."
37. Bradley, "Saudi Jihadis Aping Iraq Rebels."
38. Ibid.
39. Ibid.

Gwenn Okruhlik

The Irony of *Islah* (Reform)

Along the surface of Saudi Arabia's political terrain, there are municipal elections, the trial and imprisonment of noted intellectuals, and weekly shoot-outs between jihadis and state security forces. The tendency has been to focus on the discrete events themselves rather than on the complicated process in which they are embedded. That process, with historic roots in 1979 and 1991, reveals a larger struggle about making a nation or a community of belonging that gives meaning to its members.[1] Beneath the surface in Saudi Arabia, people are asking: who or what constitutes the nation? Competing narratives exist inside Saudi Arabia on what it means to belong—what it means, if anything, to "be Saudi" and how that relates to the larger Arab and Muslim world.

It is a contest over the prevailing norms that form the very bases of political and social life. These encompass the relationships among the state, ruling family, religion, and citizenry. More precisely, it is a contest over the substantive terms of citizenship, or the appropriate distributions of rights, obligations, and resources and the appropriate uses of force and wealth. Citizenship (*muwatana*) and nation (*'umma*) are sites of privilege,

Gwenn Okruhlik is a visiting scholar in the department of government at the University of Texas at Austin and a visiting researcher in political studies at The American University of Beirut. The author would like to thank Patrick Conge for his invaluable contributions to this project and to thank the many Saudi Arabians who generously shared their insights.

The Washington Quarterly • 28:4 pp. 153–170.

exclusion, and marginalization.[2] Among diverse populations such as that of Saudi Arabia, full and equal inclusion is a sensitive subject.

The ruling family, the al-Saud, is far from neutral and has long endorsed its own narrative to establish the proper meaning of citizenship—its own civic mythology. The al-Saud now reinforces its version to push the citizenship debate into the social realm and away from its distinctly political dimensions. Reform (*al islah*) is carefully choreographed to consolidate the ruling family's centrality in national political life and reassert its authority. The state crackdown on jihadi forces remains intense. By capitalizing on the fear of jihad and Al Qaeda, the regime also continues to crack down not only on national, liberal, and Islamist discourse but also, perhaps most importantly, on any cooperation between social forces. Although meaningful reforms are being implemented, none address the essential question of political power. Genuine political change is absent.

Narrating Citizenship

What exists inside Saudi Arabia today goes beyond the usual material contests. There is also a larger contest of ideas over the proper relationship between rulers and ruled and over the character of the just state and the just society. These underlying narratives fuel the discourse on citizenship.

The Official Civic Mythology

The official narrative meticulously weaves together the power of Islam and the al-Saud family as protector of Saudi Arabia's moral integrity. It equates the modern state with the fusion between the ruling family and a particular manifestation of Islam. This dominant narrative views people as subjects (*ra'ya*) following a shepherd (*ra'y*) who cares for them and to whom they are loyal (*wala'*).[3] Long disseminated in textbooks, by the media, and in museum exhibitions, it tells a story about the unification of the tribes under the banner of Islam and the wise leadership of Abdulaziz. The official narrative has produced a civic mythology in which citizenship has four social and economic components: family, personal behavior, Islam, and welfare.

The first component, identity with and loyalty to one's family, is of critical importance. Loyalty to the family structure is linked with loyalty to the state under the al-Saud; the private family reinforces the public family. The second component, expected norms of social behavior, is defined fairly rigidly, and women bear the brunt of social expectations. Some behavior is declared taboo on religious grounds (*haram*), while other behavior is circumscribed by social norms of shame (*'ayb*). This fuses social norms and religious interpretation, and the state identifies itself in turn with this fusion. The protection of a woman's honor is aligned with the protection of the family unit, which, as society's core institution, is expected to serve and obey the state. The third component refers to the regime's association with Islamic values. The regime promotes itself as the protector of the faith. The Koran is Saudi Arabia's constitution, and the *shari'a* is the law of the land. The state merely upholds these. The fourth component concerns the population's access to economic benefits provided by the state. With the oil-driven expansion of the economy in the 1970s through the mid-1980s, the number of foreign workers grew until they constituted about 95 percent of the private sector's labor force. The state began to codify what it meant to be Saudi to distribute the windfall benefits of oil revenues. Citizenship was defined in a way that differentiated the local population from the millions of foreign workers brought in to staff the country's burgeoning economy.

In sum, belonging was historically defined in social and cultural terms. An economic component was added during the frenzied growth spurred by the oil boom. "I am Saudi" came to mean "I am not an imported laborer." Belonging was based only on this negative frame of reference and was expressed through cultural, social, and economic qualities. Neither inclusive nor mutable, this dominant narrative could not grow with the nation.

Counter–Civic Narratives

Other narratives have been developed that contest the dominant historical account on the kingdom's founding. These versions are coherent, intricate, and internally consistent; they are woven from a fabric of cultural symbols and language that resonates among the population. Many social groups relay alternative narratives about the domination of regions rather than their unification, violence rather than wisdom, and the exploitation of Islam rather than its embrace. The memories on which such versions are based form the backdrop for the current effort to construct a national narrative that is more inclusive and less arbitrary than the official version.

The explicitly political qualities of citizenship are missing in the official interpretation. As it is currently envisioned, being Saudi is to be devoid of political power, its distribution, and its use. All people value the primary subjects of social and economic citizenship—family, Islam, social relations, and welfare—but the regime has borrowed the potency of these ideas and used them to devalue the explicitly political components of citizenship, such as fairness, accountability, and freedom of expression. Various social groups now offer counternarratives that contest this devaluation, revise the official civic mythology to incorporate political qualities, divorce the social and economic components from allegiance and subordination to a particular ruling family, and transform people from subjects (*ra'ya*) into citizens (*muwatinun*). These social groups also attempt to define a positive frame of reference that emphasizes who Saudis are, rather than focusing on who they are not. What makes Saudi Arabia's diverse population a nation? What does it mean to "be Saudi," the very name being a problem for many people? People want their rights as citizens.[4]

The importance of these narratives is that they emanate from multiple sources, across sect, region, gender, and ideology and, because they do, provide an indication of the skepticism with which the official narrative is received. Nationalists, Islamists, and their many permutations seek to create a community of belonging that provides individuals with meaning and membership, although they define community differently. A community could be considered the Muslim nation (*'umma islamiyya*), the Arab nation (*'umma 'arabiyya*), a sovereign territorial entity (*al dawla al 'umma al ssayida*), or the believers within a territory. Although tension may exist among such affinities, they are not necessarily mutually exclusive.

Counternarratives in Saudi Arabia are imbued with moral dimensions. There are many principled orientations toward the middle and away from the contending extremes of jihad and secularism. Many Saudis do not question the coexistence of religion and the state. Instead, they ask which manifestations of religion have what relation to the state. Islam is part and parcel of an entire discourse on progress and nation. It is ultimately an issue of accountable governance. For almost everyone, the ruling family must serve the state and the nation, not be the state and the nation. Its members cannot be above the law, whether one values shari'a or civil law. Further, corruption is not just a material issue; it is regarded as morally wrong. The stakes have risen. Today, it is less about "I want mine" and more about "we want ours—as a people, as a nation, and as a community (*mujtama'*)." Contentious voices resonate against Saudi Arabia's exclusionary structure of governance. From above, the sprawling religious and political bureaucracy does not represent the heterogeneity of the population. From below, there is precious little room for people to organize and contest the state. In between, old social contracts that linked the ruling family and the citizenry, however tenuously, are no longer relevant. The domestic struggle is further complicated by regional crises and U.S. hegemony.

Prelude to Contemporary Struggles

People contest the state on moral grounds because of corruption and authoritarianism, on material grounds because of inequality, on national grounds because of a lack of true representation, and on religious grounds with charges of deviation from the Koran and sunna. Today's struggle did not arise in a historical vacuum. There is a tendency to emphasize September 11, 2001, as the critical date in Saudi Arabian development. This is a mistake. Saudi Arabian domestic politics must be understood within the context of two watershed years, 1979 and 1991.

Four dramatic events unfolded in 1979: the Islamic revolution in Iran toppled the shah; a Sunni rebel, Juhaiman al-Utaibi, forcibly took control of the Great Mosque in Mecca; the Shi'a community rioted throughout Saudi Arabia's Eastern Province; and Saudi Arabian youth began to wage jihad in Afghanistan against Soviet Communists. The regime's panicked response to these events ushered in two decades of political paralysis and social stagnation. The regime chose to embrace rather than confront religious radicalism to protect the centrality of the ruling family in national life. King Fahd wrapped himself ever tighter in the mantle of official Islam, changing his title from "Your Majesty" to "Custodian of the Two Holy Cities." Seeking to bolster his family's legitimacy in a time of crisis, King Fahd sought to appropriate the power of Islam and to bind religion and state institutionally.

Throughout the 1980s, religious conservatives were entrenched in institutions, as evidenced by university funding and in the expansion of the religious bureaucracy, both of which the state funded generously even during the mid-decade downturn in oil revenues. The Islamic University in Mecca, Imam Muhammad bin Saud University in Riyadh, and Umm al-Qurra University in Mecca continued to grow even as other programs were cut back. That generation of students now serves as bureaucrats, police officers, judges, professors, and preachers.[5] The entrenchment of extreme conservatives was coupled with the return of young, ideologically driven, and battle-hardened Saudi Arabian mujahideen from Afghanistan. Although the conservatives were empowered in the 1980s, this religious resurgence was transformed in 1991 with the Gulf War when an Islamist social movement took root to oppose the U.S. military presence in Saudi Arabia. In the previous decade, the resurgence of Islam was largely inchoate, private, inwardly focused, and concerned with the purity of social norms and religious practice. With the Gulf War, however, the private became public, the spiritual became political, and individual efforts became organized. Religious believers became political activists.[6]

To bring this transformation full circle, the Gulf War gave popular power to the sheikhs of the *al sahwa al islamiyya* (Islamic Awakening) and an Islamist social movement that challenged the regime. A crisis arose in the old relationship between the *ulama* and ruling family. The *sahwa* sheikhs were jailed during the domestic turmoil following the Gulf War. In their absence, a new generation of more radical, fiery sheikhs arose who expanded the ideas of jihad, or struggle, and *takfir* (to declare someone an infidel). Later, the September 11 attacks and the ensuing war on terrorism ushered in fears of U.S. occupation or even division of the country. The jihadis engaged in the war in Iraq are returning to Saudi Arabia much younger and perhaps more independent than the mujahideen who returned from Afghanistan in the 1980s. Religious extremism and royal authoritarianism are the extremes within which the battle for the soul of the nation is being waged today.

Saudi Arabian domestic politics cannot be decontextualized. Resistance to U.S. hegemony in the Arab and Muslim world resonates among all segments of the population. It would be a mistake to underestimate this sentiment. Nevertheless, there is great uncertainty over what will happen when the thousands of Saudi Arabian jihadis in Iraq return home. The regime can respond with a wide variety of measures, ranging from amnesty, rehabilitation, and co-optation to arrest, punishment, and violent confrontation. The extent of the response and its effectiveness, however, will almost certainly depend on whether the jihadis return in triumph or defeat. What happens in the region, therefore, and particularly in Iraq matters greatly for the struggle to make a nation in Saudi Arabia.

Complex Contemporary Struggles

On the ground, in everyday politics, the political terrain is complex. Few people are satisfied with the status quo and, in one way or another, everybody is a reformist (*al islahiyyun*). The sociopolitical landscape is messy, with competition and cooperation between different groups. The division is not simply Al Qaeda versus the al-Saud family, but a nuanced field in which many participants offer different concepts of what it means to belong to the nation. The terrain cannot be described as a spectrum of right to left or top to bottom. It is not a set taxonomy but instead is fluid and mutable. People have multiple affinities and may move around the map as a strategic ploy, as a result of being co-opted by the regime, or in some cases after profound self-examination. Real power dynamics are also at play in Saudi Arabia, and it is not always clear, even to the players themselves, who is using whom. At a moment of crisis, whether prompted by succession, assassination, U.S. maneuvers, or other exogenous shock, the most organized will likely triumph.

In general, the political landscape contains four broad categories, each of which has multiple parts. The first is the Saudi Arabian state.

It consists of the al-Saud family, whose members show some differentiation, and the instruments of official Islam, all of whom are employees of the state and include the religious authorities (*ulama al dawla*), the enforcers of public moral behavior (*al mutawa'a*), and the Ministries of Islamic Affairs, Education, and the Judiciary. Over the decades, the ulama have shaped the official discourse on religion and politics and codified trivial social absurdities into law. These religious authorities were further discredited by their ruling during the Gulf War that allowed foreign forces on holy soil. They then lost their only respected leaders with the deaths of two sheikhs in recent years. There are also a wide array of state organizations, including the consultative assembly (*majlis al shura*) and the Human Rights Association. Although each is made up of skilled, bright individuals, they operate within strict parameters and are unlikely to alter the status quo.

The second category consists of the many Islamist social forces not under the rubric of the state. Perhaps largest in number are the people of the awakening (*ahl al sahwa*), often described as an effective combination of the Muslim Brotherhood's organization and the *al salafiyya*'s ideology. People of the sahwa seek to transform society. An activist argues that sahwa is, in practice, a political party because it has a radio station, a satellite channel, and the power of the mosques. In reality, the term "sahwa" is used very loosely and now refers to widely divergent groups and ideas. There are many shades and hues of sahwa. There are also neo-*salafi* (*al salafiyyun al judud*) who seek to revive what they consider a purer Islam, one free from centuries of accretions. They are more politicized and oppose the regime. Jihadis—extremists who use violence—directly confront the regime and seek to end U.S. hegemony in Saudi Arabia and the region. The intellectual counter to jihadis are those who refer to themselves as *al 'aqlaniyyin* (rationalists) or *al tayyar al tanwiri al islahi* (adherents to an enlightened reformist trend).[7] All these extraordinarily divergent social forces are Islamists (*islamiyun*) at some level.

The third category in the political landscape includes the nationalists (*al wataniyun*) who struggle for equal participation in a just and strong nation-state. These diverse voices often reflect different regions and come from marginalized social groups; various ideologies such as old-fashioned

Arab nationalists (*qawmiyuun*) and humanists (*insaniyun*); both genders; and all religious groups, including Ismailis, Shi'as, Sufis, and other Sunnis. A small but potentially influential domestic player was a tenuous and ad hoc network made up of Islamists of several orientations and nationalists of all orientations that came together in 2003 and 2004 to articulate dissatistfaction with the status quo.

The fourth category is Saudi Arabia's silent majority. Its members tend to be religiously devout, socially conservative, and mostly apolitical. Nonetheless, parents and youth alike want a better future. Many complain that girls are bored, that boys are unemployed, and that they are weary of corruption. According to a man from the center of Saudi Arabia, "The mainstream is religious and nonpolitical, but the issues that concern them are things like corruption, how people get jobs and positions, and why princes get privileges in hospitals."

Saudi Arabia's political landscape exhibits many visions of the nation and of citizenship. The Islamists and nationalists and the tenuous network between parts of them offer some of the most articulate counternarratives to the official version of belonging, making them vital to political discourse. Unfortunately, it also makes them targets of the regime's efforts to co-opt, coerce, or neutralize alternative voices.

The Irony of Islah: Reforms That Consolidate Power

A perennial problem in Saudi Arabia is that, once the government finally moves to institute a change, after years of study and committee work, social forces on the right and on the left have typically moved far beyond what is implemented. The regime's actions are always too little, too late and often represent lost moments of opportunity. The irony of islah is that, for the most part, "reforms" consolidate the power of the al-Saud family in political life.

For example, the basic law introduced in 1992 established a consultative assembly (*majlis al shura*) and provincial administrations. Nevertheless, it also consolidated the centrality of the ruling family rather than broadening political participation. The majlis remains fully appointed and has only an advisory role. The number of majlis members has recently increased, but the expansion was designed for the assembly "to represent all tribes." Yet, a significant portion of the population is not tribal, and even if it were, this justification casts light on parochial identities rather than on something larger and more inclusive.

The press has been given more leeway since 1998 but still faces red-lines that cannot be crossed. Primary among these are direct criticism of the ruling family, the official religious establishment, and especially the fusion between them. There are several recent cases of journalists, including Hamza al-Mizeini, Abdullah al-Bikheit, Hussein al-Shobokshi, Jamal al-Khashojji, and Qinan al-Ghamdi, who have found themselves in trouble for pushing the boundaries. In addition, journalist Khaled Suleiman al-Omair was arrested after he appeared on Al Jazeera television prior to the elections in the spring of 2005; he reportedly began a hunger strike in prison. The National Dialogue forums (*muntadiat al hiwar al watani*) initiated by Crown Prince Abdullah in June 2003 were a step toward tolerance, but they turned out to be a controlled dialogue to direct frustrations into acceptable channels rather than meaningful communication between social forces and the ruling family.

Municipal Elections: Why the Ambivalence?

Elections for about 1,700 seats on 178 municipal-level councils were held throughout Saudi Arabia over recent months, demonstrating to doubters that Islam and democracy are compatible, the state is technically ready for elections, and the people are ready for participation. Yet, there was also a marked ambivalence about these elections in many quarters in Saudi Arabia: only about 20 percent of the overall eligible electorate voted. (The turnout was higher in the eastern part of the country where the Shi'a minority resides. They effectively used the elections to assert their presence.)

In the months preceding the actual casting of ballots, civil servants were warned, in no uncertain language, that they would face disciplinary measures, including the loss of their jobs, if they criticized state policies or any governmental programs.[8] To say the very least, this pressure inhibits democratic dialogue. Women were not allowed to participate. In addition, although outside observers celebrated the municipal council elections, three men who called for an electoral process and a constitutional monarchy, Matruk al-Faleh, Ali al-Dumaiyyni, and Abdullah al-Hamad, remain in jail. The ideas they promote offer one version of how to embark on the national project.

The elections themselves were for only half of the council seats; the government will appoint individuals to the remaining half of the seats across the country. According to activists who have worked for elections for years, "We had elections 40 years ago! And they were for 100 percent of the seats on the council!" One man lamented that "the struggle was never about this. People did not get into this fierce struggle for this ... not for half of municipal councils." In addition, the elections were only for seats on municipal-level councils, which are likely to be concerned with issues such as street paving, the size of billboards, and parking. Even though these are certainly important issues, especially in Saudi Arabia, where the infrastructure has not kept pace with population growth, activists fear that these meager reforms may distract people from the larger issues at hand, such as the current lack of freedom of expression. Although for dissenters elections are only a means to an end, from the regime's perspective the elections are a means and an end, aimed at diffusing dissent and satisfying international pressure.

In these unwieldy elections, voters had to choose perhaps six candidates from a ballot of several hundred. The sahwa sheikhs effectively used instant messaging and e-mail to circulate so-called golden lists (*al qawa'im al dhahabia*) of candidates, those whom religious leaders deemed acceptable and portrayed as "pleasing to Allah." These candidates swept most of the elections. Their credentials are certainly not in doubt; by all accounts, these individuals make up a highly competent group. Nevertheless, there are different ways to interpret what has been called "the Islamist sweep." The fact that these men are devout Muslims does not mean that they are all "political Islamists." In addition, for many supporters of the winning lists, the results show how democracy works. They would argue that democracy reflects a society and their society is very conservative, Islamists played the game better and won, and liberals and nationalists never got their act together to put forward leadership.

Yet, in reality the explanation may be more complex. In short, the playing field is not level in Saudi Arabia. Conservative religious figures are frequently granted more leeway to shape discourse than are liberal, national, and moderate Islamist reformists. Each time they put forward potential leadership, the individuals are arrested, jailed, or intimidated. They are prohibited from criticizing the status quo, especially the fusion of official religious orthodoxy with the state. Although there is some room to discuss social issues, political discussion is met with intimidation. In March 2004, 13 reformists were arrested after they promoted the idea of a constitutional monarchy in a petition and then met to form a human rights association. Most of these men were eventually released after signing a pledge to avoid discussing politics in public. Three men refused to sign the statements and remain in jail, charged with threatening national unity, challenging those in authority, criticizing the educational system, and inciting public opinion. Their trial started and stopped several times and was eventually conducted behind closed doors. The men were handed down strict sentences in May, with each now serving six to nine years. As a result, for the duration of the elections, some of the most articulate nationalist voices were in jail or had been released only after signing a statement in which they pledged not to engage in public politics again. Yet, through the golden lists, some sheikhs were allowed to engage in politics. Perhaps the ambivalence and cynicism surrounding the elections arose because they took place without the supporting norms of freedom of expression and assembly. After all, elections require not only an outward form, but also a civic sense of national belonging.

Reassertion of Authority

The completion of municipal elections notwithstanding, it has been suggested that, on one hand, the legitimacy of the ruling regime is now very weak, even to the point where cracks seem to be appearing in the state apparatus. These observers point to such issues as the domestic jihadi campaign, the string of assassinations in al-Jouf, parts of cities where the police cannot enter and where state authority has no relevance, and a military that includes many oppositional Islamists. On the other hand, the same people painfully acknowledge that the regime has successfully reasserted itself. How can cracks in the state occur simultaneously with a reassertion of the ruling family's authority?

Saudi Arabian social forces are engaged in a fight to fashion a moral order. A just political economy would contain corruption, cease princely land grabs, attach accountability to shari'a and/or civil law, and end arbitrary governance. The ruling family, however, has yet to reassert itself in moral terms or alter the behavior of some family members. Instead, it has reasserted itself through coercive power and material wealth. The ruling family arrested and jailed the liberals, nationalists, and participants in network politics; it also co-opted some articulate voices of sahwa and the rationalist Islamist trend. Most importantly, Saudi Arabia's rulers renewed their relationship with the official religious orthodoxy and with sahwa clerics.

What allows the regime to hinder the social forces engaged in nation-making? How does the regime frame its reform efforts to make them fit the legitimate cultural repertoire?[9] In its renewed relationship with religious authorities, the regime postures itself as the "Guardian of Virtue and Custodian of Change," which is reminiscent of its response to the events of 1979. When the ruling family feels threatened, it empowers the very forces that may pose a great challenge to them. This seems to be a reaffirmation of the old civic mythology and its emphasis on the al-Saud family as protector of the moral integrity of the nation. Once again, the regime uses this mythology to enhance its Islamic credentials and to keep its traditional religious constituency happy, to take the steam out of oppositional religious forces. Rather than quell debate after 1979, however, it fueled it. Likewise, although the regime may have silenced competing voices today, this is a temporary measure that may ultimately backfire yet again.

Indeed, the regime has empowered the clerics who may later become the official ulama of the state. These men may be the *sahwa al sultan*, so to speak. They are part of the state discourse in its fight on terrorism, providing the state with the intellectual and cultural means to fight jihad. If and when clerics become part of the state, they risk losing their voice and credibility with the population. Once co-opted by the state, the sheikhs can no longer challenge the prevailing (im)moral order over which the ruling famly that appointed them presides. Hence, their co-optation will later become a source of popular dissent.

Deflecting Attention from Internal Politics

When the ruling family renews its relationships with religious orthodoxy and sahwa clerics, it placates those who are troubled by changes to the domestic social order, especially in matters of gender, education, and religious practice. Nevertheless, it is important to recognize that only the sociocultural aspects of the sahwa are given safe space in the country. The political aspects of sahwa are instead directed outward toward, for example, Iraq, Chechnya, and Afghanistan. The consequence is that the debate over political reform is deflected to foreign issues rather than focusing on domestic issues. In the context of regional crises, it has proven relatively easy to deflect attention outward.[10]

At the same time, the permissible domestic debate is about social issues, such as gender, media, globalization, and "reforming Wahhabism," rather than the more difficult, explicitly political issues such as reforming the al-Saud or the fusion of official religious orthodoxy with the state. It is much easier to offer an intellectual critique of the excesses of official religious orthodoxy than it is to talk about the excesses of some ruling family members. There is much dancing around politics.

There was a vibrant time in 2002 through early 2004 when fear of state retribution for political activism declined. Social forces took advantage of the intense international attention paid to their domestic circumstances and took more chances in pushing for political change. This vibrancy was squelched, however, with a crackdown once the regime felt secure and the United States was bogged down in Iraq. Since the arrests in March 2004, elites are frightened, liberals are tired, and nationalists are worn down. The loose national reformist network, active only two years ago, is today largely silent. Religious television programming has increased significantly. The regime has made dubious moves, jailing reformists, appeasing conservative religious authorities, empowering the social sahwa, and frightening the vast majority of the population into silence.

On the ground, nationalist and Islamist activists, as well as interesting combinations thereof, working to forge a meaningful, larger community, have been met with resistance from above. Social forces try to lay the groundwork for nation-making, but the state resists such efforts. Using its coercive power and material wealth, the regime set out to diminish or neutralize any sense of belonging that was larger than itself and any collective sense of being that is not directly dependent on the regime. The al-Saud family eliminates what it cannot control and diminishes the resonance of larger belongings. Given uncertainty about the future of the region, there is something of a corresponding resurgence of local identities in region, tribe, sect, or other communities that may provide a sense of security in crisis.

The regime has returned to its quadruped of tried-and-true methods: coercion, co-optation through disbursement of oil revenues, renewed relations with religious orthodoxy, and playing social forces against one another. At the same time, it has resurrected negative aspects of the rentier condition, where skyrocketing oil prices generate more revenue which may be used to co-opt dissenters and placate the population's material wants without addressing the messy political and social problems.

Imagining Saudi Arabia

Labels and categories must be used with caution. Many Saudi Arabian activists and intellectuals take offense at the very idea of labels because they are routinely bandied about in domestic debates as a way to discredit people. Terms such as "*al zaydi*," "*al mani*," "*al liberali*," or "*al wahhabi*" can all be manipulated with tone to serve as an insult or epithet to incorrectly mean, respectively, Shi'a, secularist, Americanized, or irrational fundamentalist. Each of these terms has a respectable meaning but also can be a pejorative label used as a mechanism to exclude a person from contemporary discourse.

The words "conservative," "liberal," "religious," and "secular" do not adequately capture political sentiment in Saudi Arabia. Similarly, the terms "sahwa" and "Islamist" are too all-inclusive to be truly meaningful in any analysis of the political landscape. The term "Wahhabi" can be used only with several explanatory footnotes.[11] "Nationalist," however, may be a more appropriate word to capture the wide, though still shallow spectrum of people who plead for an inclusive nation and an accountable state, demonstrated by the steady flow of petitions and demands to the al-Saud regime from multiple sects and regions, representing both genders. Yet, the nationalist framework has never been given a safe space in which to grow, whether one speaks of a Muslim nation, an Arab nation, or a Saudi Arabian nation (*al dawla al 'umma al 'arabiyya al sa'udiyya*).

Mythologizing 'Conservatism'

It is often argued that Saudi Arabian society is more conservative than the ruling family and that leaders seeking to initiate progressive change are held in check by a deeply conservative society. Yet, for three reasons, caution must be exercised before accepting this claim. First, political attitudes cannot be inferred from social attitudes. Much of Saudi Arabian society is generally conservative in social and religious affairs, particularly in the center of the country, less so along the coasts. Nevertheless, there are no necessary links among religious devotion, social behavior, and political beliefs. One does not always imply or lead to the other. There are political liberals who are social conservatives and social liberals who are political conservatives. Social conservatism and religious devotion do not translate into support for political authoritarianism. Saudi Arabian society is diverse and can largely be characterized as devout in religious terms, traditional in social norms, and mostly apolitical in terms of activism. Yet, most citizens have a desire for fair distribution of resources and the rule of law.

Second, it is the ruling family that systematically empowers the most conservative elements of society, giving them institutional and public space in which to operate, for example, in the sprawling bureaucracy and the educational arena. For decades, other voices were forced to remain on the periphery of discourse and power. The state is not a neutral vessel. Instead, its representatives structure the playing field so that only one voice is heard and only one voice is safe to support.

Third, the problem in Saudi Arabia is not conservative interpretations of Islam, conservative clerics, or even "Wahhabism." The difficulty lies in the monopoly that extreme "Wahhabi" doctrine has over the interpretation of religion and its fusion with the state. Although denied, many people argue that *al madhab al wahhabi* is indeed the sect and jurisprudence (*fiqh*) of the state.[12] Further, the problem is not with conservative morality but that morality has been trivialized. It is conflated with the codification of social absurdities, demonstrated by religious rulings that regulate the plucking of eyebrows, the use of nail polish, and the length of gowns, rather than grapple with explicitly political issues that revolve around distributive fairness, governmental accountability, and social justice.

Ideas of social justice and political accountability are not peculiar to Western liberals. Indeed, in critiquing the harsh sentences imposed on the three men who called for a constitutional monarchy, writers have specifically invoked Islam to defend freedom of expression, debate, and tolerance of divergent opinions.[13] In sum, neither the al-Saud nor "Wahhabism" alone is the full story. Rather, it is the excesses of each, the fusion of both, and the exclusion of all others that inhibits meaningful nation-making.

The Conundrum of Political Progressives

Progressives in Saudi Arabia, alternatively called liberals, nationalists, or moderate Islamists, often refuse to use direct and explicit language to confront the regime. They have tended to criticize the religious radicals only. An intellectual observes that "[t]hey must take on the state too! But how can they subvert a state that is their protector? They are compromised from the start." This has been the long-standing conundrum for progressive social forces. The relationship between the ruling family and Saudi Arabia's politically progressive forces was historically a convenience for the former and a necessity for the latter. A nationalist argues that progressives "often served as a shield or a fence for the ruling family. But this is less true now. After the arrests and certainly the sentences handed down, the relationship changed." Now, progressives no longer defend the ruling family so easily.

Nevertheless, progressive forces lack the four critical attributes that conservative forces have long possessed: a safe space in which to operate, ideological coherence, social connections, and organization. The regime keeps it that way by choice and capability. Clamping down on progressives has been less costly for the ruling family; it is more complicated to circumscribe conservative religious forces, on whom the ruling family so intimately depends. Ironically, in its desire to prevent any alternative leadership from arising among progressives, the regime may have actually sent an unintended message when it handed down harsh sentences. For some, there may be a painful recognition that legal and respectful dialogue will not be effective in producing political change in Saudi Arabia.[14]

The Politics of Resistance and Reform

For several years, social forces, including Islamists of many orientations, nationalists, women, representatives of various regions, and courageous networks of social groups, presented their visions of a just state and a just society to the government in the form of petitions. In the absence of real expression or elections, they articulated their vision in the form of advice and letters. What some people, both activists and nonactivists, say about the ruling family is that the question is not whether they govern but how they govern. The problem lies less in their authority and more in their abuse of authority. Whereas committed jihadis oppose the ruling family itself, many others contest the choices made by the al-Saud family over the decades to exploit religion for its own ends.[15]

People want rules of the game; a needed structural change in Saudi Arabia is simply to have structure. Some consensus exists that much popular resentment and anger would dissipate if the ruling family were reduced and regularized, its privileges and immunities were curtailed, private property were respected, new advisers who represent the country's diversity were brought onboard, and institutional constraints were placed on the behavior of all state officials, including members of the ruling family.

Two common concerns are the lack of an independent judiciary and a legal, publicly known system for determining succession. When King Fahd's death seemed imminent, there were renewed family power struggles, particularly among the king's brothers—Naif, Sultan, and Abdullah—as well as with Fahd's son, Abdulaziz. People want to know ahead of time not only how succession is to proceed among the brothers but when and how the next generation is to be involved.

There are other commonly held practical and principled concerns. The former include jobs, health, and education; the latter include free expression and assembly, respect for private property, transparency in public accounts, increased participation in government, respectful behavior on the part of the ruling family, and fairer distribution of goods. Many people point out that, if the principled reforms were implemented, especially expression and assembly, the practical problems would be more easily resolved.

There are real steps forward in Saudi Arabia, but they often go unnoticed abroad. Cinema was recently approved in the Eastern Province after decades of prohibition. Premarital genetic counseling is now mandatory, a significant reform in a country where negotiated marriages between first cousins are common. Identity cards will be required for all women, who no longer need male family members' permission to obtain one. An important religious authority, Sheikh Abdulaziz Al Sheikh, ruled against forced marriages for women. It is critical to note that none of these are explicitly political; explicit political reform remains peripheral.

In the end, tremendous respect is due to social forces that reach out across traditional barriers of tribe, region, sect, gender, and principled belief. People are taking risks to make a nation. Ordinary people want to participate in their country's development, particularly in meeting a young, booming population's need for education, housing, and employment. They want to write a new narrative on belonging that is moral and political. Saudi Arabians do not want to be tended by a caretaker. Instead, they want to be active citizens and long for a sense of control over their own lives.

Notes

1. This analysis is not about "nation building" as embodied in U.S. policies. It refers to a serious, internal process that goes far beyond the imposition of institutions under foreign occupation. The fieldwork for this analysis was largely conducted in January–August 2003 in Riyadh, Jeddah, and several cities in the Eastern Province. The work was supported by a Fulbright Research Grant and supplemented with later interviews. More than 200 interviews crossed sect, gender, region, age, principled belief, and tribal/nontribal populations. All quotations are taken from these interviews.
2. On citizenship and nation-making, see Suad Joseph, ed., "Gender and Citizenship in Muslim Communities," *Citizenship Studies* 3, no 3 (1999); Nils Butenschon, Uri Davis, and Manuel Hassassian, eds., *Citizenship and the State in the Middle East* (New York: Syracuse University Press, 2000); Sarah Radcliffe and Sallie Westwood, *Remaking the Nation: Place, Identity and Politics in Latin America* (New York: Routledge and Kegan Paul, 1996); Sheila Croucher, "Perpetual Imagining: Nationhood in a Global Era," *International Studies Review*, no. 5 (2003): 1–24. On myths, see Rogers Smith, "Citizenship and the Politics of People Building," *Citizenship Studies* 5, no. 1 (2001): 73–96; Madawi al-Rasheed, "God, the King and the Nation: The Rhetoric of Politics in Saudi Arabia in the 1990s," *Middle East Journal* 50, no. 4 (Summer 1996): 359–371.
3. This is conveyed in the hadith sharif "kulukum ra'yi wa kulukum mas'ul 'an ra'yiatih," roughly translated to suggest that "you are all shepherds and you are responsible for your dependents (or flock)." It is given political meaning in the oath of allegiance "al baiy'a 'ala al sam' wa al ta'a," giving allegiance to hear and obey the ruler.
4. On citizenship in Saudi Arabia, see Fouad Ibrahim, "Al muwatana fi mujtama' ta 'addudi: halat al sa' udiyya" [Citizenship in a pluralistic society: the case of Saudi Arabia], *Qadaia al khalij* [Gulf issues], http://gulfissues.net/; Yusif Makki, "Al muwatana wa al wihda al wataniyya" [Citizenship and national unity], *Qadaia al khalij* [Gulf issues], http://gulfissues.net/; Khaled al-Rasheed, "Hal hunak hawiyya wataniyya sa'udiyya?" [Is there a Saudi national identity?], *Shu'un sa'udiyya* [Saudi affairs], no. 3 (April 2003): 26–27; Wajiha al-Howaida, "Fuduha sira" [Stop this talk], June 1, 2005, http://www.hrinfo.net/.
5. Gwenn Okruhlik, "Networks of Dissent: Islamism and Dissent in Saudi Arabia," *Current History*, January 2002, pp. 22–28.
6. On the aftermath of 1979 and Islamism as a social movement, see Gwenn Okruhlik, "Making Conversation Permissible: Islamism and Reform in Saudi Arabia," in *Islamic Activism: A Social Movement Theory Approach*, ed. Quintan Wiktorowicz (Bloomington, Ind.: Indiana University Press, 2004), pp. 250–269.
7. For an early and widely disseminated analysis, see "Kharitat al Islamiyyin fi al Sa 'udiyya wa Qossat al Takfir" [The Islamist map and the story of Takfir], February 27, 2003, http://elaph.com/.

8. Hebah Saleh, "Saudi Warning to Critical Civil Servants Dents Hopes of Political Reform," *Financial Times*, September 16, 2004.

9. For provocative work on the notion of a legitimate cultural repertoire, see Rhys Williams and Timothy Kubal, "Movement Frames and the Cultural Environment: Resonance, Failure and the Boundaries of the Legitimate," in *Research in Social Movements, Conflict and Change*, eds. Michael Dobkowski and Isidor Wallimann (Stamford, Conn: JAI Press, 1999), pp. 225–248.

10. The United States is complicit in this deflection. It emphasizes reforms of education, banking, the WTO, and gender. It does not press for meaningful and explicit political power sharing. On the U.S. role in this process, see Ali al-Ferdan, "The Prison of Reformers and the Reality of the Saudi Government," *Arabian News*, May 16, 2005.

11. A linguistic note: "Wahhabi" seems to have taken on a hegemonic meaning in the international press that does not accurately reflect its usage in Saudi Arabia prior to September 11, 2001. Believers would never refer to themselves as Wahhabi, as that implies worshipping someone—Muhammad ibn 'Abd al-Wahhab—other than God. They prefer instead to call themselves *muwahhidun* or *ahl al-tawhid*, to emphasize the centrality of monotheism, or Salafi, to emphasize the purity of their beliefs based on the precedent of the Prophet. Usually, Salafi is a broader category than Wahhabi and the latter implies less tolerance of diversity than the former. It is a confusing state of affairs as the term means different things to different people. It may be useful to think of three meanings of Wahhabism: as a religious practice grounded in time and place, as a set of social norms dominant in the Najd, and as a type of jurisprudence. There is an emphasis on what actions are *haram* (prohibited) or *bid'a* (heresy). Wahhabism is opposed to Sufism, saint worship, and folk religious traditions. It is exclusionary, carefully delineating boundaries that distinguish believers from others. Believers reject sectarian divisions and perceive Wahhabism as the one, true Islam. To refer to those people who have broader political aspirations directed against the hegemony of the West, the more appropriate term is *al salafiyyun al judud* (neo-salafi).

12. Hamad Saleh al-Misfr, "Ittako Allah Ya ma'shara al Kodatt Fi Ahkamikum" [Fear God, oh judges, as you make decisions], *Al Quds Al Arabi*, May 23, 2005. Al-Misfr asks, "Do the judges [who sentenced the three men] know what they are doing or are they ordered by the sultan?"

13. In the above article, al-Misfr refers to "al amen al fikri fi sunnat Allah" [the security of ideas in the way of God]. See Muhammad Mafouz, "Watania wa 'adala al siyasia" [Citizenship and political justice], *Majala al Kalima*, May 27, 2005.

14. See Faiza Amba, "Saudi Crackdown on Dissenters," *Christian Science Monitor*, May 16, 2005; Mai Yamani, "How to Make Violence Inevitable in Saudi Arabia," *Daily Star*, June 2, 2005.

15. Madawi al-Rasheed constructs five "political heresies" that this fusion (*al salafia al sultania*) has produced. Madawi al-Rasheed, "Muhakamat duat al islah fi al sa'udiyya" [The judging of the reformists], *Al Quds Al Arabi*, May 17, 2005.

Part II:
Syria

Eyal Zisser

Bashar Al-Assad: In or Out of the New World Order?

When President Bashar al-Assad inherited power following the death of his father, Hafiz al-Assad, on June 10, 2000, many Syrians hoped that he would transform Syria into a more politically, economically, and culturally open society. Such speculation was based largely on contrasts between the father and the son: the gap in their ages, the dissimilarity in their educational backgrounds, and the difference in their degree of exposure to the West. At the start of the twenty-first century, amid dismal socioeconomic and political conditions, Syrians needed to hope. Toward the end of the 1990s, the ruling Ba'ath regime in Damascus seemed to have reached a dead end. Hafiz al-Assad had always been convinced that time was on his side, that there was no need for reform.[1] His son, however, seemed aware of his country's dire situation and of the need to initiate genuine reform to ensure the regime's survival. He also appeared aware of the need to bridge the deep gulf between Syrian and Western society, primarily in the realm of technological and scientific progress, but also in the political and the economic spheres, and thus enable Syria to integrate into the new world order.[2]

In mid-2005, however, five years after Bashar came to power, it has become increasingly evident that he is finding the conduct of a signifi-

Eyal Zisser is a professor and chairman of the Department for Middle Eastern and African History at Tel Aviv University.

The Washington Quarterly • 28:3 pp. 115–131.

cant change of course difficult and has still not freed himself from his late father's shadow. Moreover, many observers argue that, if any difference does exist between the two men, it has less to do with their policies and outlooks than with the fact that the father was perceived as an authoritative and powerful leader, while the son's image remains that of an upstart. In domestic and foreign policy spheres, Bashar still seems to lack sufficient legitimacy and charisma, as well as the experience needed to achieve genuine change. In fact, all of Bashar's efforts to introduce reforms, even limited ones, have clearly failed, from his early efforts to permit a certain degree of political openness to his attempts to liberalize the Syrian economy. Even Bashar's efforts to improve Syria's standing regionally and internationally have not succeeded, and the country remains more isolated and threatened than ever.

When probed during a 2003 interview with the *New York Times* about the gap between the promises and hopes that arose on his coming to power and the reality more than two years later, Bashar responded that the problem does not lay with his world view, determination, or ability to make difficult decisions. Rather, the trouble stems from Syria's lack of reformist cadre with the knowledge and experience necessary to introduce genuine change. Bashar added that, although he would continue moving toward reform, he would proceed at the "Syrian pace," a pace sufficiently slow and gradual to guarantee political stability.[3] Yet, Bashar may no longer have that luxury. Syria's failures to cooperate fully with the United States in the war on terrorism and to cope with the results of the war in Iraq, as well as with the dramatic recent events in Lebanon, are liable to bring Bashar's regime to a point at which it will have to make painful decisions in domestic and foreign policy, decisions that it has delayed making for years. The regime will have to make them if it hopes to survive.

Is Bashar a Different Assad?

Bashar's reign came when Syria faced a crossroads, if not an impasse, in light of a series of political, social, and economic policy challenges. The ability of the Ba'ath regime, which has ruled Syria since the Ba'ath Revolution of March 8, 1963, to continue in its present form was and is being questioned. The Ba'ath Party was founded in Damascus in 1947 as an all-Arab party with branches in other Arab countries, such as Lebanon, Jordan, and Iraq. The Iraqi branch of the party separated itself from the Syrian branch to become a totally different party, although ostensibly committed to the same basic principles of Pan-Arabism. The Ba'ath regime in Syria, established in the wake of the 1963 revolution, however, soon became embroiled in an intense internal power struggle that ended when Hafiz took control of the regime in November 1970. By all accounts, one of Hafiz al-Assad's (1970–2000) most definitive achievements was to establish a strong, stable regime, even if it was also highly repressive. With such unprecedented political stability, Hafiz was able to transform the country from a weak, ineffectual entity into a regional power of stature and influence.[4]

By the late 1980s, however, cracks began to appear in the secure image that Hafiz projected during his rule. A series of factors were responsible for this setback, including the collapse of the Soviet Union, Syria's close ally and patron; the ascendance of the United States as the world's sole superpower; the spread of globalization, the effects of which became palpable even in Syria; a spiraling birth rate as well as a stagnant economy during the 1990s; and Hafiz's deteriorating health, which led to his seclusion.[5]

A False Spring in Damascus

The Syrian people thus welcomed Bashar's rise to power as a refreshing wind. From the little that people who had met him reported, as well as from newspaper interviews Bashar so sparingly granted, the new president appeared to be an open-minded and intelligent young man with a modern, Western worldview who recognized the need for reform. His prolonged stay in London, where he was a resident in ophthalmology at a local hospital, as well as his deep familiarity with the Internet—knowledge in which he took great pride—were all signs for optimism.

At the beginning of his rule, Bashar made some hesitant efforts to encourage greater open-mindedness, including some moves, although rather limited in scope, toward economic and political reform. Observers noted these developments and coined the term "Damascus Spring" to refer to this new era of progress. Bashar even encouraged intellectuals to form cultural and political forums throughout Syria in a relatively open atmosphere, touching on the need to advance democracy in Syria. Bashar's support for the forums encouraged Syrian intellectuals to speak out and level criticism at the political system prevailing in the country.[6]

This tendency toward political openness was quickly curbed. Aside from Bashar's lack of experience, leadership skills, and charisma, he also appears to have been too weak to take on his father's close associates in the regime's leadership who had remained in office. The Old Guard was supported by Syria's true powerbrokers: commanders of the Security Services and the army units, all of whom are members of the Alawite community, a heterodox Muslim sect, which account for roughly 12 percent of the Syrian population; political bosses and other members of the Ba'ath Party; and the government bureaucrats who controlled Syria's socioeconomic life. They were all determined to maintain the political and social order that had existed in the country for an entire generation.

In mid-2001, just a year after assuming power, Bashar found himself leading, or perhaps impelled to lead, a counterattack of the regime against supporters of reform. Spokespeople for the regime and even Bashar himself quickly labeled the reformists as "Western agents whose only aim was to undermine Syria's internal stability from within, in the service of the state's enemies."[7] At the peak of this counterattack, the regime issued orders to terminate the forums, and several reform-camp activists who stood out for their criticism of the regime were imprisoned.

An Economic Burden

Bashar also quickly found himself confronting an economic crisis, the first signs of which had already become evident toward the end of his father's rule. The crisis centered on several key problems, the first being demographic. Syria held the dubious distinction, during the 1970s and 1980s, of having one of the highest rates of natural population growth in the world. Estimates put its population at the start of 2003 at 20 million, compared to six million when Hafiz al-Assad came to power in 1970 and three million in 1946, the year Syria had gained independence.[8] Subsequently, in the late 1990s, Syria's economic growth rates froze and then dropped; government services available to citizens regressed; the already overloaded infrastructure was further strained, causing water and electricity stoppages; unemployment rose sharply, especially among entry-level workers; illiteracy increased; and unprecedented signs of poverty appeared on the city streets.

In light of these difficult economic circumstances, Bashar's regime decided to focus its efforts on advancing economic reforms, even if only limited in scope. The government attempted to encourage the development of private banking, an industry that had not existed in the country until the beginning of 2000. Moreover, the regime began slowly to abandon the socialist terminology to which it had devoted itself for a generation. In early 2005, people in Damascus began to speak openly about the need to adopt a market economy. Yet, the collection of these reforms turned out in practice to be quite limited, cosmetic, and declarative. The difficulty the regime experienced in confronting the existing power centers, such as the governmental bureaucracy and the party activists who exercised economic control in Syria, and the people close to the centers of power who controlled a significant portion of the Syrian private sector prevented any genuine reform of the Syrian economy.

The Enduring Ba'ath System

Domestic tensions within Syria have accelerated in the wake of the 2003 U.S. war in Iraq, although they do not threaten the integrity of Bashar's regime. In early March 2004, for example, a Kurdish intifada erupted in Syria's northern region of Hasaka, especially in the city of Qamishli on the Syrian-Turkish border. Three Kurdish youths were killed by the brutality of police and security forces during a fight between fans of Kurdish- and Arab-supported football teams. In protest, Kurds launched a wave of violence that included attacks on government offices and public facilities and even reached the Kurdish quarter in Damascus as well as the University of Damascus, where Kurdish students denounced violations of Kurdish rights.[9] Previously, Damascus would have responded exclusively with an iron fist as it had in repressing previous rebellions, such as the 1982 Hama uprising when the regime killed thousands. This time, although several dozen Kurdish deaths at government hands have been reported, the regime appears more willing to be conciliatory and seems to be relying on the support of Arabs, who constitute an overwhelming majority of the population.

The regime need not be overly concerned about the protests of oppositionist organizations and human rights activists that spread throughout Syria in 2004. For the time being, these groups remain a small collection of pro-reform forces lacking any real base in the broader Syrian public. In general, the regime still appears to enjoy the support of most of the pillars of Syrian society: army officers, economic elites, and the small middle class. Those elements understand better than any foreign observer that the alternative to the current regime is not necessarily a liberal democracy as envisaged by the current U.S. administration, but rather Islamist fundamentalism of the sort that would make the Ba'ath look, by contrast, positively libertarian.

In April 2004, Islamist radicals who had recently returned from fighting U.S. forces in Iraq carried out a terrorist attack at the UN headquarters in Damascus, aimed at a Western target but also at destabilizing the secular Syrian Ba'ath regime.[10] This attack, although isolated, was the first successful operation since the regime had forcibly put down an Islamic rebellion in 1976–1982. These fundamentalist elements have subsequently resurfaced, and the true scope and extent of their presence within a population throughout the country's cities that is 60 percent Sunni is unknown.[11]

The Challenge of Globalization

Although these domestic political and economic challenges do not yet threaten to undermine Bashar's regime, they have increased as globalization has accelerated. It is no wonder that Syrians began considering globalization, which has been scapegoated by the state, to be the root of all evil. Hafiz aptly reflected this perception in remarks he made when meeting with trade union representatives in March 1999: "Globalization is flooding our markets with its products and is preventing our products from reaching its markets. It forces the world into a threatening cultural and ideological mold. We are farmers, and the land belonged and will continue to belong to the farmers."[12]

In a series of interviews in the late 1990s, Bashar al-Assad displayed a more nuanced approach. Speaking to the Kuwaiti newspaper *Al-Watan*, Bashar stressed that globalization and not, for example, the conflict with Israel was the central issue of the times and would determine Syria's ability to enter the twenty-first century. Bashar was forthright in expressing his opinion that Syria must respond to this challenge and embark on the road to progress and modernization.[13]

Nevertheless, once in power, he soon adopted his father's line of thinking about the dangers of globalization. In a speech welcoming the Chinese vice president to Damascus in January 2001, Bashar pointed out that "[t]he nations of the world who work together to achieve peace, security, stability and development, today face a series of challenges topped by the challenge of globalization. This perception constitutes a flag but also a mask for those who work to bring about ... cultural and economic hegemony ... that abolishes national identity."[14]

Syria's approach to the question of globalization, and more so to the question of economic openness, reflects the regime's difficulty in adjusting to the new international reality. One sign of this was the government's method of allegedly promoting but actually controlling or even impeding the introduction of advanced communications technology into Syria. Eventually, these advances did penetrate the country, but the slow pace of the process exemplified Syria's difficulty in integrating into the global economy and the world at large.

Computers and the Internet

A Western diplomat, meeting with Hafiz al-Assad in 1995, tried to persuade him of the importance of allowing Syrians access to the Internet. Although Hafiz listened and appeared to be convinced, at the end of the meeting he said that Bashar had tried to convince him of the same but that the heads of his security bureaus, who had the final say, still opposed permitting access.[15] Indeed, in the mid-1990s, Syria's integration into the world's information revolution appeared remote.

Dramatic change, by Syrian standards, in the authorities' approach to computers, the Internet, and information technology came only after Bashar assumed power in June 2000. In 1992, there were 2,500 computers throughout all of Syria; in 1998, there were 15,000; and by the end of 2002, there were some 330,000.[16] Syria's exposure to the Internet has proceeded slowly as well, in parallel with the gradual rise in the number of computers in the country. In 1999 the government announced the first stage of a plan to link the country to the Internet, beginning with 2,500 subscribers in various government ministries. Only in 2000 did the government offer the possibility for ordinary citizens to connect to the Internet through two official servers, the Syrian Computer Society and the governmental Communications Authority. The number of Internet subscribers rose gradually, reaching approximately 8,000 by the end of 2000; 70,000 by mid-2003; and an estimated 250,000, or a little more than one percent of the population, in mid-2005.[17] Notably, many Syrians connect to the Internet through Lebanese or Jordanian servers, despite the high costs involved, because of the absence of censorship. Ordinary Syrians' access to all sites via the two Syrian servers is controlled by the authorities. Banned web pages include Israeli sites, all e-mail sites, sites that "offend morality," and all discussion groups or chat rooms. All told, the scope of Internet use in Syria remains small, estimated at 0.3 percent of the population in 2005, compared to 24 percent in Lebanon, eight percent in the Persian Gulf emirates, and 50 percent in Israel.

Cellular Telephones

Cell phones entered the Syrian market in the late 1990s. Typically, the authorities viewed them with suspicion or, more accurately, with a lack of understanding of their significance. They showed no inclination to invest in an infrastructure capable of providing the country with an advanced wireless network. Slowly, decisionmakers came to realize the economic potential of cell phone networks and began accepting tenders for the establishment of such networks through the Ministry of Communication. Prohibitively high prices initially kept consumption by the average Syrian citizen low in this service as well. By the end of 2004, cell phone subscribers in Syria numbered around two million, or about 10 percent of the population.[18]

The exposure of Syrian society to modern technology has remained slow for political reasons, but perhaps more so because of Syria's economic backwardness. Syrian journalist Yusra al-Misri has observed that "each of us must utilize the opportunity opened up by advanced technology and the communications revolution, yet the question arises as to how we, with our below modest income, can bear these costs? I acquired a computer by taking a loan from the Journalists Union, but I have no money to acquire a cell phone."[19] Even a rapid increase in the entry of Western technology into Syria, however, will not allow every household to have Internet access. Poverty and deprivation will keep the Internet, the cell phone, and even the pager beyond the reach of a significant proportion (perhaps most) of Syrian society. Globalization, however, will inexorably march on, even in Syria.

The Collapsing Foreign Policy Environment

Under the rule of Hafiz al-Assad, it was often argued that, until a solution to the conflict with Israel was reached and as long as Syria's differences with the United States were not resolved, Hafiz would preserve the status quo in Syria, avoiding any changes and reforms that would integrate Syria into the global economy and world politics. When Bashar came to power, it seemed that he was ready to move along two tracks: introducing changes inside Syria and at the same time improving Syria's relations with the outside world. Nevertheless, the result has been a total failure in both regards. Bahsar's failure at home, as described above, was due to his lack of experience and to his personal weakness as a leader. Yet, it also had to do with the international arena Bashar had to face. Some of these changes had nothing to do with Bashar's policies and decisions, such as the campaign against terrorism or the war in Iraq. Nevertheless, Syria failed to adapt to them, to address them, or to meet the challenge they posed to its regime. As a result, Syria found itself under attack, paying a heavy price for its leader's lack of experience, determination, and political power, both at home and on the international scene.

Bashar's foreign policy troubles started as early as the winter of 2000, following the outbreak of the Palestinian uprising (the al-Aqsa Intifada) and the renewal of Hizballah's activities, with Syria's blessing, against Israel's northern border. Bashar, ignoring the danger of military escalation between Syria and Israel, adopted militant and radical positions, such as allowing Palestinian militant groups to operate and plan terrorist attacks against Israeli targets from Damascus or encouraging Hizballah to carry on its attacks against Israel along the Israeli-Lebanese border. His conduct seemed to demonstrate not only the influence of Arab nationalist and anti-Western concepts, but also his lack of experience, self-confidence, and possibly even an orderly decisionmaking apparatus or experienced advisers. The young leader was venturing into places his father had refrained from going.[20]

Bashar also failed to respond to the war on terrorism declared by President George W. Bush following the September 11 attacks. As part of this war, the United States increased its pressure on Syria to separate from the remaining members of the "axis of evil": Iran, with its protégé Hizballah, and North Korea. On one hand, Damascus took steps to avoid a direct confrontation with Washington. To that end, it was prepared to cooperate with the United States in its struggle against Al Qaeda. Indeed, U.S. agents arrived in Syria early in 2002 to investigate these possibilities. Among others, the name of Muhammad Ata, mastermind of the September 11 attacks, came up, as did Mamun al-Darakzali, a Syrian-born member of Al Qaeda who was involved in handling its finances. Later, the Syrians also arrested Muhammad Haydr Zamar, a Syrian-born German citizen who apparently had recruited Muhammad Ata into Al Qaeda. The United States was grateful to the Syrians for this assistance, and Bush telephoned Bashar to thank him. High-ranking U.S. officials were quoted as implying that the information delivered by Syria enabled the deterrence of attacks against U.S. targets and saved many lives.[21] On the other hand, Damascus continued to adhere to a nationalist, pan-Arab, anti-U.S., and anti-Western worldview and adopt courses of action that contradicted a number of Washington's policies by impeding the Arab-Israeli peace process, continuing to encourage Hizballah in Lebanon to launch military attacks against Israel, aligning with Iran, and interfering with attempts to establish a pro-Western regime in Iraq.

The U.S. Occupation of Iraq

Syria's foreign policy challenges became more acute as the United States prepared for the spring 2003 war in Iraq. The conflict itself held the promise of major change in the Middle East, heightening pressure on Bashar and his regime from within to change its socioeconomic policies and from abroad, especially from Washington, to change its foreign policy (as Mu'ammar Qadhafi of Libya did) by separating from Iran, ceasing support to terrorist groups, moderating its anti-American rhetoric, and joining forces with other moderate Arab regimes in the region, such as Egypt or Jordan, who maintained friendly and close relations with the United States. Of all Middle Eastern countries besides Iraq itself, the war appears to have affected Syria most dramatically.

Initially, U.S. preparations to strike Saddam Hussein in late 2002 raised the tension level in relations between Damascus and Washington, with Syria quickly taking Iraq's side. Attempting to foil Washington's efforts to consolidate international support for its war in Iraq, Syria accused Washington of seeking to establish a new order in the Middle East for Israel's benefit and its own.[22] The United States responded quickly, accusing Syria of smuggling military equipment into Iraq and allowing Arab volunteer fighters to reach Iraq via Syria prior to the war.

The U.S. conquest of Baghdad on April 9, 2003, shocked Damascus. Syrian newspapers defined the capture of Baghdad by U.S. forces as an ignominious defeat of historic proportions, implying that the Arabs could now only wait for Syria itself to be attacked next.[23] Senior U.S. officials accused Syria of allowing Iraqi leaders to escape through Syrian territory.[24] Although the Syrians dismissed these accusations publicly, the strong language of the U.S. allegations undoubtedly disturbed them, and they were quick to subsequently close their border with Iraq.[25]

In the ensuing two years, the initial shock has been replaced by feelings of relief with realization that the United States was in no rush to and may also not be able to exploit the momentum for regional change to put military pressure on Syria. Contributing to this sense of relief was the knowledge that Washington was encountering increasing difficulties in enforcing its authority throughout Iraq; stabilizing the security situation; and establishing a secure, legitimate, and pro-Western regime. Such circumstances afforded the Syrians some leeway to refrain from responding to basic U.S. demands in Iraq, such as stopping the infiltration of terrorists from its territory to Iraq and closing all their training and logistic centers in Syria, as well as on other related issues, such as terminating support for Palestinian terrorist organizations and Hizballah.

Syria continued to play cat and mouse with the United States, with Damascus making some essentially cosmetic moves designed to avoid incurring Washington's wrath. Syria announced that it would increase its forces along the Syrian-Iraqi border and construct an embankment to foil the passage of smugglers and terrorists between the two countries. U.S. officials were also permitted to visit Damascus and examine Syria's banking system to determine whether Saddam had indeed invested money there. The Syrians subsequently announced that they were ready to return $3.5 million of the $261 million that, according to Syrian findings, Saddam had deposited in Syrian banks. According to Syrian sources, other parts of the money would be used to cover Iraqi debts to Syrian individuals and companies.[26] Damascus was also ready to cooperate with the temporary Iraqi administration established by the United States until a "legitimate" government could be established by the Iraqi people.[27]

Desperate Overtures toward Israel

As relations with the United States deteriorated, Bashar began sending signals in early 2004 of his readiness to renew peace negotiations with Israel without preconditions. Instead of directly approaching the Israeli public or its government, Bashar sent messages via intermediaries, and for the most part, Syrian official spokespeople later denied them.[28] Both Israel and the United States dismissed such tentative signals, which they considered to be an indication of the pressure and distress that Bashar felt rather than a true and honest desire for peace.[29] Israel instead viewed Syria's actions, such as continued assistance to Hizballah as well as to the Palestinian terrorist organizations operating out of Damascus, rather than these tentative words as indications of Damascus's true policy. In the summer of 2004, Israel made an attempt on the life of the senior Hamas activist in Damascus, once more directing the spotlight on Syria's involvement in terrorism, for example.

Five years after Bashar's ascent to power, Syria still appears to be committed to the peace process as the preferred route to retain the Golan Heights occupied by Israel in June 1967. Nevertheless, it appears that both states and especially their leaders still have a long road to travel before they could renew the talks between them, for several reasons. First is Bashar's need to secure his status as his country's ruler. So long as Bashar does not feel his rule to be stable, his ability to promote a concrete process with Israel, much less sign a peace agreement, is doubtful. Bashar, therefore, is likely to respond to U.S. pressure to renew the talks with Israel and project a moderate attitude but is unlikely to reach any final decision before he feels confident in his own status. In addition, Bashar's moves and especially his pronouncements, at least during the first years of his rule, have not demonstrated an ability to adopt a realistic or pragmatic policy unaffected by emotion or youthful impulsiveness. His late father required a similar maturation process too before he was ready to embark on peace talks with Israel.

Second, it has required an Israeli dialogue partner prepared to accept the Syrian demand for a complete withdrawal from the Golan Heights back to the June 4, 1967, lines, that is, back to the eastern shore of the Sea of Galilee. Finally, even the U.S. administration, a key player in promoting the peace process, has not appeared to be overly enthusiastic about lending the full measure of its weight to promote Syrian-Israeli peace. After all, the United States is not interested in promoting its relations with a Syrian government that they view as a threat and as one of a series of evil regimes, in contrast to the U.S. view of Damascus after the Persian Gulf War in the early 1990s, when Syria was viewed as a potential U.S. ally.

U.S. Patience Expires

Meanwhile, throughout 2004, as attacks against U.S. troops grew more frequent, U.S. anger at Syria increased. In the spring, the U.S. Congress passed the Syrian Accountability Act, which levels sanctions against Damascus. The legislation had been discussed since 2003, but pressure from the administration to allow time for its direct political dialogue with Damascus convinced Congress to postpone its adoption several times. In early 2004, the administration accepted that its efforts had failed and lifted its opposition to the legislation, which Congress passed in April 2004 and the president signed into law in May. Although Washington applied only a small portion of the permissible sanctions, their effect was greater than either the United States or Syria had expected.

The sanctions against the Syrian Trade Bank, the largest and most important of Syria's banks, in particular made it difficult for Damascus to carry out financial transactions with the international banking systems and drove off investors. Moreover, the Syrian Accountability Act was not a one-time action but rather an ongoing process, providing a mechanism that examines the degree of Syria's accession to Washington's demands every few months. Depending on the results, the United States has the option to increase its sanctions against Damascus.[30] The U.S. sanctions damaged and even blocked Syrian efforts to integrate into the global economy. It deterred investors from investing in Syria and created a negative economic atmosphere that worsened Syria's failing economy.

In early November 2004, the U.S. assault on Fallujah, a major center of activity for the anti-U.S. forces of Al Qaeda member Mus'ib al-Zarqawi, revealed evidence that exacerbated tensions between Damascus and Washington even further. According to U.S. sources, documents seized during the assault bore witness, albeit not always directly, to Syrian connections to terrorist activities in Iraq. They showed, for example, that some of the anti-U.S. terrorists had come from Syria, former Iraqi Ba'ath leaders were coordinating the struggle against the United States from within Syria, and Syria had allowed or at least ignored the establishment of training camps for terrorists.[31] The tone of U.S. media rhetoric escalated, with more than one writer attacking the U.S. administration, especially the Department of State, for its weak policy toward Damascus. Reports emerged that U.S. forces fired on Syrian forces along the Syrian-Iraqi border, and rumors increased that the Pentagon was preparing military plans to strike Syria itself.[32]

Checkmate: Lebanon

Events in Lebanon at the end of 2004 also reflected the disastrous results for Syria of its worsening relations with the United States, as well as the Syrian failure to integrate politically and economically into the new world. The United States and France, working together for the first time since their schism over the Iraq war, sought to expel Syria's presence from Lebanon. Syrian troops first entered Lebanon in 1976 to bring to an end the civil war that erupted in Lebanon the previous year. Since then, nearly 40,000 Syrian soldiers have been deployed in Lebanon to ensure Syria's political, military, and economic interests in that country. When the civil war in Lebanon came to an end following the signing of the Tai'f accord in October 1989, the Syrian troops remained, ensuring that the emerging Lebanese state would follow Syria's dictates. When Bashar came to power in June 2000, he ordered the redeployment of Syrian troops in Lebanon, leaving in early 2005 almost 15,000 soldiers and security agents that were able to maintain control over Lebanon's politics as well as its economy.

On September 3, 2004, the Lebanese parliament approved 96 to 29 (with three absences) an amendment to the Lebanese constitution enabling pro-Syrian president Emile Lahoud to extend his term for another three years, for exceptional reasons. Because Lebanon's constitution limits presidents to a single six-year term, the country's political elite had been busy for several months trying to divine who would be picked to replace Lahoud. The concept of a single six-year term was viewed as virtually sacrosanct in Lebanon, and all previous efforts to change it were met with firm opposition.

Although Syria's complete political and military control of Lebanon is no secret, conventional wisdom in Beirut had been that Damascus would not try to coerce locals into accepting an extended term for its ally, Lahoud. Instead, it was assumed that Syria would try to promote the candidacy of a friendly successor through quiet dialogue with various Lebanese political factions, complemented by efforts to reach a tacit understanding on the issue with France and, if possible, the United States. Eventually, Syria settled on Lahoud, a weak leader with no substantial power bases either domestically or outside of the country, in contrast to Prime Minister Rafiq al-Hariri, who had close ties to Saudi Arabia and key Western states. Lahoud's weakness was his greatest asset in Syria's eyes, causing Damascus to ignore or simply not predict the possible outcome of such an uncalculated decision.

The parliamentary vote in Lebanon came only a day after the UN Security Council adopted Resolution 1559, calling for the respect of Lebanon's sovereignty and constitution, withdrawal of all foreign forces from Lebanon, and dismantlement within Lebanon of all Lebanese and non-Lebanese militias.[33] Thus, Syria and its Lebanese allies chose to challenge the international consensus on Lebanon as consolidated by France and the United States, signaling that Syria was not willing to give up its hegemony over Lebanon.

Yet, Syria's troubles in Lebanon did not end with Lahoud's reelection. On February 14, 2005, former Lebanese prime minister al-Hariri was assassinated in Beirut, and the Lebanese opposition was quick to blame Syria for the murder. Hariri had, after all, played a central role behind the scenes in crafting the U.S.-French axis that produced Resolution 1559.[34] Unprecedented protests against the Syrian occupation in Lebanon erupted and were encouraged by the international (primarily U.S. and French) reaction to Hariri's death. Although Washington was careful not to charge Syria with direct responsibility, it quickly recalled the U.S. ambassador in Damascus for "consultations." French president Jacques Chirac, meanwhile, visited Beirut to pay condolences to Hariri's family but pointedly refrained from meeting any senior pro-Syrian Lebanese government officials. Together, the United States and France initiated a demand by the Security Council to bring the killers to justice, and UN secretary general Kofi Annan dispatched an independent team to investigate the circumstances of the assassination. The team's findings placed indirect blame for the murder on Syria for its contribution to the tense atmosphere created in Lebanon before the assassination and on Bashar himself for threatening Hariri's life in the last meeting the two held in the summer of 2004.[35]

Looking to the Future

From his rise to power until the present, Bashar al-Assad has not succeeded in filling the void left by his father. He has not managed to obtain the same level of reverence, legitimization, and public support, but there is no evidence of any immediate danger to his rule. The experience of similar Arab regimes indicates that they are able to manifest an impressive ability to survive even in the face of a large array of domestic challenges and that only a serious external threat, such as a U.S. military undertaking, is capable of overthrowing them. Yet, the price of Bashar's survival has meant his refraining, for the time being, from confronting the challenges facing his country, particularly globalization, democratization, and rising U.S. influence and hegemony in the Middle East.

Five years after Bashar's rise to power, Syria is a weaker and more isolated state, subject to an intensifying cluster of domestic and external pressures. The strategic distress that Syria confronts today is not an unavoidable phenomenon. Rather, it is a direct result of the faulty manner in which Syria's regime has governed in recent years, including its deteriorating relations with the United States. It has been the result of inactivity, stemming in no small degree from Bashar's weakness as a ruler.

In the spring of 2000, Bashar was a young leader with a bright future, who seemed to be endowed with a firm grasp of events, curiosity, and a readiness to learn. More importantly, he appeared to understand the need for change, observing that "[t]he difference between my father and my grandfather was amazingly slight, for life changed slowly then. In contrast, the difference between me and my father is very great, and the difference between me and those younger than me by only a decade is even greater."[36]

Hafiz was not endowed with an abundance of charisma either, yet the Syrian people came to revere him and governments abroad respected him. Will Bashar similarly grow to be a worthy and admired leader who radiates power and steadfastness, or will Bashar's era become a passing, marginal episode in Syrian history, with the Assad dynasty coming to an end after just two generations? The course of U.S.-Syrian relations in the coming months or, to be more specific, Bashar's decision on whether to integrate into the new world order may provide the answer to this question. Imagining any improvement in Syria's foreign policy environment, U.S.-Syrian relations, or the advancement of Syria's integration into a globalizing world without genuine reform of Syria's domestic and foreign policies is difficult, yet it remains unclear whether Bashar has the power to implement these needed reforms.

In the meantime, Bashar has chosen to forestall the increasing domestic and international pressures being placed on him. After all, that was what his father used to do during his 30 years in power. Although domestically his regime can survive due to the lack of any organized opposition and many Syrians' fear of the emergence of radical Islamist groups, such passive conduct may not help Bashar overcome his deteriorating relations with the United States, which has come to see the Syrian regime as an antithesis to all that it is trying to achieve in the Middle East. Even if Bashar's regime survives its current crisis, however, the Syrian people will pay the heavy price of their leader's failure to integrate the country into the new globalizing world.

Notes

1. See "The President's Speech to the Nation," *Tishrin* (Damascus), March 12, 1999, p. 2.
2. See *Al Jazeera*, May 1, 2004 (Bashar al-Assad interview); "Bashar al-Assad Speaks to al-Sharq al-Awsat," *al-Sharq al-Awsat*, January 10, 2005, p. 3.
3. *New York Times*, December 30, 2003.
4. See Patrick Seale, *Assad of Syria—The Struggle for the Middle East* (London: I. B. Tauris, 1988).
5. Eyal Zisser, *Assad's Legacy: Syria in Transition* (New York: New York University Press, 2000).
6. Eyal Zisser, "A False Spring in Damascus," *Orient* 44 (January 2003): 39–62. See Alan George, *Neither Bread nor Freedom* (London: Zed Books, 2003).
7. "Syrian President's Interview to al-Sharq al-Awsat," *al-Sharq al-Awsat*, February 8, 2001, p. 2.

8. Onn Winckler, *Demographic Developments and Population Policies in Ba'thiser Syria*, (Brighton: Sussex Academic Press, 1999). See al-Jumhuriyya al-'Arabiyya sl-Surriyya (the Syrian Arab Republic), Ri'asat Majlis al-Wuzara (the Prime Minister's office), al-Maktab al-Markazi lil-Ihsa, al-Majmu'a al-Ihsa'iyya liSanat 2000, pp. 59–60 (annual statistics for 2000). For the 2002 figures, see "The Natural Growth in Syria," *al-Thawra* (Damascus), August 10, 2002, p. 6.
9. *Al-Hayat*, March 13–14, 2004; "Kurdish Protest in Syria Continues," *Al-Hayat*, May 4, 2004, p. 3.
10. *Al Jazeera*, April 27–28, 2004; "Attack in Damascus," *Al-Hayat* (London), April 29, 2004, pp. 1, 3.
11. *Al Jazeera*, April 28, 2004; See Eyal Zisser, "Syria, the Ba'ath Regime and the Islamic Movement: Stepping on a New Path," *Muslim World* 95, no. 1 (January 2005): 43–66.
12. "President Assad on Globalization," *Ha'aretz*, March 31, 1999, p. 9. See Radio Damascus, March 11, 1999 (cited in SANA [Syrian Arab New Agency], March 11, 1999).
13. "Syrian President: We Are to Meet Our Challenges," *Al-Watan*, April 4, 2000, pp. 1–2.
14. "President Welcomes Chinese Guest," SANA, January 11, 2001.
15. Unnamed U.S. diplomat, interview with author, Washington, D.C., June 23, 1998.
16. "On the Computer Revolution in Syria," *Tishrin*, February 8, 2003, p. 8.
17. "The Internet in Syria," *Al-Ba'th*, May 17, 2002, p. 6; "On the Computer Revolution in Syria," p. 8.; "Syria Moves Forward," *Al-Hayat*, September 25, 2003, p. 3.
18. "Internet Services in Syria," *Al-Ba'th*, March 2, 2002, p. 6; "Internet for Whom?" *Tishrin*, February 8, 2003, p. 7.
19. Yusra al-Misri, "An Opinion," *Tishrin*, March 4, 2001, p. 10.
20. See Eyal Zisser, *In the Name of the Father: Bashsar Al-Assad's First Years in Power* (Tel Aviv: Tel Aviv University Press, 2004), pp. 206–243. See also Eyal Zisser, "The Return of Hizballah," *Middle East Quarterly* 9 no. 4 (Fall 2002): 3–12.
21. "American Agents to Syria," *Al-Hayat* (London), April 21, 2002, p. 1; "Washington Thanks Syria," *Al-Hayat*, November 25, 2002, p. 1.
22. See "What Is Behind American Policy in Our Region," *Tishrin*, March 10, 2003, p. 9.
23. See Syrian TV, April 9–10, 2003. See also "The Fall of Baghdad," *Tishrin* (Damascus), April 10, 2003.
24. Associated Press, March 28, 2003; Associated Press, April 13, 2003; Fox News, March 14, 2003.
25. "Syria Will Fulfill Its Commitments," *Tishrin*, April 12, 2003, p. 1.

26. "Iraqi Delegation Visits Syria," *Al-Ba'th*, May 15, 2003, p. 1; "Syria to Return Iraqi Deposits to Iraq," *Al-Ba'th*, June 1, 2004, p. 2.
27. *Al Jazeera*, May 1, 2004.
28. "Bashar Al-Assad Signals to Israel," *Ha'aretz*, April 27, 2004, p. 1.
29. "Interview With Syria's President," *New York Times*, November 30, 2003, p. 1; *Al Jazeera*, June 1, 2004.
30. "American Sanctions Against Damascus," Reuters, May 12, 2004; *Al-Hayat*, May 26, 2004, p. 1.
31. "Mosques Sending Fighters to Iraq," *Daily Telegraph*, December 2, 2004, p. 1.
32. See "America May Strike Ba'athists in Syria," *Jerusalem Post*, December 24, 2004, p. 1; "Getting Serious About Syria," *Weekly Standard*, December 20, 2004.
33. Reuters, September 2, 2004; Reuters, September 3, 2004; Reuters, September 15, 2004; Reuters, October 15, 2004. See "Lahoud Was Elected President," *Al-Hayat*, September 4, 2004. p. 1.
34. Reuters, February 14, 2005; "Lebanon Mourns Hariri," *Al-Hayat*, February 16, 2005, pp. 1–3.
35. Reuters, February 14, 2005. See *Al Jazeera*, February 15, 2005; *Al Jazeera*, March 27, 2005; Reuters, March 26–27, 2005.
36. "Interview With Syria's President," p. 1.

Dennis Ross

U.S. Policy toward a Weak Assad

Bashar al-Assad's rule of Syria has been characterized by vacillation and a constant pattern of miscalculation. Whether his regime can survive its most profound error and the potential loss of its control of Lebanon remains to be seen. For now, U.S. policy, while emphasizing the need for full implementation of UN Security Council Resolution 1559 to withdraw all foreign forces from Lebanon, should avoid engaging with the Syrian leadership before its future becomes clearer. In the meantime, the United States should also engage with Syria's neighbors in discrete contingency discussions to deal with the possible regional consequences of Syrian instability.

In 24 years of dominating Syria, Bashar's father, the late Syrian president Hafiz al-Assad, never put himself in such a precarious political position. Over the years, I spent countless hours with Hafiz al-Assad negotiating the smallest details of the Middle East peace process. He was not an easy person to negotiate with because he treated every point raised as a contest. Assad had a conspiratorial background: he was part of a minority sect, the Alawites—a heterodox offshoot of Islam who compose approximately 10 percent of the Syrian population; he had been

Dennis Ross is a counselor and Ziegler Distinguished Fellow at the Washington Institute for Near East Policy. He served as special Middle East coordinator under President Bill Clinton and authored *The Missing Peace: The Inside Story of the Fight for Middle East Peace*.

The Washington Quarterly • 28:3 pp. 87–98.

involved in coups and countercoups with the military and the Ba'ath party; and he had a history of paranoia, seeing enemies everywhere. His zero-sum mindset and perception of the negotiations as a process of attrition, rather than a give-and-take, should not have been surprising. Although Assad's attitude that no issue was too small to debate might have been numbing and frustrating, there was never any doubt about his grasp of Syria's interests as he defined them. His main priorities included regime survival and stability, controlling Lebanon, recovering the Golan Heights, and preserving Syria's centrality in decisions that affected the region. Even if one disagreed with how Hafiz safeguarded these interests, at least his behavior was predictable.

Hafiz was guided by a belief that Syria must never reveal its weaknesses. Because he recognized Syria's vulnerabilities and feared their exploitation, he placed great importance on maintaining his leverage and was loath to surrender any of it. I would often remind Assad that his connection to Hizballah, Hamas, and Islamic Jihad was undermining his professed desire to reach a peace agreement with the Israelis. For Assad, however, relinquishing these "cards" meant giving up his leverage. In his eyes, the influence of Damascus on these groups gave the Israelis a crucial incentive to deal with him; he would give them up only for a price. My arguments that Syrian support for these organizations was convincing the Israeli public that Assad had no real interest in peace and that acts of terrorism by these groups were subverting every opening for peace had precious little impact on him. Peace was acceptable only on Assad's terms and, in any case, was secondary to securing his interests. Without leverage, he was convinced that Israel would seek to have its way, the Lebanese would break away, the Saudis or Jordanians might think they could ignore Syria, and the United States might come to believe that Syria did not matter or, worse, that it could be coerced and Syria would be threatened.

Assad was also a good calculator of power. He was very careful not to cross certain thresholds with those who could hurt Syria. Although he might not give in to the Israelis, he understood the danger of provoking them. He knew when to challenge and when to stand back. In 1970, during "Black September," the period when King Hussein decimated the Palestine Liberation Organization (PLO) and ultimately expelled it from Jordan, Assad would not commit the Syrian air force to rescue the PLO once Israel signaled its readiness to intervene in the event of Syrian involvement. Later, beginning in 1976, he would not deploy Syrian forces to Lebanon, below the Israeli redlines, lest he trigger an Israeli response. Following Syria's disengagement agreement with Israel in 1974 until he died in 2000, he never permitted acts of terrorism to be launched from the Golan Heights in order to avoid giving the Israelis any pretext for direct retaliation. Ironically, its border with Syria has been Israel's safest and most secure since 1974. Many more deadly incidents have occurred on Israel's borders with Egypt and Jordan, even after they signed peace treaties.

Assad used Hizballah, Hamas, and Islamic Jihad to apply terrorist pressure on Israel, but he always maintained his deniability and never permitted the Syrian territory to be used as a springboard for attack. He was ready to use these groups when they served his purpose and dispense with them when they did not. During our negotiations, the Syrians made it very clear that these terrorist groups would be simply shut down if peace was achieved. U.S. negotiators were baldly told that no one could threaten Syria's national interests and, if the Israelis and Syrians reached an agreement, these groups would not be permitted to threaten its terms.

The Syrian negotiators also frequently reminded us that Assad always kept his word. In fact, he delighted in drawing a contrast between himself and Yasser Arafat in this regard. Assad was a responsible leader who fulfilled his commitments, unlike Arafat, who made commitments easily but rarely followed through on them. All this was part of the persona of a leader who understood the limits of his power but was certain to exercise the authority he had to preserve Syria's interests as he defined them.

The Generation Gap

Hafiz al-Assad's rule was marked internally by intolerance, intimidation, and coercion; externally, it was characterized by caution, largely covert threats against neighbors, and meticulous calculation. Yet after nearly five years in power, his son and successor, Bashar al-Assad, has exhibited neither the strength nor the calculating ability of his father.

Domestically, Bashar's initial promise of a new openness, which resulted in initiating "salons for discussion" on political liberalization throughout Syria, was quickly reversed, and the salons and other civil society forums were shut down in early 2001. Similarly, his plans to modernize Syria's economy and reorient it away from its statist moorings have failed to materialize. In his foreign policy, Bashar al-Assad seems to have none of his father's guile and appears to have an extraordinary capacity for miscalculation.

To be fair, it is unknown what Hafiz al-Assad would have done, for example, after Israel's withdrawal from Lebanon created a new reality and reinforced Hizballah's strength in Lebanon (Assad died within weeks of the Israeli pullout), the eruption of the intifada, or the September 11 attacks, much less how he would have responded to the toppling of Saddam Hussein by the United States. Although some of Hafiz's reactions would likely have been similar to those of Bashar, it is still easy to discern some fundamental differences between father and son.

For one, Hafiz al-Assad never had any illusions about Hizballah. He saw the group as a useful tool to advance Syrian interests, but not as a reliable force. Hearing Bashar describe Hizballah's leader, Sheikh Hassan Nasrallah, as a democratic figure who understood broad social and public forces and from whom he could learn a great deal—as I did in 2000—reflected what appeared to be Bashar's genuine admiration for Hizballah. Bashar even invited Nasrallah to speak at a ceremony in his family's village on the first anniversary of Hafiz's death. Hafiz would have understood the value of Hizballah up to a point, but he would never have made himself or Syria's interests beholden to Nasrallah. Hafiz never even met him personally. In fact, during our meetings, the elder Assad left very little doubt about his basic distrust of Hizballah. His relationship of convenience with the organization was based on the logic that the enemy of my enemy is my friend. Bashar seemed far more affected by Hizballah's success in driving the Israelis out of Lebanon and the importance of Hizballah for him and for Syria.

Bashar has also differed substantially from his father in dealing with the Israelis. Hafiz would have seen the intifada as a form of pressure on the Israelis. He would not have shied away from dealing with the Israelis, provided of course that he received something in return. After Dr. Baruch Goldstein's killing spree in the Ibrahimi Mosque in Hebron in 1994—with the Israeli-Palestinian negotiations suspended and much of the Arab world up in arms—it was Hafiz who, at Washington's request, resumed talks with the Israelis. Bashar, however, failed to recognize when his readiness to deal with the Israelis might have gained something. After the 2000 Camp David summit and possibly after the beginning of the intifada, when Israel's government under Prime Minister Ehud Barak might have been open and forthcoming to Syria, Bashar shied away from contact, believing that he could not deal with the Israelis either in the late summer or in the politically heated atmosphere of the fall of 2000. His potential for accomplishing anything was bound to be far less with the Israeli government under Prime Minister Ariel Sharon, who took office in 2001. Later, beginning in late 2003 and after apparently deciding to try to improve relations with the United States (rather than genuinely working toward peace) Bashar reversed course, stating Syria's willingness to resume negotiations with Israel. It is an approach that his father might have considered in comparable circumstances, but Hafiz would have first used private channels to gauge Washington's interest before publicly shifting his policy without a guarantee of a positive U.S. response, which in this case never came.

The difference between the two leaders was also demonstrated by Bashar's response to the September 11 attacks, which was essentially a caricature of what his father might have done. Like Bashar, Hafiz would have certainly recognized the immediate value of cooperating with the United States in its fight against Al Qaeda. Yet, Bashar failed to understand how the terrorist attacks transformed the Bush administration strategically and shaped its approach to the world. Hafiz certainly would also have been tempted to get by on the cheap with the U.S. government, hoping to change little of his behavior and policies in the process, but he understood the fundamental realities of power. He fully grasped that the United States is a "hyperpower" with no peer and would have known to tread carefully in a situation where the United States had suffered a great trauma. With the Bush administration preoccupied with the war on terrorism, Hafiz would likely have compelled Hizballah, Hamas, and Islamic

Jihad to temper their behavior and halt attacks for an extended period of time. He would not have wanted to give Washington a pretext for placing Syria in the enemy category.

In contrast, Hizballah, Hamas, and Islamic Jihad escalated their attacks between the fall of 2001 and the spring of 2002. After a cooling-down period in the late summer of 2001, Hizballah resumed limited attacks on the Sheba farms border region with Israel in October, just a month after the World Trade Center fell, and then began ratcheting them up in subsequent weeks.[1] Suicide attacks in Israel by Hamas and Islamic Jihad also escalated dramatically from November 2001 to April 2002, with the groups' leaders in Damascus pressing for more attacks. In addition, Hizballah helped to facilitate Iran's sale of $100 million worth of arms to be smuggled into Israel to Palestinian militants on the *Karine A*. Even though the Israelis intercepted this particular shipment, there were others, all of which sought to upgrade Palestinian capabilities for conducting the intifada dramatically (by adding rockets, for example). Even if Bashar did not mandate these behaviors, he did nothing to stop them; his father would not have allowed these groups to put Syria in a potentially vulnerable, exposed position with a U.S. administration determined to fight terrorism worldwide.

Yet another distinction between Hafiz and Bashar can be seen in the latter's mishandling of the Lebanon issue. Although Bashar at least initially sought to create a "kinder, gentler" Syrian approach to Lebanon by reaching out to some of the Maronite opponents, allowing some exiled Lebanese critics of Syria to return home, and reducing the Syrian troop deployment in Lebanon, he also increased the size and presence of the Syrian intelligence apparatus and undermined Lebanese prime minister Rafik Hariri's efforts to foster greater Lebanese autonomy. Although Hariri tested the limit of what reforms and autonomous behavior Syria would tolerate, he nonetheless always stayed within the Syrian redlines of preserving its dominance in Lebanon. Bashar crossed Hariri's own redlines, however, by imposing a change in the Lebanese constitution in 2004 permitting the extension of pro-Syrian president Emile Lahoud's term—an overt act against Lebanese independence.

This ham-handed maneuver pushed Hariri to join the opposition and support the September 2004 passage of UN Security Council Resolution 1559, requiring that foreign forces such as the Syrian military and intelligence apparatus withdraw from Lebanon completely. Hariri was assassinated shortly thereafter, in February 2005. Perhaps Syria's Old Guard, fearing a loss of control in Lebanon, was responsible for the assassination without Basher's direct command. Regardless, the miscalculation took place on Bashar's watch. Hafiz would have been no more willing to surrender Syria's control in Lebanon, but it is difficult to believe that he would have let the situation deteriorate to the point that a clumsy Syrian intervention would isolate Damascus both regionally and internationally.

Furthermore, it is difficult to imagine that Hafiz would have played Syria's response to the U.S. invasion of Iraq in the way that Bashar has. If nothing else, Hafiz would likely not have been providing military material and dual-use equipment to Saddam right until the eve of the U.S. invasion.[2] Moreover, Hafiz's own interest in bringing down Saddam would have tempered any impulse to oppose the United States publicly as Bashar did. During the first two weeks of the war, Bashar seemed to be anticipating that Saddam would survive and wage an extended resistance. Bashar's public posture made him appear completely out of touch with the reality on the ground. Even worse, his misreading of the situation and subsequent willingness to provide a sanctuary for remnants of Saddam's regime, permitting them to transmit money, material, and fighters across the border, was a dangerous undertaking for Syria.

It is difficult to see Hafiz playing with fire in quite the same way. Of course, even with all his antipathy toward Saddam, Hafiz would still not have felt comfortable with the idea of Washington ousting a secular, Ba'athist regime next door. Yet, Hafiz would have been far more subtle in supporting those elements capable of tying U.S. forces down in Iraq, at least until he saw how Washington might respond and whether the administration was threatening him. In addition, Hafiz would have probably worked with the Saudis and others to try to influence the role of the United States in post-Saddam Iraq. In 1990–1991, Hafiz al-Assad's actions during the Persian Gulf War demonstrated that he grasped the realities of power very differently than his son understands them today. He joined the U.S.-led coalition and even sent Syrian forces to Saudi Arabia at Washington's request. At the time of the 2002 war in Iraq, Hafiz would have looked for a deal with the Bush administration and, like Bashar, might have found only U.S. demands in response.

The current Bush administration eschewed engagement with Syria, instead insisting that it stop busting the sanctions regime and halt the oil shipments from Iraq, end its material supply relationship with Saddam, cut its supply lines to Hizballah, close down the operations of Hamas and Islamic Jihad in Damascus, ease its control over Lebanon, and terminate all programs to develop weapons of mass destruction (WMD). Of course, once the United States went to war in Iraq, the administration understandably also demanded that Syria close down its border with Iraq to stop the movement of material and volunteers supporting the insurgency. All of Washington's demands were legitimate, but the administration gave them little priority, and even less thought was given to what might be done if the Syrians were willing to respond in part or completely. To make matters worse, Washington did not clarify the specific consequences it would impose if the Syrians failed to respond. The United States warned the Syrians repeatedly, but ultimately the only real penalty the administration sought to impose was the passage of the 2003 Syrian Accountability Act. Yet, this legislation alone offered little more than a symbolic penalty on Syria. To materially add to the sanctions that being on the terrorism list already imposes, the Syrian Accountability Act would have to have prevented all U.S. investment in Syria. Moreover, because the sanctions are only unilateral, Syria can turn to other trading partners in Europe and Asia to mitigate the consequences.

The strategic differences between Hafiz and Bashar would have taken effect at this point. Without U.S. attention to Syrian behavior, Hafiz al-Assad would have undoubtedly come to believe that the costs of challenging the United States were limited and the gains of cooperating were nonexistent as long as Syria could avoid being isolated by the rest of the region and the world. In this context, he would have attempted to show Washington the price of its approach, especially in places such as Iraq, but with an eye toward gaining something from the United States in return for stopping that which Washington opposed. Parallel to such an effort, Hafiz would have also made much more of an effort to align himself with the Europeans as well as with the Saudis and the Egyptians. Bashar's policies in this regard have been inept: he slow-rolled negotiations with the EU on an economic cooperation agreement that would have blunted the impact of U.S. sanctions, and his efforts with President Husni Mubarak and Crown Prince Abdullah have left both leaders unwilling to go to bat for him.

Bashar's Bizarre World

In fact, one often gets the sense from the Egyptian and Saudi leaders that Bashar simply does not get it. Certainly, his public posture since becoming president has, at a minimum, suggested a remarkably skewed view of the world. From the outset, he has had a penchant for making extreme statements, which some suggest was his way of trying to appeal to the broader Arab public. However, these statements produced a series of public relations disasters. In his initial address to the Arab summit in October 2000, he offered a harsh description of the Israelis reminiscent of rhetoric from the 1950s. When he hosted Pope John Paul II—the embodiment of reconciliation among all religious faiths—he chose to speak of the treacherous mentality of the Jews, declaring that they had "betrayed" and "tortured" Jesus Christ.[3] At the Arab summit in Beirut in March 2002, although he declared support for the Saudi peace initiative, he announced that any Israeli was a legitimate target for attack[4] and declared that, "as much as we are concerned about peace, we should also be eager to remain steadfast and maintain the intifada [sic]."[5]

When Bashar spoke about the situation in Iraq just prior to the war, his comments bordered on the hysterical. At one point, he noted that a disaster on par with the creation of the state of Israel and the British betrayal of the Arabs after World War I would befall the Arab world if there was war in Iraq. After the war began, he declared that Arab friendship with the United States was "more fatal than its hostility."[6] Bashar's rhetoric has continued to remain incoherent and infused with a sense of conspiracy. In a speech he delivered to the Syrian parliament on March 5,

2005, after the assassination of Hariri and the resignation of the Lebanese government, he referred to the "assassination" of Arafat.[7]

The consistency of such public statements, rather than suggesting a calculated effort to establish himself as a radical to take advantage of growing anti-U.S. sentiment, instead points more to Bashar's bizarre perception of reality. Just as Arafat was guided by his own mythologies, which prevented him from seeing the changes in the surrounding regional landscape, Bashar's reality must be recognized for what it is: his own. This does not mean that there is no way to influence him because he has demonstrated that he does draw back when pressured and the threat of danger, as he defines it, becomes clear. For example, in October 2003, Syria mustered only a tepid rhetorical response after Israel bombed an alleged Palestinian terrorist training camp in Syria. Similarly, as international and regional pressure builds for Syrian troops to get out of Lebanon, Bashar has taken steps to try to defuse the situation by reaching an agreement with Terje Larsen, UN secretary general Kofi Annan's personal representative, on a general timetable for withdrawal. Although he hoped to keep the timing of withdrawal vague, he has given in to continued pressure and agreed to withdraw all Syrian military and intelligence personnel by the end of May. Once again, Bashar's perceptions and miscalculations appear to be imposing a heavy price on Syria.

One has to wonder what will happen in Syria now. How will the Old Guard react to missteps that, if not reversed, could cost Syria much of the leverage it has in Lebanon? Perhaps Bashar, working with and becoming increasingly dependent on Hizballah, will be able to preserve a measure of Syria's position in Lebanon. Such an outcome might secure his leadership for the time being and allow him to continue to muddle along until economic problems, including the depletion of oil resources and the loss of Lebanon as a financial lifeline, mount and change can no longer be avoided. Alternatively, some of the senior Alawi figures in Syria's security and military apparatus could decide that Bashar's rule is jeopardizing their future and carry out a coup against him. Perhaps the world will learn that Bashar knew nothing about the plans to assassinate Hariri. In this case, Bashar may conclude that the Old Guard is threatening his hold on power. He could then seize on their miscalculation to remove the remnants of his father's regime and strike out on his own course.

U.S. Policy toward Bashar's Weak Leadership

In light of all the uncertainties about Syria's future, now is not the time for the United States to launch a major new policy initiative. Instead, Washington should focus on getting the situation in Lebanon right. What happens there will affect Syria and the Middle East more broadly as Arab populations throughout the region watch to see if people like themselves can in fact shape their own future. So far, the Bush administration's course of action has been correct, emphasizing the importance of Resolution 1559. Preserving an international and regional consensus on the resolution and insisting on its full implementation should remain the administration's first priority. Fostering a consensus on the consequences of a Syrian-backed military crackdown on the Lebanese public, should that occur, is also worth considering, not only to convey those consequences to Syria but also to other regional states who may face a similar dilemma in the future.

The United States should go to some lengths to make it clear that it will accept whatever decision the Lebanese people make about their future, even if Hizballah may be a part of that future. Emphasizing this theme will force Hizballah to decide which state's agenda it is going to serve in the future: Lebanon, Syria, or Iran. Hizballah, led by Lebanese Shi'a, has always sought to become politically dominant in Lebanon. How will it look if Hizballah is serving Syrian or Iranian interests at the expense of Lebanon's? If Nasrallah is as politically clever as Bashar believes him to be, under current circumstances he will have to choose Lebanon or lose a significant part of his support.

Why not integrate such a policy into a broader carrot-and-stick approach toward Syria to cease Syrian support for terrorism and separate it from Iran? Before the Hariri assassination, such an approach seemed to be the best policy option. The problem was that neither the gains nor losses conveyed to Bashar were ever really spelled out or very impressive. Too many questions remained: If Bashar really did shift course on Iraq and stop Hizballah, Hamas, and Islamic Jihad from using terrorism to disrupt any hope of peace, what would Bashar and Syria get in return? How would Syria benefit economically? How would relations between Syria and the United States have changed? Would Washington make a serious effort to resume the Israeli-Syrian negotiating track, and if so, would the United States reembrace the principle of land for peace as it related to withdrawal from the Golan Heights?

Alternatively, if Bashar did not alter his behavior on either Iraq or on terrorist groups, what price would Syria pay? Was the United States prepared to encourage more direct military pressure on Syria by permitting hot pursuit of insurgents by U.S. forces across the border from Iraq? Was Washington open to greater military pressure from Israel in response to acts of terrorism? A lesser effort such as the Syrian Accountability Act was unlikely to persuade Bashar unless the Europeans were also prepared to apply sanctions, which was not possible prior to Hariri's assassination and the Lebanese demonstrations. They are possible now, however, especially given the tough French position in the aftermath.

Even if Bashar is presented a clear, unified package of carrots and sticks, he may not be capable of making the tough decisions to accept such a bargain. To hope to change any leader's behavior, Washington must clearly signal what can potentially be lost or gained by pursuing a particular course of action. Reluctant leaders will not make painful choices without knowing their consequences and being able to justify such choices to their key constituencies. If a leader is strong, such a clear choice is both necessary and likely to be effective. If a leader is weak, however, uncertainty is much greater. A weak leader may not be capable of, or perhaps even interested in, affecting change. In Bashar's case, although I perceived that he was weak even prior to the Hariri assassination, the opaque nature of Syria's reality before February 2005 argued for testing him for no other reason than the possibility that such an assumption about him was wrong.

Today, the uncertainty of Bashar's future argues for not testing or engaging him. Whether or not he survives, the United States can always adopt the carrot-and-stick approach later. For now, the White House should not throw Bashar a life preserver or try to sink him and should deal with him through the UN. If Bashar survives, his interest in engaging the United States will increase, and he can be dealt with at that time.

If Bashar fails to survive, it is impossible at this point to predict with any confidence who or even what is likely to succeed him. Syria could return to a strong ruler like Hafiz al-Assad, perhaps led by Bashar's brother-in-law, Assaf Shawqat, the head of Syria's military intelligence. Alternatively, even though a more enlightened Alawi-Sunni coalition of officers might come together to replace Bashar, Sunni extremists could also possibly trigger an uprising and shape Syria's new leadership or produce ongoing instability in the country. Given these uncertainties, the U.S. administration needs to position itself to contain possible instability in Syria as well as its consequent regional fallout. That strategy argues for beginning a discreet set of dialogues with Syria's neighbors to plan for different contingencies. Certainly, instability in Syria could affect Turkey, Israel, Jordan, and Iraq in different ways. Turkey, for example, will be very concerned if the Kurds in Syria suddenly begin to push hard for autonomy. Israel will worry that leadership instability could increase Syria's incentive to create a crisis with Israel to forge a domestic coalescence. The United States needs to coordinate strategies with Syria's neighbors carefully to prevent potentially destabilizing interventions and to shape approaches to whatever emerges.

Ultimately, a new reality will likely emerge in Syria due to Bashar's ineffectiveness and his inability to gain the respect that his father had at home and abroad. The United States should make clear to whomever assumes leadership in Syria, including Bashar if he survives and consolidates his power, what will continue to create problems in U.S.-Syrian relations, as well as what could offer genuine opportunities for a more productive future. The logic of a carrot-and-stick approach has probably always made sense in dealing with Syria. To be successful, however, that tactic requires the United States to define what it is prepared to do both on its own and with others to make Syria's gains or losses meaningful. Perhaps the situation unfolding in Lebanon will give U.S. policymakers a reason to develop a more explicit policy vis-à-vis Syria and to adopt a strategy to make it work.

Notes

1. Flynt Leverett, *Inheriting Syria: Bashar's Trial by Fire* (Washington, D.C.: Brookings Institution Press, 2005), pp. 112–120.
2. Ibid., pp. 134–142.
3. Quoted in Eyal Zisser, "The Damascus Blood Libel," *Tel Aviv Notes*, no. 18 (May 10, 2001).
4. Quoted in Eyal Zisser, "Does Bashar Al-Assad Rule Syria?" *Middle East Quarterly* 10, no. 1 (Winter 2003): 19.
5. "Syrian President Addresses Beirut Arab Summit," BBC Monitoring International Reports, March 27, 2002.
6. Quoted in Eyal Zisser, "Syria and the United States: Bad Habits Die Hard," *Middle East Quarterly* 10, no. 3 (Summer 2003): 34.
7. For the full text of the speech, see http://www.sana.org/english/reports/assad.htm.

Daniel Byman

Confronting Syrian-Backed Terrorism

U.S. policymakers rightly blast Damascus for backing Palestinian, Lebanese, and other terrorist groups, but they often fail to grasp the Syrian regime's ambivalent relationship with several of its clients and the nuanced way it manages them. Over the years, Syria has aided a daunting array of terrorist groups, but it seldom has been an ardent supporter. Damascus has both bolstered and weakened the Palestinian cause, encouraged and constrained Hizballah in Lebanon, abetted and arrested Iraqi insurgents, and otherwise demonstrated considerable care and variance in how it uses terrorist groups. Syria also tries to portray itself as part of the solution to terrorism, demonstrating not only its efforts to halt Al Qaeda but also its ability, for the right price, to shut down the very groups it sponsors. As Middle East expert Michael Doran contends, "Ever since the 1980s, Syria has played this game of being both the arsonist and the fire department."[1]

Syria's Deadly Relationship with Palestinian Militants

Damascus has long staunchly supported various Palestinian movements and, for just as long, sought to control, limit, manipulate, and thwart

Daniel Byman is an assistant professor in the Security Studies Program of the Edmund A. Walsh School of Foreign Service at Georgetown University and a nonresident senior fellow at the Saban Center for Middle East Policy at the Brookings Institution. This article is based in part on a chapter in his book *Deadly Connections: States That Sponsor Terrorism* (forthcoming July 2005).

The Washington Quarterly • 28:3 pp. 99–113.

them when they threatened Syria's interests. This ambivalence has led Damascus to champion the Palestinian cause and provide various violent Palestinian movements with a wide array of support even as it dealt bloody blows against these same elements at other times. Today, Syria remains an important supporter of several Palestinian terrorist movements but does not control the cause as a whole.

Origins under Hafiz Al-Assad

Syria's ambivalent relationship with the Palestinian cause took shape during the reign of Hafiz al-Assad, who ruled Syria from 1970 until his death in 2000. As Patrick Seale contends, "In theory [Hafiz al-Assad] was with it heart and soul, in practice it was a constant source of trouble."[2] Hafiz held a genuine ideological commitment to the Palestinian cause, but he also sought to use the Palestine Liberation Organization (PLO) and other Palestinian factions as a weapon against Israel. He aimed to regain the Golan Heights, which Syria had lost to Israel in the Six-Day War in 1967, and more generally to demonstrate Syria's continued opposition to Israel.

Hafiz al-Assad turned to terrorism in part because Syria's armies had failed him. Israel's rout of Syria in 1967 and its lesser but still decisive victories in 1973 and 1982 demonstrated that Damascus had no conventional military options against Israel. For Hafiz to achieve any of his strategic goals, he needed a means of inflicting pain on Israel. Only then, in his eyes, could Damascus force the Jewish state to make concessions on the Golan Heights or otherwise accommodate Syria.

In addition to using the Palestinians against Israel, Syria also used Palestinian factions in its rivalry with its Arab neighbors. Syria supported the Palestinians in their struggle against Jordan's King Hussein in 1970. As the Syrian-Jordanian rivalry continued in the 1980s, Hafiz employed the Abu Nidal Organization, a radical and exceptionally murderous Palestinian splinter group, to intimidate King Hussein by attacking Jordanian officials in Europe. The Syrian intimidation campaign contributed to Jordan's decision to back away from initial efforts to work with Israel and the PLO to reach a deal on the West Bank.[3]

Despite its utility in the struggle against Israel and for regional leadership, the Palestinian cause was a double-edged sword. Palestinian guerrilla attacks against Israel could escalate into an all-out war that Syria would lose. In addition, enthusiasm for the Palestinian struggle could inflame the passions of the Arab world, leading to pressure on Arab regimes to act and even to popular revolts against the existing leaders. Because these options would be disastrous for Syria, the regime had to control as well as exploit the Palestinian cause. Control was particularly important after Hafiz consolidated power and Syria gave an impressive showing in the 1973 war with Israel, becoming far more of a status quo power.[4]

From the PLO's point of view, Syria's attempts to dominate the movement and control its actions were a grave threat. The Palestinians were concerned both about Damascus's desire to dominate Lebanon, the PLO's main base from 1970 until 1982, and about its eventual opposition to the PLO's claim to be "the sole legitimate representative of the Palestinian people."[5] Palestinian leaders tried to resist Syrian dominance, which in turn led to violent clashes. Most devastatingly, in Lebanon in 1976, Syria militarily intervened against the Palestinians and their allies to prevent their victory over Christian forces in the civil war. After the Israeli invasion in 1982 and the subsequent expulsion of much of the PLO leadership from Lebanon, Syria also worked with the Palestinian rivals of PLO leader Yasser Arafat to foster an all-out struggle for power within the Palestinian movement, a struggle that left Arafat in power but gravely weakened, particularly in Lebanon.

The Syrian regime also leaned heavily on the Palestinian cause to bolster Damascus's weak legitimacy. Hafiz al-Assad had taken power in a military coup and never institutionalized his rule, despite repeated attempts. Syria lacked strong political parties, an efficient bureaucracy, respected courts, and other basic institutions. In essence, Hafiz ruled through the military, the security services, the Alawi community (followers of the Alawi sect of Islam, representing only 11 percent of Syria's population), economic cooptation, and family ties, all of which undermined efforts to build strong institutions.

The sectarian nature of the regime was a particular problem. Many Sunni Muslims, who make up more than half of Syria's population, consider the Alawis to be heretics. When the Syrian Muslim Brotherhood challenged the government from 1976 until 1982, it was opposing what it declared to be an apostate Alawi regime. Although the regime brutally crushed the uprising, its sectarian nature remains a problem. Foreign rivals of Hafiz's regime, such as the Ba'athist regime in Iraq and at times King Hussein's regime in Jordan, played on this theme of illegitimate Alawi domination in their criticism of the Syrian government.[6] As expert Raymond Hinnebusch notes, "Resentment of Alawi dominance remains the main source of the regime's legitimacy deficit."[7] Hafiz was thus forced to embrace the Palestinian cause as the *sina qua non* of Arab unity.

Until 1986, Syria was also quite active in using its own agents for operations. These agents attacked Syrian dissidents, Palestinians who sided with Yasser Arafat, Iraqi officials, and moderate Arab state officials, as well as Israeli and Jewish targets. After outside pressure grew in response to several terrorist outrages, in 1986 Syria refrained from using its own operatives to mount clandestine attacks and tried generally to minimize its direct hand in any violence. To allow itself deniability, it decided to use terrorist groups exclusively instead of its own agents. Pressure from the United States and several European countries made Damascus fearful that using its own operatives would greatly increase that pressure and perhaps even lead to military strikes. Outsourcing terrorism reduced these risks. As the U.S. Department of State report noted at the time, "Damascus utilizes these groups to attack or intimidate enemies and opponents and to exert its influence in the region. Yet at the same time, it can disavow knowledge of their operations."[8] This deniability served a useful purpose, enabling Syria to distance itself when necessary from the actions of its proxies.

After the Cold War ended and the peace process gained momentum, Syria supported an array of violent anti-Israeli movements that rejected the peace process. In 1991, after the Madrid peace conference that brought Israel, Palestinian leaders, and various Arab states together, Hamas and other militant Palestinians, mostly secular and Marxist, established the "Ten Front" in Syria to oppose negotiations.[9] The Popular Front for the Liberation of Palestine (PFLP), the Democratic Front for the Liberation of Palestine (DFLP), the Popular Front for the Liberation of Palestine–General Command (PFLP-GC), the Palestine Islamic Jihad (PIJ), Hamas, and Hizballah all attacked Israel, the latter three being particularly active before as well as after the second intifada broke out in September 2000. Some of these groups used terrorism, while others, particularly Hizballah, also use guerrilla warfare.

Syrian leaders supported and strengthened these groups, even though they seldom shared the specifics of the groups' agendas. Syria, of course, rejected the Islamist groups' visions of governance. Even more importantly, Damascus often seriously engaged in peace negotiations with Israel, which had a heavy U.S. role to boot, using its backing of terrorism to extract concessions from Israel on the particulars of the border or to ensure that Syria itself was not excluded from any settlement. Ironically, Damascus viewed terrorism as vital to its peace negotiations strategy. Having built its legitimacy on being the most steadfast Arab regime, however, backing away from the more militant Palestinian groups was difficult. Domestic critics of Hafiz's regime were often quick to seize on any perceived softening toward Israel.[10]

The impact of terrorist attacks by groups with ties to Syria was considerable, going far beyond the death toll they inflicted. The attacks demonstrated the inability of the Palestinian Authority to completely stop the violence, although the latter's cooperation with Israel did reduce terrorism for many years. In turn, this fed Israeli suspicions of Arafat and made the Israeli public far more skeptical that any concessions would lead to peace.

Continuity under Bashar

Despite initial hopes that he would prove to be a reformer after his father died in 2000, Bashar al-Assad has made at best cosmetic changes to open up Syria's political system or change its basic foreign policy orientation. Like his father, Bashar openly ties his regime to the Palestinian cause. The State Department reports that Syria still provides political and material support to numerous Palestinian rejectionist movements, including Hamas, the PIJ, the PFLP, and the PFLP-GC.[11] The sanctuary these groups find in Syria, even though Damascus itself is often not directly involved in their actions, allows them to coordinate their activities, organize, and otherwise operate with little interference. Given Israel's highly skilled military and impressive counterterrorism capabilities, Palestinian groups have benefited considerably by being able to conduct these activities with limited Israeli interference at most.

Syria claims that these and other Palestinian groups are a legitimate, armed resistance movement, not terrorists. Damascus also contends that these groups only conduct political activities from Syrian soil, a claim that is hotly disputed.[12] Ambassador Cofer Black, when he was State Department coordinator for counterterrorism, testified that the United States has "seen evidence that some of these offices are, in fact, used for operational purposes."[13] The State Department reports that the PIJ receives "limited logistic support assistance from Syria," as does the PFLP and PFLP-GC.[14] Syria also provides the PFLP-GC with military support and Hizballah with diplomatic, political, and logistical support.[15] The United States contends that Hamas and the PIJ do not receive funding or arms directly from Syria but that Syria probably allows them to raise funds and buy or receive arms from others with little interference.[16] Such claims suggest that Syria helps these groups sustain and organize themselves, even though several of them, particularly Hamas, would remain potent organizations even without a major Syrian role.

The logic for Syrian support remains consistent with the past, but if anything, Bashar appears to be in a weaker domestic position that makes him even more dependent on terrorist groups for legitimacy. His father steadily consolidated power, ruling for 30 years in the face of numerous domestic and foreign challenges. As such, he had a strong power base within his regime and considerable credibility as an opponent of Israel. Bashar, in contrast, was rushed into senior positions by his father and has not built up the same authority and credibility. He holds power in part by not challenging any of the country's main factions,[17] and his utterances are largely a mask for strategic and domestic concerns. As the International Crisis Group notes about Bashar, "His approach is ideological in the sense that ideological fidelity is an important ingredient in a pragmatic strategy of regime survival. This has meant avoiding any radical departure from his father's approach, which would have exposed him to strong domestic criticism."[18]

Syria and Hizballah

In addition to its long-standing ties to Palestinian movements, Syria is also a major backer of Hizballah, a terrorist and guerrilla group active in Lebanon since the early 1980s. Syria allows Hizballah to enjoy a sanctuary in Lebanon, where it also allows Iran to arm and train Hizballah's members. Using Hizballah as a proxy allows Damascus some degree of deniability, enabling it to strike at Israel or other targets without risking the confrontation that direct military action would entail.

Hizballah has proven a remarkably effective force against Israel. Although the United States knows Hizballah best as the terrorist organization responsible both for the devastating attacks on U.S. diplomats as well as military forces and for taking Western hostages in Lebanon in the 1980s, Hizballah in the 1990s became one of the world's most formidable guerrilla forces. As one Israeli officer noted, "Hizb'Allah are a mini-Israeli army. They can do everything as well as we can."[19] By 2000, Hizballah had forced Israel out of Lebanese territory, marking the first time that Arab arms ever forced Israel to concede territory.

Hizballah also helps Palestinian terrorist groups become more lethal. Since the outbreak of the current Al Aqsa intifada in September 2000, Hizballah has stepped up its support for Hamas, the PIJ, and other anti-Israeli groups. This support includes guerrilla training, bomb-building expertise, tactical tips such as how to use mines against Israeli armor, and propaganda from Hizballah's radio and satellite television stations. Hizballah operatives have also been caught smuggling weapons to Arabs in Israel, and its experts have helped Palestinian groups build deadly bombs.

As with the Palestinians, support for Hizballah also offers the Syrian regime domestic political benefits, largely due to Hizballah's lionization in much of the Arab world. Bashar in particular has sought out the blessing of Hizballah's leader, Hassan Nasrallah, suggesting that the traditional dominance Damascus exerted over the organization may be more limited today.

Hizballah responds to the Syrian regime's needs. In March 2005, Hizballah orchestrated a massive counterdemonstration in Beirut to oppose calls for Syrian forces to withdraw from Lebanon. When Damascus wants to avoid a confrontation, Hizballah will also lie low. When Hafiz met with President Bill Clinton in January 1994, for example, Hizballah refrained from attacks on Israel. During January–August 2003, when U.S. pressure on Syria heated up before and after the war in Iraq, Hizballah again halted attacks on Israel to avoid getting its patron into any more hot water.

As the above fluctuation in Hizballah's activities suggests, Damascus appears to exercise a veto power over Hizballah's military operations in Lebanon. Indeed, many observers believe that the road to south Lebanon runs through Damascus. As Human Rights Watch notes, "By controlling Hizballah's prime access to arms, Syria appears to hold considerable influence over Hizballah's ability to remain an active military force in the south."[20] Syria's potential influence is even greater. Damascus fears unrest in Lebanon, and recent protests indicate that the fear is legitimate. As a result, its intelligence on the country is superb. Damascus knows the identity and location of Hizballah's core membership and many of its sympathizers. Moreover, Syria has repeatedly proven it will be ruthless and is willing to inflict thousands of civilian casualties to root out any opposition. Syria's large military and intelligence presence could even act directly against Hizballah if Damascus deemed it necessary.

The Next Front? Syria and the Iraqi Insurgency

Syria has provided a range of support for Iraqi anti-U.S. insurgents of various stripes but has done so in a way that ensures a degree of deniability. In essence, Damascus has acted as a passive supporter, helping former regime elements and even jihadists by not aggressively policing its borders or controlling its territory. Damascus walks the line between undermining the U.S. position in Iraq and incurring the full brunt of Washington's wrath.

Although details are scarce, Iraqi insurgents appear to exploit Syrian territory in several ways. Senior members of the former Iraqi regime organized and controlled parts of the insurgency from Syrian territory, with little interference from Damascus. Although Damascus has turned over some leading insurgent leaders (Saddam Hussein's half-brother and

29 other former regime officials, for example, in 2005) as a concession to U.S. pressure and to gain U.S. goodwill on issues such as the Syrian position in Lebanon, U.S. military leaders responsible for Iraq still characterize Syrian cooperation as "very unhelpful."[21]

In addition, Syria is a transit point for money and fighters, most of whom were raised outside Syria, traveling to Iraq.[22] In October 2003, the Defense Intelligence Agency described Syria as a "major point of access" for jihadists and noted that Syrian border police gladly look the other way if they receive a bribe.[23] Although some of this access may relate to a regional tradition of smuggling, made worse by the networks developed to elude sanctions in the 1990s, Syria has in the past demonstrated that it can exert considerable control over its territory when it chooses, something it has done at best intermittently so far. To be clear, the activities Syria tolerates are not essential to the insurgency's survival, but they do make the anti-U.S. opposition stronger and more difficult to counter.[24]

As with the Palestinians and Hizballah, Damascus is playing a careful game. On one hand, Syria wants the United States to get bogged down in Iraq and, more generally, to abandon regime change as a policy. Damascus also seeks to have its proxies become stronger in Iraq, fearing that rival countries, particularly those with ties to Turkey, Israel, or other Syrian enemies, might dominate the opposition. Finally, the Syrian leadership wants to placate domestic sentiment, which is strongly against the U.S. intervention, and even allowed demonstrations in support of the insurgents, an unusual move for a regime fearful of any popular agitation.[25] On the other hand, Syria does not want unrest, particularly Islamist unrest, to spill over into its territory. Damascus also remains fearful of a U.S. military response and recognizes that too much or too blatant support for the insurgency would be a dangerous course.

On Balance: Mixed Rewards for Syria

Although the costs are daunting, support for terrorism offers Syria many benefits. Through terrorism, Syria has helped undermine a comprehensive Arab-Israeli peace. In particular, it was able to prevent a separate Israeli-Palestinian peace, which would have left Syria isolated and with few levers to use in pursuit of regaining the Golan Heights. Syria has at times also successfully used terrorism to intimidate its neighbors. Its campaign against Jordan through the Abu Nidal Organization and others for many years made Amman less willing to cut a deal with Israel and the Palestinians that Damascus opposed. This campaign also demonstrated to Washington that any regional deal had to include Syria.[26] Syria's tough stand against Israel and support for the Palestinian cause also paid off for the regime politically. Over time, the regime gained considerable credibility as a steadfast opponent of Israel, and even many of Hafiz al-Assad's opponents supported his approach.[27] Syria also gained protection from outside challengers to its legitimacy: Hamas has never challenged the Ba'ath party, despite its shared heritage with the party's Islamist opposition.[28]

Support for terrorism, however, has had considerable costs for Syria. Backing Palestinian rejectionists led Syria into clashes with Israel, some of which were disastrous. In 1967, Israel's forces devastated Syria's military, leading to the loss of the Golan Heights and regime instability. In 1982, Syrian and Israeli forces engaged in a limited conflict in Lebanon after Israel invaded, but the result was equally one-sided. In addition, Syria's backing for the latest round of violence that began in September 2000 has met with a limited military response. In April 2001, Israeli forces killed four Syrian soldiers when Israel bombed a Syrian radar station in Lebanon following a Hizballah attack. Under similar circumstances, it struck another Syrian radar station in July 2001. In October 2003, Israeli warplanes bombed a training camp for Palestinians in response to a suicide attack by the PIJ.[29] The U.S. response to Israel's strikes was supportive, with President George W. Bush declaring, "We would be doing the same thing."[30]

In Syria's negotiations with Israel over the Golan Heights, terrorism was both a benefit and a curse. Terrorism helped lead Israel to the negotiating table. Without the pain inflicted by terrorism, Israel would have had few incentives to surrender territory. On the other hand, terrorism caused the Israeli public to distrust Syria. After a series of suicide bombings in 1996, the Israeli public became skeptical of the possibility for peace. Syria's refusal to shut down the headquarters of groups such as the PIJ or even publicly express sorrow made both the Israeli people and government doubtful that Hafiz truly wanted peace.

For the Israeli government, Damascus's unwillingness to distance itself from terrorists increased the difficulty of forging a peace that it could sell to its own people. By the late 1990s, for example, a window of opportunity may have opened up as negotiations had reached a point where only minor material issues separated the two parties. Yet, Israeli leaders were often hesitant to make concessions, in part because mistrust of Damascus in their country was so widespread. By 2000, that window had closed. As Hafiz's health deteriorated, he became more focused on the smooth succession to his son Bashar and less willing to make concessions that might have led to criticism at home.[31]

Support for terrorism also damaged the Syrian regime's reputation with the United States. Syrian-backed Palestinian terrorism often had little direct impact on U.S. citizens, but it did affect the security of Israel, an important U.S. concern. By contrast, Syrian support for Hizballah did contribute to the deaths of hundreds of U.S. citizens in 1983 and 1984, but Damascus has not been implicated in a Hizballah attack that has killed U.S. citizens in recent years. More broadly, various U.S. administrations have considered support for terrorism inherently objectionable and have limited their contacts with Damascus as a result. Because of Syria's ties to terrorism, many of the financial inducements that kept Jordan and Egypt at the negotiating table were not available to Syria. Moreover, as noted below, the United States has imposed sanctions and otherwise worked against Syria, in part because of the latter's support for terrorism.

Syria's actions in Iraq since the fall of Saddam have proven particularly egregious in Washington's eyes. After the September 11 attacks, Damascus provided considerable cooperation in the fight against Al Qaeda. Rather than reap the benefits of being an ally in the campaign against terrorism, however, Syria is often cited as the next possible target for a U.S. attack, due both to its historic ties to terrorists and its actions in Iraq. There is a cyclical chicken-and-egg quality to this issue. Damascus did not reap the full benefits of cooperation because the United States saw it as linked to other terrorist groups such has Hizballah and Hamas. Because the United States at times scorned Syria, particularly in public, Damascus was probably more willing to support anti-U.S. forces in Iraq, fearing that a failure to bog the United States down there could lead to its own disaster.

Limited Success in Curbing Syrian Sponsorship

The United States and Israel have both tried to halt Syrian-supported terrorism, with little success. Backing down in the face of limited Israeli pressure would be both a strategic and domestic political disaster for the Ba'ath regime. Strategically, support for terrorism is one of the few assets the Syrian regime enjoys in its struggle against Israel. If Israel could neutralize this with its conventional military power, Damascus would have no way of compelling Israel to make concessions on the Golan Heights or other issues. The domestic political impact would be even greater. The regime's legitimacy hangs heavily on its Arab nationalist credentials, which in turn depend on its opposition to Israel. Backing down in a public manner with nothing in return would eliminate what little appeal the Ba'ath regime enjoys among the Syrian public.

Yet, Syria does modulate its pressure to avoid provoking an Israeli response that it could not withstand. As such, it tries to preserve deniability and use Lebanon as a base for many of the terrorist groups it supports, both of which maintain the fiction that Syria itself has at best limited involvement in anti-Israeli violence. Moreover, it restricts the operations and arms it provides, ensuring that the bloodshed does not rise to a point that forces Israel to respond due to domestic pressure. Modulating the violence and preserving deniability also keep regional states behind Syria, making it more difficult for Israel to gain the diplomatic support it needs to act. Given Israel's many other pressing security problems, only some of which are linked to Damascus, stopping Syrian backing for rejectionist groups is often not a priority.

The United States too, despite many years of pressure, has failed to persuade or coerce Syria into ending its support for terrorism. Syria was a charter member of the 1979 list of state sponsors of terrorism and has long suffered a range of U.S. diplomatic and economic pressure to end support for terrorism. Following the 1979 legislation, the United States cut off all economic aid to Syria. The United States has restricted arms sales, economic assistance, and access to dual use items and also opposed funding for Syria through multilateral economic institutions.[32]

In part, the inconsistent U.S. response to Syrian-backed violence undercuts U.S. coercion. Washington has maintained diplomatic ties with Syria, in contrast to other countries officially identified as state sponsors of terrorism. The United States has also allowed trade and investment in Syria. In addition, the United States did not respond directly against Syria for such acts as the 1983 bombing of U.S. and French forces in Lebanon, despite boasting by Syrian officials years later that they approved the operation.[33] The United States also worked with Syria in Lebanon in the late 1980s and afterward, effectively accepting a Syrian satrapy there.

What explains this U.S. caution? Assad, both father and son, have tried to preserve their reputations as pragmatic and realistic negotiating partners, avoiding the ideological blindness that at times characterized other terrorism sponsors, such as Iran, Afghanistan under the Taliban, and Sudan. Moreover, the prospect of Israeli-Syrian peace also proved a major source of U.S. caution. For much of the 1990s, U.S. efforts to end Syrian support for terrorism were bound up in the Middle East peace process. As former Clinton and Bush administration official Flynt Leverett has testified, "[O]ur outstanding bilateral differences were to be resolved as part of a peace settlement between Israel and Syria. For example, it was generally understood that, as part of such a settlement, Syria would have no need for, and would sever its ties to, Palestinian rejectionists and disarm Hizballah fighters in southern Lebanon."[34]

When the peace process collapsed at the outset of the second intifada in September 2000, pressure on Syria was initially limited as U.S. officials sought to restart the peace process. After the September 11 attacks, however, Damascus's ties to terrorist groups became far more important to U.S. officials than what was seen as an increasingly frail hope of reviving the peace process. As a result, the United States also stepped up the rhetorical heat on Damascus. In June 2002, Bush demanded that Bashar "choose the right side in the war on terror."[35] He later demanded that Damascus close terrorist training camps. Other senior U.S. officials echoed the president's line.[36] For its part, Congress passed the Syrian Accountability and Lebanon Sovereignty Restoration Act, which increased economic restrictions on Syria.

Damascus has responded to the pressure by limiting its proxies and providing some cooperation on terrorism in general, but not by clamping down completely. In 2003, for example, Syria closed the "media offices" of several Palestinian groups in Damascus. It also had urged Hamas and the PIJ to sign a cease-fire agreement with Israel. At the same time, however, senior Palestinian rejectionist leaders remained in Syria and continued to use cell phones and computers to direct operations from there.[37] During the run-up to the 2003 U.S. war in Iraq, Syria also was able to convince Hizballah to limit its guerrilla attacks and temporarily to halt supplies of Iranian arms to the group.[38] Yet, even as Syria made concessions, it opened the tap in Iraq. This combination was another way of reminding the United States that Syria can be both a valuable friend and a lethal enemy.

Syria's favored proxies have changed over the years, but Damascus's purposes have remained consistent: to gain additional strategic leverage against its foes and to shore up the regime's limited legitimacy at home. Syria has achieved these objectives, but this success has proved costly. The Ba'ath regime damaged its reputation with the United States and diminished its ability to make peace with Israel. Given the benefits of terrorism and the risks to the regime's legitimacy by abandoning these groups, however, the inability of either Israel or the United States to convince the Syrian leadership to mend its ways should come as no surprise.

Yet, recognizing the reasons for Syria's intransigence does not mean passivity should be U.S. policy. Damascus's support for terrorism is not the sole cause of continued Israeli-Palestinian violence or of U.S. problems in Iraq, but it does make a resolution more difficult. Continued pressure through U.S. leadership and multilateral, particularly Arab, action can help push the Syrian regime in the right direction. Syrian sponsorship is not motivated by ideology, which makes it more amenable to outside pressure. Indeed, Damascus has repeatedly demonstrated that outside pressure will lead it to curtail its support for terrorists, even though its responses are halting, grudging, and often short-lived.

For now, Damascus is on the defensive. The stirring of the "Cedar Revolution" in Lebanon serves as both an opportunity and a model. A combination of U.S. leadership and multinational pressure, including France and several Arab leaders, such as Crown Prince Abdullah of Saudi Arabia, proved particularly effective in convincing Damascus that it had no friend who would help it. As a result, Syria is drawing down its forces, at least for now, and the possible diminishing of its influence opens up opportunities in the long term to turn Hizballah away from terrorism. The terrorist group will have to respond more to Lebanese realities, several of which mitigate continued terrorism. The Lebanon experience is also a model. As it did after the assassination of former Lebanese prime minister Rafiq Hariri—effected almost certainly at Damascus's behest, if not necessarily by Syrian officials wearing official insignias—Washington should end the fiction of deniability that Syria has enjoyed in Lebanon. Because Damascus exercises such influence there, its support for terrorist proxies via Lebanon should not be tacitly accepted.

Should Syria move away from its Lebanese, Palestinian, and Iraqi proxies, easing pressure on Damascus is also appropriate. If the Syrian regime does move away from terrorist groups, the regime will need to produce economic results or otherwise restore some of its lost legitimacy, which is something that the international community can help bolster. Given the Syrian regime's poor track record, however, carrots should wait until sticks produce verifiable and lasting results.

Notes

1. As quoted in John Burns, "Syria Turns Over a Top Insurgent," *New York Times*, February 28, 2005, p. 1.
2. Patrick Seale, *Asad: The Struggle for the Middle East* (Berkeley, Calif.: University of California Press, 1990), p. 282.
3. Ibid., pp. 464–466; William B. Quandt, *Peace Process: American Diplomacy and the Arab-Israeli Conflict Since 1967* (Washington, D.C.: Brookings Institution, 1993), pp. 354–356; U.S. Department of State, "Syrian Support for International Terrorism: 1983–1986," *Special Report*, no. 157, December 1986, p. 2.
4. Itimar Rabinovich, *The War for Lebanon, 1970–1985* (Ithaca, N.Y.: Cornell University Press, 1989), p. 51.

5. Ibid., pp. 52, 86; Dilip Hiro, *Lebanon: Fire and Embers* (New York: St. Martin's Press, 1992), p. 37.
6. Nikolaos Van Dam, *The Struggle for Power in Syria: Politics and Society Under Asad and the Ba'th Party* (New York: I. B. Tauris, 1996), pp. 96, 106, 116–117.
7. Raymond Hinnebusch, *Syria: Revolution From Above* (New York: Routledge, 2001), p. 72.
8. U.S. Department of State. "Syrian Support for International Terrorism," p. 1.
9. Shaul Mishal and Avraham Sela, *The Palestinian Hamas: Vision, Violence, and Coexistence* (New York: Columbia University Press, 2000), p. 87.
10. Itamar Rabinovich, *Waging Peace: Israel and the Arabs, 1948–2003* (Princeton, N.J.: Princeton University Press, 2004), pp. 135–136.
11. U.S. Department of State, *Patterns of Global Terrorism 2003* (Washington, D.C.: U.S. Department of State, 2004), p. 93.
12. Ibid., pp. 120, 130–132.
13. Cofer J. Black, "Syria and Terrorism," testimony before the U.S. Senate Foreign Relations Committee, October 30, 2003.
14. U.S. Department of State, *Patterns of Global Terrorism 2003*, p. 130.
15. Ibid., p. 122.
16. House Committee on International Relations, *Syria: Peace Partner or Rogue Regime*, 104th Cong., 2d sess., 1996, pp. 8–11 (statement by Philip Wilcox) (hereinafter Wilcox statement).
17. Volker Perthes, *Syria Under Bashar al-Asad: Modernization and the Limits of Change* (London: International Institute for Strategic Studies, 2005); International Crisis Group, *Syria Under Bashar (II): Domestic Policy Challenges* (Amman/Brussels, February 11, 2004), p. 5.
18. International Crisis Group, *Syria Under Bashar (II)*, p. 6.
19. As quoted in Clive Jones, "Israeli Counter-Insurgency Strategy and War in South Lebanon, 1985–1997," *Small Wars and Insurgencies* 8, no. 3 (Winter 1997): 92.
20. Human Rights Watch, *Civilian Pawns: Laws of War Violations and the Use of Weapons on the Israel-Lebanon Border* (New York: Human Rights Watch, 1996), p. 22.
21. Ann Scott Tyson, "Iraqi Insurgency Is Weakening, Abizaid Says," *Washington Post*, March 2, 2005, p. A5.
22. Douglas Jehl, "U.S. Said to Weigh Sanctions on Syria Over Iraqi Network," *New York Times*, January 5, 2005, p. 1; Thomas E. Ricks, "Rebels Aided Allies in Syria, U.S. Says," *Washington Post*, December 8, 2004, p. A1; Bradley Graham and Walter Pincus, "U.S. Hopes to Divide Insurgency," *Washington Post*, October 31, 2004, p. A1.
23. Edward T. Pound, "Trouble on Another Front," *U.S. News and World Report*, November 22, 2004, p. 45.

24. Neil MacFarquhar, "At Tense Syria-Iraq Border, American Forces Are Battling Insurgents Every Day," *New York Times*, October 26, 2004, p. 11.
25. Ibid.
26. Laurie Brand, *Jordan's Inter-Arab Relations: The Political Economy of Alliance Making* (New York: Columbia University Press, 1994), p. 177; Rabinovich, *War for Lebanon, 1970–1985*, p. 188.
27. Perthes, *Syria Under Bashar al-Asad*, p. 33.
28. Khaled Hroub, *Hamas: Political Thought and Practice* (Beirut: Institute for Palestine Studies, 2000), p. 166.
29. Gal Luft, "All Quiet on the Eastern Front? Israel's National Security Doctrine After the Fall of Saddam" *Saban Center Analysis Paper*, no. 2, March 2004, p. 19, http://www.brookings.edu/fp/saban/analysis/luft20040301.pdf.
30. As quoted in International Crisis Group, *Syria Under Bashar (II)*, p. 5.
31. Dennis Ross, *The Missing Peace: The Inside Story of the Fight for Middle East Peace* (New York: Farrar, Straus, and Giroux, 2004), pp. 244, 583–587. See Jerome Slater, "Lost Opportunities for Peace in the Arab-Israeli Conflict," *International Security* 27, no. 1 (Summer 2002): 96–97; Rabinovich, *Waging Peace*, pp. 130–131.
32. Wilcox statement, p. 6.
33. Ely Karmon, "Syrian Support to Hizballah: The Turkish Lesson," November 27, 1998, http://www.ict.org.il/articles/articledet.cfm?articleid=68.
34. Flynt Leverett, "Syria-U.S. Policy Directions," testimony before the Senate Committee on Foreign Relations, October 30, 2003.
35. Office of the Press Secretary, The White House, "President Bush Calls for New Palestinian Leadership," June 24, 2002, http://www.whitehouse.gov/news/releases/2002/06/20020624-3.html.
36. "Powell Urges End to Hezbollah Border Presence," *Ha'aretz*, May 5, 2003.
37. International Crisis Group, *Syria Under Bashar (II)*, p. 9.
38. Ibid., p. 13.

Emile El-Hokayem

Hizballah and Syria: Outgrowing the Proxy Relationship

Terms such as "proxy" and "client" are often used to characterize the power dynamic between Hizballah and its allies Iran and Syria. These states' vital resources and indispensable political sponsorship elevated Hizballah to the position it enjoys today. They each played a central role in past decisions of momentous importance for Hizballah. Today, however, this image of Hizballah as a client of Iran and Syria has become obsolete due to the power base the Shi'ite group has nurtured and expanded in Lebanon and the growing political capital it has acquired in the Middle East thanks to at least the perception of its military victories, be they real or not, particularly in the summer 2006 war against Israel.

By holding its ground against Israel, the region's strongest military, Hizballah demonstrated its capacity to shake the Lebanese and regional political landscape. Hizballah resisted Israel's onslaught without substantive Syrian support. By partnering with Hizballah, Syria hoped to defy isolation and reclaim its role as a pivotal power in the region, as well as give the Asad regime a new lease on life. The shifting dynamics of this relationship, however, with Hizballah asserting itself as a more-autonomous actor, have considerable implications for policies aimed at engaging or isolating Syria, as well as for dealing with the Hizballah challenge.

Emile El-Hokayem is a research fellow at the Henry L. Stimson Center in Washington, D.C.

The Washington Quarterly • 30:2 pp. 35–52.

Hizballah has acquired a degree of autonomy and flexibility in recent years vis-à-vis Syria. Long gone are the days when Damascus's rules and influence determined Hizballah's activities, guaranteeing the predictability and restraint that prevented full-blown war. Hizballah has emerged as a more-independent player able to operate in Lebanon and the wider Middle East on its own terms.

Syria and Hizballah maintain complex relations that have evolved considerably over the past 25 years, shifting to fit their strategic interests and ideological agendas. Yet, two crucial changes, one in the early 1990s when Syria established itself as the unquestioned dominant player in Lebanon and the other ongoing since 2000 as Hizballah gradually grows stronger, have redefined how they interact and led them to reassess their relative positions. Hizballah has acquired enough confidence and prestige to become more than just a pawn for Syria to manipulate. Today, for strategic and ideological motives, Syria is more pro-Hizballah than Hizballah is pro-Syria.

Hizballah's Initial Volatile Relationship with Syria in the 1980s

Lebanon's Hizballah was born from a long process of Shi'ite awakening made possible by the political activism of charismatic clerics and by urbanization and rose from the chaos of the Lebanese civil war. It has emerged as the foremost and most famed Shi'ite organization in the Sunni-dominated Arab world.[1] The Islamic Republic of Iran's commitment to exporting its revolution and Israel's 1982 invasion of Lebanon to dismantle the Palestinian guerrilla infrastructure in Lebanon and install a friendly regime gave Hizballah its central and crucial raison d'etre—*muqawama*, or resistance against a formidable occupier, Israel—that would transcend political and sectarian rifts and shape its political outlook.

Syria had a direct but not determining role in Hizballah's birth, allowing Iranian units to enter Lebanon to provide organizational, logistical, and operational support for guerrilla operations. An in-depth examination of the Hizballah-Iran connection falls outside the scope of this paper,[2] but unlike Tehran, Damascus did not anticipate Hizballah's evolution into Lebanon's foremost guerrilla organization, nor was it comfortable with the prospect of managing an Islamist organization with clear transformational goals. Given its own experience with Islamists, Damascus was concerned about a potential loss of control over this new movement.[3] Hizballah's ideology, Iranian political sponsorship, independent resources, and tight discipline made it problematic for Syria to exert the kind of control it had over its other Lebanese clients, including Amal, the Shi'ite community's initial champion and Syria's favorite proxy.

Yet, after the weakening of Syria's position in Lebanon following the Israeli invasion and the deployment of the multinational force composed of U.S. and European troops, Hizballah was instrumental in facilitating Syria's reentry into the Lebanese arena. Lacking a strategy and resources, Damascus was in no position to confront the multinational force and Israeli occupation forces in Lebanon head-on to protect its Western flank and interests in Lebanon. It therefore relied on local allies to reestablish influence, and many willingly cooperated. Hizballah complied mostly on tactical grounds because its interests intersected with those of Syria. It did not initially accept the Syrian logic of co-opting or coercing Lebanese leaders from all political and religious persuasions into accepting its domination without questioning Lebanon's sectarian-based political system. Nonetheless, Syria appreciated the potency of Hizballah's asymmetric warfare and willingness to spearhead both the anti-Israeli resistance and efforts to expel the multinational force. At the same time, Syria went to great lengths to avoid irrevocably alienating Western powers by posing as a moderating force and cultivating deniability, especially during the hostage crisis.[4] What Syria would not do, Hizballah and others did.

Syria's uneasiness with Hizballah showed in its efforts to sideline the group's political outreach. Hizballah was notably absent from several unsuccessful efforts to negotiate a comprehensive settlement of the Lebanese war, including the Syria-engineered Tripartite Agreement of December 1985. Hizballah was also involved in deadly clashes with Syria and Syrian allies over control of West Beirut in the 1980s. By the end of the decade, Hizballah's future was still far from guaranteed. Much would hinge on the nature and quality of its relations with Syria, by then the dominant player in Lebanon, whose strategic environment and preferences were quickly changing with the rise of the United States as the uncontested external power in the Middle East.

Hizballah Adapts to Syrian Domination in the 1990s

Major regional realignments and international acceptance of Syrian domination of Lebanon in the early 1990s paved the way for the first turning point in Syrian-Hizballah relations. Persuaded by U.S. diplomacy, Syria joined both the U.S.-led coalition against Iraq and the Arab-Israeli peace process in 1991. Almost simultaneously, the death of Ayatollah Ruhollah Khomeini in 1989 and Iranian fatigue of revolutionary radicalism resulted in a pragmatic reorientation of Iranian foreign policy that gave Syria a freer hand to maneuver regionally. Syria became the uncontested power in Lebanon.

Syria's Strategic Leverage

The official framework for Syria's presence in Lebanon was based on the 1989 Taif Agreement, which reaffirmed the centrality of Lebanon's sectarian power-sharing structure while calling for its deconfessionalization. The agreement crushed Hizballah's idealistic goal of an Islamic state and should have spelled its end as an armed organization, as it also required the disarmament of all militias. Hizballah's conundrum was that Syria had become the Taif Agreement's godfather, and rejecting it would inevitably lead to confrontation. This new political reality compelled Hizballah, after intense internal debates, to accept Lebanon's confessional system and to work out an arrangement with Syria to preserve its weaponry.[5] Conveniently, Syria had a use for this arrangement. Syrian president Hafiz al-Asad sought to recover the Golan Heights lost to Israel in 1967 and to obtain a peace agreement that acknowledged Syria's pivotal role in the region. Hafiz had few avenues for exerting pressure, and he quickly grasped the value of relying on Hizballah as an armed group to improve Damascus's negotiating position vis-à-vis Israel.

The writings of prominent U.S. and Israeli peace negotiators as well as interviews with Syrian officials confirm that Hafiz sincerely desired a negotiated settlement with Israel, contingent on the full recovery of the Golan Heights in exchange for a flexible mechanism for its return, including mutual security guarantees, water arrangements, and diplomatic relations.[6] Although Hafiz hoped to orchestrate an Arab front to strengthen his own negotiating position, the collapse of the elusive Arab front after the 1993 Oslo accords and the 1994 Israeli-Jordanian peace agreement forced Syria to look elsewhere for leverage.

Lebanon, firmly anchored in the Syrian orbit, served as Damascus's strategic depth. It guaranteed good-faith negotiations over the Golan Heights from a position of relative strength. The Western and Israeli assumption underlying Syrian-Israeli talks was that Damascus would constrain and eventually disarm Hizballah once peace was reached. As former Western and Arab diplomats put it, there was an informal understanding that once peace between Syria and Israel was signed, a treaty between Israel and Lebanon would follow, providing a framework for Hizballah's disarmament and the integration of its fighters into Lebanon's regular armed forces.[7] Yet, Hizballah's future was never explicitly put on the table, and there is no clear indication that Syria was asked to offer written guarantees to that end. Hizballah's own statements were contradictory enough to wonder whether its leadership even knew the endgame. Hizballah's ambiguous rhetoric might have been aimed at augmenting pressure on Israel and increasing its own value as a Syrian asset.[8]

Syria's official position on Hizballah's activities in Lebanon relied on the disingenuous argument that Hizballah was a legitimate actor operating with the full consent of the Lebanese nation without Syrian intervention. Syria thus could not determine the post-peace future of Hizballah for Lebanon or publicly acknowledge any need for continued Hizballah attacks against Israel if Israel withdrew unconditionally from southern Lebanon under UN Security Council Resolution 425. In reality, to preserve the linkage with the Golan Heights, Syrian leverage on Israel through Hizballah depended on the continued Israeli occupation of southern Lebanon. This explains why the Lebanese government and Hizballah, with heavy Syrian prompting, raised the contentious issue of the Shebaa Farms, a strip of land whose real ownership remains unclear but which Lebanon claims. This delicate and confusing game on Lebanon contrasted with the clarity of the Syrian position regarding bilateral Israeli-Syrian issues, especially the necessity for Israel to return the Golan Heights.

The informal understanding on Hizballah's future after a peace settlement fell short of a guarantee that Hizballah would disarm. Given the absence of a simultaneous Israeli-Lebanese negotiation track, which was deemed unnecessary because Syria called the shots, Lebanon could not assure Israel and the United States that Hizballah would relinquish its weapons. Moreover, even if Syria were prepared to enforce Hizballah's disarmament in principle, former Syrian officials are at loss to describe what steps, if any, Syria would take to promote and facilitate this implementation or whether Syria felt confident that it could deliver on such a commitment.[9] Would Syria's presence, under the pretext of negotiating its end, be even more entrenched by linking it to an effective and permanent disarmament of Hizballah? Would renouncing Hizballah's weapons require a new negotiation over power-sharing in Lebanon to give the Shi'ite community a greater share of power? Could the Lebanese polity cope with such dramatic changes without being closely associated with their formulation? Hafiz probably hoped that Syria's role in Lebanon could continue beyond a peace settlement to prevent the Shi'ite militia from becoming a spoiler.[10] Therefore, Hizballah would have served as a pretext for perpetuating Syrian control over Lebanon, which remained the ultimate prize for Damascus.

Hizballah embraced the label of national resistance to circumvent the Taif Agreement and to differentiate itself from other militias. This meant that Syria had to manage two conflicting projects in Lebanon.[11] Hassan Nasrallah, the young and charismatic secretary-general of Hizballah, articulated an agenda of steadfast resistance against Israel aimed at transcending Lebanon's political and sectarian divisions. On the other hand, Rafik Hariri, a wealthy businessman and prime minister from 1992 to 1998 and 2000 to 2004, envisioned Lebanon as a hub for regional trade and finance and a prime real estate market, as well as a magnet for tourism, and relied on the expectation of imminent regional peace.

Syria resolved this quandary by facilitating an informal bargain.[12] Hizballah obtained autonomy and absolute exclusivity in carrying out its resistance against Israel from Lebanese territory with official cover but agreed to minimize its participation in Lebanese economic and political affairs. Hariri was given considerable authority over reconstruction and domestic and economic policies but little or no say over resistance strategy and policy.

This deal had obvious limitations for these Lebanese actors. Whenever Israel and Hizballah clashed, the fighting jeopardized Hariri's economic plans by reminding international investors and donors of the continuous instability plaguing Lebanon.[13] Tensions between Hizballah and Hariri were frequent, sometimes erupting in public arguments that were quickly contained by Damascus.[14] Yet, despite the difficulty of managing this arrangement and the need to preserve a clear but delicate division of roles, it served Syrian interests well. Damascus relied on Hariri to project a reassuring image to the West, other Arab states, and much of the Lebanese public and to generate revenue and growth in Lebanon, which would sustain Syria's own economy. Hizballah's growing power also checked Hariri's ambitions, most notably by limiting government reach into Hizballah-controlled areas and serving as a reminder of Syria's overriding authority. By retaining a decisive say in all security and foreign policy matters, Syria acted as the ultimate arbiter of disputes.

At the same time, support for Hizballah and other Damascus-based Palestinian groups allowed Syria to play up its pan-Arab, anti-Israeli credentials and avoid harsh criticism for its involvement in the peace process. Importantly, Hafiz demonstrated calculated caution, being careful not to meet personally or in public with Nasrallah and relying heavily on his intelligence apparatus to run Hizballah. This approach was primarily shaped by Hafiz's prudence, distrust of Hizballah's ideology, and genuine investment in peace negotiations with Israel.

Hizballah Struggles for a Future

Hizballah was expected to channel and moderate the frustrations of its Shi'ite constituency. It did so by developing an extensive network of social services that reflected its social vocation (*da'wa*) and compensated for the lack of government resources and presence, instead of promoting Shi'ite rights within the framework of the state. Doing so would have created friction with other Lebanese sects and jeopardized the Syrian-engineered consensus on the muqawama. This arrangement ironically boosted Hizballah's domestic profile over time, shielding it from the Lebanese population's wide rejection of the corrupt Lebanese political elites, highlighting its principled agenda compared to their parochial interests, and allowing for gradual political integration without sharing the blame for the country's many ills. Therefore, instead of contributing to the country's reform, Hizballah subordinated significant Lebanese concerns to its resistance agenda, arguably a priority given the continued Israeli occupation of southern Lebanon.

Hizballah remained closely aligned with Syrian diplomatic posturing, alternating lulls and uptakes in armed conflict as needed. It drew comfort from the fact that Syria differentiated between the concepts of peace and normalization. Whereas peace meant the end of the state of war and the establishment of normal diplomatic relations, normalization went further, calling for broader cooperation on a variety of economic, cultural, and social issues. The hope was that a peace with Israel would allow Hizballah to endure as a national guard. If Hizballah could no longer resist Israel militarily, its carefully nurtured society and culture of resistance would prevent the rapprochement of Israeli, Syrian, and Lebanese societies, keeping Israel regionally ostracized despite a formal end to war.[15]

Midlevel Hizballah officials were naturally concerned about the future of their movement when the much-publicized land-for-peace formula assumed the dismantlement of its armed branch. Yet, they also held a belief, born from Hizballah's political successes, that Hizballah could genuinely transform itself into a political party if need be.[16] Ironically, while Hizballah's military successes in 1993 and 1996 raised its value as a Syrian asset in negotiations, they also gradually transformed it into a more autonomous player with enhanced Lebanese and regional prestige, creating some confidence that it would survive any Syrian-Israeli peace.

Ultimately, of course, there was no grand bargain between Syria and Israel. In its place, after repeated Israeli failures to degrade Hizballah and to break Syria's linkage of southern Lebanon to the Golan Heights, a set of rules were formulated in 1993 and formalized in 1996 to manage the escalation of violence and enforce redlines in Lebanon. Hizballah agreed to limit its attacks on Israeli forces and their surrogates in southern Lebanon, while Israel pledged not to strike Lebanese civilians. These rules augmented Syria's leverage by formalizing its role as a guarantor of stability in the area.

Bashar's Search for Legitimacy since 2000

The second major turning point in Syrian-Hizballah relations came at the turn of the century with a change in Syrian leadership. Israeli prime minister Ehud Barak had hoped to break the Syria-created linkage between the Golan Heights and southern Lebanon when he ordered an unconditional withdrawal from southern Lebanon in May 2000, only to see Hafiz al-Asad's death in June and the unexpected issue of the Shebaa Farms thwart this calculus. Syria's ability to reach peace heavily depended on Hafiz's power and commitment. Bashar al-Asad, Hafiz's younger son not cultivated for statecraft, came to power with no serious leadership or management experience and no anti-Israeli or military credentials. He lacked legitimacy and credibility at home as well as in the region. To be sure, his youth and softer image quickly endeared him to the Syrian public, but this hardly granted him the authority or strength to guarantee his hold on power and to pursue peace. To compensate, he sought to acquire these traits by associating himself with allies whose regional prestige was built on a record of anti-U.S. and anti-Israeli opposition.

Enter Hizballah, the Lebanese guerrilla movement and political party that had scored its biggest victory to date, Israel's withdrawal, just weeks before Hafiz died and months before Bashar succeeded him. The group could easily provide Bashar with the credentials that he needed to gain credibility, initiating a process of legitimization by association. By associating himself with Hizballah's strength and resolve, Bashar hoped to counter perceptions that he was either a weak leader manipulated by hidden interests or an aggressive one prone to strategic miscalculations.[17] Bashar reasoned that if the victorious Nasrallah was thanking him for Syria's support of efforts that led to Israel's withdrawal from southern Lebanon, the Syrian and Arab publics would view him as the legitimate heir to his father's legacy. To justify his own attitude on major regional developments, including his opposition to the U.S. invasion of Iraq, Bashar relied heavily on Hizballah's own principled hostility to U.S. designs.

Breaking with his father's cautious handling of Hizballah, Bashar cultivated a close personal relationship with Nasrallah and made certain that the praise they lavished on each other was well publicized. Perhaps the most trivial but revealing illustration of this shift has been the sudden flurry of posters featuring Hafiz, Bashar, and Nasrallah plastered across Syria and Lebanon since 2000. A former regime insider, now a low-key critic of Bashar, remarked half-jokingly that the senior Asad, were he able to rise from the dead, would use these posters as fuel to burn his own son.[18]

To be fair, Bashar's decision may have been vital to his regime's ability to overcome the many domestic and regional crises he has faced since his ascent to power. What some have branded a necessary learning curve or a typical consolidation of power, however, has in fact been a slow but willing conscription of Bashar as Hizballah's ideological partner. Pressed by deteriorating regional conditions, from the second Palestinian intifada to the U.S. invasion of Iraq, Bashar grew from a follower of Hizballah by necessity into a faithful admirer and willing captive of Hizballah's confrontational outlook when U.S. pressure on Syria intensified in 2003. By overtly partnering with the region's steadfast resistance group par excellence, Bashar lost the plausible deniability that his father had cherished so much. With that, he jeopardized Syria's ability to maneuver diplomatically without dangerously alienating his Western partners and Israel.

Nasrallah's influence on Bashar is apparent in the latter's public remarks. Bashar borrows from Nasrallah's repertoire, rhetorically espousing Hizballah's worldview, appealing to audiences beyond Syria, and framing his resolute opposition to U.S. policy as part of a larger struggle against imperialistic oppression. Bashar has also revived a waning pan-Arab, nationalist, and strongly anti-Western rhetoric in an attempt not only to recast himself as his father's legitimate successor but also to defy U.S.-allied Arab leaders and pander to their anti-U.S. publics.

Syria's mostly symbolic gains from its partnership with Hizballah became tangible and political ones in 2004. After the September 2004 passage of UN Security Council Resolution 1559, which demanded Hizballah's disarmament and Syria's withdrawal from Lebanon, and the February 2005 assassination of Hariri, Syria relied heavily on Hizballah's outrage to counter rising U.S. and French pressure and to portray the resolution as an international diktat with no Lebanese or Arab legitimacy.

During this tense period, Hizballah emerged as Syria's honorable and reliable ally. Under heavy scrutiny from Western and Arab countries as well as intense criticism inside Lebanon, Syria could not resort to its usual unsavory proxies to mount a credible defense of its record in Lebanon. A Syrian official remarked in May 2005, "Many of our allies in Lebanon have thrived since 1990 thanks to Syria, but they have lost their credibility with their people. Not Hizballah."[19] Nasrallah stood out as Syria's champion, organizing a massive "good-bye but thank you" demonstration on March 8, 2005, and presenting the departing head of Syrian intelligence with a peculiar if telling gift of gratitude for Syria's support for the resistance: an Israeli rifle seized by Hizballah.[20] The photo op served to mitigate the humiliation of Syria's forced withdrawal and to shore up Bashar's profile at home. The positive relationship with Hizballah, a Shi'ite party with a seemingly nonsectarian attitude and a glorious anti-Israeli record, became the key achievement that Bashar wanted to highlight domestically and regionally. His eagerness to do so demonstrated that the tables had turned. Rather than Hizballah deriving great benefits from Syria's support, Syria now reaped more benefits from its association with Hizballah.

Hizballah Today

Syria's departure from Lebanon considerably changed the strategic environment in which Hizballah operates and presented it with challenges and opportunities. The key challenge was to preserve a consensus on its weapons and retain a special status in Lebanese politics. The key opportunity was to finally overcome its image as a Syrian pawn and capitalize on its achievements and credibility. This process was fraught with considerable difficulties, and domestic and regional developments conspired against it.

Hizballah's actions since the 2005 Syrian withdrawal from Lebanon are often presented as an extension of Syrian and Iranian policy.[21] To be sure, its interests often coincide and reinforce those of Syria and Iran, but many overestimate the influence that they have over Hizballah's decision-making and preferences. Syria today is more pro-Hizballah than Hizballah is pro-Syria. Hizballah is no longer a card or a proxy; it has become a partner with considerable clout and autonomy.

Paradoxically, there is little love today for Syria among Hizballah's supporters.[22] They see Syria as having constrained Hizballah's political potential. The Lebanese Shi'ite community also suffered from Syrian workers competing for the same jobs. Furthermore, Hizballah owes no particular heritage to Syria, contrary to Iran, which remains a supreme religious and ideological reference. An anecdote making the rounds in Beirut has Hizballah militants comparing Syria to a ring and Iran as a finger on Hizballah's hand. The ring can fall off or be taken off willingly, whereas the finger can only be severed.[23] This contrasts with the attitude of the Syrian public, which identifies with Hizballah. Syrians view the Lebanese as fractious, greedy, and ungrateful for Syrian sacrifices in Lebanon, but they see Hizballah as righteous and animated by a just, pan-Arab cause.

Hizballah's objectives are often misunderstood. Hizballah's raison d'etre has become the very idea of perpetual but not necessarily active muqawama against Israel. A former Hizballah activist put it this way: "Resistance is like a one-wheel[ed] bike that Hizballah is riding. If it stops pedaling, it falls."[24] Yet, the muqawama refers not only to guerrilla operations, but also to a culture of resistance based on social mobilization and an associated political and social discourse that transcends religion, territoriality, and nationalism, although it is rooted in all three. Therefore, Hizballah has no tangible ultimate objective such as advancing Shi'ite demands, reforming Lebanon's governance system, or liberating Israeli-occupied Arab territories. It will undoubtedly accept those as valuable by-products of its resistance efforts, but they do not constitute Hizballah's core purpose.

Contrary to its initial goals and to the fears of many, Hizballah no longer actively seeks to impose an Islamic agenda on Lebanon and even prefers not to govern the country if it can rely on amenable allies from various sects in parliament and government.[25] Hizballah has genuinely adjusted to the sectarian fabric of Lebanon's society, gradually emphasizing muqawama instead of Islamism in its rhetoric and ideology. Hizballah has not abandoned its Islamist ideal, but to the extent that this goal complicates its ability to pursue muqawama or erodes its image, Hizballah is willing to do away with it.

What Hizballah today wants most is to ensure that nothing, especially Lebanese domestic considerations, can constrain its ability to conduct its resistance agenda in the time frame and form of its choosing. It developed a two-tiered political strategy to anchor Lebanon firmly in a rejectionist axis formed by Iran, Syria, and radical Palestinian groups. It has placed itself within Lebanese society through its political activities and much-praised social services. It has simultaneously positioned itself above society by defining muqawama, preferably but not necessarily endorsed by a national consensus, as a fundamentally supranational vocation.[26] In practical terms, this focus on resistance shapes how Hizballah operates as a political actor, determining its degree and nature of political involvement, its choice of alliances, and even the decision and timing of its operations against Israel.

Hizballah, which thrived as a guerrilla force mostly equipped with small and light weaponry to resist Israeli occupation, became a more-sophisticated force as its main mission shifted to deterrence based on rocket and missile capabilities. Syria's departure from Lebanon meant that Hizballah could no longer count on an external enforcer to protect its weapons. This left Hizballah with three options: build alliances with other forces and deepen its political engagement to eventually govern the country, manipulate sectarian politics to create a Shi'ite shield, or a combination of the two. All of these options are highly dissatisfying. They turn Hizballah into a political party like the others and conflict with the nonsectarian image it cultivates for national and regional purposes.

This fear of the end of a national consensus over its armament prompted Hizballah to enter the Lebanese government for the first time in 2005 and to obtain a formal Cabinet statement endorsing the resistance as "a sincere and natural expression of the Lebanese people's right to defend its land and dignity in the face of Israeli aggression, threats, and ambitions as well as of its right to continue its actions to free Lebanese territory." Hizballah's concern was quickly validated as its rationale for remaining armed came under heavy domestic criticism. The necessity of reaffirming the value of its arsenal led Hizballah to launch the fateful July 12 operation that started the summer 2006 war with Israel with the stated objective of obtaining the liberation of the remaining Lebanese prisoners in Israeli jails. For its supporters, the war validated the need to preserve Hizballah as a militia to defend Lebanon. For its critics, it illustrated the dangers of Hizballah's continued resistance.

In the aftermath of the summer war, constrained by new strategic realities, namely the deployment of Lebanese and UN-mandated troops in southern Lebanon, and undoubtedly exhausted by the fight, Hizballah redirected its efforts toward Beirut, hoping to capitalize on its "divine victory." Faced with the reluctance of the anti-Syrian Lebanese parliamentary majority to offer the expected substantive political gains, angry at the government's alleged connivance with Israel, and concerned that Hizballah's victory would bring no tangible results and leave it weakened in southern Lebanon and in Beirut, a victorious yet apprehensive and frustrated Hizballah stepped up the pressure on the central government to obtain a government reshuffle and a veto right.[27] A senior Hizballah official confirmed this in December 2006: "Now we are demanding [a greater government share] because our experience during the war and the performance of the government has made us unsure. On several occasions they pressured us to lay down our weapons while we were fighting a war."[28]

The U.S. government and others, including Lebanese politicians, misrepresent Hizballah's push to obtain more governmental power as a Syrian- and Iranian-engineered attempt to overthrow the Lebanese government. True, Syria in particular benefits from paralyzing Lebanese government activity as it seeks to obstruct the international tribunal that will try the suspects in the Hariri and other assassination cases and to avoid the institutionalization and expansion of its isolation under a

UN umbrella.Yet, Hizballah pursues this objective for a different motive: guaranteeing an institutional cover for the resistance by seizing a veto over government decisions in order to prevent a further erosion of its domestic position. The confluence of the two crises means that the vital interests of Damascus are intrinsically linked to those of Hizballah, even though it abhors being identified with a Syrian goal.

Engaging Syria?

The deteriorating U.S. situation in Iraq and the summer war in Lebanon have given new life to the idea of enlisting Syria to help stabilize Iraq and restrain Hizballah. Powerful voices have called for a more-inclusive diplomatic strategy in the Middle East. Those advocating engaging Syria stress the value of luring Damascus away from Tehran, thereby countering Iran's spreading influence in the region.[29] Former U.S. secretary of state James Baker, the architect of the peace process in the 1990s, confidently argues, "If you can flip the Syrians, you will cure Israel's Hizballah problem."[30] At the same time, a piecemeal approach runs the risk of being turned down. The International Crisis Group argues that "[i]f the idea [of engagement] amounts to politely asking what up to now has been curtly demanded, [it is] better not even to try."[31] In any case, the Bush administration remains loath to pursue such a course due to the fear of projecting weakness by engaging foes and due to the high price Syria would be expected to extract. Nevertheless, engaging Syria might be worth trying on its own merits, but only if assumptions about peace talks are revised, the relative power of the parties is well understood, and expectations are kept low.

The summer 2006 war reinforced Syria's position on several levels. Syria derived much pride and prestige from the perceived achievements of Hizballah. It hoped that the war illustrated the pacifying role that Syria had played in Lebanon since 1990 and persuaded many of the mistake of pushing it out of Lebanon. The war also reminded Israel of Syria's enduring power of nuisance when ignored or mistreated. Nevertheless, the reasoning behind engaging Syria should not be uniquely driven by the hope that it can somehow stabilize Lebanon in a durable manner.

If talks were to begin, Bashar would be expected to demonstrate his willingness and ability to constrain Hizballah and then to disarm it once an agreement is reached. Syria's withdrawal from Lebanon has eroded its capacity to deliver on both counts. Syria could theoretically cut off the supply of Iranian weapons to Hizballah as required by UN Security Council Resolution 1701, which ended the summer 2006 war with Israel. Further, Hizballah could still be negatively affected by changes in Damascus, particularly if Bashar awakes to the precariousness of his position. To be sure, Damascus retains leverage over Hizballah because it receives logistical support from Syria. Yet, although Hizballah and Iran give Bashar short-term legitimacy and strategic confidence, they cannot offer him regional and international acceptance or much-needed economic assistance.

The Syrian regime, despite some bombastic statements during the summer war, cannot embrace Hizballah-style resistance because it has a lot more to lose to an Israeli attack than Hizballah does. Syria is also nervous about growing Iranian power in the Levant, a powerful constraint on its diplomatic options. Such a course of action, however, ignores the reality that Hizballah thrives as a guerrilla force; its power is not just a result of the high-technology weaponry supplied by Iran and Syria. It would also be politically dangerous for Bashar to try to outsmart his Iranian ally. Moreover, Hizballah could turn the tables on Syria if it felt outmaneuvered, most likely by provoking Israel without Syrian knowledge but at Syrian expense. Testing Syrian intentions without a clear process and end goal could therefore backfire.

In reality, despite encouraging signs from Damascus, including high-profile interviews of Bashar in Western media and meetings with U.S. senators, Syria is in no position to respond constructively to potential U.S. overtures anyway. A Syrian list of demands and apparent readiness to talk do not amount to a coherent and encouraging negotiating posture. Bashar welcomes the process of dialogue mainly because it replaces the narrative of 2005 as Bashar having systematically miscalculated with a new one of Bashar having correctly positioned Syria to take advantage of the rapidly changing landscape in the Middle East. Moreover, calling for dialogue while knowing that the other side will not respond makes Damascus seem open to compromise and makes Washington look intransigent and arrogant. Bashar may well calculate that, were he to survive the next two years and wait for the next U.S. administration to adjust to the many U.S. failures in the Middle East, he would emerge on top, stronger and vindicated.

Although Syria could negotiate peace in good faith during the 1990s because of its strong strategic position, the loss of Lebanon as its economic and political depth and the apparent international consensus on preventing its return to Lebanon suggest that Syria will not sacrifice its ties to its few remaining strategic partners, Iran and Hizballah. Bashar is prisoner to the radical outlook he has espoused in order to gain domestic and regional legitimacy. He can hardly jump ship in the current regional environment. Syria is in a position of relative weakness vis-à-vis its partners. Bashar does not enjoy the same degree of popular legitimacy as Nasrallah, Iranian president Mahmoud Ahmadinejad, Hamas political leader Khaled Meshaal, or Palestinian prime minister Ismail Haniyeh, all of whom are either elected leaders or leaders of successful political parties legitimized by elections. Regime survival against domestic challengers, though weak and divided, continues to top Bashar's priorities. His narrow sectarian base, though loyal, is hardly expandable; and Syria's crippling economy, sectarian fabric, and domestic discontent are a recipe for internal instability.

The new relationship between Syria and Hizballah profoundly impacts how peace should be pursued in the region. Seeing Hizballah only through a regional prism and assuming that Syria will systematically determine Hizballah's behavior is flawed. Lebanon's fabric and conditions must inform Hizballah-specific policies. As counterintuitive and cliché as it seems, the priority should be political reform. As long as Hizballah subordinates everything to its resistance agenda, it will not play a positive role in reforming Lebanon. This paradoxically provides an opportunity to expose Hizballah's dilemma. Although many Shi'ites see Hizballah as their champion, the latter, to preserve its raison d'etre, does not prioritize Shi'ite demands, a dilemma one Shi'ite intellectual calls Hizballah's "schizophrenia." Even within Hizballah, there is a rift between a powerful core committed to permanent resistance and the midlevel political cadre willing to focus exclusively on political participation.

The underlying assumption that Israeli peace with Syria will lead to Hizballah's disarmament must also be reassessed. There is no more symmetry in what to expect from Syria with regard to Hizballah. Today, Syria probably retains the power to ignite Hizballah and hopefully to restrain it, but it has lost the power to disarm it. This prospect alarms Israeli strategic thinkers and explains their measured enthusiasm for the Syrian withdrawal from Lebanon. The summer 2006 war between Israel and Hizballah even suggested to some that the predictability of a deterrable Syria controlling Lebanon is better than the alternative of an unbound Hizballah.

What Next for Hizballah?

Despite its summer 2006 victory, Hizballah's position in Lebanon remains precarious, with a risk that it might overplay its hand. Its domestic alliances might not outlast the current cycle of political unrest for tactical and ideological reasons. Its Christian allies do not adhere to Hizballah's strong anti-Western outlook and would not settle for an indefinite postponement of a discussion over Hizballah's weapons.[32] Sectarian dynamics have forced Hizballah to resort to its Shi'ite shield, eroding its cross-sectarian appeal in Lebanon and hurting its image in the Arab world.

More recently, however, Hizballah has tried to regain a wider support base by publicly articulating political and economic demands instead of focusing exclusively on the muqawama. Further, in the midst of deadly clashes in Lebanon in early 2007, Nasrallah offered to widen the ranks of the muqawama to include non-Shi'ite factions in an attempt to polish its Lebanese credentials and counter sectarian criticism. Hizballah seems willing to part with its cherished monopoly over anti-Israeli resistance in order to regain national, multisectarian cover and legitimacy.

The need to avoid domestic strife, which would durably taint Hizballah, could lead it to respond positively to Iranian or Arab pressure to accept an unsatisfactory political compromise, although Syria could emerge as an obstacle to such a settlement. If a compromise is not reached, a politically weakened Hizballah could redirect its efforts to the south and pressure the UN peacekeeping forces there. Hizballah is also in the process of reframing muqawama to include the United States, now seen as an existential threat to be countered. Given this emerging reality, an overly aggressive U.S. posture will only reinforce Hizballah's rationale for pursuing the muqawama instead of undermining it. This is why reaching a political accommodation with Hizballah, as unpleasant as it may be, is so essential.

The fates of Syria and Hizballah are intertwined, but addressing the challenges they pose requires differentiated approaches. Hoping that Syria is the key to Hizballah ignores the reality that although Syria retains some influence, Hizballah has gained leverage and independence over its former patron. Although Syrian and Iranian nods, as unlikely as they may be, would go a long way in containing Hizballah, confrontation by proxy is no longer enough. Rather, only the Lebanese political process, as messy and imperfect as it is, can constrain Hizballah. Political reform and progress on some of Hizballah's demands, including those related to the Lebanese-Israeli track, will undermine its main levers of power and influence. This is of course fraught with considerable risks and is premised on the capacity of the Lebanese polity to demonstrate adaptability and farsightedness. Nonetheless, this is the approach that the international community should promote to prevent another dramatic explosion of violence.

Notes

1. For a discussion of Shi'ite awakening and rise in Lebanon, see Fouad Ajami, *The Vanished Imam: Musa Al-Sadr and the Shia of Lebanon* (Ithaca, N.Y.: Cornell University Press, 1986); Augustus Richard Norton, *Amal and the Shi'a: Struggle for the Soul of Lebanon* (Austin: University of Texas Press, 1987).
2. For a discussion of the Iran-Hizballah relationship, see Graham E. Fuller, "The Hizballah-Iran Connection: Model for Sunni Resistance," *The Washington Quarterly* 30, no. 1 (Winter 2006–07): 139–150.
3. Former Syrian intelligence officer, interview with author, Beirut, summer 2003.
4. See Magnus Ranstorp, *Hezbollah in Lebanon: The Politics of the Western Hostage Crisis* (New York: St. Martin's Press, 1997).

5. See Amal Saad-Ghorayeb, *Hizbu'llah: Politics and Religion* (Sterling, Va.: Pluto Press, 2002); Nizar Hamzeh, "Lebanon's Hizballah: From Revolution to Parliamentary Accommodation," *Third World Quarterly* 14, no. 2 (1993): 321–337.
6. Dennis Ross, *The Missing Peace: The Inside Story of the Fight for Middle East Peace* (New York: Farrar, Straus, and Giroux, 2004); Itamar Rabinovich, *Waging Peace* (Princeton, N.J.: Princeton University Press, 2004); Helena Cobban, *The Israeli-Syrian Peace Talks: 1991–96 and Beyond* (Washington, D.C.: USIP Press Books, 1999).
7. European and Arab diplomats, interviews with author, Paris, Beirut, and Damascus, summer 2003 and May 2005; former U.S. negotiator, interview with author, Washington, D.C., December 2006.
8. Eli Carmeli and Yotan Feldner, "Lebanon and the Armed Struggle After Israel's Withdrawal," *MEMRI Inquiry and Analysis Series*, no. 26 (March 31, 2006), http://memri.org/bin/articles.cgi?Page=archives&Area=ia&ID=IA2600.
9. Syrian official, interviews with author, Beirut, summer 2003; former Syrian official, interview with author, Europe, November 2006.
10. European and Arab diplomats, interviews with author, Paris, Beirut, and Damascus, summer 2003 and May 2005.
11. Nadim Shehadi, "Riviera vs. Citadel: The Battle for Lebanon," openDemocracy.net, August 22, 2006, http://www.opendemocracy.net/conflict-middle_east_politics/riviera_citadel_3841.jsp#.
12. Judith Palmer Harik, *Hezbollah: The Changing Face of Terrorism* (New York: I.B. Tauris, 2004), p. 47.
13. Ibid.
14. Ibid.
15. For an examination of the society and culture of resistance, see Mona Harb and Reinoud Leenders, "Know Thy Enemy: Hizbullah, 'Terrorism,' and the Politics of Perception," *Third World Quarterly* 26, no. 1 (February 2005): 173–197.
16. Hizballah officials, interviews with author, Beirut, July 2003.
17. Syrian analyst, interview with author, Damascus, May 2005.
18. Former Syrian official, interview with author, Paris, November 2006. See Volker Perthes, "The Syrian Solution," *Foreign Affairs* 85, no. 6 (November/December 2006): 33–40.
19. Syrian regime insider, interview with author, Damascus, May 2005.
20. Seth Colter Walls, "Striking a Syrian Pose?" *Weekly Standard*, November 17, 2005, http://www.weeklystandard.com/Content/Public/Articles/000/000/006/369xrvlb.asp?pg=1.
21. See Office of the Press Secretary, The White House, "Statement on Condemnation of Hizballah Kidnapping of Two Israeli Soldiers," July 12, 2006, http://www.whitehouse.gov/news/releases/2006/07/20060712.html.

22. Hizballah militants, interview with author, Beirut, May 2005.
23. See also Augustus Richard Norton, "Hizballah in a National and Regional Context, From 2000 to 2006," *Journal of Palestine Studies*, no. 141 (Fall 2006), http://www.palestine-studies.org/final/en/journals/issue.php?iid=141&jid=1&vid=XXXVI&vol=203.
24. Former Hizballah activist, interview with author, Beirut, November 2006.
25. "Nasrallah New TV Interview Excerpts," Mideastwire.com, September 4, 2006, http://www.mideastwire.com/topstory.php?id=10401.
26. Emile El-Hokayem, "Hizbollah's Enduring Myth," *Arab Reform Bulletin* 4, no. 9 (November 2006), http://www.carnegieendowment.org/publications/index.cfm?fa=view&id=18857&prog=zgp&proj=zme#hizbollah.
27. Hizballah official, interview with author, Beirut, November 2006.
28. Scheherezade Faramarzi, "Hezbollah Seeks More Power in Lebanon," Associated Press, December 15, 2006.
29. Itamar Rabinovich, "Courting Syria," *Ha'aretz*, November 30, 2006, http://www.haaretz.com/hasen/spages/791583.html.
30. David E. Sanger, "Dueling Views Pit Baker Against Rice," *New York Times*, December 8, 2006, http://www.nytimes.com/2006/12/08/world/middleeast/08diplo.html?th&emc=th.
31. Robert Malley and Peter Harling, "Talks With Iran and Syria Will Not Be an Easy Ride," *Financial Times*, December 13, 2006, http://www.ft.com/cms/s/f03dea38-8ad8-11db-8940-0000779e2340.html.
32. Christian demonstrators allied with Hizballah, interview with author, Beirut, December 2006.

Part III:
Iraq

Carlos Pascual and Kenneth M. Pollack

The Critical Battles: Political Reconciliation and Reconstruction in Iraq

By now it should be apparent to even the most hermetic observers that untangling the problems of Iraq will be a monumental task. As the January 2007 National Intelligence Estimate on Iraq highlighted, the country suffers from a variety of dangerous, complicated, and intertwined problems, including terrorism, pervasive organized and unorganized crime, an insurgency, a failed state, a security vacuum, and a civil war.[1] U.S. policy toward Iraq must come to grips with all of them if it is to have any chance of engendering an environment that leads to a sustainable peace.

Recognizing that Iraq is a failed state is fundamental to understanding that it lacks the capacity to fix itself, no matter how much pressure the United States applies. Rebuilding the political, economic, and bureaucratic institutions of a failed state requires considerable resources and a long-term commitment, both of which are only possible in a secure environment. This is why fixing Iraq's security vacuum is critical to creating the conditions under which economic, political, and social institutions can begin to reemerge.

Carlos Pascual is vice president and director for the Foreign Policy Studies Program at the Brookings Institution and former coordinator for reconstruction and stabilization at the Department of State. Ken Pollack is director of research at the Saban Center for Middle East Policy at the Brookings Institution and former director for Persian Gulf affairs at the National Security Council.

The Washington Quarterly • 30:3 pp. 7–19.

Any U.S. strategy, including the Bush administration's spring 2007 troop surge, will thus be most successful if it can influence the dynamics on the ground to create political latitude for action. The best case is that a strategic approach such as the surge will create a secure space in which to start to rebuild Iraq's shattered political, economic, and social institutions and thus threaten Iraq's warlords enough to force them to make compromises for a political settlement, just as radical Shi'a cleric Muqtada al-Sadr was forced to join Iraq's political process in 2004 when he lost control of Iraq's streets to a determined coalition offensive.

If it is going to have any chance to succeed, the surge or any other U.S. effort to stabilize Iraq cannot be left as simply a military strategy. To sustain any gains in stability, it will also be vital to forge a complimentary political agreement to achieve a sustainable peace and set in motion processes to begin to rebuild Iraq's capacities for self-governance and economic regulation. Without a truce that gets the warring parties to stop fighting, neither the United States nor the Iraqi state will be able to provide sustained security and a better life for the Iraqi people. Even the most wildly successful military strategy can do no more than create the space in which diplomatic, political, and economic efforts can build a viable new Iraq. The United States' lack of such exertions is key to the failure of its previous efforts in Iraq and essential to what is almost certainly the last chance to do so.

Learning from Experience

Before Iraq and Afghanistan, the United States had been engaged in major conflicts in Bosnia, El Salvador, Haiti, Kosovo, Nicaragua, Somalia, Sudan, and elsewhere. It has learned about the difficulty of transforming centrally controlled states and building market-based democracies with a rule of law in central Europe and the former Soviet states. Whatever happens on the ground in Iraq, U.S. policy should take into account at least six previously learned principles of peacemaking and peacekeeping.

First, civil wars generally require political solutions. External military forces can help create pressure for a political agreement, but they cannot usually impose peace on warring parties. If at least one party has the money and recruits to sustain guerrilla tactics, it is difficult for governing or external groups to stop violent attacks solely through force, as shown in Bosnia, Kosovo, Northern Ireland, and Sudan.

Second, such political solutions themselves require a "ripeness" that typically only emerges when all sides are exhausted by the fighting, a stronger external force compels them to cease, or the circumstances change in a way that makes it more compelling for the warring parties to make real compromises than to keep fighting. Unfortunately, Iraq's warlords—its Sunni insurgents and Shi'a militias—are still full of fight, and compelling them to cease would require a far-greater force than even what the troop surge provides. Without a political agreement that creates a stake in peace, the incentive will be to disrupt and fight. Ending this logjam requires eliminating the security vacuum and rebuilding the failed state, thereby threatening the warlords' hold on the Iraqi people, in the expectation that doing so will persuade the warlords to make compromises that they otherwise would not for fear of losing everything. At this late date, that will not be easy, but the easy options in Iraq disappeared a long time ago.

Third, political agreements need to achieve a truce on core grievances among fighting factions to buy time for parties to build trust and to achieve a longer-term solution. In Bosnia, Kosovo, and South Africa, for example, political settlements took root in stages. Although the transitions did not always work as planned, full settlements would have never worked at the outset. In Iraq, the core grievances include the sharing of oil revenues, federal-regional relations, and minority rights. Usually, there must be an amnesty for most combatants, or they have no incentive to end the fighting.

The prospect for a political solution is complicated by the constitution that the United States helped to broker in 2005 in order to demonstrate the progress of democracy. The ill-conceived provisions on oil set back the prospects for a viable political solution in Iraq and enraged the Sunni community by holding out the prospect that the Shi'a and Kurds will be able to control the development of future energy resources. A last-minute condition brokered by U.S. ambassador Zalmay Khalilzad created a provision for future revisions to the sections on energy developments that has not been fully acted on. At this stage, however, it may be necessary to suspend the constitution in favor of modest interim arrangements. The Shi'a and Kurds may have no interest to do so unless they are pressed by regional actors who are either their key supporters or actors who can block their ambitions to develop and retain energy wealth. The Sunnis will have to concede on some level of regional autonomy in return for guarantees on sharing oil wealth.

Fourth, a solid security environment sustained by the presence of adequate security forces is required to facilitate governance and economic activity. In Bosnia, for instance, 19 international troops were deployed per 1,000 civilians to implement the Dayton accords. In Kosovo, the ratio of security personnel to civilians was 20 to 1,000.[2] By contrast, the troop concentrations in Iraq of 7 to 1,000 in 2003 and in Afghanistan of 1 to 1,000 in 2001 have made it easier for insurgencies and militias to take root.[3]

If there is a political settlement in Iraq, force concentrations comparable to Bosnia and Kosovo would suggest boosting deployment from the current 150,000 troops in Iraq to as many as 250,000 to 450,000 in order to sustain stability. Iraqi forces should not be counted as part of this external troop requirement. International experience in building indigenous police and military forces has demonstrated that typically it takes three to five years to develop reliable indigenous capabilities. With Iraqi forces distrusted or seen as a tool of sectarian factions by large segments of the population, the presence of international troops would be critical in the process of capacity and trust building.

Fifth, the United States and the international community must be prepared to sustain external forces and economic support for eight to 10 years after a political settlement. The international community was still providing assistance in the Czech Republic, Hungary, and Poland in 1995, six years after the fall of the Iron Curtain. Russia and Ukraine, both with massive resources, went through virtually eight years of economic contraction before they began to grow, and Russia was helped by soaring oil prices that masked structural imbalances.

With peace, Iraq has potential parallels to Russia in 1991: a well-educated population, massive energy resources, and a defunct command economy. Yet, not only does Iraq have a ruptured society, war has also destroyed much of its infrastructure, perhaps undoing as much as was invested by the United States and others. Not all U.S. investments in Iraq were wasted, and lessons have been learned about the need to rely more on Iraqi capabilities. Nevertheless, massive funding will be needed, particularly to create jobs. Those resources will ideally come from Iraq's own oil revenues, but outside support may still be necessary. It will be difficult, if not impossible, for Iraq's crippled bureaucracy to move local investments from central to provincial coffers and to the private sector.

Sixth, stabilization and reconstruction efforts must be multilateral, preferably under a UN mandate, to achieve legitimacy and sustain the levels of international support needed over eight to 10 years. At present, the trend is moving in the other direction. The United States' international partners in Iraq see failure, and domestic pressures are forcing them out as quickly as possible. Although the United Nations continues to provide a mandate for U.S. troops, at this point its impact on legitimacy is meaningless. The only way to renew multilateral support is through a new initiative that begins with a political and diplomatic agreement that creates a truce among Iraq's warring factions and unites regional and international actors in an effort to stem international terrorism.

Filling the Security Vacuum, Fixing the Failed State

Iraq is a failed state dominated by a sectarian war that encompasses Sunni and Shi'a militias, al Qaeda in Iraq, and, potentially, armed Kurdish fighters. Iraq's government is dominated by Shi'a militias, most notably Sadr's Mahdi Army and the Badr Organization of the Supreme Council for the Islamic Revolution in Iraq, a militia trained and organized by Iran that controls key cities in southern Iraq. The militias gain their strength by providing protection, both voluntary and involuntary, as well as basic services such as food, medicine, money, employment, gasoline, and even electricity to Iraqis who cannot count on the central government to do so.

They provide these services in return for political support, which has allowed them virtually to sweep Iraq's elections and thereby dominate

Iraq's government. As members of the ruling coalition, the militias have taken over Iraq's ministries, ensuring that they do not provide basic security and services, lest they undermine the popular support for the militias. The militias run these ministries like patronage networks, in which graft is the norm and government agencies function as private fiefdoms. Naturally, in this environment, crime of all sorts becomes a constant presence, adding to the mayhem and to popular reliance on the militias.

The situation of the Sunnis differs from that of the Shi'a only in that they are largely in opposition to the Shi'a- and Kurdish-controlled government. The early, mistaken decisions of the United States regarding de-Ba'athification and the constitution of Iraq's first few governments convinced Iraq's Sunni tribal population that the reconstruction of Iraq was meant to come at their expense, causing them first to shelter deadly Salafi jihadists such as al Qaeda in Iraq and then to support a full-blown insurgency against the central government, which the Americans had allowed to exclude Sunni interests early on. This state of affairs then became self-perpetuating when the Shi'a militias took control of Iraq's streets and with them its elections.

Iraqi combatants may just not be ready to accept that a peace settlement is their best option, but the Bush administration can make better use of the tools at its disposal to increase the incentives and prospects to make a political agreement viable. The military elements of the surge strategy correctly but much belatedly build on the lessons of past counterinsurgency and stabilization campaigns. The goal of the current plan is to secure Baghdad by blanketing the city with U.S. and Iraqi security personnel, working in joint teams with the primary mission of protecting the civilian population and making the streets safe, something coalition forces have rarely bothered to do over the previous four years.

The United States has a smart and realistic secretary of defense in Robert Gates. In General David Petraeus, it has a commander of U.S. forces in Iraq who has spent more time than any other U.S. general learning the lessons history has to teach about how to make an operation such as this succeed. Under Petraeus's leadership, U.S. and Iraqi forces have radically altered their tactics in Iraq and are seeing some success in establishing the kind of security that could create the time and space for civilian efforts to gain traction on politics and economics.

The plan and the implementation are much weaker when it comes to the various political and economic steps that will be needed to turn temporary military successes into lasting peace and stability. Although the administration has talked about increasing the numbers of civilian personnel operating outside the relative security of the Green Zone, it is at best unclear from where those people are going to come. The U.S. government has not mobilized the people and resources for a major civilian initiative, lacking the numbers of people needed with the requisite skills.

In contrast to the 150,000 troops that will be in Iraq, there are only about 6,500 Foreign Service officers posted everywhere in the world. The president has proposed to double the number of civilians in Provincial Reconstruction Teams (PRTs) to about 450, but that number will still fall well short of the hundreds of personnel desirable for an operation of this size, and they will have to operate within military units for protection, greatly hindering their ability to complete their mission.

Furthermore, without a change in security, it will be difficult to entice U.S. and international nongovernmental organizations (NGOs) to return to Iraq. The Civilian Reserve Corps proposed by the administration may be a useful supplement for future conflicts, but it is not even proposed in the president's fiscal year 2008 budget. Only a fraction of the needed civilian capabilities will be available or able to operate in Iraq in 2007.

Perhaps the only community that could provide the numbers of personnel with the skills needed to shoulder the burden of political, economic, and social reconstruction in Iraq are the international NGOs and certain agencies of the UN, yet all along they have been notably absent from the administration's planning. Enticing them to greater participation will doubtless require a secure environment in which they can do what they do best by getting out among the Iraqi people. Even if Petraeus succeeds in creating such an environment in the greater Baghdad area, NGO personnel will likely also want an international political framework led by the UN or other international institutions, such as they have traditionally had in similar operations elsewhere around the world. This will require the administration to allow UN or UN-authorized personnel to play a much greater role in reconstruction than they have in the past.

Moreover, current U.S. operations remain badly hobbled by the absence of an integrated command structure in which U.S. and Iraqi personnel both from the military and civilian sides are able to closely coordinate their operations. Again, part of the problem is simply the lack of civilians, skilled or otherwise, to fill out a proper chain of command. Without the capacity to field civilians on the ground, it is not surprising that civilian and military agencies have not worked out how to cooperate effectively. Civilians in PRTs must depend on the military to move about in their areas. They typically get access to just a fraction of the projects they support. With at best only a handful of civilians on any PRT, it is almost impossible to have the necessary skill sets to make a difference.

Oddly enough, the Department of Defense, which under Secretary Donald Rumsfeld famously disdained nation building in favor of war fighting, is now the only U.S. bureaucracy that has the thousands of personnel, security capabilities, and funding to take this critical mission to heart. Increasingly, most other U.S. government personnel want little to do with what is seen as a failing mission in a dangerous environment with little effort being made to exercise core diplomatic competencies to seek a political settlement. The result is, not surprisingly, rising frustration and distrust a sense among the military that they are alone and a sense among civilians that it was military incompetence that dragged the United States into this mess. As the United States learned belatedly in Vietnam, an effort such as the reconstruction of Iraq requires complete and constant coordination between the military and civilian elements of government, along with resources for the political, economic, and social programs that are equally if not more important than the military campaign.

Securing a Political Settlement

If the first steps of the surge do their job, they will improve the security climate in Baghdad and begin to build up the capacity of various elements of the Iraqi government. In doing so, they will threaten the power of the militias and insurgent groups by taking away their access to the populace and creating an alternative and preferable source for security and services. This threat could make those militia leaders willing to make real compromises on power sharing and revenue distribution—the very compromises they see no need to make now.

Hence, the bottom-up elements of the surge (taking back the streets and building government capacity) are designed to help the top-down approach (breaking the political logjam in Baghdad) that could make a real political settlement among the warring parties a tangible prospect for the first time. That political settlement would greatly assist securing the rest of the country, further aiding the process of capacity building. In other words, if it works, it will become a self-reinforcing process.

Another key gap in the current surge is the underdeveloped plan to forge just such a political settlement. In parallel with the surge, the United States must begin what the Iraq Study Group called a "diplomatic offensive" to put in place an international process to broker a deal among the warring parties when they are most vulnerable and willing to make compromises.[4] Particularly because of the weak civilian side of the effort, Petraeus's work to improve security may quickly come under strain, putting a premium on moving forward with political negotiations designed both to take advantage of that improved security situation and to reinforce it.

In other words, the United States cannot afford to wait for the bottom-up approach to succeed before starting the top-down one. Because of the difficulties facing both, the process of brokering a political settlement needs to begin immediately and long before the other elements of the surge have secured Iraq's streets and rebuilt its government capacity precisely to assist that process.

A Framework for Progress

The immediate goals of a political settlement would be to stop the fighting among the militias, control or dismantle al Qaeda in Iraq, and establish at least a five-year truce that provides time and political space to work out a viable long-term constitutional arrangement. The critical necessary element is an agreement among sectarian groups, endorsed and enforced by international actors. Its longer-term goals would be to rationalize oil development and revenues, federal-regional relations, minority rights, control of militias, and amnesty for combatants. Militias would have to be disbanded or folded into formal security structures. A framework would need to be created for representative local government.

An increase in U.S. forces without an effort to forge such a political agreement is unlikely to significantly stabilize the situation for long, if at all. If properly sized and employed, a military force can create a secure space for political compromise and civilian development. Without these follow-on efforts, however, it will become increasingly difficult and eventually impossible to sustain the secure environment. Likewise, increased economic assistance without a political agreement and greater stability would have little sustainable impact because of the eventual return of instability and violence. Infrastructure investments would likely be destroyed. Wasted resources would later make it even more difficult to mobilize additional support if a political agreement were reached.

Many factors will make it difficult to secure a political agreement. No one clearly understands what now motivates the militias—politics, power, religion, personal greed, or all of the above. Some of the issues that sparked the Sunni insurgency, such as exclusion from oil profits and de-Ba'athification, are clear, but restraining the insurgency has become more complicated than redressing these grievances. In particular, the sectarian violence is now propelled as much by revenge for past killings and fear of future ones as it is by instrumental desires to achieve specific political goals. For these reasons, involving Iran, Syria, Turkey, and the neighboring Sunni states in this process will be critical to convincing them to use their influence to pressure militias to stop fighting. No one should expect that Iran and Syria will cooperate in good faith. A determining factor will be whether Iran sees danger in an uncontrolled war.

The process and structure of political and diplomatic negotiations will be complicated. For the United States, one of the most difficult points to accept may be that it cannot run such a process because it is seen as an actor with a stake in the outcome and without the neutrality needed to broker deals. The UN would need to lead, call the parties together, and broker disputes. To make that possible, the UN would need a completely new team for Iraq, led by someone with the experience and stature of former Finnish president Marti Ahtisaari, who brokered agreements in Kosovo and Aceh, or the UN special coordinator for the Middle East peace process, Terje Roed Larsen. Putting this task in the hands of the UN's current placeholder team in Iraq, which is seen as inexperienced and lacking international stature, would lead nowhere.

A credible and reconfigured UN initiative might make it politically possible for the United States and Sunni states to join a process with Iran. Under the UN, the key external players—the European Union, Iran, Jordan, Kuwait, Saudi Arabia, Syria, Turkey, and the United States—will need to form a contact group to manage the process. A wider circle of countries and organizations, such as the Arab League, Gulf Cooperation Council, China, Japan, and Russia, will need to be engaged, but it would be logistically impossible to involve all of them in each step of the negotiations. As a starting point, all non-Iraqi participants in the negotiations should commit to securing a political deal and to exert pressure on all Iraqi factions to participate.

To achieve a meaningful outcome, it will be necessary to secure the participation of all key Iraqi leaders. They will need to go into the discussions accepting that the goal is a five-year truce, not a permanent solution. A massive public education campaign led by Arab radio and television networks outside Iraq should make the broad base of regional engagement in the process clear in order to stimulate grassroots Iraqi interest and generate bottom-up support for a settlement that stops the fighting. If the process stalls or proves counterproductive, the international actors must be ready to call off negotiations on Iraq and refocus on handling the regional consequences of war.

The proposed agreement should be kept as simple as possible, recognizing that it is temporary and that excessive detail will stall both its negotiation and chances for implementation. In some cases, it may be best to revert to aspects of earlier arrangements such as the Transitional Administrative Law, the protoconstitution that governed Iraqi administration prior to the adoption of the constitution in 2005, or independent policy proposals. Key elements of an agreement would include provisions for core compromises, absorption of militias, battling transnational terrorism, freezing the political process, Iraqi security and jobs, and regional peace and security.

Core compromises would include a formula for revenue sharing,[5] a formula to balance federal and regional responsibilities, national guarantees for minority rights, and amnesty for combatants. Sectarian factions should agree to fold their militias into the national army or police forces. That said, Iraqi security forces would have to be restructured so that they do not become official sectarian weapons. All participants in a conference, Iraqi and international, would need to commit beforehand to their opposition to al Qaeda in Iraq. There needs to be a clear international and national message that al Qaeda serves no Iraqi interest.

It may be necessary to freeze elections for three to five years to provide a space for governance. Although this may seem antidemocratic, post-conflict experiences have shown that democracy has a better long-term prospect if elections are not immediately imposed on war-torn societies. Officials involved in Bosnia, for example, argue that the heavy schedule of elections in the Dayton accords served to legitimize criminal leaders rather than facilitate political stability. In Iraq, Fareed Zakaria argues that "elections had wondrous aspects, but they also divided the country into three communities and hardened these splits. To describe the last four years as a period of political progress requires a strange definition of political development."[6]

In the meantime, the international community would need to sustain support for security and to create jobs. The United States should seek to internationalize security forces under a UN mandate. Finally, the Israeli-Palestinian issue will remain a destabilizing factor around which both Sunnis and Shi'a will rally. A sensitive yet critical part of a political process for Iraq will be to offer a dialogue to regional actors on peace and security in the region. Yet, any regional security dialogue could be divisive, and it will be necessary to keep these differences bounded so that they do not detract from a possible agreement on Iraq.

Leaving No Stone Unturned

There are many reasons why such a political and diplomatic initiative could fail. It cannot be assumed that political or militia leaders will act out of concern for the greater good. At present, no leaders among either the Sunni or Shi'a Arabs can speak for and compel behavior from the welter of vicious militias, in contrast to the Bosnian war in which ethnic leaders controlled their forces by 1995, making the Dayton accords possible. Sectarian identity is increasingly taking over Iraqi identity as sectarian militias take over the streets. The Shi'a and possibly their Iranian backers think that they can win. Moderate Sunni states will likely increase support to Sunni extremists in Iraq if they think that the Shi'a will attain control. Actions, politics, and rhetoric in Iran and the United States every day make it more difficult for both sides to sit at the same table without appearing to capitulate. A political settlement will require the United States and other international forces to make it viable, and the political will to provide them may have already been eclipsed.

Even if the probability of success of a political and diplomatic initiative is low, so is the relative cost. A failed diplomatic initiative may at least stir some international goodwill, and it will not add to an already common international perception of failure in Iraq.[7] Experience suggests that reaching a political settlement takes time and generally involves backsliding on the part of those involved, so a quick result will not be possible. That said, the act of engaging conflicting parties could put pressure on them to stop fighting. If done in a way that engages the UN, key regional actors, and other international actors, it could be a critical bridge to international cooperation to contain regional spillover.

As more time passes and violence escalates, the more difficult it will be to achieve a political settlement. The United States must cooperate with regional players, the UN, and other international partners to create leverage over Iraqis who might restrain the militias and reach a political compromise. The chances for success are low, but this is one of the few options that have not been tried, despite the imperative suggested by international experience with civil wars. Failing to try essentially amounts to accepting civil war in Iraq.

A Least Bad Option

The reconstruction of Iraq has been a four-year-long disaster. As a result, there simply are no good options left. As one U.S. soldier in Iraq put it in 2005, "[T]he problem with Iraq is that we can't stay, we can't leave, and we can't fail."[8]

Nevertheless, some policy options are worse than others. Withdrawal from Iraq would almost certainly condemn the state to all-out civil war that could destabilize the vital Persian Gulf region, either by allowing internal instability to spread or by plunging Iraq's neighbors into a regional war. Proposals to partition Iraq appear premature at best and would likely require either massive bloodshed or massive U.S. force levels to sort out the populations and convince them to accept divisions that very few Iraqis currently would accept. In the event of full-scale civil war in Iraq, the United States could shift to a posture of containment to try to prevent the spillover that traditionally accompanies such wars,[9] but Washington should not readily adopt this option unless clearly there is no chance to stabilize the country.

This brings the focus back to the troop surge. It would have been much easier to apply the core concepts of the surge three years, two years, or even one year ago. At this late date, it is something of a "Hail Mary." If it is going to have any chance to succeed, it cannot be left as simply a military strategy. It must be understood that the purpose of stronger military force is to create an environment for civilian efforts to revive Iraq's economy as well as rebuild government capacity and to forge a political settlement among the warring parties. If the revised military approach cannot gain political and diplomatic traction, then it too will fail, leaving only the worst options.

Notes

1. National Intelligence Council, "Prospects for Iraq's Stability: A Challenging Road Ahead," January 2007, http://graphics8.nytimes.com/packages/pdf/politics/20070203_intel_text.pdf.
2. Seth G. Jones et al., *Establishing Law and Order After Conflict* (Santa Monica, Calif.: RAND, 2005), pp. 19, 202, http://www.rand.org/pubs/monographs/2005/

RAND_MG374.pdf.

3. Ibid., pp. 184–185.
4. James A. Baker III and Lee H. Hamilton, *Iraq Study Group Report* (New York: Vintage Books, 2002), pp. 44–46.
5. Kenneth M. Pollack, "A Switch in Time: A New Strategy for America in Iraq," *Saban Center Analysis Paper*, no. 7 (February 2006), pp. 71–75, http://www.brookings.edu/fp/saban/analysis/20060215_iraqreport.pdf.
6. Fareed Zakaria, "The Limits of Democracy," *Newsweek*, January 29, 2007, http://www.fareedzakaria.com/articles/newsweek/012907.html.
7. "World View of U.S. Role Goes From Bad to Worse," *World Public Opinion*, January 22, 2007, http://www.worldpublicopinion.org/pipa/articles/home_page/306.php?nid=&id=&pnt=306&lb=hmpg1.
8. U.S. soldier, interview with author, northern Iraq, November 2005.
9. See Daniel L. Byman and Kenneth M. Pollack, "Things Fall Apart: Containing the Spillover From an Iraqi Civil War," *Saban Center Analysis Paper*, no. 11 (January 2007), http://media.brookings.edu/MediaArchive/fp/jan2007iraq_civilwar.pdf.

Michael O'Hanlon and Nina Kamp

Is the Media Being Fair in Iraq?

The Bush administration has complained about the tenor of media coverage of the war in Iraq ever since the April 2003 looting that followed the fall of Baghdad. Ambassador Paul Bremer criticized the media frequently during the first year of the U.S. presence in Iraq. Secretary of Defense Donald Rumsfeld and Vice President Dick Cheney have often asserted that the media have a proclivity to overemphasize violence and to dwell on negative news stories. The complaint that the public hears only the bad news has become increasingly prevalent among members of the U.S. armed forces as well.[1] This problem is potentially serious. Many critics of the media believe that negative coverage could cost the United States the war. By their reasoning, the United States could fail in Iraq only if our national resolve falters, which could only happen if the American public gets an unfairly pessimistic view of the situation as a result of the media's fixation on violence and other bad news. If the United States and its coalition partners do not prevail, however, the failure will most likely result from events on the ground there, not from an untimely wavering of domestic political support. In

Michael O'Hanlon is a senior fellow and Nina Kamp is a senior research assistant at the Brookings Institution in Washington, D.C. They are the coauthors of Brookings' Iraq Index, located at http://www.brookings.edu/iraqindex. O'Hanlon and Kurt Cambpell of CSIS are the coauthors of the forthcoming *Hard Power: The New Politics of National Security*.

The Washington Quarterly • 29:4 pp. 7–18.

fact, more than three years into the campaign, the U.S. body politic remains surprisingly tolerant of the mission in Iraq and, in general, resists calls for immediate withdrawal, despite far more bad news than anyone in the administration forecast or even thought possible when the war was first sold to the nation and launched. Given the facts, the U.S. public's view of the situation in Iraq is arguably just about where it should be. The public is exceptionally impressed by U.S. troops but depressed about the general lack of significant progress on the ground. They are upset, moreover, with the Bush administration for overpromising and underpreparing in regard to the war.

It seems that the people of the United States remain committed to the effort in Iraq, having reelected in 2004 the president who took them to war, because all of the alternatives look worse. Indeed, even as President George W. Bush's personal popularity among the U.S. population has declined to well below 40 percent, a Pew poll conducted in the spring of 2006 found that 54 percent of U.S. citizens still expected some level of success in establishing a democracy in Iraq.[2] If the media are so consistently reporting only bad news and creating an image of a failure in the works, it is not clear on what information this 54 percent is basing its guarded optimism.

Measuring the Media's Reporting of Iraq

To evaluate the claim of media bias systematically, we constructed a simple methodology for reviewing the reporting from Iraq over the last three years. First, we selected several news outlets that are considered among the most important in the United States and that also span its political spectrum, at least in the outlets' editorial instincts. Specifically, we assessed coverage by the *New York Times*, the *Wall Street Journal*, and NBC News and also looked at the *Washington Times*, *USA Today*, ABC News, and Fox News in more limited ways. This approach not only served to provide raw data that could help answer our basic question of whether media coverage is slanted but also helped to assess the degree to which the typical tone of stories might vary across organizations and thus the degree to which the reporting might reflect the political agendas of publishers, owners, editors, editorial writers, news anchors, and other key media figures.

Second, to make the analytical task more tractable, we selected a few specific months for examination. The goal was not to cover the whole three-year time period but to take only a random sampling of months. Specifically, we examined January, April, and May, the choice of the latter two months allowing for four years' worth of data for each year since the invasion of Iraq in March and April 2003.

We then used standard media search engines to obtain the headlines of all stories from each outlet for each month in question. This review allowed us to score the tone of each headline as positive, negative, or neutral. For example, a story about the killing of Abu Musab al-Zarqawi, the completion of a hospital construction project, or the high percentage of Iraqi voters going to the polls would be considered positive, whereas a story about violence against Iraqi citizens or U.S. forces, corruption, or economic mismanagement would be scored as negative. In rating the headlines, we assumed that headlines accurately reflected story content or, perhaps more importantly, at least for newspaper articles, that the tone of headlines influenced most readers at least as much as the tone of the article content did.

Without question, our exact count of positive, negative, and neutral stories is subject to some imprecision. Someone else scoring the headlines would undoubtedly come to at least a slightly different result (we, of course, would be delighted if others would perform their own assessments as a check on ours). Moreover, the very stories we chose to examine required some degree of arbitrariness in the way we queried the search engines to find stories. Most notably, short news clips that mentioned Iraq only once or twice, such as those characteristic of the news summaries in the *Wall Street Journal* as well as many stories with just a few paragraphs of text in other papers, were generally not counted in our approach. For this reason, there were very few entries for three or four of the 10 months we examined in the *Wall Street Journal*. Therefore, caution should be applied in interpreting our specific statistics about the tone of that paper's coverage. Overall, however, this methodology was straightforward to apply and fairly convincing in the general story line it seemed to generate.

Does It Depend on the Source?

Negative stories in the U.S. media have indeed outweighed positive ones by a factor of roughly 2.5 to 1 across several major outlets and in the course of the three years of the U.S. presence in Iraq. This number is a reasonable approximation averaged across the three major news sources we examined in detail and did not vary enormously from one outlet to another. That said, within print media, the *New York Times* was indeed somewhat more critical in its coverage than the *Wall Street Journal* was, as most media observers would predict, given the former newspaper's reputation as more left-leaning than the latter (see chart 1). The difference between the two, however, 2.8 negative stories for every 1 positive story in the *Times* and a ratio of 2.4:1 for the *Journal*, was hardly drastic.

A smaller but still notable difference was the overall tenor of coverage of Iraq by the *Washington Times*, also viewed as a conservative news outlet, at least editorially, which may have been somewhat more optimistic. Our assessments of this paper were more limited, but in April 2006 it carried 10 negative headlines, 6 positive headlines, and 12 neutral headlines. In May, the paper carried 13 negative headlines, 10 positive ones,

Table I: Assessment of Coverage by the *New York Times*

	Negative	Neutral	Positive	Total	Ratio of Negative to Positive	Percent Neutral
May 2003	72	52	58	182	1.2:1	29
January 2004	46	14	27	87	1.7:1	16
April 2004	93	44	27	164	3.4:1	27
May 2004	128	51	40	219	3.2:1	23
January 2005	70	35	30	135	2.3:1	26
April 2005	40	8	13	61	3.1:1	13
May 2005	51	10	18	79	2.8:1	13
January 2006	43	7	12	62	3.6:1	11
April 2006	42	11	12	65	3.5:1	17
May 2006	39	6	14	59	2.8:1	10
Monthly Average					2.8:1	

and 10 neutral. The *Washington Times*' overall ratio of about 1.5 negative stories to 1 positive story was considerably more positive during those two months than the headlines that appeared in either the *New York Times* or the *Wall Street Journal*, and the tone was somewhat more positive than NBC's coverage. For the same two months in 2006, the overall ratio of negative to positive stories in *USA Today* was about 2.3:1.

Nonetheless, the data do vary more notably from month to month than from newspaper to newspaper. In other words, for some months, the news was far worse than it was for others. This variation suggests that events on the ground drove the tone of coverage much more than the emotional, professional, or political predilections of editors and journalists.

Television may have had a somewhat greater proclivity to show bad news than newspapers had to report it. Specifically, data samples show that NBC's coverage of the war, as reflected in major story headlines across various shows at various times of day, was more negative than reporting by the *Times* or the *Journal*, especially in the early months of U.S. occupation (see chart 1). After the first year, however, less divergence was evident. As another check, we looked at ABC News for April and May

Table 2: Assessment of Coverage by the *Wall Street Journal*

	Negative	Neutral	Positive	Total	Ratio of Negative to Positive	Percent Neutral
May 2003	15	17	17	49	0.9:1	35
January 2004	7	7	5	19	1.4:1	37
April 2004	45	11	16	72	2.8:1	15
May 2004	31	21	8	60	3.9:1	35
January 2005	19	6	12	37	1.6:1	16
April 2005	10	5	5	20	2.0:1	25
May 2005	5	5	3	13	1.7:1	38
January 2006	5	3	1	9	5.0:1	33
April 2006	9	2	8	19	1.1:1	11
May 2006	4	3	1	8	4.0:1	38
Monthly Average					2.4:1	

Chart I. Ratio of Negative to Positive Stories

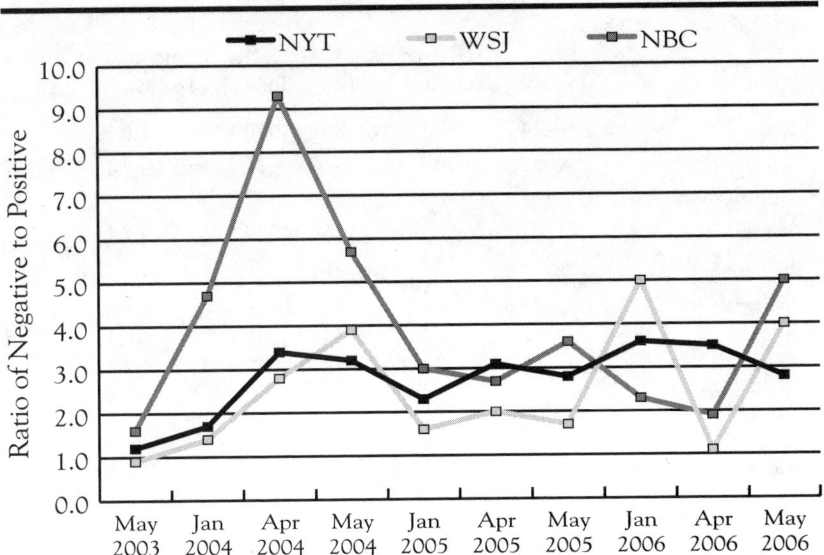

of 2006. Its ratio of negative to positive stories for that period was about 3.5:1, again somewhat more negative than the main newspapers we examined but not dramatically so.

Another point to consider is that newspapers grab attention with headlines, whereas television speaks most loudly with images. Violent imagery on television makes a greater impression on audiences than words or even photographs in a newspaper. It is therefore plausible that television coverage of the war in Iraq has conveyed an even more negative tone than the data suggest.

We found that Fox News, which is widely considered conservative leaning, had a far larger number of news stories about Iraq that were neutral in tone, whereas the other three outlets had comparable and much lower numbers of neutral headlines. The story headlines used by Fox News, regardless of time of day or program, do not lend themselves to the type of scoring that could be done as fairly straightforward as it was for headlines in the *New York Times*, the *Wall Street Journal*, and NBC News. No doubt, a network that wishes to convey a different tone

Table 3: Assessment of Coverage by NBC News

	Negative	Neutral	Positive	Total	Ratio of Negative to Positive	Percent Neutral
May 2003	24	31	15	70	1.6:1	44
January 2004	52	13	11	76	4.7:1	17
April 2004	112	53	12	177	9.3:1	30
May 2004	102	89	18	209	5.7:1	43
January 2005	79	34	26	139	3.0:1	24
April 2005	41	6	15	62	2.7:1	10
May 2005	47	23	13	83	3.6:1	28
January 2006	42	12	18	72	2.3:1	17
April 2006	33	9	17	59	1.9:1	15
May 2006	45	24	9	78	5.0:1	31
Monthly Average					4.0:1	

than the one adopted by the rest of mainstream media is capable of doing so. These initial assessments are entirely consistent with the possibility that Fox News made a decision to do just that.

Getting into Issues

Consider how things are going and how they are being reported in each of the three major areas in Iraq: politics, economics, and security. On the former, the coverage has been thorough and fair of Iraq's impressive steps toward democracy, notably the transfer of sovereignty in June 2004, the interim elections in January 2005, the constitutional referendum in October 2005, the full-term elections in December 2005, and the formation of a new Iraqi government in the spring of 2006. The U.S. media have also accurately reported the horse trading, backroom dealing, and political maneuvering that abound in liberated Iraq, as they do in most of the world's democracies.

To be sure, there are not enough probing media stories about Iraq's economic situation. From what the data show, however, it is hardly clear that the additional accounts, if told, would be mostly positive. In a coun-

Chart 2. Percentage of Neutral Stories

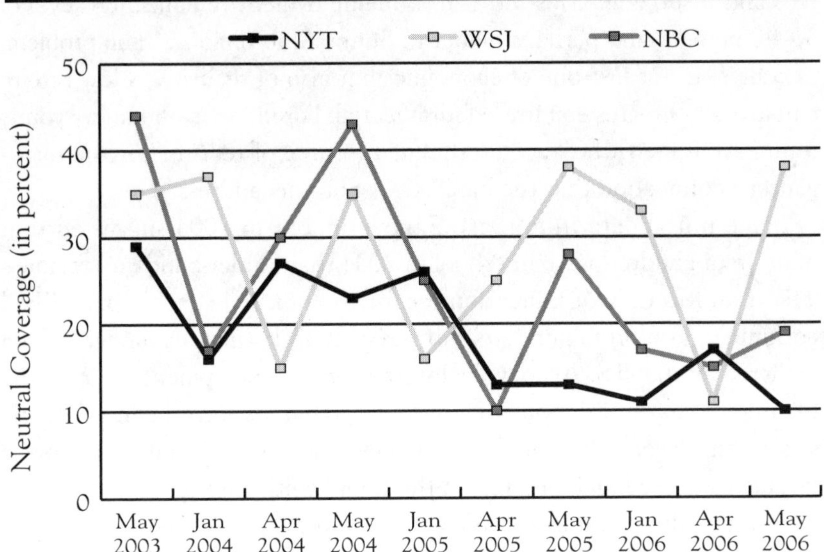

try of 25 million people with more than $5 billion a year spent by the United States and large revenues brought in by high oil prices, there are countless incidents of new businesses successfully growing, schools opening, telephone services mushrooming, and satellite TV dishes sprouting. If the media should view their job as bucking up the morale of the U.S. public, the media could perhaps be criticized for not telling enough of these stories.

Despite some economic progress, however, the overall reality is simply not that good. Iraq's gross domestic product has been largely flat since the initial months of the post-Saddam period. The country's infrastructure remains at or below the pre-invasion levels in oil production, electricity production and distribution, water and sanitation services, and transportation. Additionally, the availability of heating and cooking fuels has declined substantially below estimated requirements.[3]

Corruption remains a widespread problem, and to date, only modest progress has been made to stem or eliminate it altogether. Consumer subsidies, although reduced somewhat this year, remain very high and create black markets in scarce goods, providing financial opportunities for criminals and insurgents. Most critically, unemployment remains at a level of 30–40 percent and perhaps higher in Sunni Arab regions.[4] The problem, of course, is not just one of economics but also of security. A low rate of employment creates embittered, disaffected, bored, poor, and angry young Sunni Arab men who become the main source of recruits for the insurgency, a connection that the media does not fully address.

Some initial data from the U.S. government in 2004 suggested that more Iraqi children were in school in 2004 than under Saddam's regime.[5] The Iraqi Ministry of Education recently confirmed that the trend had continued, as a prominent story in the *New York Times* explained.[6] Data gathered by the U.S. Agency for International Development indicate the likelihood that childhood vaccination campaigns have been relatively successful. Beyond that piece of good news, however, available data make it difficult to see much progress in the Iraqi health care sectors.

In the realm of security, the media have perhaps covered the violence in Iraq excessively, as they do at home. Some mistakes have been conceptual, for example, fixating on how many Iraqi units are in the top state of readiness (typically one or no battalions at any given time in the last year) rather than on the more significant indicator of how many Iraqi forces are at least reasonably competent to maintain security in the country. As of the early summer of 2006, Iraq has some 60,000 indigenous security personnel, most of them in the army and a few thousand in the police force, whom the United States government assess as capable of taking the lead in carrying out most security tasks, relative to an effective starting point near zero two years ago.[7] Proficiency is a more appropriate standard by which to judge Iraqi security forces, rather than the unrealistic ideal of maintaining the highest state of readiness.

Yet, the Bush administration itself bred skepticism about the training and equipping of Iraqi security forces by constantly overstating the progress that was being made in the first year after liberation. Thus, it has taken a while for the journalistic corps to build up confidence in the training programs undertaken by Gen. David Petraeus and Gen. Martin Dempsey since the spring of 2004. Now, however, that story is getting out; and in fairness, this should happen more widely and more often.

Nevertheless, this progress hardly constitutes unblemished success. Iraqi units may currently be more proficient technically, but they are poorly integrated ethnically and not yet dependable politically. These factors pose huge risks at a time when Prime Minister Nouri al-Maliki rightly identifies Iraq's ethnic militias as among his country's most worrisome security problems, militias that, in fact, are often tolerated by security forces of similar ethnicity.

Moreover, the rate of sectarian strife has grown significantly in 2006 with an average of 10 violent incidents a day occurring throughout the first half of the year, most notably including the February 22 bombing of the Golden Mosque in Samarra, compared with only one or two per day previously.[8] The increased level of sectarian violence suggests that, even though improved security forces are necessary, they may also pose a danger to Iraq because of the possibility that they could ultimately take up arms against each other in a civil war. In fact, one analyst has gone so far as to argue that the intense programs to train these forces create more risk than they are worth.[9]

Just as in the case of Iraq's high unemployment rate, the media do underreport some negative security issues. For example, over the past year Iraqi security forces have been suffering about three times the number of monthly fatalities of the U.S.-led foreign coalition forces, whereas in the early months after liberation, Iraqis suffered fewer fatalities than the foreign forces.[10] One encouraging aspect of this grisly statistic is that at least the Iraqis are willing to fight and die for their country, but the extent of the bloodshed underscores just how dangerous the environment remains.

Leaving aside the war per se, Iraq has far and away the highest criminal murder rate in the greater Middle East. Although it is difficult to give precise figures, in Baghdad the criminal murder rate is estimated at nearly one murder victim for every 1,000 people per year.[11] That rate is roughly 10 times the typical murder rate in inner cities in the United States. Kidnapping is another huge issue. Stories about kidnappings tend to be told only when a U.S. citizen, such as Jill Carroll or Nicholas Berg, is abducted, but kidnapping of foreigners is just the tip of the iceberg. The stunning reality in Iraq is that an estimated 30–40 Iraqis—professionals, political figures, doctors, lawyers, wealthy merchants—are kidnapped each day.[12]

Many if not most are released once ransom is paid; few are killed through grisly beheadings or other such spectacles. Yet, the rate of kidnapping, probably the highest per capita rate in the world, is tremendously disruptive to life in Iraq.

On balance, Iraq is easily the most violent country in the broader Middle Eastern region. Leaving aside a couple of extreme examples, such as Sudan, Iraq is one of the most violent countries in the world. According to the best documented estimates, at least 1,000 civilians in Iraq have been killed by acts of war on a monthly basis since the invasion, a figure consistent with the estimate Bush offered in 2005.[13] The reality could potentially be two to three times that number. For most people, Iraq is actually a much more dangerous place to live today than it was in the later years of Saddam's reign (although the country is much better than the Iraq of the 1980s, when a brutal war against Iran was followed by Saddam's genocidal rampages against first the Kurds and then the Shi'a). These depressing facts are often not reported quite so starkly. If anything, the media typically underreport just how violent Iraq now is compared with the broader region and its own recent past.

Finally, the frequency of coverage of Iraq overall has dropped by roughly a factor of two over the last two years for the two newspapers and one television network examined. A recent analysis published in the *Chicago Tribune* reaffirmed the same result for a wider set of newspapers.[14] Again, the notable point is that trends on the ground do more to determine the nature of U.S. media coverage of Iraq than any biases of reporters. Recent news is less interesting, given that it increasingly reads like a repetition of previous news, at least in terms of the security and economic environments.

Undoubtedly, the quality of media coverage about Iraq is uneven. Some reporters are simply more entrepreneurial, courageous, or careful to address the inherent challenges of counterinsurgency warfare than others. As viewers of almost any nightly news broadcast know, televised news reports in particular tend to lead with violence rather than with positive stories. Thus, at some level the media do emphasize the negative more than the positive, especially when visual imagery is required. Moreover, the media must keep looking for creative ways to report the bravery and sacrifices of U.S. soldiers. The public wants to hear such stories, and they help counter potentially misleading images that arise from isolated tragedies such as the Abu Ghraib prison scandal and what appears to have been a massacre at Haditha.[15] But to level these specific critiques and suggestions is one thing, to allege systematic media bias quite another.

What Is a Journalist's Job?

When assessing the media's coverage of the war in Iraq, many critics seem to have in mind an earlier era, when the nation was firmly united in common cause against a clear enemy, such as during World War II. At that time, journalists were effectively part of the team, reporting on the march against tyranny and shoring up the faith, resolve, and morale of the public back home.

It is true that morale and patience are important in war. It is natural and appropriate, therefore, for the country's leaders to work to build up the confidence and optimism not only of the troops but also the public supporting them. (Clearly, the role of critics and dissenters is important too, especially when badly conceived or poorly led military operations are involved.) Without strong political leadership, the country would fail to marshal all elements of national power in support of a military mission, the national will could suffer, and enemies could target the nation's psyche as their main strategy. In the casualty-averse days of much of the 1980s and 1990s, this concern seemed especially serious.

But is it really the media's job to shore up public morale? Some columnists and talking heads can and should do so. Yet, reporters, editors, and news anchors do not have that same task. Their most important job is to provide independent and objective information and assessments. When news reporting is in accord with what political leaders are saying about a given situation, the messages reinforce each other, the government gains credibility, and the nation gains resolve. When media reports conflict with political messages, leaders are kept accountable; they are obliged to explain the reason for the dissonance and perhaps to reassess the thrust of their own policies. Other political leaders then also gain more grist for developing policy alternatives. These basic dynamics are not only natural but essential to the healthy functioning of a democracy.

This natural and generally accepted role of the media as the Fourth Estate of political life in the United States underscores why coverage of the Iraq war should be critical. The war has gone far worse than the Bush administration had predicted or led the country to believe it would. The more the public learns about the administration's overconfidence that Iraq would remain peaceful after Saddam was overthrown, an overconfidence that conflicted with the predictions of most outside experts and that led the government to underprepare for the difficulty of the mission, the more natural it is for the Fourth Estate to be tough in reporting the operation.[16]

The Media Is Not the Problem

The broad argument voiced by critics of the media in the United States is often badly overstated. Even though the overall image of Iraq conveyed by the mainstream media may be somewhat more negative than reality, it is not incredibly dissimilar from the situation on the ground. Iraq is a war zone in which progress has been largely elusive. Given this reality, accurate reporting naturally places more emphasis on the negative aspects than on the positive ones.

Journalists are missing quite a few stories in Iraq, but the ones they miss are just as often bad as they are good. If the journalists have faults, as they surely do, it is because they are more inclined to be ultracompetitive to beat their media rivals to a good headline than to work against the interests of the U.S. government deliberately. Even though the reporters in Iraq are not facing the same risks as those confronting the front-line troops, the journalists display remarkable commitment and courage, and they have been incurring casualties at substantial rates.[17] More than 100 journalists have died in Iraq, although most of them have not been from the United States. More U.S. journalists have lost their lives in Iraq, however, than field-grade officers of the U.S. armed forces.

It makes little sense to expect people reporting from a war zone to have a particularly happy set of messages to convey. Sometimes the reporters do get it wrong, and it is legitimate to hold them accountable when that happens and also to suggest specific ways they can improve their reporting. Rather than habitually berating the media in sweeping terms, we should read their critical stories for insights into where U.S. policy may be failing and how it can be improved in a war that we truly must win yet could still lose, on the ground in Iraq.

Notes

1. See L. Paul Bremer, *My Year in Iraq: The Struggle to Build a Future of Hope* (New York: Simon and Schuster, 2006), pp. 112–113.
2. The Pew Global Attitudes Project, "America's Image Slips, but Allies Share U.S. Concerns Over Iran, Hamas," Washington, D.C., 2006, p. 14, http://pewglobal.org/reports/pdf/252.pdf.
3. "Iraq Index: Tracking Reconstruction and Security in Post-Saddam Iraq," Brookings Institution, Washington, D.C., http://www.brookings.edu/iraqindex.
4. Ibid.
5. Ibid.
6. Sabrina Tavernise and Sahar Nageeb, "Amid Iraqi Chaos, Schools Fill After Long Decline," *New York Times*, June 26, 2006, p. A1.
7. U.S. Department of Defense, "Measuring Stability and Security in Iraq," Washington, D.C., May 2006, pp. 45–48.
8. Ibid., p. 40.
9. Stephen Biddle, "Seeing Baghdad, Thinking Saigon," *Foreign Affairs* 85, no. 2 (March/April 2006): 2–14.
10. "Iraq Index."
11. Ibid.
12. Ibid.
13. Office of the Press Secretary, The White House, "President Discusses War on Terror and Upcoming Iraqi Elections," December 12, 2005, http://www.whitehouse.gov/news/releases/2005/12/20051212-4.html.
14. Timothy J. McNulty, "Has the Iraq War Disappeared From the Front Page?" *Chicago Tribune*, June 11, 2006, p. 7.
15. Frank Schaeffer, "In This Paper, War Heroes Are MIA," *Los Angeles Times*, June 11, 2006. See Kathy Roth-Douquet and Frank Schaeffer, *AWOL: The Unexcused Absence of America's Upper Classes From Military Service—and How It Hurts Our Country* (New York: Harper Collins, 2006).

16. On these latter points, see Kurt Campbell and Michael O'Hanlon, *Hard Power: The New Politics of National Security* (New York: Basic Books, 2006); George Packer, *The Assassins' Gate: America in Iraq* (New York: Farrar, Straus and Giroux, 2005); Michael R. Gordon and General Bernard E. Trainor, *Cobra II: The Inside Story of the Invasion and Occupation of Iraq* (New York: Pantheon Books, 2006).
17. "Iraq Index."

Brian Fishman

After Zarqawi: The Dilemmas and Future of Al Qaeda in Iraq

Although they worked together nominally, the central Al Qaeda network, as led by Osama bin Laden and Ayman al-Zawahiri, and the late Abu Musab al-Zarqawi's terrorist group in Iraq held vastly different conceptions of jihad. The U.S. invasion and occupation of Iraq minimized the magnitude of that ideological clash, enabling Zarqawi's limited cooperation with Al Qaeda in the Iraqi arena. Although they used each other for tactical support, publicity, and recruiting purposes, their doctrinal differences made them only allies of convenience rather than genuine partners, and as Zarqawi's tactics grew more extreme and indiscriminate, Al Qaeda chose to distance itself from his handiwork.

The U.S. air strike that killed Zarqawi on June 7, 2006, deprived Al Qaeda in Iraq (AQI) of its strategic leader. But the knowledge that U.S., Iraqi, and Jordanian intelligence effectively penetrated AQI to gather information on Zarqawi's whereabouts is just as important to the group's future as Zarqawi's elimination. The coalition's demonstrated ability to gather accurate intelligence is likely to frighten and sow distrust among AQI's remaining members. This heightens the leadership challenge for

---

Brian Fishman is an associate in the Combating Terrorism Center at the United States Military Academy at West Point and an instructor in the Department of Social Sciences. The views expressed in this article are those of the author and do not represent those of the U.S. Military Academy, the Department of the Army, or any other department or agency of the U.S. government.

The Washington Quarterly • 29:4 pp. 19–32.

AQI's new emir, identified only under the alias Abu Hamzah al-Muhajir. His response to the internal security questions and the lingering doctrinal impasse with Al Qaeda proper will determine the organization's future trajectory.

The challenge for Muhajir is to strike a balance between appealing to secular and tribal Sunnis in Iraq, some of whom likely provided intelligence that helped doom Zarqawi, while maintaining an insular terrorist network that can sustain potentially weakening criticism from Islamic, Arab, and Western sources. During his tenure, Zarqawi discovered that these two goals require unique ideological and operational strategies that may be mutually exclusive. A moderate ideology allows for mass appeal, whereas a more extreme ideology that emphasizes the moral imperative of separation from society increases group cohesion but impairs recruiting. Zarqawi developed a controversial strategy to sidestep this contradiction, which ultimately widened the rift between his group and bin Laden's. Now, Muhajir or whoever ends up at AQI's helm must clarify AQI's focus to counter increasing factionalism. This is easier said than done. Muhajir has done little to clarify AQI's strategic future in the months since Zarqawi was killed. The United States can seize on this turning point to manipulate AQI's points of instability.

Enemies Near and Far

After being released from a Jordanian prison in 1999, where he was held for five years on terrorism-related charges, Zarqawi traveled to Afghanistan to establish his own terrorist training camp. He did not, however, join Al Qaeda. Sayf al-Adl, a senior Al Qaeda leader, explained that Zarqawi's disagreement with Al Qaeda, or more specifically, bin Laden, was ideological: "The controversial issues with [Zarqawi] were neither new nor uncommon.... The most important issue with [Zarqawi] was the stance regarding the Saudi regime and how to deal with it in light of the Islamic laws that pertain to excommunication and belief."[1] The disagreement between Zarqawi and Al Qaeda over Saudi Arabia hinted at what would become their fundamental discord: whether jihadi-salafists should prioritize attacks against the "near enemy" or the "far enemy." This debate would not be easily resolved. Even three years later, when Zarqawi was building a terrorist network in Iraq called Tawhid wal Jihad, he did not join Al Qaeda.

Zarqawi and Al Qaeda based their versions of jihad on their divergent understandings of their enemy's center of gravity. Bin Laden's Al Qaeda saw U.S. support (the far enemy) for Arab governments in funding, the granting of legitimacy, and weapons sales as the source of apostate political power and therefore prioritized attacks on the United States. In contrast, Zarqawi focused on apostate cultural and political influence within the Islamic world (the near enemy), which he considered a separate issue from U.S. governmental support. Thus, the two parties employed different strategies of warfare even as they shared the same ultimate goal: the reestablishment of the caliphate, a single, transnational Islamic state.

This ideological dispute between Zarqawi and Al Qaeda was never resolved, which explains much of the tension between them even after Zarqawi swore allegiance to Al Qaeda. Zarqawi and bin Laden put aside their differences because the U.S. invasion of Iraq and its subsequent intimate relationship with the new Iraqi government conflated the near and far enemy. The functional implications of the ideological gap between Zarqawi and Al Qaeda were reduced greatly by the invasion, enabling them to cooperate operationally even as they continued to disagree ideologically. In 1999, when Zarqawi operated in Afghanistan, his ideological differences translated into different tactics. At that time, Al Qaeda's focus on attacking the U.S. homeland required very different planning than an attack on an Arab regime or apostate cultural site. In present-day Iraq, however, the operational implications of the two strategies are not so distinct. An attack on a U.S. patrol or an Iraqi police station requires similar planning and is a direct blow against both an apostate government and a critical U.S. foreign policy goal.

Zarqawi's agreement to join Al Qaeda in the fall of 2004, 18 months after the invasion of Iraq, did not mean that he immediately acceded to Al Qaeda's ideological and operational strategy. In a book released online in May 2005, the chief of Zarqawi's *shari'a* committee, Abu Hamzah al-Baghdadi, explicitly contradicted Al Qaeda's doctrine by restating Zarqawi's focus on the near enemy: "Apostasy is a greater transgression than original disbelief, and the apostate is a greater enemy.... [T]he enemy who is close to the Muslims is more dangerous. When you fight him, you avert his evil and the evil of those who stand behind him. If the Muslims occupy themselves with fighting the far enemy, the near enemy will seize the chance to hurt the Muslims."[2]

During Zarqawi's tenure as emir, AQI's relationship with Al Qaeda was a function of strategic convenience rather than doctrinal agreement. For Al Qaeda, attaching its name to Zarqawi's activities enabled it to maintain relevance even as its core forces were destroyed or on the run. Zarqawi, meanwhile, used the Al Qaeda brand to facilitate recruiting. This nominal relationship was never truly robust; its weaknesses became increasingly apparent when Zarqawi ignored instructions from Al Qaeda to cease attacks against civilian and Shi'a cultural targets, which could not easily be interpreted as strikes against the far enemy. This decision was not taken lightly, and it was largely a function of AQI's second dilemma.

The Gharib Paradox and Shi'a Strategy

All terrorist groups face an important ideological paradox. Their ideas must appeal to a popular audience, but they also must be insular enough to maintain internal group cohesion in the face of external criticism. The latter effect is often achieved by denigrating the masses that do not belong to the group, which naturally limits mass appeal. Zarqawi dealt with this paradox by favoring internal group cohesion over popular appeal, a tendency illustrated by his long-standing nickname, al-Gharib, or the Stranger, a common *nom de guerre* among jihadists.

Zarqawi's adoption of Gharib in the early 1990s was a means of steeling himself for the isolation of the long fight on which he had embarked. This definition of identity—an outsider from mainstream society—embraces and expropriates isolation from the majority so that, instead of being a source of despair and weakness, seclusion promotes unity and strength.[3] The gharib identity informed Zarqawi's activities until his death. In October 2005, he paraphrased scholars and *hadith* to argue that God smiles on strangers because they adhere to Islam even as the masses abandon God:

> The strangers ... are the good few among the evil many.... These various descriptions of the strangers by the prophet, may God's peace and blessings be upon him, while explaining the great role of these strangers in their places and during the times of their alienation, namely their role of implementing and adhering to the orders of God, also explains the immense pain and suffering of these strangers and their great patience in facing them.[4]

Zarqawi used the gharib identity to explain the disadvantaged political position of jihadists and to suggest that their isolation and criticism indicated the moral rectitude of their path. Zarqawi cultivated this identity within his organization to prevent discouragement and disillusionment, stating that "[t]hose who belong to the victorious group can tolerate the bleakness of their path and they are not alarmed when they see that only few men take such a path. They are only compared in this with the best of creation and the eminent prophets and messengers."[5]

Zarqawi's approach to the gharib paradox made AQI resilient but impeded his ability to build a social consensus in the Sunni community that would be strong enough to assert any real political control in Iraq. An inflexible, extremist ideology that relishes violence and embraces criticism as an indicator of ideological correctness is always going to alienate more people than it attracts, a trend that played out as Iraq's tribal Sunnis increasingly rejected Zarqawi.

Back in 2004, Zarqawi made a critical choice about how to deal with Iraq's Sunni tribes. At the time, Zarqawi believed that increasing cooperation between Sunni tribal leaders and U.S. as well as Iraqi government forces left him with two bad options and one long-shot hope for building an alliance with the tribes. The first option was to attack the tribal chiefs directly despite the probability of alienating Sunnis in his base areas. The second was to abandon Iraq to fight elsewhere.[6] Because neither option was palatable, Zarqawi reasoned that his only hope of making common cause with the tribal leaders was to instigate widespread Shi'a-on-Sunni violence.[7] Zarqawi hoped that provoking a Shi'a backlash against Sunnis would convince moderate and tribal Sunnis that the Iraqi government was simply a veil of legitimacy disguising a coordinated Shi'a plot to attack Sunnis. This, Zarqawi hoped, would compel secular Sunni groups to ally with him and adopt his ideology and methods. In other words, Zarqawi believed that it was not necessary to moderate his ideology and strategy to become attractive to moderate Sunnis because he believed that he could quickly radicalize the Sunni population. He would solve the gharib paradox by dramatically changing the underlying conditions.

Six months before joining Al Qaeda, Zarqawi explained this Shi'a strategy to its leaders, saying that

> targeting [Shi'a] in religious, political, and military depth will provoke them to show the Sunnis their rabies ... and bare the teeth of the hidden rancor working in their breasts. If we succeed in dragging them into the arena of sectarian war, it will become possible to awaken the inattentive Sunnis as they feel imminent danger and annihilating death at the hands of the Sabeans.[8]

This is not to say that Zarqawi opposed attacking Shi'a targets as a worthwhile goal in and of itself. The killings were intended to punish the Shi'a for theological offenses, to correct historical injustice, and to penalize collaboration with U.S. forces. Yet, Zarqawi's policy had a grander strategic purpose of building popular support for Zarqawi in the Sunni areas of Iraq without moderating the ideological extremism that insulates the movement from outside criticism.

Zarqawi's problem was that not all criticism of his strategy came from outside the jihadist movement. In the summer of 2005, Ayman al-Zawahiri, Al Qaeda's second in command, criticized Zarqawi's Shi'a strategy, claiming that attacks on Shi'a targets distorted the image of jihadists and distracted them from their most important enemy, the United States. This disagreement pertained to more than just the Shi'a; it reflected the older disagreement over whether or not attacks should be focused on the near enemy or the far enemy. Zarqawi's attacks on Shi'a cultural sites and civilian institutions were more difficult to justify as damaging to the U.S. far enemy than attacks on U.S. or Iraqi security forces. As Zarqawi's attacks grew more indiscriminate, the operational nexus between the near and far enemies that was created by the U.S. presence in Iraq dissolved, and the alliance of convenience between Zarqawi and Al Qaeda broke down.

Zarqawi's Strategic Failure

Zarqawi's response to the two fundamental dilemmas facing AQI was internally inconsistent and ultimately self-defeating. First, although AQI built a nominal relationship with Al Qaeda based on the U.S. presence in Iraq, Zarqawi pursued an operational strategy premised not on the U.S. occupation but on the underlying sectarian divisions in Iraqi society. That operational strategy ultimately undermined the confluence of interests that had enabled the original alliance. Second, Zarqawi designed an insular ideology that would complement his brutal operational strategy. This ideological decision was ill conceived precisely because AQI's controversial operational strategy ensured that the most damning criticism would come not from outside the jihadi movement but from inside Al Qaeda itself.

The best illustration of Zarqawi's self-defeating strategy was the November 2005 coordinated bombing attack of three hotels in Amman, Jordan. The attack was widely derided in Jordan, particularly after the revelation that one bomb had detonated amid a wedding party. Although there is no public record of Al Qaeda condemning Zarqawi for this attack, in retrospect its silence was deafening. On April 13, 2006, six months after the Amman bombing, Zawahiri released a video that, in part, praised Zarqawi.[9] This was striking because Zawahiri's tape appears to have been made in early November 2005, just before the Amman hotel attacks. In the video, Zawahiri suggests it was intended to mark the anniversary of the infamous Tora Bora battle in Afghanistan, which occurred in November and December of 2001. He also referred to the September 2005 reelection of Egyptian president Husni Mubarak and the October 2005 earthquake in Pakistan as recent events.

The delay between taping and release was perhaps an attempt by Zawahiri to distance Al Qaeda from the Amman attacks because of the negative reaction they generated in the Arab world. That Zawahiri did not mention Zarqawi by name in any of his statements during the interim period is further evidence that Al Qaeda did not want to be associated with an unpopular attack that did not serve its operational and ideological strategy. Although Zarqawi also tried to distance himself from some of the carnage of these attacks, he clearly considered the premise of attacking Jordanian hotels consistent with his modus operandi of attacking civilian apostates. To Al Qaeda's leaders, however, the Amman attacks demonstrated that the functional implications of Zarqawi's ideological and strategic differences with Al Qaeda remained significant despite their confluence of interests in Iraq.

Al Qaeda's Uncertain Future in Iraq

Many major issues drive factionalism inside AQI, including the basic questions of power and influence. The most important strategic question is a function of AQI's two critical dilemmas discussed above. Should AQI continue to conduct excruciatingly brutal attacks, particularly against Shi'a civilians, or should it fall in line behind Al Qaeda's leadership and refocus attacks on the far enemy? In other words, should AQI respond to the gharib paradox by following Zarqawi's teaching or bin Laden's?

One man that seems to be firmly in the Zarqawi camp is Abdallah bin Rashid al-Baghdadi, the emir of the Mujahidin Shura Council (MSC). The MSC, which was formed in January 2006 as an umbrella media group for several jihadist groups in Iraq, may play an increasingly important role now that the jihad's greatest media champion, Zarqawi, is no more. On June 9, 2006, Baghdadi reiterated his determination to continue Zarqawi's jihad against Iraq's Shi'a. Baghdadi's intentions were further clarified on June 21, 2006, when the MSC's legal committee authorized the execution of four Russian hostages.[10] A video of their beheadings was circulated online four days later.[11]

Baghdadi's statement stood in stark contrast to the first official jihadi statement made after Zarqawi's death. In that statement, the deputy emir of AQI, Abu Abd al-Rahman al-Iraqi, pledged to continue bin Laden's strategy in Iraq.[12] Iraqi ignored the fact that bin Laden's strategy had never been followed in Iraq and that doing so would represent a major strategic shift for the organization. His attempt to ignore this reality was likely an attempt to position himself as a close intellectual ally of bin Laden.

In this internal debate, the Zarqawi camp is likely to have the upper hand. Maintaining strategic momentum will be simpler than changing it midstream. Furthermore, the apparent penetration of AQI by U.S. and Iraqi intelligence, as indicated by the U.S. ability to pinpoint Zarqawi's advisers and track them to the safe house where he was killed, will compel the group to close ranks ideologically and operationally. In an environment of internecine warfare and distrust, the pressure to respond to the gharib paradox by increasing the brutality of attacks and demonizing all nongroup members is very high. AQI will attempt to increase group solidarity through shared participation in brutal acts and will use both ideological and operational participation in such behavior as a means of vetting members. The increase of sectarian violence in Iraq since Zarqawi's death will only reinforce this tendency.

Another question regarding Zarqawi's successor is whether AQI should be led by an Iraqi or another foreigner like Zarqawi. The appointment of Muhajir as the new emir, whose pseudonym implies he is not an Iraqi, suggests this question has been decided, but that does not mean all of the issues surrounding it have been resolved. One critical issue is the vulnerability of AQI to penetration by U.S. and Iraqi intelligence. If Iraqi intelligence brought Zarqawi down, foreign fighters in the group may lose trust in their Iraqi comrades. Likewise, the revelation that Jordanian intelligence, which worked closely with Iraqi tribes to gather information on Zarqawi, contributed to Zarqawi's demise may sow distrust of foreigners among Iraqi elements of AQI.[13] Although AQI's ideology eschews nationality, having foreign leadership certainly did not help the group win friends among Iraq's Sunni population. In the wake of Zarqawi's failed attempt to radicalize large numbers of Iraqi Sunnis, some AQI members will likely advocate reaching out to them by elevating Iraqi members of the organization.

The third question concerns how much AQI should expand its area of operations outside of Iraq. Zarqawi's Shi'a strategy was a long shot to avoid pursuing the only other strategies that he felt were available: confront the tribal leaders head-on or leave Iraq. The Shi'a strategy was clearly failing even before Zarqawi was killed, which accounts for the increase in attacks on tribal leaders and helps explain AQI's effort to build infrastructure for jihad outside of Iraq.[14] Even setting aside the November 2005 Amman hotel attacks, the evidence that Zarqawi was planning to expand the jihad beyond Iraq is robust. Jordanian sources report that up to 300 terrorists trained in Iraq have since returned home to await orders.[15]

Zarqawi's final missive focused on a regional Shi'a conspiracy against Sunnis and threatened Lebanon's Hizballah in particular.[16] A document found in the safe house where Zarqawi was killed outlined a plan to incite a war between Iran and the United States. One possible tactic was to frame Iran for attacks in the West itself.[17] The debate within AQI over operations outside of Iraq will inevitably be tied to the question of whether AQI's future revolves around attacking the near enemy, like Zarqawi advocated, or the far enemy, as bin Laden argued. Even though Zarqawi was toying with the idea of blaming Iran for attacks on Western targets, his long-standing doctrine suggests that AQI's primary focus would likely have remained apostate Arabs in the Middle East. Zarqawi's death may actually strengthen the negotiating position of jihadists dedicated to attacking the U.S. homeland.

Decoding Muhajir

After Zarqawi's death, Muhajir has assumed the responsibility of leading AQI. His primary challenge is to consolidate control over AQI's various elements while providing strategic guidance on these critical strategic questions, which will not be easy. From the moment Muhajir was appointed, U.S. forces, AQI members, and online sympathizers speculated about the emir's real identity. Some sympathizers maintained it was Iraqi, AQI's deputy emir, whereas Maj. Gen. William Caldwell declared that Muhajir was really Abu Ayyub al-Masri, an Egyptian with long-standing ties to Zawahiri. Meanwhile, another group hoped to build support around Baghdadi, emir of the MSC. As of this writing, confusion over the identity of AQI's new emir has not been definitively resolved, a fact that alone demonstrates how Zarqawi's death was a significant blow to AQI. In his wake, Muhajir must harangue disparate factions into accepting his authority, but more substantively, he must address the distinct strategic perspectives within AQI. Further, he must do all of this in a very difficult operational environment. Zarqawi's killing demonstrated that AQI had been penetrated, and Muhajir must redefine AQI's strategic direction within an organization that he cannot completely trust.

During his tenure as AQI leader, Zarqawi used public statements released online to convey determination, ideological fervor, and strategic purpose to followers, enemies, and pole-sitters. These statements provided strategic context for AQI's attacks, which might otherwise be perceived as simple acts of sadism rather than military instruments designed to achieve specific outcomes. They also encouraged widely dispersed AQI members to sustain criticism and suffer the hardships of jihad. Without a central node defiantly explaining the group's strategic purpose, AQI as we know it would have ceased to exist.

The most striking attribute of Muhajir's tenure thus far is the fact that he has chosen not to define either his own identity or his strategic vision for AQI clearly. Muhajir must have good reasons for this silence because the costs of such strategic ambiguity are very high. Muhajir is likely foregoing the benefits of strategic clarity in order to mollify different factions within AQI. His silence prolongs the internal debate within AQI over the group's future strategy. Muhajir is unlikely to force a resolution until he is certain he will win. In a covert organization that depends on the cooperation of many members, the standard for victory is not simply a majority, it is near consensus.

Predicting Al Qaeda's Next Move in Iraq

In the long run, it may be better to let disagreements fester within AQI rather than to eliminate all potential targets immediately.[18] Striking kinetically at an organization's leadership is not always the best way to destroy its effectiveness. Asking who will be the next emir of AQI is a useful intellectual question, but it may be somewhat misleading. Asking which leader within the jihadist movement in Iraq will be Zarqawi's intellectual successor may be a better way to frame the issue than focusing on the AQI organization specifically. Despite this ambiguity, some broad conclusions can be reached about the future of AQI and the wider jihadist movement in Iraq.

First, Al Qaeda in Iraq will fragment. Other Islamic groups in Iraq, notably Ansar al-Sunnah and the Islamic Army of Iraq, will collect some of

AQI's inevitably disaffected derivatives. Zarqawi's greatest strength was not his ideological prowess, it was his personal leadership skills. Muhajir, whether he is the Egyptian Masri or someone else, is unlikely to be commensurately capable. Some elements of AQI will likely leave the organization, both in response to doctrinal disagreements and to fears that the group has been penetrated by coalition intelligence operatives. In order to build unity within AQI, Muhajir or whoever ultimately takes control will most likely continue Zarqawi-esque attacks but will at least temporarily reduce AQI's anti–Sunni-apostate rhetoric.

Zarqawi may be dead, but the gharib identity will live on, either in AQI itself or in some derivative organization. Although Zarqawi was rightly and frequently derided as an ill-educated leader, he combined ideology and action in a manner that will continue to inspire many in and outside of Iraq. His ideology had teeth. As damaging as AQI's brutal anti-Shi'a attacks may be to Al Qaeda's image, a public rift would be even more traumatic. Despite continued strategic tension, neither party will provoke a dramatic falling-out.

Second, AQI's new emir will try to attack outside of Iraq. AQI's long-term focus on the near enemy suggests it is best positioned to attack Arab countries, rather than the United States or European targets. Although a specific location will not be Muhajir's first concern, he will look for a place with established support networks, a large Sunni population, historical Sunni-Shi'a tension, and an unpopular apostate government. The most likely targets are Lebanon and Syria, where a dramatic and bloody attack on Shi'a targets would be extremely destabilizing. Although attacks on Israel are the lowest common denominator of terrorist act in much of the Islamic world and moving in that direction is, to some degree, an act of desperation, organizing a successful attack on Israel could bolster the credibility of AQI's new emir more than any other action. Zarqawi's successors will be heartened by the fighting between Israel and Hizballah. Although they would prefer to see a Sunni group, rather than Shi'a Hizballah, be the champion of militant anti-Zionism, they will see war between two of their biggest enemies as a positive development and a potential opportunity.

Attacks on the United States or Europe are possible, but this would signify a greater degree of subordination to bin Laden and Al Qaeda proper. No matter where AQI chooses to focus geographically, it will attempt to exploit events in the region. One of the most provocative would be a U.S. or Israeli strike on Iran. Although Iran itself is not a good arena for jihad, Muhajir and the AQI leadership would welcome a fight between the United States and Iran's Shi'a leaders. If the United States attacks Iran because of its nuclear program, the network will actively attempt to heighten the tension regionally, perhaps by staging dramatic attacks in Syria or Lebanon and blaming either Iran or the United States.

Whatever the specific target, AQI's network outside of Iraq will begin to freelance. Communications problems will make it more difficult for AQI to exert bureaucratic control over its global network. In lieu of direct bureaucratic control, ideological homogeneity and group insularity are very important for organizational cohesion.[19] Although Muhajir, like his predecessor, will eventually develop a strategic media presence to distribute ideology, Zarqawi's death will loosen the personal and ideological bonds connecting the dispersed jihadis to AQI. These individuals will maintain a kinship to the Iraqi jihad but may be less directly tied to the AQI network.

Implications for U.S. Withdrawal

Wittingly and unwittingly, U.S. policy shapes the political terrain on which the jihadi-salafist network, including AQI, is built. By employing a selective use of force, a carefully designed political and military presence in the Middle East, and information operations, the United States can design the battlefield to be as disruptive to the jihadi-salafists as possible. Generally speaking, measured actions are best. AQI, like other terrorist groups, would like to provoke unhelpful overreactions.

U.S. policymakers must always think holistically about U.S. interests before embarking on any initiative. No single approach is correct, and policymakers must carefully analyze the costs and benefits of all options. Although disrupting the AQI–Al Qaeda nexus is a critical foreign policy goal, it should not be pursued at the expense of all others. Protecting U.S. economic interests and containing Iran's nuclear ambitions are but two examples of more important priorities than driving a wedge in Al Qaeda.

Nevertheless, in order to increase the discord inside AQI and between AQI and Al Qaeda, the United States should increase the distance between the near and far enemies by minimizing public support—military, economic, and moral—for "apostate" Arab regimes, including Iraq's. To divide Zarqawi's ideological successors from the bin Laden sympathizers, the United States should aggravate the functional implications of their ideological disagreement by disengaging from Iraq as much as possible.

Strategically, disengagement means beginning the process of moving troops out of Iraq and explicitly guaranteeing that all U.S. forces will leave eventually. Even if credibly separating the near and far enemies in the short term is not possible, the United States can complicate jihadist long-term planning by forcing on them a debate about how to proceed once the near and far enemies are less obviously linked. The U.S. debate over Iraq has been focused on means for too long, specifically the timeline-for-withdrawal debate, to the neglect of the most important issue, the end state, i.e., complete withdrawal versus a semipermanent presence. To disrupt the jihadists, U.S. strategic direction must be very clear, and talk must be supported by visible action. This is not a call for U.S. troops to run for the exits immediately but for the United States to make its strategic intentions to withdraw completely apparent. If that is not its intention, the United States must be prepared for Americans to die in Iraq in perpetuity.

Critics will rightly question whether the benefit of upsetting AQI's relationship with Al Qaeda justifies a strategic reorientation. If the war on terrorism is our primary concern, it very well may. The sectarian violence wracking Iraq is extraordinarily disruptive but does not necessarily translate into increased support for Al Qaeda and its affiliated movements. Iraq's violent mobs and numerous secular insurgents will not target U.S. interests beyond Iraq's border, but AQI and Al Qaeda will. The argument that we must prevent Iraq from becoming a haven for terrorists is certainly potent, but its impact is mitigated by the fact that Iraq is already serving that purpose. If the war in Iraq is but one front in a wider war on terrorism, then the campaign there should be designed to disrupt those elements that threaten U.S. interests around the world. Furthermore, the functional aspects of the strategic reorientation, in the short term, need not be overly dramatic. Although the timeline is protracted, Gen. George W. Casey's reported plan to reduce U.S. combat brigades in Iraq from 14 to six over the next 16 months is the right kind of thinking, as long as it is coupled with an unambiguous strategic message.[20]

Most importantly, U.S. planners should resist the temptation, in an attempt to avoid the psychological costs of defeat, to pursue middling strategies that have little hope of bringing victory but carry significant costs in blood and treasure. If the long-term outcome in Iraq resembles what many now consider victory in Afghanistan, the United States will be in a very precarious situation indeed. Maintaining a small U.S. force to advise and support an Iraqi government that can assert continuous authority only in some of Iraq's provinces would be a very expensive strategy to give Zarqawi's successors and other jihadists exactly what they want: access to U.S. troops, ungoverned space in the heart of the Middle East, a means of draining the U.S. Treasury, and a recruiting boon.

Although a decisive, complete withdrawal of troops is vital, the inverse principle is just as important. If the United States is determined to remain in Iraq, it should maximize the opportunity to crush the insurgency by increasing the number of troops on the ground. Calls for maintaining current troop levels or a phased drawdown of troops without a clear, strategic end state are well meaning but will ultimately serve our worst enemies' interests rather than our own. In other words, strategic action must be resolute.

Getting Al Qaeda Out of Iraq

The United States should take advantage of AQI's differences with Al Qaeda rather than criticize AQI's ideology, overtly or covertly. Zarqawi's gharib identity will live on in AQI. Directly criticizing the network will be counterproductive, particularly in the months after his death, because the group's ideology will manipulate criticism from the outside into solidarity within. Perhaps most importantly, the United States must be aware that neither Zarqawi nor AQI were ever the center of gravity of the Iraqi insurgency. AQI will be less dangerous without Zarqawi, but its derivatives will metastasize and grow. Secular, Sunni, and Shi'a groups will continue to kill Americans and disrupt the Iraqi government. Nevertheless, the United States can improve its overall prospects in this long war by sowing division within AQI and between AQI and Al Qaeda by simply avoiding actions that unite these rivals despite their ideological divisions.

Notes

1. Abu Hamzah al-Baghdadi, "Why Do We Fight, and Whom Do We Fight?" June 2005, http://www.tajdeed.org.uk/forums.
2. Ibid.
3. The nickname also invokes an Arabic literary tradition that celebrates the lonely traveler longing for the simple comforts of home. See Abu 'L-Faraj al-Isfahani, *The Book of Strangers*, trans. Patricia Crone and Shmuel Moreh (Princeton, N.J.: Markus Wiener Publishers, 2000).
4. Abu Musab al-Zarqawi, audio lecture, September 30, 2005, http://www.world-news-network.net (appears to be derived from the Sahih Muslim, *Kitab al-Iman* [The book of faith], chap. 66.
5. Ibid.
6. Abu Musab al-Zarqawi, letter released by the Coalition Provisional Authority, February 12, 2004, http://www.cpa-iraq.org/transcripts/20040212_zarqawi_full.html.
7. Ibid.
8. Ibid.
9. Ayman al-Zawahiri, "Four Years After the Tora Bora Battles; From Tora Bora to Iraq," *Global News Network*, April 13, 2006, http://www.w-n-n.net.
10. Mujahidin Shura Council, untitled video, June 21, 2006, http://www.hanein.net.
11. Mujahidin Shura Council, untitled video, June 26, 2006, http://www.muslm.net/vb.
12. Abu Abd al-Rahman al-Iraqi and the Mujahidin Shura Council Media Committee, "Statement Untitled—Acknowledging Zarqawi's Death," June 8, 2006, http://www.tajdeed.ork.uk/forums.
13. Borzou Daragahi and Josh Meyer, "'We Knew Him': Jordanian Spies Infiltrated Iraq to Find Zarqawi," *Los Angeles Times*, June 13, 2006, p. A1.
14. "Al-Qaeda in Iraq Situation Report," Harmony document no. IZ-060316-01, http://www.ctc.usma.edu/harmony_docs.asp. This document was written by an aide in Zarqawi's organization. The document was captured in Iraq by U.S. forces in early 2006.
15. Michael Slackman and Scott Shane, "Terrorists Trained by Zarqawi Went Abroad, Jordan Says," *New York Times*, June 11, 2006, p. A1.

16. Abu Musab al-Zarqawi, "Has the Story of the Rejectionists Reached Thee?" *Islamic Renewal Forum*, June 1, 2006, www.tajdeed.org.uk/forums.
17. For a document found in a safe house and released by Iraqi national security adviser Mouwafak al-Rubaie, see Sameer N. Yacoub, "Al-Qaida in Iraq Sought War Between U.S. and Iran," *North County Times*, June 15, 2006, http://www.nctimes.com/articles/2006/06/16/news/nation/15_01_226_15_06.txt. As this document was released just after Zarqawi's killing by the Iraqi national security adviser, some have questioned its veracity. Whether authentic or not, the claim that Zarqawi hoped to instigate hostilities between the United States and Iran is likely accurate.
18. Combating Terrorism Center at West Point, Department of Social Sciences, U.S. Military Academy, "Harmony and Disharmony: Exploiting al-Qa'ida's Organizational Vulnerabilities," February 14, 2006, http://www.ctc.usma.edu/aq/Harmony%20and%20Disharmony%20--%20CTC.pdf.
19. Ibid.
20. Michael Gordon, "U.S. General in Iraq Outlines Troop Cuts," *New York Times*, June 25, 2006, p. A1.

Part IV:
Iran

Michael McFaul, Abbas Milani, and Larry Diamond

A Win-Win U.S. Strategy for Dealing with Iran

In its nuclear negotiations with the rest of the world, the Islamic Republic of Iran has been pursuing a strategy of "heads you lose, tails we win." In its carefully crafted and creatively ambiguous response to UN Security Council Resolution 1696, the Iranian regime claims that it is willing to negotiate on all issues, including suspension of enrichment activities, but will not accept any precondition for such negotiations. Their strategy is clear: delay, obfuscate, and prevaricate to buy time to race ahead with technical efforts to master the complex uranium-enrichment process. At the same time, by appearing flexible, they offer China and Russia enough ammunition to impede the West, the United States in particular, from pursuing any serious coercive action endorsed by the United Nations.

The regime's response places Western leaders in a difficult situation. If they do nothing or make empty threats, Iran will become a nuclear-weapon power within a decade or possibly sooner. If the West loses patience with this game and seeks to impose UN sanctions, the Iranian mullahs reason that they can divide Russia and China from the rest of the Security Council and thus prevent any serious sanctions regime

Larry Diamond, Michael McFaul, and Abbas Milani are fellows and coordinators of the Iran Democracy Project at the Hoover Institution at Stanford University. McFaul is a member of *The Washington Quarterly*'s editorial board.

The Washington Quarterly • 30:1 pp. 121–138.

from ever being approved, let alone enforced. They may be right. Moreover, if the United States loses patience with the ineffectual sanctions road and eventually opts for preventive military action, the mullahs, as well as most international experts, believe that Europe will drop out of the coalition as well. A preventive strike would probably kill many innocent civilians, destroy revered cultural sites, and rally much of Iranian society behind the decrepit regime, giving it a new lease on political life and a more compelling pretext to crack down savagely on what remains of the democratic opposition. So, the current rulers in Iran win no matter which of these strategies the United States pursues.

We need a new approach. It is time for the United States to get smart in dealing with Iran and frame its own win-win proposition, which we propose here: a sophisticated two-track policy that deals boldly and directly with the regime as well as the Iranian people on all issues in the bilateral relationship. By expanding the agenda to include not only the control of nuclear technologies but also Tehran's support for terrorism, the lifting of sanctions, democracy and human rights, and even diplomatic relations, U.S. policymakers could radically change the very limited parameters of the stalemated debate with Iran in a way that would serve arms control and democratization.

The Failures of Current U.S. Strategy

Formulation of a new strategy for dealing with the Iranian threat must begin with an honest assessment of past and current failures. Since Ayatollah Ruhollah Khomeini and his supporters seized power in 1979, four objectives have dominated the U.S. policy agenda concerning the Islamic Republic of Iran: limit Iran's aggressive assertiveness in the region, halt Tehran's support for terrorism, promote Iranian democracy and human rights, and stop Iran from obtaining nuclear weapons. Progress toward any of these goals has been shockingly minimal. Iran is more assertive in the region today than arguably any time in the last two decades. Through support for Shi'ite militias in Iraq, Hizballah in Lebanon, and now even Hamas in Palestine, Iran's hegemonic reach in the Middle East has grown appreciably in the last several years.

Over the past 25 years, the United States has imposed economic sanctions, armed Iraq to fight Iran, supported a variety of opposition groups to the regime, and orchestrated international efforts to isolate it, including a campaign to keep Iran out of the World Trade Organization (WTO). None of these strategies has produced any measurable progress for the core objectives of U.S. policy toward Iran. In many ways, the Iranian regime is in a better strategic situation today than it has been at any time since the revolution.

The Sanctions Dead End

The current policy pursued by the Bush administration does not inspire hope either. After flirting with radically different policy options in its first term, the administration has settled on a narrowly defined policy of arms control in its second term. If Iran suspends its enrichment activities, the United States would join forces with European allies, particularly France, Germany, and the United Kingdom, to enter into negotiations with Iran. The newfound unity among China, Europe, Russia, and the United States on Iran was a big success for the Bush administration.

Yet, how this symbolic victory of unity in the international community and isolation of Iran will eventually lead to a suspension of Iran's nuclear program is not at all clear. In characteristic form for Iranian negotiators, Tehran has refused U.S. and European offers while hinting of compromise just enough to delay any serious attempt to assemble an effective UN sanctions regime. Further, if the Security Council ever does acquiesce to U.S. pressure for sanctions, the result is unlikely to be a robust sanctions regime that includes the export of oil and gas or the import of gasoline, which would cripple Iran's economy and those of many other countries with it. China recently signed a multibillion-dollar oil and gas agreement with Iran, making Beijing a very unwilling participant in a serious sanctions regime. Russia is also unlikely to agree to tough sanctions. Russian defense minister Sergei Lavrov recently bluntly stated, "We cannot support ultimatums that lead everyone to a dead end and cause escalation, the logic of which always leads to force."[1] Russia, in addition to the Bushehr reactor that it has helped to build over the last decade, has many other economic interests in Iran, not the least of which is the hope that Bushehr will be the first of many lucrative contracts to build Russian nuclear power plants in Iran. Even the French and British will be reluctant to back sanctions that would hurt their economies. A sanction that includes oil exports will hike oil prices to levels that the Islamic republic wagers is unbearable for Europe.

Moreover, even if a new UN-backed sanctions regime did win approval, Iran has threatened to withdraw from the Non-Proliferation Treaty (NPT). As the success of the nuclear weapons programs in India and Pakistan prove, a state determined to acquire this technology will do so at any cost. In the long run, the only solution to Iran's nuclear threat is the emergence of a democratic Iran. In the short run, the sole way to mitigate the Iranian nuclear threat is to alter Tehran's motivations for acquiring these weapons.

Finally, the economic pain of sanctions would fall on the masses, not on government elites. Limited travel and financial sanctions targeted on regime elites would be worth pursuing in the absence of other tools, but they will only raise the costs of defiance. Broad new economic sanctions, such as an embargo on gasoline imports, would hurt the very people that the West is trying to empower, a flaw that even Secretary of State Condoleezza Rice has acknowledged.[2] Although such measures would increase resentment, much of it might be directed against the West, not the government in Tehran. In contrast to democratic leaders in South Africa during apartheid, Iranian democrats have argued consistently that the people of Iran should not be hurt as a means to try to punish the regime.

Illusory Military Options

When sanctions fail, some are already arguing that President George W. Bush, as a last resort, must then order military strikes against Iran's nuclear facilities, including the enrichment complex in Natanz, the Bushehr reactor, and perhaps some other facilities in Tehran and Isfahan. Proponents of this option cite Israel's successful air strike against Iraq's nuclear complex at Osirak in 1981. A U.S. or Israeli strike would not end Iran's aspirations, but it would, so the argument goes, either slow down the process and make the mullahs reconsider the costs of trying to restart the program again or at least buy time for regime change.

The costs and uncertainties of a military strike are enormous. Air strikes are unlikely to succeed in destroying Iran's nuclear facilities, as experts have estimated the number of nuclear sites to be far more than the 18 the regime claims, with many buried deep underground.[3] Others may not yet have been discovered. In addition, even if the military operation were successful in slowing down the nuclear program, it would only induce Tehran to redouble its efforts at building a bomb and to withdraw from the NPT altogether.

Moreover, because Iran's facilities are spread out and located in urban areas, a preventive military strike could kill hundreds, if not thousands, of innocent Iranians and destroy ancient buildings of historical and religious importance. Isfahan is the central headquarters of Iran's nuclear program, but it is also Iran's most beautiful city and home to many precious civilizational landmarks. Widespread air attacks on Iran's nuclear facilities and other military assets—they would have to be massive and widespread to have any chance of success—would rally the Iranian people around the mullahs, strengthen the regime, and undermine the considerable admiration and goodwill Iranians now feel for the United States. Whatever time such strikes purchased in setting back Iran's nuclear program would be more than offset by the extended lease on life they would give to the regime. Needless to say, a unilateral strike against Iran would only further damage the United States' standing in the world at a time when U.S. prestige internationally is at an all-time low. Finally, such a strike would provide ammunition to the arsenal of fanatics in the Muslim world, including some in the Tehran regime, who see an ongoing "crusade" by the Judeo-Christian West against the Muslim East. The Iranian government has often threatened that, in the case of an attack, it would mobilize its militia and terrorist proxies in Iraq, Lebanon, and the rest of the Middle East to attack U.S. forces and interests around the world, including Iraq. No doubt this would include Afghanistan, where there are already signs of escalating Iranian mischief.

Some U.S. proponents of military confrontation argue that Libyan leader Colonel Mu'ammar Qadhafi's recent decision to dismantle Libya's nuclear weapons program means the threat of military force will induce the Iranian mullahs to give up their nuclear program like Qadhafi gave up his. This analogy is false. Qadhafi yielded as much from inducements offered, including a promise not to pursue regime change, as he did from threats. Moreover, Libya's investment in a nuclear program and its capacity to sustain and develop the technology were only a fraction of Iran's. Qadhafi also had good reason to fear a U.S. air strike because such an attack could have eliminated not only his nuclear weapons programs but also his entire armed forces and maybe even himself and his regime. Iran, on the other hand, is a much larger and more complex country, with 70 million people, more than 10 times Libya's population and a hydra-headed regime not organized around one leader and his family. Especially with U.S. forces overstretched and bogged down in Iraq, Iranian leaders do not fear a full-scale invasion, and any other kind of strike would benefit them politically.

A final, most radical option floated by some is violent regime change, either through invasion or support for an external fighting force such as the Mujahedin-e Khalq (MEK), which advocates the overthrow of the Islamic republic. Founded in the 1960s in Tehran and expelled after the Iranian Revolution, this once-popular terrorist organization, whose ideology is an eclectic mix of Marxism and Islamism, sided with Saddam Hussein during the Iran-Iraq War and has been headquartered in Iraq since the 1980s. The MEK has lost almost all of its popular support inside Iran, however, and possesses next to no military or organizational capacity, especially now that its primary funding source, Saddam's regime, is defunct. Equally absurd is the idea of supporting ethnic minorities or "national liberation" movements. These groups also have no capacity whatsoever to bring down the Iranian regime.

These scenarios are simply preposterous. The U.S. government has neither the military means nor the domestic political support to invade Iran. Such an assault would be impossible to justify morally or legally. The continued empty threat of a military invasion to topple the regime only works to strengthen the hands of radicals such as President Mahmoud Ahmadinejad and his cabal. Nor are there forces already in the country ready to take up arms for this purpose. In fact, genuine democratic activists and human rights groups are extremely reluctant to accept financial support from the U.S. government or even U.S. nongovernmental organizations (NGOs).[4] They fear regime repression and the stigma of being labeled U.S. pawns. The domestic conditions that made external assistance to Serbian, Georgian, and Ukrainian opposition forces so effective during the Colored Revolutions of 2000–2004 simply do not exist inside Iran today.

A New Policy for Dealing with Iran

Given past and present failures, we need a radically new approach. It is time for the United States to offer the Iranian regime a deal it cannot refuse. Washington should propose to end the economic embargo, unfreeze all Iranian assets, restore full diplomatic relations, support the initiation of talks on Iran's entry into the WTO, encourage foreign investment, and otherwise move toward a normal relationship with the Iranian government. In return, Tehran would have to agree to three conditions: a verifiable and indefinite suspension of activity that could feed into a nuclear weapons development program, including all enrichment of uranium, with a comprehensive and intrusive international inspections regime administered by the International Atomic Energy Agency; an end to support for terrorist groups and activities, including training, intelligence support, and weapons shipments for Hizballah, Hamas, and radical Shi'ite militias in Iraq; and affirmation of basic human rights principles under international covenants and a recognition of the legitimacy of international and domestic efforts to monitor those conditions. The nuclear terms would have to "freeze the construction of more centrifuges and heavy-water reactors that could produce plutonium," although they might ultimately allow a small, face-saving research program of enrichment.[5] Included in the accord should be a mutual pledge that neither side will use military force against the other or initiate the use of force against their neighbors.

The negotiations would have to proceed with a few minimal conditions. So that the regime could not manipulate the truth of what was offered and so the Iranian people would not fear that the United States was about to sell out their aspirations for democracy, the broad parameters of the U.S. proposal should be announced publicly from the start. To prevent Iran from dragging out the negotiations indefinitely to stall for time to perfect and expand its nuclear weapons program, a time limit should be placed on the negotiations, open to extension only if the two sides agree that they are making genuine progress toward a deal. Third, the new bilateral talks should proceed alongside and in coordination with, not in place of, the ongoing discussions conducted by the EU-3 (France, Germany, and the United Kingdom). Finally, although in principle we favor unconditional negotiations, in the current context at least a limited and temporary suspension of uranium enrichment must be obtained to prevent the regime from trumpeting the U.S. offer to negotiate as a victory for its intransigent stance.

Any broad agreement with Iran must include provisions for restoring full diplomatic relations. As the Cold War demonstrated, the United States does not need to like, approve of, or even trust a regime to find mutual benefit in dealing with it and engaging its people and culture.[6] With diplomatic relations, Washington could open an embassy in Tehran and hopefully consulates in several Iranian cities, and vice versa. U.S. mass media, universities, and NGOs could open offices in Iran, establish ties with Iranian counterparts, and promote educational and scientific cooperation, cultural exchanges, a freer flow of information, and increased travel and study in the United States by Iranians. Should the United States declare a willingness to admit many Iranian students and travelers and deploy the large number of consular officials necessary to handle the demand, the massive lines outside U.S. consulates would vividly testify to the real feelings of the Iranian people.

As the United States seeks to engage the Iranian regime in direct negotiations, it must also seek to engage the Iranian people directly. We should stress our admiration for Iranian history and culture, our respect for the Iranian people, and our sincere desire to have a thriving and mutually beneficial relationship. In proposing direct negotiations, the Bush administration should outline why the prospective deal would so clearly be in the interest of the Iranian people, bringing badly needed economic development, foreign investment, increased employment, new educational prospects at home and abroad, and more generally an end to Iran's international isolation.

At the same time, our public diplomacy must emphasize the benefits of such an agreement for regional security and peace as well as the severe dangers of Iran's continued pursuit of nuclear weapons. Strangely, little has been done to convey to the Iranian people the practical and geopolitical dangers and real economic costs of the nuclear program. For one thing, there are serious safety concerns with Iran's plans. Although Russia has helped to build a relatively safe Bushehr plant, Iranian democrats claim that the recently revealed clandestine program has relied on secondhand equipment bought on the black market, sometimes put together with the help of rogue engineers from the former Soviet Union, and built at the juncture of two of the world's most deadly fault lines. Moreover, the nuclear program is unnecessary for electric-power generation and is eating up significant financial resources that could be much more productively spent on modernizing the country's infrastructure and economy.

In addition, it is an illusion to think that the nuclear program will give the Iranian people greater security. Rather, Iran's acquisition of a nuclear weapon would probably trigger efforts on the part of Sunni Arab regimes such as Egypt and Saudi Arabia to acquire the technology as well. Then, Iran would be facing the prospect of living in a region with several nuclear-weapon states, some of which lack political stability and could eventually come under the sway of radical, if not apocalyptic, Sunni Islamist political forces. Overnight, regimes who, by the sheer size of their territory or population, are incomparably weaker than Iran would achieve parity through the deterrence of nuclear power, just as Pakistan did with India.

The United States should endorse the creation of a regional security organization in the Middle East that could provide security guarantees among states, much like the Conference on Security and Cooperation in Europe did during the Cold War. The Iranian regime desperately wants these security assurances, including an explicit statement of nonaggression from the United States. If provided in a multilateral context, these security guarantees could be part of a more comprehensive legal and normative framework that would address human rights issues as well, much like the Helsinki process in the 1970s allowed for parallel conversation on "basket one" security issues and "basket three" human rights issues.[7] Most importantly, this new international institution must legitimize and provide some mechanism for the monitoring of human rights conditions and pledges among the member states, just as the Helsinki accords did 30 years ago. Without this constant emphasis on human rights issues and support for the democratic aspirations of the Iranian people, the package of incentives will simply be pocketed by the regime.

Fanciful Folly or Bold Vision?

These policy suggestions do not fit neatly within the polarized debate in Washington about Iran. To oversimplify, the "arms controllers" usually call for negotiations with the Iranian regime about the narrow topic of nuclear enrichment and reprocessing. They deliberately seek to keep other issues, such as democracy, human rights, and terrorism, off the agenda. Some in this camp believe that bilateral negotiations between the United States and Iran could lead to rapprochement and stable relations. The "regime changers" usually call for no contact whatsoever with the illegitimate regime in Tehran but instead advocate coercive measures to topple the Islamic republic. Some in this latter camp even believe that the use of military force against Iran will hasten the demise of the mullahs' theocracy.

Our view does not fall into either of these two camps. In a Manichean world between those that seek to preserve the status quo and those that seek to change it, we are firmly in the latter group. Yet, our recommended strategy for promoting such change is not invasion, military strikes, or even sanctions. It is rather to fully engage the regime and thus connect with Iranian society, which in turn will ultimately facilitate democratization. This approach is predicated on three major hypotheses. First, a democratic Iran would pursue foreign and national security policies different from the current regime, policies that would benefit or at least not seriously harm the United States and its allies and ultimately the Iranian people. Second, the prospects for Iranian democratization are greater than commonly assumed. Third, constructive engagement would advance the causes of arms control and democratization. All three of these hypotheses are contentious and deserve further elaboration.

Many believe that a democratic Iran will still aspire to be a nuclear Iran. Iran's aspirations for nuclear weapons predate the Islamic republic, with the U.S.-allied shah developing the technology in the 1970s. Why, therefore, would a democratic Iran be any less of a threat to the United States and its allies than the current regime? Of course, the foreign and national security policies of a democratic Iran cannot be predicted with any certainty. Other instances of democratization, however, triggered an end to nuclear weapons programs in countries such as Brazil, South Africa, and Ukraine, and Iran's historic relationship with the West gives cause to be optimistic about a fundamentally different regional security environment.

In large measure, Iran's leaders seek nuclear weapons to deter a U.S. attack. The regime's refrain about Iran's "inalienable right" to nuclear technology in the name of scientific progress is hollow, given the regime's contempt for every other right of the Iranian people and its pseudoreligious assault on social progress. At the same time, there is also an element of prestige associated with joining the nuclear club and a desire to become the dominant power in the Persian Gulf. These factors will to some extent persist in a democratic Iran, but a democratic Iran would not feel threatened by the United States or Israel and could well be an ally. Moreover, a democratic Iran will be a more rational and responsible country, drawn much more to development through economic and social integration with the West than to regional dominance through weapons.

Prospects for a Democratic Iran

In the last few years, through electoral manipulation, fraud, and a host of other coercive means, Iran's Islamist hard-liners have consolidated their grip on all the major sources of institutional power. Soaring oil and gas prices have endowed the regime with resources to buy off local challengers and arm external proxies, such as Hizballah. All of the regime's major external enemies are much weaker today than just a few years ago. Courtesy of the United States, two of Iran's most formidable enemies, Saddam and the Taliban, have been toppled from power.

Despite these short-term gains for the autocratic regime, Iran exhibits many structural and strategic features that make it conducive to democratization. Social scientists have a poor track record of predicting regime change, and Iran's complex system of government makes prognostications about the future even more risky. Yet, the assumption of authoritarian stability made by many in the wake of Ahmadinejad's dubious electoral victory in 2005 is based on a shallow understanding of Iranian history and politics.

More Than a Dream

Structurally, Iran's middle-income status; its reasonably high levels of education and information; and its relatively strong national identity, drawing on a 5,000-year history, all augur well for Iran's democratic prospects if a transition were to begin. The legitimacy of the regime is already weak and declining among the broad bulk of the population. Dictators have a much greater probability of maintaining autocratic rule if they sustain either an ideology or a project that morally justifies their form of rule. In the first years of the Islamic republic, Khomeini championed such an ideology, which enjoyed popular support. He also internationally pursued an ideological mission that helped to create enemies abroad and thereby increase popular support for defending the regime at home. Today, however, Khomeini's ideological creed offers the existing regime little or no legitimacy. The cataclysmic toll of the war with Iraq from 1980 to 1988 exhausted popular support for revolutionary ideas and the regime that propagated them.

The blatant and increasing corruption of the revolutionary leaders has further undermined the legitimacy of the regime's ideology, especially in the eyes of many Iranians who fought bravely in the Iran-Iraq War and returned home to discover many in the political leadership enriching themselves through corruption, graft, and kickbacks. Today, many of the regime's most active opponents are from the ranks of university Islamic associations, which were once the bastion of solid support for the regime. In 1997 and 2001, the resounding electoral victory of reformist presidential candidate Muhammad Khatami demonstrated the society's unequivocal rejection of the regime's ideology. Some of Khatami's most energetic supporters came from the ranks of the disgruntled, erstwhile supporters of the discredited revolutionary ideology. Although Khatami later disappointed his supporters by failing to secure enduring democratic reforms, public opinion polls show little support for those in power today and mass support for ideas antithetical to those of the revolution.

Moreover, the regime's leadership itself has abandoned the cause of the revolution, much like Soviet Communist Party officials in the 1970s and 1980s who simply went through the motions of building and exporting communism while focusing on staying in power and enriching themselves. In contemporary Iran, the ruling mullahs have the same two obsessions. During the last presidential election, every candidate, including eventual victor Ahmadinejad, ran against the corrupt status quo. In fact, both Khatami and Ahmadinejad won as protest candidates, running as reformist "outsiders."

Nonideological autocrats who have largely squandered popular legitimacy can stay in power if they produce enough economic growth to pacify or buy off potential opposition. China is the economic model that so-called pragmatic mullahs look to emulate. In reality, however, these rulers do not have the know-how or resources to deliver the kind of economic prosperity that their Chinese counterparts have produced.[8] To be sure, high oil prices have fueled positive economic growth rates over the last several years. Nonetheless, the regime's corruption, incompetence, and crony capitalism have created massive unemployment and widespread dissatisfaction.

Even the sudden windfall of oil revenues has not helped the regime solve its structural economic problems. In fact, during the windfall period, more capital left Iran than came in as oil revenue. This shows how little trust Iranian businesses have in their government. The expanding middle class and especially the swelling ranks of Iranian youth, unemployed, with no hope for the future, no ideological attachment to the regime, and much sympathy for the United States and democracy, constitute a real latent challenge to the establishment.

As a presidential candidate, Ahmadinejad promised to fight corruption and help the poor. As president, he has yet to demonstrate any serious strategy for tackling these tremendous issues. Instead, he has distracted his electorate by promising to remove Israel from the planet, "liberals" from the universities, and television satellite dishes from the rooftops. These confrontational policies abroad and draconian social policies at home do not find deep support within Iranian society. Rather, popular support for his Khomeini renaissance is shallow. His populism and image as someone who has yet to be corrupted by office have been the only positive elements in his record to slow the rate of disaffection.

An additional factor that offers hope for a regime transition is the deepening of divisions within the ruling elite. In one camp is Ahmadinejad, his supporters in the Iranian Revolutionary Guards Corps and the Basij paramilitary, and messianic fundamentalists inspired by the teachings of a powerful conservative cleric, Ayatollah Muhammad Taghi Mesbah-Yazdi. In the other camp are Iran's embattled democratic movement and an array of forces that benefited from the status quo before Ahmadinejad came to power, including Ali Akbar Hashemi Rafsanjani, the head of the Expediency Council. The Revolutionary Guards, not at all a united force, are demanding a bigger share of political power and thus of the economic spoils.

The clergy are also deeply divided in their allegiances. Some advocate reform, others support the Ahmadinejad camp, and those who are more traditionalist are dismayed by Ahmadinejad's overt messianism. Clerics are growing more daring in their public challenges to the authority of Supreme Leader Ayatollah Ali Khamenei. Some of the clerics supported Rafsanjani's failed candidacy in the June 2005 presidential election, and others adamantly opposed it. The intensely competitive maneuvering between Khamenei and Rafsanjani is one striking manifestation of the regime's widening cracks.

The Ahmadinejad victory has only aggravated them. Ahmadinejad's personal allegiance to archconservative Mesbah-Yazdi and Ahmadinejad's attempt to replace all top-level and most midlevel bureaucrats with his cronies have created new alliances and factions within the regime. Rafsanjani's decision in October 2006 to make public a secret Khomeini letter outlining Khomeini's rationale for ending the war with Iraq has created an open rift between commanders of the Revolutionary Guards and clerics such as Rafsanjani. Finally, Ahmadinejad's success in appointing his closest ally and confidante Hashemi Samere to the post of undersecretary of the interior ministry and therefore to be in charge of elections has further widened the factional rifts. These divisions can create an opening for a new period of political liberalization.[9]

A Civil Society Renaissance?

The presence of a vigorous and inventive, albeit constrained, civil society in Iran also enhances prospects for democratization. Iran's democratic movement remains fractured and demoralized in the wake of Khatami's failure as a reformist president. Many in his own camp and many more in society at large think that he betrayed their trust and failed to live up to his promises. Highly undemocratic parliamentary elections in 2004 and the presidential election of 2005 delivered new blows to Iran's democrats. The opposition could do little to stop the gross electoral manipulation, and attempts by reformist members of parliament to protest the rigging by organizing sit-ins in the parliament were met with popular apathy. The parliamentary election results and the victory of Ahmadinejad further deprived the democrats of key institutional beachheads for promoting democratic change.

At the same time, however, more than 8,000 NGOs continue to function; human rights lawyers are battling the state; select, relatively independent media outlets are still in business; and an estimated 75,000 bloggers—one of the highest numbers anywhere in the world—have exploded onto the political scene. Imprisoned dissenter Akbar Ganji, an investigative journalist who survived six years in jail and an 80-day hunger strike, has emerged as a democratic hero who could play a unifying and catalyzing role for another democratic movement in the future.

More generally, society performs subtle acts of resistance every day. Women wear their scarves higher and higher on their foreheads and dress in bright colors, students gather at home to drink alcohol and listen to Western music, and youth seek out a wide range of independent (and subversive) information and ideas on the Internet, radio, and television. The regime's recent attempt to remove satellite dishes from tens of thousands of homes was met with popular defiance. Moreover, sizable bus-driver strikes in Tehran in late 2005 and early 2006 as well as rising ethnic unrest in several provinces indicate that the regime has many structural vulnerabilities.

None of this means the regime's collapse is imminent. On the contrary, when compared with the transitions from semi-autocracy in Serbia in 2000, Georgia in 2003, and Ukraine in 2004, Iran's political condition still lacks several key ingredients for change.[10] First and foremost, Iran's regime has more aggressively deterred reformers from seeking office and been more ruthless in shutting down independent media outlets and civil society organizations.

Second, Iranian democrats must alter the constitution significantly to democratize Iran. To varying degrees, democrats in Serbia, Georgia, and Ukraine either pursued or threatened to pursue extraconstitutional means to achieve democratic breakthroughs as a means of enforcing the constitution. Yet, when they did so, their aim was to make sure that the formal laws embodied in the existing constitutions were actually followed and no longer abused by corrupt governments. By contrast, Iran's constitution itself is not democratic. Guaranteeing its enforcement would not produce a democratic breakthrough; it must be completely rewritten. In particular, the position of the supreme leader must be eliminated, as should the role of the Guardian Council and Council of Experts, both clergy dominated by law. Despite having a reformist president in power and a significant number of reformist deputies in parliament from 1997 to 2005, Iran's reformist movement could not democratize the current regime from within. Some kind of rupture with the existing constitutional system will be necessary to bring about democracy in Iran.

Third, as a consequence of the aforementioned bitter experience of playing by the current regime's rules and losing, Iran's democratic movement has been demoralized. Some activists are disenchanted with politics, and the movement is in disarray.

With the exception of the constitution, all of these impediments to democracy are the result of human decisions and actions, or inaction, in Iran's recent history. They are not deeply rooted cultural or socioeconomic structural barriers to democratic change. The current confidence of the regime and malaise within the democratic movement needs an exogenous shock to jump-start a new, more dynamic process of change. That exogenous shock should come from Washington.

Why Engagement, Not Isolation, Works

For many advocates of regime change living outside of Iran, the very idea of interaction with Tehran's theocracy is both normatively revolting and practically counterproductive. Although their normative proclivity against interaction is understandable, it is too valuable a tactic not to utilize. Above all else, opponents of normalization insist that any direct contact with Iran's dictatorship will legitimize and sustain the regime while selling out Iran's democrats. It is a legitimate worry. U.S.-Soviet détente in the 1970s may have prolonged Soviet oppression, although skyrocketing oil prices in that decade were the more direct cause of regime endurance. The opening of diplomatic relations with the People's Republic of China three decades ago has not yet produced any real loosening of Communist Party domination. Needless to say, the United States maintains diplomatic relations with many dictatorships around the world without pressuring these regimes to change. The recent Bush administration flirtation with "transformational diplomacy" toward Egypt produced some small steps toward democratization, followed by even greater moves back toward autocracy.[11] Perhaps most poignantly, few in Washington seem to worry much about Libyan democracy now that Qadhafi and Bush have cut a deal.

The dynamic of normalization between the United States and Iran, however, and Iran's deeper integration into the world economy would be different than any of these historical analogies. Iran's economic structure differs sharply from the Soviet and Chinese command economies. Markets, private property, and a capitalist middle class are already present, and the tradition of trading and interacting with the West is long and well established. The potential for U.S. businesses to find willing and able partners in Iran's truly private sector is enormous.

Despite the deepening tensions between the two governments, there is still a great reservoir of Iranian popular goodwill toward U.S. society. The appearance of U.S. citizens, businesses, and goods would mark a major economic, cultural, and social moment in Iranian society. Moreover, the Iranian-American community is large, wealthy, and pro-democratic. They could play an immediate and powerful role in strengthening the nonstate sectors of the Iranian economy, which in turn would help to nurture Iranian civil society. WTO rules would constrain the Iranian regime's ability to siphon rents and subsidize economic practices beneficial to its cronies.

To be successful, the U.S. overture toward the Iranian regime will have to be structured carefully and executed nimbly. The main interlocutor on the Iranian side must be the supreme leader and his administration and not Ahmadinejad, who is neither the real head of state inside Iran nor a person who deserves to sit at a negotiating table with U.S. officials.

As negotiations proceed, U.S. diplomats must state clearly and often that they will not abandon their concerns about human rights violations as a quid pro quo for an arms control agreement. Instead, both issues must be addressed simultaneously.[12] If negotiations eventually produce a breakthrough and the United States is allowed to open an embassy in Tehran, Department of State officials should resist all attempts by the Iranian government to restrict their interactions with Iranian people. Tehran's mullahs need to understand that with formal diplomatic relations come certain obligations, including the free and equal flow of U.S. and Iranian citizens. U.S. diplomats charged with interacting with their Iranian counterparts must make the registration and operation of U.S. NGOs inside Iran a high priority. To be sure, such policy positions will cause friction in the bilateral relationship, but the purpose of bilateral relations is closer contact with the people and official but not necessarily always cordial ties with the regime.

The trigger for democratization will come from within Iran. Nonetheless, the United States could make an important contribution by helping to create a more favorable environment. A new kind of diplomatic relationship with Tehran would not be a concession to the mullahs but a step toward opening, liberalizing, and ultimately democratizing Iran. The end of the current sanctions coupled with a U.S. diplomatic presence in Tehran would allow much greater contact between U.S. and Iranian businesspeople, civic leaders, academics, and elected officials committed to democratic change. A more secure Iran would create better conditions for the reemergence of a pro-Western, peaceful, democratic movement inside the country. The specter of armed conflict with the United States only helps Ahmadinejad consolidate his power. The United States loses nothing in trying to pursue a comprehensive agreement.

The Offer Is the Key

If the logic of our argument is so clear, why wouldn't Khamenei, Ahmadinejad, and their followers also understand it and therefore reject any U.S. gesture? They might, and they might not. Either way, U.S. national security interests, as well as the interests of the Iranian democratic movement, would be served.

If they rejected such an offer, the regime in Tehran would pay a significant price domestically. The vast majority of the Iranian people yearn for more engagement with the West and the United States in particular. Iran's economy urgently needs foreign investment, new technologies, and greater trade opportunities for the nonenergy sectors. A government that openly rejects such inflows will face a potent popular backlash. Even within the regime, some who have made their fortunes by controlling rents generated by the state would now like to privatize these assets through greater integration into the world economy. Of course, allowing corrupt and repressive mullahs to transform themselves into "respected" capitalists is unfair and odious. Yet, as in eastern Europe, it may be a necessary price to pay if the result is a serious challenge to the existing political order. Paradoxically, some of these corrupt mullahs have a shared interest with Iran's democratic movement in developing deeper ties to the West and the United States.

In addition to Iranian popular resistance, the ruling mullahs would face a more internationally legitimate U.S. foe if they rejected this comprehensive agreement. After offering everything outlined above but receiving no positive response from Tehran, Washington would be in a better position internationally to pursue tougher policies, including serious sanctions against the Iranian regime.

Iran's current leaders might not reject the offer. They might believe they have the ability to manage greater interaction with the United States and the West. They might judge that such a direct dialogue with the United States would vindicate their previous policies and legitimate their regime at home and abroad. They might opt for the considerable practical benefit to Iran of everything being offered. In other words, the United States would gain if Tehran either rejects or accepts a comprehensive agreement.

In the long run, the payoff of a democratic Iran would be even greater. Soviet leader Leonid Brezhnev thought he was securing legitimacy and a long life for the Soviet Union when his government signed the Helsinki accords in 1975. Because the West finally recognized post–World War II borders at Helsinki, including Soviet territorial gains, Brezhnev and Western critics of the accord saw this as a major Western concession to growing Soviet power. Both Brezhnev and these critics were wrong. Similarly, no one can predict the timing of democratization in Iran or the role that a new U.S. policy toward Iran might play in accelerating the process.

Perhaps our best guide for what might help Iranian democratization is the ideas of Iran's own democratic leaders. Our strategy is precisely the course advocated by most leaders within the democratic movement inside Iran. No major figure in the Iranian opposition supports sanctions, let alone military action. On the contrary, according to Ganji, arguably the country's most important moral advocate of democracy, the vast majority of Iran's democratic leaders and thinkers believe that normalized relations with the United States and greater integration of Iran into the world's institutions will strengthen their democratic cause.[13] After a quarter century of policy failure, is it not time that we heed the Iranian people's own recommendations for fostering democratization in their country?

Putting the Pressure on Tehran

The United States cannot continue to burn precious time by pursuing an incremental, limited policy for addressing the Iranian nuclear threat. Rather than tactical innovations, the United States needs to adopt a bold and fundamentally different strategy that would allow U.S. diplomats to pursue arms control and democratization at the same time.

Our proposed strategy beats the mullahs at their own game. If they accept the bargain, they will have to give up their nuclear weapons program or be exposed by a comprehensive and energetic inspections regime. A regime without nuclear weapons is a much less powerful adversary for the Iranian democrats. Meanwhile, as Iran integrates with the world economy and opens up to the West, the conditions for a peaceful transition to democracy take root. Nearly every major democratic leader inside Iran agrees that isolation only helps the mullahs at the expense of the democratic cause.

If the mullahs reject this deal publicly, however, they will further undermine their already weak legitimacy with a young, restive, and suffering people. The blunt exposure of the mullahs' obsession with defending their own power and privilege at the expense of the public could intensify popular unrest, further divide an already splintered regime, and eventually create the conditions for regime crisis and transition to democracy. Heads we win, tails they lose.

Notes

1. Steven Lee Meyers, "Russia Hints It Won't Back Penalties Against Iran," *New York Times*, September 2, 2006, p. A7.
2. "Rice Says She Would Not Back Gas Embargo on Iran," Reuters, September 26, 2006, http://today.reuters.com/news/articlenews.aspx?type=topNews&storyID=2006-09-26T055113Z_01_N26233100_RTRUKOC_0_US-NUCLEAR-IRAN-RICE.xml&archived=False.
3. Anthony H. Cordesman and Khalid R. Al-Roham, "Iranian Nuclear Weapons? The Options If Diplomacy Fails" (working paper, CSIS, April 7, 2006), http://www.csis.org/index.php?option=com_csis_pubs&task=view&id=3037.
4. Akbar Ganji, "Money Can't Buy Us Democracy," *New York Times*, August 2, 2006, http://www.nytimes.com/2006/08/01/opinion/01ganji.html?ex=1312084800&en=448e9d7dd418d001&ei=5090&partner=rssuserland&emc=rss.
5. Scott D. Sagan, "How to Keep the Bomb From Iran," *Foreign Affairs* 85, no. 5 (September/October 2006): 59.
6. For an overview of the U.S. dual-track Soviet strategy, see George Shultz, *Turmoil and Triumph: Diplomacy, Power, and the Victory of the American Ideal* (New York: Simon and Schuster, 1993).

7. Daniel Thomas, *The Helsinki Effect: International Norms, Human Rights, and the Demise of Communism* (Princeton: Princeton University Press, 2001); Natan Sharansky, *The Case for Democracy: The Power of Freedom to Overcome Tyranny and Terror* (New York: Public Affairs, 2004).
8. See Michael McFaul, "Chinese Dreams, Persian Realities," *Journal of Democracy* 16, no. 4 (October 2005): 74–82.
9. On the importance of splits within the regime for triggering a process of democratization, see Guillermo O'Donnell and Philippe C. Schmitter, *Transitions From Authoritarian Rule: Tentative Conclusions About Uncertain Democracies* (Baltimore: Johns Hopkins Press, 1986).
10. For elaboration on these key ingredients, see Michael McFaul, "Transitions From Postcommunism," *Journal of Democracy* 16, no. 3 (July 2005): 5–19.
11. Amr Hamzawy and Michael McFaul, "The U.S. and Egypt: Giving Up on the 'Liberty Doctrine,'" *International Herald Tribune*, July 3, 2006, http://www.iht.com/articles/2006/07/03/opinion/edmcfaul.php.
12. Shultz, *Turmoil and Triumph*, p. 266.
13. Akbar Ganji, "Prospects for Democratization in Iran" (lecture, Center on Democracy, Development, and Rule of Law, Stanford University, August 9, 2006).

Graham E. Fuller

The Hizballah-Iran Connection: Model for Sunni Resistance

Iran dominates conversations on the Middle East as of late, lying at the center of a spider web of pressing issues: Tehran's influence in Baghdad, its nuclear policies, and a growing fear of an emerging "Shi'ite axis" that is purported to link Iran, Iraq, Syria, and Hizballah in Lebanon. The image is designed to stir geopolitical blood and has prompted new debate in Washington and the Middle East about how to treat the nature of this "threat."

The Shi'ite tail seems to be wagging the Sunni dog once again. After all, only about 15 percent of Muslims worldwide are Shi'a, making this group clearly outnumbered by its Sunni counterparts. Only in Iran, Iraq, Lebanon, and Bahrain do Shi'a constitute a majority or plurality of the populace. Yet, two of Middle East's most active and outspoken Islamic forces, the Iranian regime and Hizballah, are Shi'a phenomena.

The summer 2006 war between Israel and Hizballah in Lebanon has recharged an ideological debate over the geopolitical relationship between Iran and Hizballah. During the Lebanese conflict, talk emerged of an Iran-Hizballah "axis" and even a "proxy war" in Lebanon between the United States and Iran. In the eyes of the Bush administration and much

Graham E. Fuller is a former vice chair of the National Intelligence Council at the Central Intelligence Agency. He is coauthor of *The Arab Shi'a: The Forgotten Muslims* (2000) with Rend Rahim Francke and author of *The Future of Political Islam* (2004).

The Washington Quarterly • 30:1 pp. 139–150.

of the Israeli establishment, Hizballah is a dangerous Iranian creation that promotes Tehran's radical ambitions and forms an integral part of a dangerous and growing Shi'a bloc across the region. This view is also shared by the leadership of embattled and autocratic Sunni regimes in Egypt, Jordan, and Saudi Arabia as well as by some Persian Gulf state rulers. Meanwhile, next door in Iraq, the Shi'a have electorally commandeered the formerly Sunni-run government in the wake of Saddam Hussein's ouster. Sunni-Shi'a sectarian violence is wracking the nation, particularly Baghdad.

Hizballah is not accumulating power in a Lebanese vacuum but rather in an environment of growing violence across much of the Middle East over several decades, sharply intensified since September 11, 2001, and the beginning of the U.S. global war on terrorism. The group's Iranian connection is profound and well established, but this link is not indicative of a burgeoning sectarian axis reinvigorated by the new power that the Shi'a have gained in Iraq. What is certain, however, is that Hizballah's growing power, although solidly rooted in Lebanon, reflects a broad intensification of resistance to the status quo throughout the Middle East. Invoking a Shi'ite axis may be a good scare tactic, but the phenomenon really signifies political change that is broader than sectarianism.

A Model of Resistance Emerges

Two historical trends have been significant to the Middle East's sociopolitical development and will continue to shape the region's future: a long-term Muslim/Arab determination to resist Western hegemony and a widening self-assertion by minorities within their own political orders. Hizballah is the product of these cultural and psychological forces that, in one form or another, persist throughout the region regardless of sect.

Resistance to Western domination can be traced back a century or more to the military and economic invasion of the Middle East by European imperialism, a process that sparked a wave of anticolonial movements across much of the globe. This resistance developed a "civilizational" character as it spread across Muslim Eurasia. States did not fight against Western dominance in isolation, but rather as part of a broader Muslim *ummah*, the global collective of Muslims who were engaged in separate but parallel struggles for independence. Growing awareness across the Muslim ummah of a seemingly common struggle against imperialism has generated an echo effect that has only been nourished and intensified by modern communications. Today, the Internet constitutes a "virtual" or "electronic" ummah, a sounding board and organizational tool for common Muslim grievances and struggles.

Ironically, this search for some kind of state power capable of resisting Western imperialism facilitated the emergence of the oppressive Middle Eastern security state after World War II. Most notably, the Arab nationalist movement under Gamal Abdul Nasser, president of Egypt from 1945 to 1970, championed Arab unity under a banner of revolutionary social change and modernization. In parallel, various pan-Arab Ba'ath parties sprang up in opposition to ongoing Western intervention in the Arab world and the creation of the Israeli state in 1947, perceived by many to be a political creation of Western Jewry on Arab soil, blessed by a West guilt-ridden over its own treatment of the Jews.

Israel's defeat of the principal revolutionary Arab states—Egypt, Jordan, Syria, and Iraq—in the 1967 Six-Day War was a turning point at which it became apparent that Arab nationalism had failed to deliver on its promises of unity, prosperity, and strength against the West. The foundering appeal of the discredited Arab nationalists gave rise to the emergence of new Islamist movements that promised an even more comprehensive transformation of society. The Islamists vowed to erase the abuses of the Arab dictatorial state while strengthening social foundations to establish greater social justice and to counter its foreign enemies more effectively.

In parallel with the rise of Islamism, religious and ethnic minorities in the Middle East were no longer willing to be suppressed within the larger authoritarian state. Berbers, Kurds, Christians, Shi'ites, Copts, and other minorities all sought to assert themselves against the modern state's forced homogenization process. Western imperial powers had used these minorities to facilitate "divide and rule" policies, making them objects of suspicion in Middle Eastern societies. Yet, the new assertiveness of minorities has contributed to instability in the social order across the region as authoritarian orders weaken. In this context, the Shi'a of Lebanon, a plurality within the country, began their long journey to political dominance in the Lebanese political order.

Hizballah: Independent Actor or Dangerous Proxy?

In Lebanon, the Arab Shi'a have long been a politically, socially, and economically marginalized minority—the "wretched of the earth." Yet, they have been present in Lebanon for at least six centuries. Despite being looked down on by many Sunnis, they nonetheless became a star in the Shi'ite crescent by playing a leading role in the Shi'i-fication of Iran in the early sixteenth century. At that time, the Safavids, a new ruling house, took over in Iran and decided to reject traditional Sunni Islam and embrace Shi'ism. The Safavids desperately needed Shi'ite jurists to help educate and impose its new creed on its Sunni Iranian public. The al-Sadr family so prominent in Iraq, which today includes the young firebrand cleric Muqtada al-Sadr and his famed uncle Ayatollah Muhammad Baqr al-Sadr, were among those Lebanese jurists who went to what is now Iran and Iraq centuries ago to answer that call.

In a turnabout in the early 1970s, the Shi'ite community in Lebanon requested that a member of that same al-Sadr family, the young cleric Musa al-Sadr, to come back to Lebanon from Iran to work with the community to strengthen its jurisprudential and educational level. Al-Sadr's personal impact on the Lebanese Shi'ite community was unparalleled for nearly 20 years, all before the Iranian Revolution. Al-Sadr forged a powerful, new communal sense of dignity and self-help by organizing schools, clinics, economic promotion, and political institutions. He was not a radical but was quite critical of Israel and the Palestine Liberation Organization, whose military confrontations in southern Lebanon were harming the Shi'ite community. Al-Sadr also called for a more equitable share of power within the Lebanese political order, which was dominated by Maronite Christians. These now legendary Lebanese Shi'ite links with Iran form the basis of contemporary references to a Shi'ite axis.

After al-Sadr's probable murder during a visit to Libya in 1978, his movement subsequently morphed into the successful Amal ("Hope") movement, a social movement that reflected and perpetuated his goals. In 1982, Israel invaded Lebanon for the second time and occupied Shi'ite southern Lebanon. In response, various Shi'ite Islamist guerrilla groups, including the more radical elements of Amal, emerged and ultimately coalesced into a formal group in 1985 called Hizballah. The movement's first goal, to end the Israeli occupation of southern Lebanon, was finally accomplished in 2000 after 18 years of guerrilla warfare. Hizballah has declared Israel to be an illegal state based on Jewish exclusivity and founded through violence on Palestinian territory that continues to deprive the Palestinians of their patrimony and land.

Hizballah has particularly close links to revolutionary Iran, drawing inspiration from Ayatollah Ruhollah Khomeini's Iranian Revolution of 1979, which called for revolution to correct injustices across the Muslim world. Today, Hizballah leader Sayyid Hasan Nasrallah follows the theological and sometimes ideological guidance of Iran's supreme leader, Ayatollah Ali Hosseini Khamenei. All major ayatollahs have formal representatives abroad, and in 1995, Khamenei nominated Nasrallah as his deputy in Lebanon.[1]

The Iranian Revolutionary Guard Corps (IRGC) has trained Hizballah forces in eastern Lebanon's Bekaa Valley and in Iran itself since Hizballah was founded. The IRGC also provides the bulk of weaponry that Hizballah has received over the years, including its missiles and rockets. Hizballah is in close and regular contact with Iran, which provides a considerable portion of Hizballah's funding, estimated by the U.S. government at tens of millions of dollars per year, funds that figure importantly in Hizballah's ability to support its wide-ranging social and philanthropic programs in the country.

Although Hizballah would not exist in its present form without the strong support of the Islamic Republic of Iran since its founding, Hizballah today does not operate at the command of the Iranian government. Over the last decade, Hizballah's own independent funds have grown, particularly from wealthy Shi'ite merchants in Lebanon and from the sizable West African, South American, and U.S. Lebanese Shi'ite diaspora.

Anthony Cordesman reported from Israel in August 2006 after the war in Lebanon that no serving Israeli official, intelligence officer, or other military officer with whom he had spoken felt that Hizballah had acted under the direction of Iran or Syria.[2]

Hizballah is thus not some foreign element grafted onto the Lebanese body politic. All Lebanese are fully aware of the group's deeply Lebanese character. Iran's support to the Shi'a elicits little surprise in the Lebanese context in which, regrettably, foreign manipulation of the political scene is nothing new. The French have supported the Maronites. The Syrians have alternately backed the Christians, Sunni, or Shi'a, depending on the geopolitical situation. Other Arab states—Egypt in Nasser's day, Saudi Arabia in more recent decades—have supported the Sunnis for long periods. Libya and Iraq have both aided Sunni political elements inside Lebanon for decades. Israel has funded the Maronites and various minor groups within the Shi'ite community to help support its own geopolitical goals. The Soviet Union actively supported a significant Communist movement in the country. The United States provided covert funding to facilitate the election of various leaders in Lebanon in the 1960s and has regularly lent support to various factions over the years.

In this context, Iran's involvement is hardly an exceptional phenomenon in the old Middle East political game—one of the reasons for the political dysfunction of the region. Iran could undoubtedly weaken Hizballah considerably as a force in Lebanon by cutting off financial assistance and arms shipments. Although Hizballah does have considerable financial resources of its own, the loss of Iranian funding would significantly constrain the organization's range of activities, especially its anti-Israeli guerrilla campaigns, even if the loss would not bring it to its knees. That strong Iranian influence, however, does not remotely mean that Hizballah is taking orders from Iran.

The two major Shi'ite movements, Amal and Hizballah, were not created to be instruments of Iranian control so much as to strengthen the independent power of the Shi'ite community and to meet its genuine security needs before and during the Lebanese civil war from 1975 to 1990. Throughout that struggle, sectarian militias were vital to the protection of all major Lebanese sectarian elements. Moreover, Hizballah's and, earlier, Amal's armed capabilities have not been used against other domestic groups since the civil war ended.

Hizballah will not readily relinquish the advantages it currently enjoys as a powerful militia for the sake of its constituency's welfare. The Lebanese state historically has never served the Lebanese Shi'a well. The Shi'a have been an ignored and deprived underclass that has never received an equal share of the Lebanese infrastructure, political representation, or economic benefits. Despite being a plurality in the country today, the Shi'a are constitutionally allocated only 27 out of 128 parliamentary seats. National power is gradually shifting toward the Shi'a in that body in part because of Hizballah's activities, but the process of power allocation in Lebanon remains highly charged. Few Lebanese aside from the Shi'a would accept the principle of one man, one vote, as this would weaken the other long-dominant sectarian groups, such as the Christian Maronites and Sunni Muslims. At this stage in Lebanon's political development, its Shi'a have little confidence that the state can or will meet their needs and thus place greater confidence in Hizballah and Amal as their political instruments. In this context, Iran's preferences on the matter are not particularly relevant to what Hizballah does.

Furthermore, Hizballah is a potential national military asset on which the Lebanese state may depend again in the event of further confrontations with Israel, a crucial resource, considering the Lebanese military's weakness. Following the mostly Hizballah-achieved Israeli withdrawal in 2000, Hizballah retained its armed militia to prevent further Israeli attacks in the south and to liberate the small territory known as Shebaa Farms, currently Israeli-occupied, internationally recognized as Syrian, but claimed by Lebanon.

These historic ties between the Lebanese Shi'a and Iran provide a clear indication that the relationship does not represent simply some latter-day development brewed up by Tehran as part of a new geopolitical weapon. Significant geopolitical implications do flow from their commonality of vision, but their impact is at least equally a result of the weakness and unpopularity of current pro-U.S. autocrats in the Arab world.

The 'Shi'a Revival's' Political Appeal to Sunnis

In Washington's search for a silver bullet with which to dispatch anti-U.S. movements within the Islamic world, much has been made of a split between the Shi'ite and Sunni world in the face of a reviving Shi'ite threat. Threatened Sunni regimes echo this concern. Yet, such a portrayal of the geopolitical situation in the Muslim world misses the big picture.

Serious historical rifts exist between Sunni and Shi'a Islam, whose origins trace back to a 1,300-year-old dispute over the Prophet Muhammad's rightful successor. Yet, in practice, there is little serious theological difference between the two sects; their divisions have more to do with practice. As in the rift between Protestants and Catholics in the West, religious differences have shaped separate communal existences over time.

Friction between the Sunni and Shi'a today manifests itself primarily in areas in which the two communities live in close proximity. This is especially true in Iraq, where the Sunni minority has politically and socially marginalized the Shi'ite majority for hundreds of years. The communal balance of power has now drastically shifted with the overthrow of Saddam's secular but Sunni-dominated regime and the accession to power of the Shi'a via the ballot box. The conflict in Iraq is occurring on a Shi'a-Sunni axis not because of any real theological or sectarian differences, but because of a struggle for concrete political power and interests in a newly volatile environment between two rival communities.

In overwhelmingly Sunni Egypt, Jordan, Palestine, North Africa, and Central and Southeast Asia, the Sunni-Shi'a issue is minor. In states in which Shi'ites represent significant minorities—Turkey, India, Kuwait, the United Arab Emirates, Yemen, Afghanistan, Pakistan, and Saudi Arabia, in rough order of their degree of successful minority integration—similar tensions arising from communal proximity do exist. In these states, however, democratization is a much less volatile process from a Sunni point of view because even the ballot box will not overturn the balance of political power that rests with the Sunni majority. Syria remains a major exception. There the 'Alawi Shi'ite minority, representing 13 percent of the population, rules over the Sunni majority, an arrangement that will eventually break down. Outside of rivalries between close-proximity communities, anti-Shi'a feeling among Sunnis elsewhere is largely theoretical and minimal.

Nonetheless, since the shift in the balance of power in Iraq, some extraordinary, near-hysterical pronouncements have come from Arab states that scarcely possess any meaningful Shi'ite minorities among their population. In December 2004, Jordanian King Abdullah II paraded fears of a new "Shi'ite crescent" cutting across the Middle East.[3] In April 2006, Egyptian president Husni Mubarak, in reference to Shi'a living in Arab states, darkly opined, "Most of the Shi'ites are loyal to Iran, and not the countries they are living in."[4] Then, at the outset of the July–August 2006 Lebanese-Israeli war, the Egyptian, Jordanian, and Saudi heads of state astonishingly all publicly opposed Hizballah's actions, suggesting that it and Hamas were engaged in reckless adventurism that endangered Arab interests.

These statements were surely not motivated by sympathy for Israel but rather by these rulers' fear of rising national resistance forces under the rubric of Islamism. Sunni leaders do not actually fear adherents of Shi'ism per se but rather the growing power of popular radical or revolutionary forces craving change, which is now emerging from within the Shi'ite world. The real regional fault line is thus not along a Sunni-Shi'a axis. Instead, we witness entrenched, threatened authoritarian rulers supported by the United States who are opposed by domestic populations that seek to dislodge these rulers, end the U.S. and Israeli occupations of Muslim lands, and resist overall U.S. policies. Sunni public opinion is galvanized at the prospect of changing the hated status quo through Hizballah's and Iran's unyielding posture toward Washington. Hizballah's ability, nearly unprecedented in Arab history, to stand up to the punishment of a powerful Israeli military machine and force it to a truce is electrifying.

Despite the bombastic statements of pro-U.S. Arab leaders, it is difficult to make the case that Shi'ite forces in modern history have acted in pursuit of narrow sectarian interests, at least on the international level. On the contrary, Shi'ite political movements generally possess a pan-Muslim or pan-Arab political vision that avoids invocation of Shi'ism. Autocratic Arab rulers actually fear the empowering forces of organizations such as Hizballah and Hamas, which seek to enable communities or the masses to take control of their own destiny. This self-empowerment in recent decades has mostly emerged through Islamist organizations; almost no other contenders exist.

The struggle of the Arab autocrats against Islamist fundamentalism thus more accurately translates into a struggle against spontaneous, civic-based activism and resistance that the state cannot control rather than a Sunni backlash against Shi'a. This is not to say that Islamist actions automatically equate to democracy in action, but they are closer to democracy than most other currently existing political forces, which are manipulated and controlled by the state. Regimes' references to "Islamic fundamentalism," "Iranian ambitions," or "Shi'ite ambitions" are code words that they know will resonate in Washington, bringing continuing political support even as the Bush administration speaks of bringing democracy to the Middle East.

Iran's Resistance Model Today

Iran challenged the ruling status quo in the Arab world in the fervid early years of the Iranian Revolution, calling for the overthrow of U.S.-supported despotic rulers. Khomeini called for social and political justice, especially for the Palestinians, who are Sunni. He inveighed against the imperialist United States, or "Great Satan." He expelled the shah, the top U.S. ally in the region; seized U.S. hostages; and bested the U.S. government's ill-fated military rescue operation, all wildly popular events across most of the Muslim world. Iran generally presumes to speak for pan-Muslim causes, rarely invoking its own Shi'ite character except to condemn injustices committed by repressive Sunni regimes on occasion.

Today, Tehran is determined to strengthen its resistance to the U.S. agenda in the Middle East by insisting on its right to master the nuclear fuel cycle and calling for political change across the region in ways that no Arab ruler dares. President Mahmoud Ahmadinejad's violent diatribes against Israel are directed as much at the wider Arab world as at the Iranian population. Most Arab populations even seem to view the prospect of Iran's acquisition of nuclear weapons with some equanimity. Not even a nuclear-armed Shi'ite regime worries most Middle Eastern regimes as much as the populist drawing power of the Iran, Hizballah, and Hamas combination, which challenges these rulers' domestic control. In September 2006, in solidly Sunni Cairo, two of the most popular figures were Ahmadinejad and Nasrallah.[5]

Iran champions genuinely popular issues that resonate across the Muslim world. It reflects a revolutionary spirit of resistance with deep appeal to populations who feel impotent and who crave bold leadership that will assert their dignity against the United States and Israel. Iran itself, of course, is no longer a truly revolutionary state. It accepts and works with the status quo when needed and is quite pragmatic in its foreign policy. Ironically, its present ability to win broad regional sympathy would quickly fade if the leading Arab states were to be taken over by popularly elected leaders who would predictably express more outspoken opposition to unpopular U.S. policies. Iran would in that case lose its monopoly on the fiery stance that gives them so much popular support, at present only enjoyed by other Islamists, Sunni and Shi'a alike. These forces of resistance to the United States run deep. It is only a question of who will ride them.

Can Hizballah Be Contained?

Hizballah is cast from the same mold. Its character is mainstream Shi'ite, but its rhetoric focuses on Arab unity, the illegitimacy of the Israeli state, and the need for change in Arab leadership. Hizballah champions the (Sunni) Palestinian cause and cooperates closely with Hamas, a preeminently Sunni Islamist organization. Hizballah's kidnapping of the two Israeli soldiers in July 2006 was also partially in support of the newly elected Hamas government that has been struggling under a U.S.- and Israeli-led boycott. Lebanese Sunnis as well as Shi'a fully approve of this aspect of Hizballah's policies.

These policies, its successful 18-year-long guerrilla war against the Israeli occupation of southern Lebanon, and its impressive ability to withstand the Israeli onslaught in the summer of 2006 enabled Hizballah to win the hearts and minds of most Sunnis on the street. These publics have been exhilarated by these demonstrations of Arab bravery, sacrifice, and military skill. It makes no difference that members of Hizballah are

Shi'ites; they are perceived to be on the right side of vital Arab national issues. Admiration for the Shi'a is more restrained only in states where the communities live in close proximity, especially in Lebanon, where the entire country had to bear the brunt of Israel's punishment. Even in Iraq, most Sunni Islamists called for support of Hizballah against Israel. Even Ayman al-Zawahiri, the number two leader of Al Qaeda, an organization known for its clear anti-Shi'ite sentiments, stated that all Muslims should support this just cause in Lebanon.[6]

Hizballah is thus a manifestation of deeply entrenched geopolitics of resistance and revolution in the Muslim world. Its growing influence and popularity have long-term historical and ideological roots, and its ambitions and actions are neither exclusively Shi'ite nor anti-Sunni in character. It represents a powerful regional current that is larger than itself and thus cannot be easily suppressed or disarmed.

Washington classifies Hizballah as an international terrorist organization and targets it with broad sanctions. Although Hizballah has undeniably engaged in a number of terrorist acts, this generalized label and approach are not a recipe for success. Hizballah is a vastly different creature from Al Qaeda, for example. The latter is a globally focused network that promotes the sweeping, violent elimination of all Western influence, the overthrow of virtually all existing governments of the region, and the imposition of ultra-fundamentalist forms of Islamic governance. Yet, the U.S. government treats the two groups as functionally identical phenomena.

Despite its widespread popularity and Iranian connections, Hizballah is a basically local organization with goals primarily in the immediate region. It has operated almost exclusively within Lebanon and against military or foreign government installations. Aside from two anti-Israeli terrorist attacks in Argentina on Jewish targets, the organization has not engaged in any violent activities in the United States, Canada, or anywhere else outside Lebanon except across the border against Israel, although it has engaged in fundraising activities and efforts to gain political support in North and South America among Lebanese Shi'ite communities there. Hizballah's basic lack of involvement in out-of-state guerrilla operations is indicative of its essentially Israel-Lebanon-Palestine orientation and concentration on local grievances. There is little credible evidence that Hizballah has ties to Al Qaeda, which is generally strongly anti-Shi'a and whose version of radical Salafism is responsible for killing large numbers of Shi'ites in Iraq, Afghanistan, and elsewhere.

Disarming Hizballah is not currently realistic in the context of present regional power politics. The players who exert the greatest influence over it have little incentive to surrender a key element of their geopolitical power package. Iran, for example, has absolutely no reason to weaken the vitality of this long-standing link, particularly when Tehran perceives Washington as determined to whittle down Iran's regional power sharply. Nor can Syria be ignored in this equation. Damascus has routinely facilitated passage of Iranian weapons to Hizballah and has provided some of its own weapons as well, because Hizballah's power helps to divert Israeli pressure away from Syria and supports Syrian aspirations to regain the lost Golan Heights from Israel.

If the United States seriously desires to weaken the Iran-Hizballah nexus, it must deal with a range of regional problems as a unit and engage in unprecedented thinking about the region. The Middle East is a graveyard of failed attempts to achieve salami-style solutions that seek to isolate and pick off smaller and weaker elements of the problem without dealing with the crux of the issue. Israeli occupation of the Golan Heights and Palestinian territories since 1967 is the very node of the complex of problems from which nearly all other calculus proceeds. A genuine and equitable regional peace settlement would drastically change the internal calculus for Hizballah, Hamas, and all other regional players.

Even among the Shi'a, many, most notably a growing and gradually prospering middle class, at present reluctantly support Hizballah but aspire in the longer run to a more modern and unitary Lebanese state. In this sense, once a regional settlement has been reached, Hizballah will largely have fulfilled its own historic mission and, even for most Shi'a, will have little reason to exist as anything except a local political party. Meanwhile, Washington's jealous monopoly on the peace process over three decades has dramatically failed to bring an end to this fundamental fact of occupation, an issue to which so many other regional issues are held hostage.

The Iran-Hizballah nexus is very real, has deep historical roots, and will not likely be crushed by transient squeeze plays by Washington or Tel Aviv. A campaign designed to exacerbate Sunni-Shi'a hostility as currently promoted by Washington and its nervous acolytes in Saudi Arabia, Egypt, and Jordan will be hard pressed to succeed when Iran and Hizballah are seen by Sunni publics as pursuing popular Arab national issues. Only an Iranian war of aggression against an Arab state or states might whip up enough Sunni regional emotion to deflate the influence of this Shi'ite entente. Such an action does not seem likely, given Iran's basic lack of territorial aggression for more than two centuries. Even nervous Gulf sheikhdoms know that a hostile U.S. policy toward Iran will not serve their long-term interests, even though they seek political counterweight to Tehran's influence.

Washington has few longer-range options other than dealing with the reality of Iranian influence and Hizballah's established role in Lebanon, withdrawing its hated military presence from the region, and bringing about a just settlement of the Palestinian situation. With every passing month that the issue of U.S. and Israeli occupation is allowed to fester, the Iranian and Hizballah strategy pays rich dividends to both throughout the Sunni world.

Notes

1. Lara Deeb, "Hizballah: A Primer," *Middle East Report Online*, July 31, 2006, http://www.merip.org/mero/mero073106.html.
2. Anthony H. Cordesman, "Preliminary 'Lessons' of the Israeli-Hezbollah War" (working paper, CSIS, August 17, 2006), http://www.csis.org/media/csis/pubs/060817_isr_hez_lessons.pdf.
3. Sami Moubayed, "The Waxing of the Shi'ite Crescent," *Asia Times Online*, April 20, 2005. http://www.atimes.com/atimes/Middle_East/GD20Ak01.html.
4. Nicholas Blanford, "Shiite-Sunni 'Rift' a Worry Across Region," *USA Today*, April 13, 2006, http://www.usatoday.com/news/world/iraq/2006-04-13-iraq-rift_x.htm.
5. "Nasrallah Dates," Reuters TV, September 26, 2006, http://rtv.rtrlondon.co.uk/2006-09-27/2f0cbffc.html.
6. Daniel Kimmage, "Al-Qaeda Addresses the Jihad-Versus-Resistance Conflict," Radio Free Europe/Radio Liberty, July 31, 2006, http://www.rferl.org/featuresarticleprint/2006/07/96bd70d7-07bd-4862-8751-41f30aa14028.html.

Elliot Hen-Tov

Understanding Iran's New Authoritarianism

Mahmoud Ahmadinejad's victory in the June 2005 Iranian presidential elections and his confrontational politics highlight two remarkable aspects of Iran's political development. First, it indicates that Iran is in fact undergoing a gradual process of regime change, not moving toward democratization but rather modifying Iran's brand of authoritarianism. It constitutes the beginning of a marked shift from the existing clerical theocracy toward a more conventional authoritarian regime. Two threats have created the need for more effective authoritarian governance to secure Iran's clerical regime: the internal challenge by the reformist opposition and the external threat of U.S. intervention posed to Iran in the post–September 11 world. This transition will therefore see remnant democratic features erode as the evolving regime concentrates power among a small number of key decisionmaking centers. Similar to other authoritarian regimes, the role of the military-security apparatus will be enhanced, as will the regime's dependence on tools of patronage or repression to assert full control.

Second, in contrast to many ill-fated predictions regarding Iran, the domestic political economy underpinning the regime is surprisingly stable in the medium term. Profound structural problems in Iran's economy

Elliot Hen-Tov is a doctoral candidate specializing in contemporary Iranian and Turkish affairs in the Department of Near Eastern Studies at Princeton University.

The Washington Quarterly • 30:1 pp. 163–179.

will prevent the leadership from implementing the China model—authoritarianism with high economic growth—but Iran's oil-based economy nevertheless provides the regime with sufficient resources to satisfy its supporter base and discourage opposition. If anything, the potential but unlikely international isolation of Iran if Tehran mishandles its apparent quest for nuclear weapons represents a greater threat to regime stability than Iran's economic condition.

Conservatives Consolidate Their Gains

Starting with Ayatollah Ruhollah Khomeini's death in 1989, Iran underwent a limited, gradual liberalization process culminating in the Khatami presidency (1997–2005) and a reformist-led parliament, the Majlis. During their years in power, reformists used control over budget and legislation to publicly challenge the legitimacy of the theocratic pillars of the Islamic republic, particularly the supreme leader. After years of reformist meddling, however, the conservatives used antidemocratic measures to recapture municipalities in 2003, the Majlis in 2004, and the presidency in 2005. Now, as the conservatives control all branches of government once again, power is increasingly concentrated in the hands of Supreme Leader Ali Khamenei. Khamenei's emergence as the "absolute" supreme leader, as named in the constitution, was not a reflection of his superior juridical or intellectual credentials.[1] Hence, he has relentlessly shored up his leadership by cultivating different supporters and shrewdly playing Iranian politics.

Khamenei's clout was limited during the Rafsanjani presidency, from 1989 to 1997, as there were plenty of actors competing for the heritage bequeathed by the death of Khomeini, the leader of the 1979 Islamic Revolution. For Iran's populace, the 1990s were an era of unfulfilled hopes after the dreadful decade of postrevolutionary chaos and the Iran-Iraq War (1980–1988). By the time of the 1997 presidential elections, this disappointment resulted in a landslide victory for the reformist cleric Muhammad Khatami, compounded by the reformist takeover of the Majlis in the elections three years later. Simultaneously, the loss of executive and legislative positions of power forced conservatives of various factions to coalesce around the supreme leader. This meant that conservatives operated against the Khatami administration primarily through state bodies supervised or appointed by the supreme leader. In practice, conservatives utilized the upper house of parliament (Council of Guardians), the judiciary, and paramilitary forces to stifle reformist opponents. Because of conservative dependence on the office of the supreme leader, Khamenei became the true figurehead of conservative leadership.

Eventually, conservative forces applied the tools provided by Khamenei to engineer electoral successes and regain formal power in the legislative and executive branches. The defeat of reform efforts through constitutional means from 1997 to 2005 not only demoralized reformist politicians but also alienated the broader population from political life. Due to the failure to reform the Islamic republic effectively, Iranian sentiment increasingly has become one of political apathy. Instead of politics, Iranians increasingly focus on economic progress.[2]

The June 2005 presidential elections bore more resemblance to elections in other semicompetitive authoritarian regimes. Although antidemocratic in nature, the elections did offer an array of choices. The restricted candidacies allowed only one explicitly reformist candidate to run against five conservatives of varying shades, Ahmadinejad being the most conservative and supposedly closest to Khamenei. Virtually nonexistent in polls before the election, his second place in the first round and landslide victory in the second round resulted both from his campaign platform and his political connections. As a former Revolutionary Guard commander and Basij militia instructor, he could rely on the Revolutionary Guards and Basij to engage in serious voter mobilization as well as outright vote rigging.

This partially legitimizes calls that Ahmadinejad was artificially installed, but genuine popular support for Ahmadinejad's campaign was extensive. In contrast to other candidates tainted by wealth and corruption, his anti-establishment image appealed to average Iranians struggling with economic difficulties. Moreover, his aim to counter corruption and address Iran's deteriorating income inequality captured voters' primary preoccupations. Yet, from a structural perspective, the most noticeable element in the election campaign is Ahmadinejad's position within the regime. He is the first noncleric to hold the presidency and is both the supreme leader's preferred choice and the candidate with the most influence in Iran's security and paramilitary apparatus. His election is hence indicative of the nature of regime development in Iran, even if Ahmadinejad himself has proven to be a controversial leader. The consolidation of conservative power in the Iranian state is proceeding along conventional authoritarian patterns with an increasing shift of power to the state security services.

The prominent elevation of intelligence and security figures under Ahmadinejad is a product of their increased role during the Khatami years of silencing and intimidating reformist sympathizers. The prime example is Mostafa Pour-Mohammadi, Ahmadinejad's interior minister, who allegedly engineered the serial killings of intellectuals in late 1998 while serving as deputy information minister, before managing a special intelligence department in the office of the supreme leader. Although very active in intimidation, assassination, and other forms of state coercion even before Khatami's election, the security branches became the preferred tool of conservative control in recent years and a pillar of Khamenei's rule. The Iranian state security system has been subservient to more radical elements of the regime, whose spiritual leader is the fundamentalist cleric Ayatollah Mesbah Yazdi. The overlap between fundamentalists and state security became blatantly obvious in the blasphemy case of Hashem Aghajari in November 2002. In that instance, Yazdi's private supporters announced a death sentence on the Internet, and the official decision released by the judiciary a month later was identical, word for word.[3]

Following the 2005 election, Ahmadinejad filled most of the executive branch with veterans of the state security services. Moreover, even other conservative streams have increasingly been shut out of decisionmaking. This centralization of decisionmaking along with the greater prominence of fundamentalist actors is bound to reduce policymaking compromises. In 2002, Tehran University professor Hossein Seifzadeh wrote, "[T]he domestic politics of fundamentalists are more congruent with totalitarianism, though they are unable to implement its principles within the current political system."[4] Since then, fundamentalists have exercised control over Iran's domestic affairs with feeble limitations: halfhearted parliamentary oversight, muted opposition figures, and a muffled media.

Ahmadinejad and Elite Factionalism

Ironically, a major concern of traditional Iranian conservatives rests in the populist agenda of Ahmadinejad. His persona is key to understanding the emerging political class. He came of age during the 1979 revolution that intended to rectify the injustices and immorality of the shah's regime. Of a modest background himself, Ahmadinejad was immediately enamored with Khomeini's ideals and began a devoted career in service of the revolution, in particular within the state security apparatus as a Revolutionary Guard commander. An unknown figure until recently, Ahmadinejad is representative of a new group of younger ideologues that are gradually taking over within the conservative establishment. The fact that the Revolutionary Guards and Basij supported his candidacy over two older, former Revolutionary Guard commanders testifies to this emerging trend. In addition to Ahmadinejad's military nature, his populist rhetoric offers an appealing ideological variant to the flagging legitimacy of the clerical system.

The defining feature of Ahmadinejad's administration is the intertwining of formal government decisionmaking with the revolutionary military-security complex, in contrast to the conventional armed forces, which lack influence in the Islamic republic. The homogeneity of the new government's membership is striking. At an average age of 49, most of Ahmadinejad's cabinet members are middle-aged, unknown, strongly ideological, second-generation revolutionaries without any political experience. Virtually all have a background in the Revolutionary Guards or other branches of state security. Although mostly nonclerical, even the two clerics in Ahmadinejad's cabinet, Pour-Mohammadi and Ghalam-Hossein Mohseni-Ejeie, come from a career in the intelligence services and are thus equally militarized.[5] Their theological training and intelligence careers make Pour-Mohammadi and Mohseni-Ejeie unique links between the clerical ranks and the military-security personnel that constitute most of the new government. They will gradually become more influential as they channel clerical legitimacy to an ideologically bankrupt regime that increasingly resembles conventional authoritarianism. As with other selections, Pour-Mohammadi's and Mohseni-Ejeie's controversial appointments suggest the regime feels it can entirely ignore opposition, even from conservative factions.

The worldview of these particular elites is dominated by the events of 1979 and implies that Iran's current problems lay in its society's insufficient realization of revolutionary Islamic principles. In contrast, having occupied positions of power since 1979, older, traditional conservatives have recognized the limits to implementing Khomeini's radical ideas. Although Ahmadinejad is considered a loyal supporter of Khamenei, the election demonstrated the extent of disdain among these new revolutionaries for the corrupt elites within the broader conservative enterprise, particularly in the circles around former president Ali Akbar Hashemi Rafsanjani.

Since taking office, the Ahmadinejad administration has instituted rapid personnel change throughout the bureaucracy with little regard for other interest groups. For example, in November 2005, Ahmadinejad replaced 40 senior ambassadors in one fell swoop with associates deemed more ideologically rigid. Simultaneously, he has ensured the placement of fellow militarist ideologues in senior management positions throughout the central government, regional governorships, and state-owned banks. Expectations of political appointments among the Revolutionary Guards were so high that, after complaints and an official meeting, Ahmadinejad appointed additional senior Revolutionary Guards as vice interior minister and governor of Hamedan.[6] Overall, these actions suggest real regime change because the mechanism and channels of elite recruitment are being structurally changed. In other words, it is less the clerical class and its associates, but rather increasingly the militarist class around the Revolutionary Guards, that is supplying the preferred pool of candidates.

Ahmadinejad's personal style of confrontation and the structural nature of these changes have provoked a rising discomfort within the conservative enterprise of the ideological, populist, and militarist agenda. In 2005, traditional conservatives blocked Ahmadinejad's efforts to install an associate to head the oil ministry, the main source of government revenues, three separate times. Out of 290 votes, none of his crony nominees received even 120, the number of seats held by the coalition that is nominally allied with the president, known as the Abadgaran coalition.[7] In the end, the longtime deputy of the oil ministry became oil minister. Control over Iran's most valuable resource would have completed a quasi-revolution and was hence unacceptable to other conservatives.

Other examples of the threat perception within the Iranian leadership are Khamenei's decrees restricting Ahmadinejad's executive powers. A decree on June 25, 2006, created the new Strategic Council on Foreign Relations, composed of former government ministers.[8] Earlier, Khamenei empowered the Expediency Council, headed by none other than Rafsanjani, legally to supervise the new government. Outspoken about the erosion of governance norms in Iran, Rafsanjani is not only concerned about real incompetence in Ahmadinejad's administration but also about the fate of his own political and personal fortune. Reputedly Iran's wealthiest individual, Rafsanjani has built up a web of businesses through the influence of public office.

Oligarchs such as Rafsanjani have the most to fear from populist authoritarians such as Ahmadinejad, who campaigned on a platform to combat corruption and alleviate Iran's rampant income inequality. The oligarchs are the most prominent manifestations of both. Nevertheless, the much publicized drive to reduce corruption may simply become a pretext for purging opponents and competitors of the emerging ruling elite. Moreover, oligarchs such as Rafsanjani are ideal targets because they not only represent a challenge to Ahmedinejad's administration but also possess large-scale assets that could be redistributed for populist purposes. This conflict of interest has prompted tensions between Rafsanjani and Ahmadinejad, and its outcome will be a key determinant of Iran's short-term political path.[9]

Iran's internal political upheaval is occurring at the same time as the critical phase in its development of nuclear energy. Despite Tehran's denial that it is building nuclear weapons and controversial but reasonable economic arguments that it is developing a civilian nuclear energy base to free up more oil for exports and foreign earnings, there are at least three structural reasons to suggest Iran's nuclear program is not limited to civilian use. First, for purely civilian nuclear energy, it makes no economic sense to build a vast nuclear program with multiple research reactors, light- and heavy-water nuclear plants, and an enrichment facility. Second, Iran has a long record of lying about rather unimportant but nevertheless secret activities. Third, Iran's parallel ballistic missile program, involving Shahab-3 and Shahab-4 missiles, is irrational unless they will be armed with weapons of mass destruction.

One should view Iran's quest for nuclear weapons through the prism of elite factionalism and regime development. The successful acquisition of nuclear weapons would accelerate a militarization of Iran's regime. It will provide the Iranian regime with limited immunity against external threats and thus help preserve the regime, especially because domestic opposition is currently immaterial. In fact, if domestic forces do arise to challenge the regime, nuclearization, portrayed as an issue of national pride, would become one of the few powerful tools that could provide regime legitimacy and enable popular mobilization. In the meantime, the management of Iran's nuclear assets help accelerate the shift toward a more conventional authoritarianism. Like the Shahab ballistic missiles and other items of vital national security, the nuclear program is subordinate to the Revolutionary Guards, not to the conventional armed forces. Developing their nuclear program will therefore continue to enhance the very same populist forces in the military-security apparatus trying to assert themselves within the wider regime.[10]

Iran's Political Economy: Oil, Patronage, and Repression

Independently of Ahmedinejad's emergence, the surprising stability of the Iranian political economy is helping to insulate and strengthen the durability of the emerging authoritarian order. The regime appears very stable in the medium term, even if there are major political and socioeconomic challenges. Despite these issues, the regime can amass sufficient resources to maintain its patronage system and tools of repression. Specifically, the relatively high price of oil and the concentration of assets in a web of state and quasi-state control enable the regime to cultivate a loyal support base while preventing the rise of competitive social groups. Only a severe economic downturn, such as a total collapse in oil revenues if prices crash or an international embargo is imposed, could hasten the creation of serious opposition. This would force the regime to ratchet up repression levels, possibly provoking greater opposition and threatening the regime's survival. In order to prevent this scenario, Iran's leaders aim to emulate the China model: authoritarianism with rapid economic growth.

The Limits of the China Model

In China, the Communist Party has effectively maintained political control while engineering remarkable economic progress. Both its impressive economic record and nationalism help legitimize the Chinese Communists. Commonly termed the Asian/China model in Iran, this idea has gained ground among ruling conservatives. Yet, the adoption of the China model will fail in Iran due to three major obstacles: Iran's macroeconomic challenges, the concentration of economic power in the oil industry, and a lack of political commitment.

First, Iran faces a daunting set of macroeconomic challenges, including economic growth, inflation, unemployment, and income inequality. Iran managed an average of only 4.4 percent annual gross domestic product (GDP) growth for 1994–2004, although growth has surpassed 6 percent on average since 2002.[11] Simultaneously, inflation continues to be high, with average rates remaining higher than 15 percent for the past five years. High inflation hits public sector employees particularly hard because their salaries are annualized and rarely grow at inflationary rates. Even worse, although the high rate of unemployment is officially 11 percent, realistic estimates are closer to 16 percent. Youth unemployment (ages 15–24) is significantly higher than that due to the baby boom encouraged during the war with Iraq—babies who have grown up and are now entering the labor market.[12] This large generation requires the creation of 800,000 new jobs a year just to maintain the current unemployment rate, equivalent to almost 6.5 percent economic growth. A real reduction in unemployment would indeed necessitate Chinese growth rates of more than 8 percent. The alternative, high unemployment especially among youth, would generate widespread discontent. Finally, Iran has seen its middle class shrink and income inequality worsen. Among the UN Human Development Report's 124 countries, Iran is currently ranked 79, below Kenya and above Uganda.[13] By itself, such inequality constrains economic growth because of the systemic misallocation of resources among the country's industries.[14] Combined with these other economic problems, in short, Iran's economy is potentially destabilizing because of its social combustibility and inherent strains on economic progress.

Second, the nature of Iran's hydrocarbon industry actually restrains the country's overall development. Production levels have never recovered to pre-revolutionary times. At barely more than four million barrels per day (bpd), Iran is still producing 30 percent less than in 1979.[15] The government aims to raise this to 5.6 million bpd by 2010 and to 7 million bpd by 2020. These goals are ambitious, considering that without any investment in the oil industry, Iran would lose about 300,000 bpd in production capacity annually. Production levels have stagnated primarily because of a lack of technological expertise in development and exploration. Any substantial rise in production levels will require significant foreign investment and expertise. In late 2004, Iran granted Sinopec the rights to develop Iran's Yadavaran oil field, its first large agreement with a Chinese company. Due to limited technological and financial depth, however, Chinese companies are not a long-term option, and Iran will still need Western oil companies to boost national oil production.

Other endemic problems in Iran's oil industry, namely management and corruption, are directly linked to the Islamic Revolution. In a revolutionary zeal to do away with the remnants of the shah's government, Iran began to duplicate authorities because they could not do away entirely with the organizational infrastructure. This process escalated until today, resulting in two entrenched, mammoth organizations, the Ministry of Oil and the National Iranian Oil Company, as well as an endless number of subsidiaries. To illustrate the extent of duplication, Iran's oil employment numbers tell the story: 54,000 employees worked in Iran's oil industry during the last year of the shah's reign in 1979, compared to 180,000 employees today who, after 25 years of technological progress, produce about one-third less oil (see figure).[16] The cancerous growth of multiple authorities also created rampant corruption. This phenomenon will be

Figure: Iran's Oil Production and Consumption 1973–2004

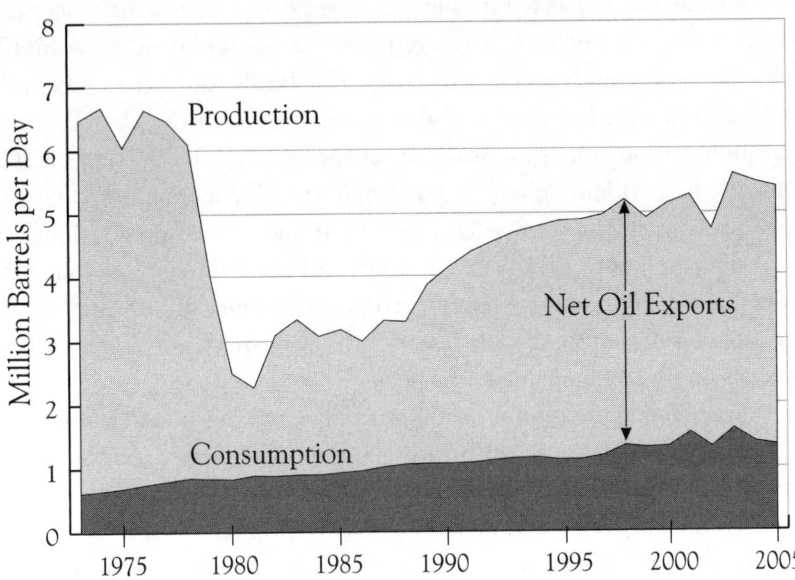

Sources: Joint Economic Committee, *Energy and the Iranian Economy: Hearing before the Joint Economic Committee*, 109th Cong., 2nd sess., 2006, http://www.house.gov/jec/hearings/testimony/109/07-25-06_iran_Simons.pdf (statement of Paul Simons, U.S. Department of State); Joint Economic Committee, *Energy and the Iranian Economy: Hearing before the Joint Economic Committee*, 109th Cong., 2nd sess., 2006, http://www.house.gov/jec/hearings/testimony/109/07-25-06_iran_Schott.pdf (statement of Jeffrey J. Schott).

difficult to stamp out because the very same corrupt officials, their unprincipled work ethos notwithstanding, are the only Iranian oil specialists with sufficient expertise to reform the country's oil industry.[17]

Overall, Iran's oil wealth has not been used to broaden the economic base, as the country remains overly dependent on its hydrocarbon industry. Instead, oil has led to distorting effects on Iran's political economy. For one, the state-managed oil sector has dominated investment decisions, thus crowding out both the private oil sector as well as other industries. Moreover, heavy state involvement in all sectors has led to rent seeking, or the purchase of government privileges, which in turn has wasted resources and lowered overall investment.[18]

Third, in addition to hard economic realities, the Iranian leadership lacks the actual political skill and will to emulate the Chinese reforms. Iran's leaders have used state bureaucracies primarily as patronage networks instead of technocratic agencies, thereby creating mass inefficiencies in the public sector. Ideologically, Iran's rulers have not fully embraced market economics; and confrontation with the United States continues to cost Iran, by at least one estimate, about 1.1 percent of GDP annually in U.S. sanctions.[19] In particular, Iran's economic potential will be stifled if suspicion of foreign investment and ownership continues to limit development of Iran's major competitive advantage: oil. As mentioned above, reducing systemic corruption in Iran's oil industry would probably result in a significant loss of technical expertise as Iran's corrupt officials do possess valuable know-how.

In Iran, economic reform would probably have to come in the form of liberalization. This would in turn precipitate a challenge to other elites whose conservative credentials have enabled them to build personal fortunes in a highly regulated market. The emerging power centers, such as the Revolutionary Guards, are major industrial players themselves that have profited from a closed statist economy. Confronting these deep-rooted interests would seriously undermine government unity and regime stability. Instead of liberalization, Ahmadinejad's agenda advocates populist redistribution of wealth. Such populism only works smoothly during an oil boom, as only oil revenues are affected by the redistribution and existing privileges are left untouched.

Regime Resources: A Well-Oiled Apparatus

In spite of these overwhelming socioeconomic challenges, actual regime survival is not threatened. The regime can rely on two factors to ensure domestic stability: higher oil prices and a highly developed system of patronage and repression. Oil constitutes the main source of government revenue, representing 80 percent of foreign earnings, about 60 percent of government revenue, and 30 percent of GDP.[20] Hence, oil prices indicate government spending power. Iran sold crude oil for $35 per barrel in 2004 and $51 per barrel just one year later.[21] In light of recent high oil prices, the regime is well financed to continue to buy social peace through a set of subsidies. These subsidies range from simple consumption subsidies, for example, gasoline still costs about $0.40 per gallon, to more complex transfer payments. Higher oil prices have also helped Iran's balance of payments and have enabled the government to reduce external debt, with the remaining debt being primarily domestic.

Moreover, the oil boom has resulted in massive payments into the Oil Stabilization Fund, created in 2000 both to provide a cushion for future oil price declines and to operate as an investment trust to promote current growth. Iranian budgets since then have not abided by the fund's original rules, and the government has liberally dipped into the fund to prop up current spending. In the long term, these populist expenditures will be regretted if oil prices do collapse. In the meantime, however, with the rise in oil prices, government revenue and spending has been able to exceed initial budgetary estimates. Non-oil exports increased 24 percent in 2005, proving that some of that capital is supporting overall growth as well.[22] The 2006–2007 budget is based on an oil price of $40 per barrel, which roughly equates to an almost 50 percent increase in public spending since last year. Hence, the persistent oil spike has delayed any moment of reckoning by many years.

The oil revenues underpin a mature system of patronage and repression that solidifies a support base and deters opposition. Loyal regime supporters can justifiably point to quality of life improvements that tend to be lost in the review of Iran's dismal postrevolution macroeconomic performance. The most evident successes are in education and health care. For example, adult literacy rates have increased from 50 percent in 1980 to 78 percent in 2002.[23] The number of physicians per capita more than doubled during the same period.[24] Moreover, the Islamic republic fares much better than the shah's regime in providing public services to rural areas, where one-third of the Iranian population lives. Nowadays, most rural areas have paved roads, are connected to the power grid, and have adequate access to sanitary water. In addition to substantive achievements, the Iranian regime has created a sophisticated web of patronage through state and quasi-state organizations. Given that Iran's formal public sector constitutes about 50 percent of Iran's GDP, public agencies and state-owned enterprises are a critical resource for dispensing jobs and cash to dependable constituencies.

The unique feature of the Islamic republic is the wide array of quasi-state foundations called *bonyads*, which are semi-nongovernmental foundations holding private companies. Following the revolution, the new government confiscated the assets of wealthy businessmen closely associated with the shah. The confiscated businesses were incorporated into large conglomerate holdings. Although bonyads are technically separate from the state, their management is chosen from the clerical order close to the supreme leader. Because they are intertwined with the regime, the bonyads have effectively displaced any independent industrial class through political pressures and economic favoritism. The bonyads even receive resource transfers from the state on top of their corporate earnings and religious donations, cementing their quasi-state status. The state channels resources to bonyads through a set of financial and legal means, including budgetary payments, interest subsidies, below-market exchange rates, special credits from state banks, tax exemption, immunity from legal restrictions, and monopoly status in various sectors. By some estimates, the total share of bonyads amounts to at least 20 percent of GDP.[25]

The nominal purpose of these foundations is to provide social services under the auspices of religious guidance. As such, their names reveal the purported target of their social services: Foundation for the Oppressed and Disabled (Bonyad-e Mostazafan va Janbazan), Martyr's Foundation (Bonyad-e Shahid), Housing Foundation (Bonyad-e Maskan), and Imam Khomeini Relief Committee (Komite Emdad-e Emam Khomeini). In reality, the bonyads are the preferred tool of social engineering for the clerical establishment. They accomplish three functions that strengthen the regime: social mobility, social security, and popular mobilization. The mass holdings of companies provide professional opportunities for members of the underclass who otherwise have no avenue for upward social mobility. The large number of recipients of social services is greatly dependent on the foundations. For example, close to three million people annually receive some form of aid through the Imam Khomeini Relief Committee. Because that same community is grateful for these foundations' efforts, the bonyads also operate as direct mobilization tools, indoctrinating and gathering masses for proregime activities.[26]

It is the range of state and quasi-state organizations that empower the state's ability to control Iranian society, while preventing the rise of an autonomous and competitive middle class. Parallel to the economic sector, there are a web of state and quasi-state organizations in the realm of public security and order. In addition to conventional military and police forces, the Islamic Revolution inspired the institutionalization of complementary armed forces and militias. The most well known are the Islamic Revolutionary Guards Corps and its volunteer counterpart, the Basij. In Iran's new authoritarianism, the army continues to be starved of investment and attention while the Revolutionary Guards and the Basij supply the recruiting pools for future leadership and the regime's local representatives. When challenged, the regime can resort to the ubiquitous presence of these armed masses to intimidate or suppress opposition.

In this context, much has been written about Iran's burgeoning youth and its discontent. The more infamous example of Basij activity is their involvement in quelling youth unrest, such as the student protests in July 1999. Even if the regime has recently had to subdue disgruntled youth, demographic trends indicate that the regime might soon not even be required to call on its coercive apparatus. As birth rates began to drop toward the end of the Iran-Iraq War in 1988, demographic pressure has been easing, with the last of the baby boomers due to enter the labor market by the end of this decade. Subsequently, the labor force growth rate will shrink to 1.7 percent, about half of the rate in 2000 and easily supported by current growth.[27] Recent evidence of Iran's economic and social order suggests that the regime does not face an imminent popular challenge and certainly has the means to confront any domestic opponents until this demographic reversal is completed.

Moreover, empirical and theoretical evidence on the durability of comparable authoritarian regimes imply astounding stability for Iran. Oil states, according to a detailed study on oil wealth and regime survival from 1960 to 1999 by Benjamin Smith, maintain remarkably durable regimes both in boom and bust periods.[28] Similarly, Eva Bellin's examination of Middle Eastern authoritarianism finds overwhelming proof that both discretionary patronage and a strong coercive apparatus are vital ingredients for the survival of authoritarianism.[29] In light of the findings above, widespread unhappiness in Iran poses no immediate threat to the regime. Rather, the Iranian public has abandoned opposition in favor of apathy, and the Iranian regime possesses the financial or coercive means to co-opt or repress any domestic challenge at least for the next decade until demographic and their related economic trends turn more favorably for Tehran.

Implications for Iran and the World

The defeat of the reformist movement has drastically reduced internal demands for change. Instead, the regime is primarily concerned with withstanding international pressure. Iran had just been slowly extricating itself from international isolation due to skilled diplomacy on part of the Khatami administration. The crackdown on reformists starting in 2003 coincided with growing international attention on Iran's nuclear program. As mentioned earlier, the achievement of nuclear status is of paramount interest to the regime in Tehran because it provides limited immunity vis-à-vis external challengers and simultaneously heightens domestic legitimacy. Viewed from Teheran, those benefits outweigh the potential costs of confrontation over the nuclear program.

Although highly improbable, a military strike against Iran would rally the Iranian population as well as the international community firmly in support of the regime. Instead, the United Nations could issue a set of sanctions against Iran. In that case, the effect would depend on the nature of the sanctions. Economically, Iran is fairly immune to sanctions in the short term. Only a limitation on oil sales would have any immediate impact on decisionmaking in Tehran. Current high oil prices are demand driven, however, and it is thus virtually unthinkable that the world would curtail the producer of 5 percent of global oil production. Similarly, at 10.5 percent of GDP, Iran's external debt is very low, so Iran cannot be compelled by debt repayment.[30] Iran needs to integrate into the world economy eventually, but it can endure its isolationist stance for the foreseeable future.

International pressure could only affect Iran's political economy in the short term if it sparked elite rivalry. This could be in the form of "smart" sanctions: travel bans, asset freezing, or economic sanctions that selectively target members of Iran's leadership and their affiliate corporations (bonyads and subsidiaries). In particular, the financial interests of pragmatic conservatives such as Rafsanjani are more affected by economic sanctions than the hawkish leadership around Ahmadinejad. Another factor provoking factionalism could be developments in the region, especially in Iraq or Lebanon, if Iran's leadership is faced to choose between pragmatism and ideology in strategic decisions. That being said, the current process of consolidating Iran's new authoritarianism is aimed precisely to reduce such factional infighting.

Iran's new authoritarianism is producing a new leadership elite, constituting a form of regime change in terms of personnel at least. These changes may not yet be structural enough to warrant claims of a change in regime type. Nevertheless, Iran is gradually undermining its unique clerical theocracy with a shift toward conventional authoritarian models. Lacking any political or economic urgency for reform, this internal regime change is likely to address its most serious structural weakness: factionalism. The constitutionality of the Islamic republic inherently produces competing power centers that demand authority based on constitutional ambiguity. Iran's new authoritarianism is gradually tackling the danger of elite rivalry by streamlining Iran's political hierarchy. The immediate winners are the office of the supreme leader and the state security apparatus, especially the Revolutionary Guards and the Basij. In this respect, Iran will increasingly resemble other Middle Eastern authoritarian regimes.

In the long term, however, there are two major challenges to the regime. First, regardless of the harmonious relationship between the supreme leader and the security apparatus today, there is no long-term guarantee of mutual loyalty. At some point, the militarization of Iran's government may directly pose a threat to Khamenei's leadership and thus provoke an internal power struggle. Second, in terms of political economy, Iran is caught in a "structural trap" in which the political system prevents the proper allocation of economic resources.[31] The fundamental retardation of Iran's economic development cannot be forever compensated by buoyed oil prices.

At some point, Iran will have to pursue a path of economic liberalization and develop a more accountable and productive mechanism for spending its oil revenues. This development in turn will undermine the elite's power bases and open space for new social forces. Furthermore, Iran's economy as a whole, especially its hydrocarbon industry, requires large levels of foreign investment. Iran's oil and gas sectors alone need more than $160 billion through 2030, multiples of Iran's current level of foreign investment.[32] Today's oil fortune may be acting like a drug on Iran's rulers, but no high lasts forever.

In the meantime, Iran's regime can enjoy political stability and increased legitimacy, courtesy of high oil prices. Oil revenues grease the wheels of the economy, finance an elaborate system of patronage, and further strengthen the machinery of repression. In Iran's case, the oil boom will facilitate the transformation of the theocratic republic into a more conventional Middle Eastern authoritarian regime. Moreover, the timing of the oil boom has been especially fortuitous, consolidating the regime until the demographic reversal begins around 2010, when lower post-1988 birth rates will slowly diminish the socioeconomic urgency of reform. The Iranian regime is changing, but not for the better.

Notes

1. Ali Ansari, "Continuous Regime Change From Within," *The Washington Quarterly* 26, no. 4 (Autumn 2003): 59.
2. "Will Iran's Presidential Election Make a Difference?" *Economist*, June 11, 2005, p. 43.
3. Hossein Bastani, "Naghsh-eh ostad dar ehdam-eh mortedan," *Rooz*, November 15, 2005, http://roozonline.com/02article/011721.shtml.
4. Hossein Seifzadeh, "The Landscape of Factional Politics in Iran," *MEI Perspective*, August 20, 2002, http://www.mideasti.org/articles/doc62.html.
5. For official biographies of each cabinet member in Ahmadinejad's government, see http://www.khedmat.ir (in Farsi).
6. Meysam Tavab, "Sepah sahm-e bishtari az dolat khast," *Rooz*, December 6, 2005, http://roozonline.com/01newsstory/012278.shtml.

7. "President's Former Right Hand Man for Oil Ministry Rejected," Iran Press Service, August 24, 2005, http://www.iran-press-service.com/ips/articles-2005/august-2005/ahmadinejad_cabinet_24805.shtml; "Oil Minister Nominee Rejected," Reuters, November 23, 2005, http://english.aljazeera.net/NR/exeres/C505AFFA-D606-4321-B223-D571C709E40E.htm.
8. "Kamal Kharrazi be reyasat-e shora-ye rahbordi-ye ravabat-e khareji mansub shod," *Aftab-e-Yazd*, June 26, 2006, p. 2.
9. Kamal Nazer Yasin, "Climactic Political Battle Between Hardliners and Pragmatists Looms in Iran," *Eurasia Insight*, November 21, 2005, http://www.eurasianet.org/departments/insight/articles/eav112105a.shtml.
10. Ali Gheissari and Vali Nasr, "The Conservative Consolidation in Iran," *Survival* 47, no. 2 (Summer 2005): 188.
11. World Bank, "World Development Indicators 2005," http://devdata.worldbank.org/wdi2005/index2.htm.
12. All employment-related figures assume no labor productivity growth. See World Bank, "Iran: Medium Term Framework for Transition," *World Bank Report*, no. 25848 (April 2003), p. iv.
13. United Nations Development Program, "UN Human Development Report 2005," http://hdr.undp.org/reports/global/2005/pdf/HDR05_complete.pdf, p. 270.
14. Stephen Knowles, "Inequality and Economic Growth," *Journal of Development Studies* 41, no. 1 (January 2005): 135.
15. Joint Economic Committee, *Energy and the Iranian Economy: Hearing before the Joint Economic Committee*, 109th Cong., 2nd sess., 2006, http://www.house.gov/jec/hearings/testimony/109/07-25-06_iran_Simons.pdf (statement of Paul Simons, U.S. Department of State); Joint Economic Committee, *Energy and the Iranian Economy: Hearing before the Joint Economic Committee*, 109th Cong., 2nd sess., 2006, http://www.house.gov/jec/hearings/testimony/109/07-25-06_iran_Schott.pdf (statement of Jeffrey J. Schott).
16. Reza Bayegan, "Iran's New Oil Disorder: Interview With Dr. Parviz Mina," *Ekbatan Observer*, August 4, 2005, http://bayegan.blogspot.com/2005/08/irans-new-oil-disorder-interview-with.html.
17. Ibid.
18. Kjetil Bjorvatn and Kjetil Selvik, "Destructive Competition: Oil and Rent Seeking in Iran" (paper, Norwegian School of Economics and Business Administration, April 21, 2005).
19. Akbar Torbat, "Impacts of the U.S. Trade and Financial Sanctions on Iran," *World Economy* 28, no. 3 (March 2005): 432.
20. Economic Research and Policy Department, Central Bank of the Islamic Republic of Iran, "Annual Review 1383 (2004/05)," September 2005, http://www.cbi.ir/default_en.aspx. For an exact analysis of Iran's public finances, see Albrecht

Frischenschlager, “How Iran Finances Itself,” *Middle East Strategies*, December 2000, http://www.mestrategies.com/finances_content.htm.

21. Energy Information Administration, U.S. Department of Energy, “Spot Prices for Crude Oil and Petroleum Products,” http://tonto.eia.doe.gov/dnav/pet/pet_pri_spt_s1_d.htm.

22. Azam Mohebbi, “Economic Focus: Non-Oil Exports,” *Iran Daily*, April 3, 2006, http://www.irandaily.ir/1385/2527/html/focus.htm.

23. World Resources Institute, “Country Profile - Iran, Islamic Rep.,” http://earthtrends.wri.org/text/population-health/country-profile-87.html.

24. Based on the total number of physicians in 1980 according to the Academy of Medical Sciences of the Islamic Republic of Iran. Reza Malekzadeh, Azarakhsh Mokri, and Pejman Azarmina, “Medical Science and Research in Iran,” *Archives of Iranian Medicine* 4, no. 1 (January 2001), http://www.ams.ac.ir/AIM/0141/malekzadeh0141.html.

25. Ali Abootalebi, “An Evaluation of 25 Years of the Revolution,” *Middle East Review of International Affairs* 8, no. 2 (June 2004): 43.

26. Ali Saeidi, “The Accountability of Para-governmental Organizations,” *Iranian Studies* 37, no. 3 (September 2004): 486–487.

27. International Monetary Fund, “Staff Report for the 2004 Article IV Consultation,” September 2004, p. 10, http:// www.imf.org/external/pubs/ft/scr/2004/cr04306.pdf.

28. Benjamin Smith, “Oil Wealth and Regime Survival in the Developing World 1960–1999,” *American Journal of Political Science* 48, no. 2 (April 2004): 232–243.

29. Eva Bellin, “The Robustness of Authoritarianism in the Middle East: Exceptionalism in Comparative Perspective,” *Comparative Politics* 36, no. 2 (January 2004): 139.

30. “Islamic Republic of Iran: 2005 Article IV Consultation,” *IMF Country Report*, no. 06/154 (April 2006), http://www.imf.org/external/pubs/ft/scr/2006/cr06154.pdf.

31. Parvin Alizadeh, “Iran’s Quandary: Economic Reforms and the Structural Trap,” *Brown Journal of World Affairs* 9, no. 2 (Winter/Spring 2003): 267.

32. International Energy Agency, *World Energy Outlook 2005*, pp. 369–370.

Karim Sadjadpour

How Relevant Is the Iranian Street?

Gauging popular sentiment in Iran is notoriously difficult. Domestically conducted independent opinion polls are rarely allowed, and the results of government-sponsored polls are often, though not always, predictably skewed. In 2003, former revolutionary hostage-taker turned prominent reformist Abbas Abdi conducted an independent poll and found that three-quarters of Iranians favored having relations with the United States.[1] He was summarily imprisoned for publishing the results, charged with "collaborat[ing] with U.S. elements and British intelligence" and conducting "psychological warfare" aimed at overthrowing the government. Not guaranteed the "freedom after speech" of open societies, Iranians, although more publicly outspoken than most peoples in the Middle East, are inherently suspicious of formal questioning, making telephone polls conducted from abroad highly unreliable. Moreover, a socially diverse population of nearly 70 million people does not lend itself easily to sweeping generalizations about "what Iranians want."

In the absence of reliable public opinion measurements, alternative means of discerning the hopes, demands, and concerns of the Iranian street include campaign platforms, voter turnout, and election results. To be sure, elections in Iran are not open. Candidates are vigorously

Karim Sadjadpour is an analyst with the International Crisis Group, based in Washington D.C. and Tehran.

The Washington Quarterly • 30:1 pp. 151–162.

prescreened and vetted by the unelected Islamic Guardian Council. Of the council's 12 members, six are appointed directly by Supreme Leader Ayatollah Ali Khamenei; the other six are appointed by the head of the judiciary, who is also selected by the supreme leader. Those deemed insufficiently sympathetic to the country's theocratic system of governance are weeded out. Candidates espousing a secular platform are barred from entering all elections, and women are barred from running in presidential elections. Once the filtering occurs, however, genuine competition and debate does take place among those permitted to run. Further, ever since the unanticipated landslide election of reform-minded president Muhammad Khatami in 1997, whose platform of democracy and social liberalization unexpectedly electrified the country's younger generation and women, successful Iranian politicians have learned to employ language that will appeal to voters.

During Iran's June 2005 presidential elections, seven candidates marketed themselves to the masses. Former president Hashemi Rafsanjani, considered the man to beat, acknowledged the country's many shortcomings—economic malaise, social restrictions, international isolation—and vowed to deliver change. Former Revolutionary Guards commander Muhammad Bagher Ghalibaf promised law and order. Moderate cleric Hojatoleslam Mehdi Karroubi claimed that he would somehow dole out 50,000 toman (about $60) per month to every Iranian. Mostafa Moin, the hope of the reform movement, ran on a platform of democracy and human rights. Tehran mayor Mahmoud Ahmadinejad, then considered a dark horse, vowed to fight corruption and put oil profits on Iranians' dinner tables.

If there was a common theme among all of the candidates, it was change. Nearly every one acknowledged the country's decrepit economy, corruption, and despair of the youth. Several, including Rafsanjani, claimed they would "fix" relations with the United States. Even hardline Ahmadinejad vowed he was not interested in pushing a religiously austere, socially conservative agenda. As one blue-collar worker in Tehran wryly commented days before the election, "Everybody is running on a platform of reform now. Does that mean they're admitting what they've been doing for the past 26 years had been wrong?"[2]

The issues not raised in campaigns were equally telling. Despite the Iranian government's fixation with Israel, no candidate vowed to champion the Palestinian cause or to pursue a hard-line policy against Israel. Indeed, Israel, or "the Zionist entity," was hardly even mentioned. Despite widespread reports both in the state-monitored Iranian media and Western media that all Iranians feel very strongly about the nuclear project, no candidate vowed to deliver Iran nuclear energy or to pursue an uncompromising nuclear posture. On the contrary, Rafsanjani's top aide, Muhammad Atrianfar, claimed that Rafsanjani would suspend uranium enrichment if elected president.[3]

Yet, despite the fact that Iran's young population likely aspires for international integration more than uranium enrichment and for conciliation with the United States rather than confrontation with Israel, Iran's foreign policy posture has in no way reflected these demands, especially under Ahmadinejad. This is due in part to the fact that the constitutional authority of elected institutions in Iran, particularly the presidency and parliament, are dwarfed by those of unelected institutions, such as the supreme leader and Guardian Council. Although it is widely believed that Khamenei makes decisions by consensus rather than decree, Iranian public opinion has never appeared to figure prominently in Khamenei's consensus-building process. This begs the question: How, if at all, do the demands of the people factor into Tehran's foreign policy? Do the Iranian people care about their government's foreign policy? If so, and their opinions continue to be ignored, will people start agitating?

Palestine: A Regional, Not Domestic, Recruiting Tool

On the surface, Iran's belligerence toward Israel is puzzling. At a time when most Arab governments, including mainstream Palestinian leaders, have come to terms with Israel's existence, non-Arab Iran continues to call for eradication of the Jewish state.[4] Ahmadinejad has attacked Israel as a "tumor" that should be "wiped off the map" or relocated, and dismissed the Holocaust as a "myth." In the face of widespread international criticism, the Iranian president has been essentially unrepentant, saying, "Western reactions are invalid.... [M]y words are the Iranian nation's words."[5]

Ahmadinejad's confidence that the Iranian public shares his intense hostility toward Israel is misplaced. Throughout nearly three decades of calls for the liberation of Jerusalem, Iran's revolutionary regime has never come to terms with essential realities. There exists no inherent reason why the Israeli-Palestinian struggle should be an issue of overriding concern to the average Iranian. Iran has no territorial disputes with Israel, no Palestinian refugee problem, a long history of contentious relations with the Arab world, and an even longer history of tolerance vis-à-vis the Jewish people. To this day, the Jewish community in Iran, numbering around 25,000, is the largest in the Middle East outside of Israel. Although the regime in Tehran continues to demonize Israel and lionize Palestine in the media, popular Iranian sentiment toward the Arab-Israeli dispute has gradually grown numb. It is a distant conflict that has insufficient tangible impact on their daily lives to cause a significant portion of the population to agitate either for or against it.

Ironically, anti-Israel sentiment among Iranians was much greater prior to the 1979 revolution, during the reign of Shah Muhammad Reza Pahlavi. The shah's cozy relationship with Tel Aviv was widely unpopular, not least because Israeli Mossad agents were rumored to have trained the shah's seemingly ubiquitous and oppressive secret police force, SAVAK. When Iran's monarchy was overthrown, the keys to the de facto Israeli embassy in Tehran were handed over to Yasser Arafat's Palestinian Liberation Organization, and the ascendant Ayatollah Ruhollah Khomeini declared that Iran's Islamic Revolution would march onward until the "liberation of Jerusalem." Exaltation of the Palestinian cause and excoriation of "the Zionist entity" quickly became one of the hallmarks of the foreign and domestic policies of the newly inaugurated Islamic Republic of Iran.

Three decades later, however, few among Iran's restive young population have much interest in marching onward to Jerusalem. Beset by double-digit inflation and unemployment, Iran's postrevolutionary generation is well aware that the ideological hubris of their parents' generation, a hodgepodge of Islamism, anti-imperialism, anti-Zionism, and Marxism, has bore the country little fruit apart from a soiled international reputation, political isolation, and economic hardship. During student protests in the summer of 2003, amidst calls for greater democracy and freedom, one popular slogan, delivered in rhythmic Persian, was "forget about Palestine, think about us!"[6]

Much of Iran's political elite, despite remaining sympathetic to the Palestinian cause, has also come to terms with the fact that the government's rhetoric toward Israel is self-defeating. Widely echoed in Tehran are the words of Ali Reza Alavi-Tabar, a strident revolutionary cum reformist who has said, "We need to reinvent ourselves. We shouldn't be chanting 'death to Israel'; we should be saying 'long live Palestine.' We needn't be more Palestinian than the Palestinians themselves." [7] The popular reformist party, the Islamic Participation Front, criticized Ahmadinejad's comments on Israel, saying, "When the country is facing an international crisis, such expressions impose a heavy burden on the country's political, security, and economic interests." Even conservative lawmaker Heshmatollah Falahatzadeh similarly claimed, "Our officials should realize that there are many facts in the world that we should not pass judgment on in a way that the world finds fault with."[8]

Iran's continued support for Hizballah and Hamas is another elite-driven policy on which the domestic public has had little or no impact. Aid workers in Iran log complaints from resentful Iranian earthquake victims who claim their government would be quicker in sending support if the earthquake had been in Gaza or southern Lebanon.[9] In the aftermath of Israeli bombings in July 2006, Iran's offer to help finance and rebuild southern Lebanon spurred resentment at home. As one Tehran resident said, "We Iranians have a saying, 'We should save our own house first and then save the mosque.' A lot of people think this way. The government should help its people first, and then help the people in Lebanon."[10]

Ahmadinejad's diatribes against Israel make more strategic sense in the regional context. Iran sees itself engaged in a battle with the United States for regional power, influence, and Arab and Muslim hearts and minds. In taking on the United States, Iran has also targeted U.S. regional allies Egypt, Jordan, and Saudi Arabia. From Tehran's perspective, these "scandalous" governments may be aligned with Washington, but their populations are ripe for recruitment. In this context, Ahmadinejad's denunciations of Israel read as calculated attempts to shame U.S.-loyal Arab leaders and score political points on the Arab and Muslim street, rather than the random musings of a deranged fundamentalist. Although such language alienates the West and falls largely on deaf ears among Iran's slogan-fatigued population, it makes Ahmadinejad's star shine in places such as Cairo, Amman, and Damascus.[11]

Currying favor on the Arab street is integral to Iran's goal of becoming the Middle East's dominant power and a bulwark against perceived U.S. imperialist ambitions in the region. Although Tehran's stock may be soaring at the moment, its ambitions to be the anti-imperialist vanguard of the largely Sunni Arab Middle East will ultimately be undermined by the fact that it is Shi'a and Persian. As 1,400 years of contentious Arab-Iranian relations have shown, Muslim solidarity has never transcended the Arab-Persian divide. Moreover, there is reason to believe the Arab masses admire Iran's Islamic republic much in the same way the Latin American street once romanticized Fidel Castro's Cuba. They praise the defiant political order from afar but do not wish it for themselves. Opinion polls show the Arab nation in which Arabs would most like to live is not religiously austere Saudi Arabia but economically thriving, socially open, and internationally integrated Dubai.

Manufacturing Support for the Nuclear Project

A similar story is told by looking at the nuclear issue. In early 2006, hundreds of Iranian schoolgirls were bused to a government-organized rally in support of the country's nuclear program. The smiling teenage girls shouted slogans and held up hand-written placards in Persian and in English for the benefit of the international media, extolling Iran's nuclear project. The next day, the *Financial Times* ran a front-page photo of a young Iranian girl holding up a sign that was intended to read, "Nuclear energy is our obvious right." The word "nuclear" was misspelled, however, and instead the unwitting girl's sign read, "Unclear energy is our obviouse right."

This incident is in some ways emblematic of the Iranian government's painstaking but often clumsy efforts to project the nuclear project internationally as popularly driven and universally supported. How strongly could a 14-year-old girl feel about indigenous uranium enrichment? As Atrianfar, Rafsanjani's adviser, said, "People have been hearing these things about having the right to have or to possess this [nuclear] capability. And, naturally, if you ask an Iranian whether [they] want this right or not, they would say they do want it. But if you ask, though, 'What is nuclear energy?' they might not be able to tell you what it is."[12]

As Tehran has presented it to the Iranian public, the goal of France, Germany, the United Kingdom, and the United States is not to prevent Iran from enriching uranium and weaponizing it but to deny Iran access to nuclear energy in order to keep it backward and dependent on the West. As lead nuclear negotiator Ali Larijani frequently says, "The West wants two classes of nations ... [t]hose that have nuclear technology and can be advanced, and nations that must be restricted to production of tomato juice and air conditioners."[13]

Even those sympathetic to Iran's nuclear project and critical of U.S. "double standards" testify to the government's manipulation of "popular opinion." As a respected Iranian intellectual said in 2005, "The regime consistently represses popular will, but when it comes to the nuclear program they conveniently invoke the name of the people."[14] In a strikingly candid op-ed in the *Financial Times* in May 2006, former Iranian deputy foreign minister Abbas Maleki dismissed the notion that the nuclear program is driven by popular demand.

> Reports suggest that Tehran's official joy over the nuclear breakthrough is shared by a large segment of Iranian society. Such reports should not be taken as evidence that the Iranian people share their government's views, and should not be used as a pretext for using force against Iran's population.... The general public does not consider the nuclear issue to be of vital importance. Nuclear technology will do little for the average Iranian; it cannot create more jobs for a country that needs one million jobs annually, it cannot change the chronic low efficiency, productivity, and effectiveness of the economy and management, and it will do nothing to improve Iran's commercial ties with the rest of the world.[15]

Christopher de Bellaigue, an *Economist* correspondent who has spent the last several years living in Tehran, has also voiced skepticism regarding popular Iranian support for the nuclear project.

> Iranians who vocally support their country's nuclear ambitions tend to be strong supporters of the Islamic Republic, and they are a minority. In today's sullenly depoliticized Iran, it is the mundane issues that animate people: the price of staple products, for instance, or changes in the terms of required military service. In the four and a half years that I have lived in Iran … I have never witnessed a spontaneous discussion of the nuclear program among average Iranians.
>
> True, the few opinion polls that have been commissioned, mostly by organs close to Iran's conservative establishment, found strong public support for the country's declared goal of becoming a nuclear fuel producer. But there is good reason to be skeptical about their findings. It would be quite remarkable if a populace increasingly disengaged from politics were suddenly energized by something as arcane as nuclear fuel and its byproducts.[16]

Adding to the uncertainty, Tehran closely controls debate and research on this topic in the domestic Iranian media. The Iranian government has successfully presented the nuclear program as one supported by all Iranian patriots and as an issue of deep national pride. Visiting Western reporters have largely followed suit, with numerous headlines declaring that all Iranians, regardless of their political creed, are united behind the country's nuclear program.[17] In the absence of solid empirical evidence, analysts and journalists cite government-sponsored surveys that indicate that nearly 85 percent of the Iranian public supports the country's nuclear program.[18] Aside from the obvious bias of government-sponsored polls, such surveys are inherently flawed because their questions imply that the nuclear program is a risk-free enterprise and offer those surveyed no alternative.[19]

Popular opinion is more nuanced than what the Iranian government would like the world to believe. To be sure, Iranians are a ferociously nationalistic people; and many, even those unsympathetic to the regime, are vocally supportive of their government's nuclear ambitions for a variety of reasons: Iran needs to prepare for life after oil resources run out; Western double standards permit India, Pakistan, and Israel to have nuclear programs; Iran lives in a dangerous neighborhood and thus need not only a nuclear energy program but also a nuclear weapon.

Yet, many Iranians also express uncertainty about the nuclear project, concerned about the direction in which the country is headed.[20] The Iran-Iraq War (1980–1988) was one of the bloodiest wars of the second half of the twentieth century, leaving about 500,000 Iranians killed or wounded. The country is still emerging from this postwar depression, both emotionally and economically, and few Iranians romanticize the prospect of conflict or militarization.

Given the tremendous effort the government has made to invoke Iranians' keen sense of nationalism, pointing out Western double standards, extolling the virtues of nuclear energy, and praising the country's scientists, the government clearly perceives public opinion as a powerful bargaining tool. Yet, ascertaining what the public really thinks about nuclearization is difficult. Few Iranians spend much time debating the merits of uranium enrichment, but any popular opposition to the government's nuclear posture has so far been negligible, given that Iran has paid few tangible costs for its intransigence. Objectively speaking, Iran has thus far seemingly outwitted Western interlocutors consumed with bloodletting in Iraq and soaring oil prices. Whereas the "dialogue of civilizations" of the Khatami era landed Iran in the "axis of evil," Ahmadinejad's uncompromising and sometimes belligerent posture has netted Iran economic and nuclear incentives from the European Union and a conditional offer of dialogue from the United States that were not offered during Khatami's eight-year tenure.

Popular Upheaval: A Bridge Too Far?

So, if Iranians do not wake up in the morning with enriched uranium or the fate of Palestine on their minds, what are they thinking about, and why are they unhappy? The simple answer is economic dignity or a lack thereof. In real terms, per capita income in today's Iran is roughly one-half what it was shortly before the shah's downfall. As de Bellaigue puts it, "For most Iranians, the price of food and the government's failure to lower it are more important [than the nuclear program]."[21] Among the older generation of Iranians, revolutionary promises of economic deliverance have gone largely unmet.

The regime's fundamental challenge, however, is not middle-aged or geriatric Iranians nostalgic for the economic and social freedoms of their youth. Rather, it is the two-thirds of the population under the age of 32 that did not experience the repression and corruption of the shah's reign and hence have no special loyalty to the 1979 revolution or the Islamic republic. At the onset of the revolution, Khomeini encouraged families to produce many offspring in order to produce a robust Islamic society, an edict that has now come back to burden the regime tremendously. These "children of the revolution" struggle to enter university and find jobs and identify very little with the austerely religious society in which they live. Many have access to satellite television and the Internet and see how their counterparts in the rest of the world, particularly in the West, are living and long for the same freedoms and opportunities.

An inability to influence their government's foreign policy positions may not be high on Iranians' list of grievances given their economic and social woes. Indeed, both anecdotal and empirical evidence suggests that popular discontent in Iran is deep seated and widespread and that the majority of Iranians aspire to see sweeping political, economic, and social reform in their country. Yet, when asked how and when this change should occur, they offer few concrete ideas aside from hoping that it occur *bedun-e khoonrizi* (without bloodshed).[22]

After the removal of the Taliban from Afghanistan, some Iranians romanticized about the prospect of a U.S. intervention in Tehran.[23] After more than three years of tumult and insecurity in next-door Iraq, however, talk of regime change is muted and a distant memory. Skepticism has increased about U.S. designs for the region. Although Iran arguably remains the least anti-U.S. population in the entire Muslim Middle East, the United States has lost considerable political capital on the Iranian street in the aftermath of the Iraq war.

Many Iranians have come to see the U.S. project in Iraq as less about democracy and more as a botched attempt to expropriate the country's oil resources. As such, no one looks to Iraq as a paradigm for change. As one middle-aged Tehran resident said, "When we look at the situation in Iraq, it doesn't appear to us a choice between democracy and authoritarianism but rather stability and unrest. Few people are happy in Iran, but nobody wants unrest."[24] Whereas prior to the Iraq war, hope for a swift and painless change of leadership in Tehran may have existed, the abstract optimism of a rapid political upheaval has been eclipsed by the fear of the unknown tumult that would follow. Given the prevailing chaos in the Middle East, millions of Iranians, even those fundamentally opposed to the Islamic republic, prefer the continuation of a flawed system to the potential lawlessness and destruction seen in Iraq and Lebanon. They are increasingly inclined to deal with the devil they know rather than the one they do not.

Although to the casual observer the depth of Iranian popular discontent appears unsustainable, facts on the ground give little evidence that change is imminent. For one, nothing close to an organized channel for the political expression of popular discontent exists, namely a credible, united opposition movement with significant support and concrete proposals. Domestically, the country's reform movement is at the moment impotent and indecisive. Its members may be dubious that the system can be reformed from within, but at the same time they are largely unwilling to take the route of reformist cum dissident Akbar Ganji in calling for a referendum on the system.[25] Although unhappiness with the government is broad and deep and there may likely be periodic hiccups of unrest, as of yet there is no easily viable mechanism for this displeasure to find a political outlet or build greater momentum.

As past pro-democracy and student protests have shown, the war- and revolution-weary Iranian populace's aversion to violence and confrontation makes it no match for the regime's intimidating and seemingly unwavering security and intelligence apparatus, namely the easily roused Basij militia and Revolutionary Guards. Moreover, few Iranians can be compelled to take to the streets given an economic situation that for many teeters between subsistence and poverty, affording people neither the luxury to risk their livelihoods waging political protest nor the "nothing to lose" desperation and rage that can result from penury. Support for the regime also comes from roughly 20 percent of the Iranian population that can be counted on to vote for conservative candidates consistently and a wealthy and powerful coterie of *bazaaris* (businessmen) and *bonyads* (religious "foundations") that are heavily invested in the status quo.

It is unclear, therefore, if the fundamental disconnect between Iranian popular sentiment and Iranian foreign policy can be sustainable over the long term. At a time when the majority of Iran's young population wants to be reintegrated in the international community, Ahmadinejad's conduct is leading Iran down a path of further isolation. At the moment, however, foreign policy is not a bread and butter issue in Iran. Although popular grumblings may exist that Iranian money, much needed at home, is being used to support Hizballah and Hamas or being defiantly poured into a nuclear program with uncertain benefits, neither issue in isolation is animus enough for Iranians to agitate.

This will likely remain the case as long as few costs in terms of domestic economic conditions are associated with the government's defiant stance. If and when domestic economic conditions in Iran begin to deteriorate, however, whether as a result of isolation, sanctions, or general economic mismanagement, the regime, in particular Supreme Leader Ayatollah Khamenei, may decide to change course. Despite often projecting an uncompromising stance, regime survival, not ideology, is paramount for the country's theocratic elite.

A recently publicized letter written by Khomeini in 1988 shows that, despite his previous avowals to continue the Iran-Iraq War until Saddam Hussein's removal from power, the Iranian public's war fatigue was a primary factor in compelling Khomeini to swallow the "poison chalice" and agree to a cease-fire—after eight years and nearly 500,000 casualties.[26] Today, Iran's leadership, faced with a larger, younger, and revolution-fatigued society, is cognizant of the fact that it cannot ask the nation to make similar sacrifices of blood and treasure in order to maintain a defiant foreign policy. At the moment, however, buoyed by soaring oil prices and U.S. difficulties in Iraq, the regime is banking on the fact that it will not have to.

Notes

1. Human Rights Watch, "Iran," *World Report 2003* (New York: Human Rights Watch, 2003), http://www.hrw.org/wr2k3/mideast3.html.
2. Iranian worker, interview with author, Tehran, June 2005.
3. Muhammad Atrianfar, interview with author, Tehran, May 2005.
4. See Karim Sadjadpour and Ray Takeyh, "Behind Israel's Hard-Line Stance on Israel," *Boston Globe*, December 23, 2005, http://www.crisisgroup.org/home/index.cfm?id=3855.
5. "Iran Leader Defends Israel Remark," *BBC News*, October 28, 2005, http://news.bbc.co.uk/2/hi/middle_east/4384264.stm.
6. Karim Sadjadpour and Afshin Molavi, "Tehran Dispatch: Change Up," *New Republic*, November 3, 2003, https://ssl.tnr.com/p/docsub.mhtml?i=20031110&s=molavisadjadpour111003.
7. Ali Reza Alavi-Tabar, interview with author, Tehran, May 2005.
8. Karl Vick, "Iran's President Calls Holocaust 'Myth' in Latest Assault on Jews," *Washington Post*, December 15, 2005, p. A1.
9. United Nations Children's Fund and United Nations Development Program employees, interviews with author, Tehran, March–June 2005.
10. Michael Slackman, "Turmoil in the Mideast: Tehran; In the Streets, Aid to Hezbollah Stirs Iranian Fear and Resentment," *New York Times*, July 23, 2006, http://select.nytimes.com/search/restricted/article?res=F30F1FFA3F5B0C708EDDAE0894DE404482.
11. Saad Eddin Ibrahim, "The 'New Middle East' Bush Is Resisting," *Washington Post*, Wednesday, August 23, 2006, p. A15.
12. Muhammad Atrianfar, interview by Margaret Warner, *PBS NewsHour*, September 6, 2006, http://www.pbs.org/newshour/bb/middle_east/july-dec06/iran_09-06.html.
13. Ali Larijani, interview with Jam-e Jam television, July 16, 2005.
14. Iranian intellectual, interview with author, Tehran, June 2005.
15. Abbas Maleki, "Iran Is Eager to Defuse the Nuclear Squabble," *Financial Times*, May 9, 2006, http://www.ft.com/cms/s/c6310ec4-df83-11da-afe4-0000779e2340.html.
16. Christopher de Bellaigue, "Think Again: Iran," *Foreign Policy*, May/June 2005, http://www.foreignpolicy.com/story/cms.php?story_id=2828.
17. See Frances Harrison, "Iranians Unite Over Nuclear Row," *BBC News*, October 20, 2004, http://news.bbc.co.uk/2/hi/middle_east/3758762.stm; Robin Wright, "Desire for Nuclear Power a Uniting Factor in Iran; Issue Seen as a Matter of Independence, Reaction to U.S.," *Washington Post*, November 14, 2004, p. A25.

18. "Eighty-five Percent of Citizens Favor Continuation of Nuclear Activities," Islamic Republic News Agency, February 5, 2006, http://server30.irna.com/en/news/view/line-22/0602058193194754.htm.
19. De Bellaigue, "Think Again: Iran."
20. See Karim Sadjadpour, "Iranians Don't Want to Go Nuclear," *Washington Post*, February 3, 2004, http://www.crisisgroup.org/home/index.cfm?id=2504&l=1.
21. Christopher de Bellaigue, "Bush, Iran, and the Bomb," *New York Review of Books* 52, no. 3 (February 24, 2005), http://www.nybooks.com/articles/17762?email.
22. International Crisis Group, "Iran: Discontent and Disarray," *Middle East Briefing*, no. 11 (October 2003), http://www.crisisgroup.org/home/index.cfm?action=login&ref_id=2324.
23. See Amy Waldman, "In Iran, an Angry Generation Longs for Jobs, More Freedom and Power." *New York Times*, December 7, 2001, http://www.iran-press-service.com/articles_2001/dec_2001/nyt_iran_81201.htm.
24. Iranian citizen, interview with author, Tehran, January 2005.
25. Akbar Ganji, "Letter to America," *Washington Post*, September 21, 2006, p. A25.
26. Nazila Fathi, "An Old Letter Casts Doubts on Iran's Goal for Uranium," *New York Times*, October 5, 2006, http://www.nytimes.com/2006/10/05/world/middleeast/05iran.html?ref=world.

Part V: Afghanistan

Peter van Ham and Jorrit Kamminga

Poppies for Peace: Reforming Afghanistan's Opium Industry

With the September 2005 parliamentary elections, Afghanistan took another important step toward democracy and stability. Over the past four years, President Hamid Karzai's government has put an end to decades of civil war and offered the Afghan people the possibility of rising from their abject poverty. These successes, however, are merely the silver lining of a massive cloud that still hangs over Afghanistan's future: the all-invasive drug industry that impedes the country's economic growth, fosters instability, and hampers its democratic aspirations. Afghanistan remains economically dependent on the illegal growth of opium poppy and the production and trafficking of drugs. Today, the Afghan drug economy generates $2.8 billion annually, or about 50 percent of Afghanistan's gross domestic product, making almost three million Afghans (12.6 percent of the population) dependent on poppy cultivation for their everyday needs.[1]

The U.S.-led invasion and reconstruction of Afghanistan since October 2001 has failed to destroy this drug-based economy. Of greater concern, Afghanistan has once again become the world's leading producer of opium, the narcotic product of opium poppies. Opium poppy

Peter van Ham is director of the global governance research program at the Clingendael Institute in The Hague and a professor at the College of Europe in Bruges, Belgium. Jorrit Kamminga is head of policy research for The Senlis Council in Kabul.

The Washington Quarterly • 30:1 pp. 69–81.

cultivation has now spread to almost every province of the country, and its crops deliver 92 percent of the opium produced worldwide, or roughly 90 percent of all heroin consumed.[2] These facts, as well as falling heroin prices on European streets, clearly indicate that Afghanistan's drug industry is again blossoming and that the international community's counternarcotics strategies are failing. The United States and the United Kingdom are leading a war on drugs in Afghanistan that is quite similar to the one in Colombia, where crops are destroyed by force without offering the local population sufficient alternative livelihoods. Despite years of extensive eradication activities, production and supply levels of illegal drugs have remained stable in Latin America, as have their purity levels and prices. This war on drugs, launched in 1971 by the Nixon administration, has cost $150 billion over 35 years and has seen the drug supply rise from 1,000 tons in 1970 to around 6,000 tons in 2006.[3]

The military counternarcotics strategy is clearly not only ineffective but even counterproductive, especially considering recent growing violence and mounting insurgency in Afghanistan's major poppy-growing areas. This strategy should therefore be replaced with a serious alternative that could be called "poppies for peace." Poppy crops can be used to produce medicines such as morphine and codeine, which are high-demand painkillers in a growing global market. The international community should help the Afghan government start a scientific pilot project to investigate further the practical implementation of a licensing system for Afghanistan. Such a system would allocate existing poppy crops for medicinal purposes, offering all stakeholders, from farmers to warlords, an opportunity to profit in a legal economy.

This alternative combines the best of both worlds. It stabilizes a crucial country in the global war on terrorism and alleviates the pain crisis in AIDS-stricken developing countries. It is not a silver bullet for Afghanistan's many troubles, but it does pave the way for the country to escape its current development and security crisis. For strategic and moral reasons, the international community should accept the poppies for peace project as a realistic and attractive alternative to current counternarcotics strategies.

Classic Counternarcotic Strategy Failures

Security and development are two inseparable components of the same reconstruction effort in Afghanistan, with opium located at the core of that nexus. Afghanistan's lawlessness breeds poverty, its poverty sustains instability, and drugs perpetuate this vicious cycle. The dependence of the Afghan economy on illegal opium production hinders economic development and poses a direct threat to the country's stability, reconstruction prospects, and establishment of the rule of law. Opium production serves as the livelihood of millions of Afghans, as well as the main source of income for the remnants of the Taliban forces. Afghan and U.S. officials have openly acknowledged that the illegal drug market "has corrupted the government from bottom to top, including governors and cabinet officials, and is financing warlords, local militias, the Taliban, and possibly Al Qaeda."[4] Although direct links between Al Qaeda and the drug trade are difficult to discern, opium clearly funds Al Qaeda indirectly, which uses drugs profits to support and maintain its terrorism network in Iraq and beyond.[5] The drug links Afghanistan directly to Iraq, one of the key countries through which opium is trafficked to Western consumer markets.[6] The stakes are high, and Afghanistan could easily slip back into chaos and insecurity if the international community does not make serious headway in tackling the country's lingering drug crisis.

Opium poppy has been officially prohibited since 2002, when Karzai declared a kind of jihad against the drug industry. The Afghan government receives considerable financial and hands-on support from the United States and key European players to eradicate opium poppy crops across the country. British Special Forces have been deployed to track down and dismantle the mobile drug laboratories that are used to convert opium into heroin. The United Kingdom is also involved in the development of alternative livelihoods for farmers, but clearly its main focus is to destroy poppy crops and drug laboratories. Germany has trained significant numbers of Afghan police officers in the use of military tactics to combat drug trafficking, and Italy is the lead country on reforming and rebuilding the Afghan criminal justice system. In 2004 the U.S. Drug Enforcement Agency set up a Central Poppy Eradication Force (CPEF) urging local leaders to destroy the poppy fields in the areas under their control.

The results of these forced eradication strategies, however, have been minimal, and the costs high. In 2005 the United States earmarked $150 million for eradication over a period of three years, but the CPEF eradicated only 250 hectares, or less than 1 percent of the relevant land, in that first year. That same year, the Afghan government managed to destroy only 5,000 hectares, which accounts for a mere 5 percent of the total poppy cultivation in 2005.[7] For 2006 the figures are even more astonishing. The first real, nationwide, massive eradication campaign has been counteracted by a bumper harvest of 6,100 tons of opium, an increase of 49 percent from 2005 and an all-time high.[8] Despite the eradication of 15,300 hectares in 2006, cultivation increased by 59 percent to 165,000 hectares.[9] The British government will have spent about $960 million from 2002 to 2007 on Afghan counternarcotics efforts, humanitarian assistance, and state building with very little to show for it.[10]

Karzai called on farmers in 2005 to halt poppy cultivation, threatening that the international community would use "all means available," possibly including aerial spraying, to eradicate the opium poppy.[11] He has so far managed to avoid aerial spraying, focusing instead on methods such as manual eradication. Nonetheless, all forms of eradication negatively impact the lives and health of farmers and wage laborers, their families, and their livestock. Doris Buddenberg, the representative of the United Nation Office on Drugs and Crime in Afghanistan, argued in 2004 that "eradication usually does not bring about sustainable reduction of poppy crop—it is a one-time, short-term effort. Also eradication usually pushes the prices up. As we have seen from the Taliban period, the one-year ban on opium-poppy cultivation increased prices enormously the following year and it became extremely attractive for farmers to cultivate poppy."[12] Kim Howells, the British minister of state dealing with Afghanistan, argued in February 2006 that "aerial spraying could cause famine [in Afghanistan], so we must be careful about it."[13]

Strong-arm eradication measures in Afghanistan would further alienate the local population without making any progress in the fight against drug production. As evidenced by the massive 2006 eradication campaign in the south, forced eradication initiatives complicate even more the already tenuous relationship between farmers and the central government. Farmers become disillusioned with the government and its policies and turn to local warlords or insurgent movements for support and protection.[14] Moreover, field research during early 2006 has revealed a direct link between forced eradication and increased hostility toward the international coalition forces and NATO-led International Security Assistance Forces in southern Afghanistan.[15] Farmers have seen no improvement in their living conditions since the 2001 invasion and are turning their backs on the local government. Meanwhile, the Taliban and other insurgent groups benefit from these misguided policies by offering support and services to farmers.[16] In sum, continuing with force-based counternarcotics policies will only fuel insurgency and terrorism, alienate farming communities, and create similar conditions to those that existed just before the Taliban movement took control of the country in the early 1990s. Forced eradication therefore remains counterproductive as long as the root causes of the opium problem, which are developmental and economic in nature, are ignored or not addressed effectively.

Some donor organizations take a different approach to the opium problem by focusing on the economic nature of the challenge. The European Union recently committed about €376 million to address Afghan opium production during 2006–2010 by stimulating alternative livelihoods.[17] The U.S. Agency for International Development and several European nongovernmental organizations have invested in new agricultural sectors and products, in some cases reintroducing crops that had previously provided many with steady incomes. Through compensation and subsidy arrangements, they are trying to promote products such as rose oil, saffron, nuts, raisins, and various fruits as alternatives to the lucrative poppy. Another strategy is to revive the Afghan carpet industry, which is trying to turn Afghanistan again into one of the world's leading carpet exporters.[18] These efforts are part of the UN-coordinated Counter Narcotics Trust Fund to finance alternative livelihoods, new government institutions dealing with drug control, a counternarcotics information campaign, local and regional drug law enforcement units, and treatment for drug addiction. The EU has already allocated €15 million to the fund, and individual EU member states are following suit.

This economics-based approach has enormous potential, but it suffers from two main weaknesses. First and foremost, alternative development takes many years to become self-supporting, profitable, and sustainable. In the meantime, Afghanistan risks tumbling back into lawlessness and instability. Second, past experiences have shown that alternative development has very limited impact on drug control. It does not drastically reduce poppy cultivation but instead indirectly benefits the country by reducing economic risk for transitioning farming communities and lending political stability to drug-affected areas. Alternative development for Afghanistan's poppy farmers is necessary but not sufficient in and of itself. Afghanistan's democracy is simply too fragile to rely solely on long-term measures.

An Alternative Path to Stability

Afghanistan should explore other ways to decrease its illicit opium economy. The Senlis Council, an international think tank whose work encompasses foreign policy, security, and development, suggests that, rather than trying to wipe out opium poppy, Afghanistan should capitalize on the expertise of poppy farmers by diverting part of the existing illegal opium industry to the domestic and international medicine markets. A humanitarian brand of Afghan morphine and codeine could be marketed in developing countries that have a serious shortage of those medicines. The council is currently building a coalition to support a scientific pilot project that will further investigate how to implement this proposal.

Although poppy licensing will be far from easy, the basic conditions for such a program exist in Afghanistan. The 2005 Senlis Council study indicates that opium licensing presents an economically viable solution to the status quo of extreme rural poverty.[19] Opium is the base material for morphine and codeine, two World Health Organization–recognized essential medicines. Given that Afghanistan has a long tradition of poppy cultivation and thus has the required knowledge and expertise, it would be possible to set up a medicine-producing industry in the short term on a small to medium scale. This project would also improve the security situation by drawing warlords and Taliban elements into a legal economy. It would decriminalize the Afghan economy, raise the government's tax base, and erode the financial basis of organized crime and terrorist groups.

If key international and Afghan players can be co-opted in this new strategy, the commercial opportunities for Afghan-made essential medicines are wide open. Globally, the demand for opium-based medicines is significant, and research suggests that the major part of this demand is not being met. Developing countries have almost no access to these medicines, and the growing HIV/AIDS crisis is increasing demand. Currently, only six countries consume 79 percent of opium-based medicines: Australia, Canada, France, Japan, the United Kingdom, and the United States.[20] Developing countries account for only six percent of global pharmaceutical opium consumption.[21] These countries, which suffer the most from the AIDS crisis, lack the financial means to buy painkillers on a commercial basis. Ironically, Afghanistan does not currently produce any opiates for its domestic medicine industry.

A special Afghan brand of morphine and codeine can be developed and promoted in the international development and humanitarian community through preferential trade agreements. Exports of Afghan medicine could become a central element of economic reconstruction and represent a positive and productive economic response to the opium problem, improving security and development. Afghanistan would reap substantial benefits at the global export level. Its medicines would address largely unmet needs for painkillers both in developed and developing countries. Preferential trade agreements between the Afghan government and current donor states would guarantee a substantial and sustainable market for these goods. For that reason, the British medical magazine *The Lancet* argued, "This may be the only chance Afghanistan has to solve its drug problem, while providing a pragmatic and dynamic solution to its future peace, and meeting the vital public health objective of supplying essential medications to the developing world."[22]

The basic idea is attractive, but important questions have to be answered regarding the practical details of such a poppy licensing system. The Senlis Council has therefore recently finalized a series of research programs to examine the details of such a system. A first practical question is whether Afghanistan's current poppy varieties are suited for the production of morphine and codeine. If a new medicinal variety needs to be introduced that is less suitable for the production of heroin, this could seriously hamper the short-term implementation of poppy licensing. Also, Afghan farmers must be provided with an adequate financial incentive for the licit production to compete successfully with the illegal drug trade. Finally, control mechanisms must be developed to ensure that a limited amount of licensed opium is diverted to the illegal drugs economy. Weak government institutions, corruption, and limited experience with such a control mechanism raise doubts about Afghanistan's ability to successfully implement this strategy. Yet, as of now, 100 percent of the Afghan opium supply "leaks" to the illicit market, so there is plenty of room for improvement. Still, the concern about the level of diversion to illegal channels has important implications. Pharmaceutical companies will be reluctant to participate unless the complete cycle, from poppy crop to medicine, is fully assured and controlled.

This proposal can be modeled on similar projects in Australia, France, India, and Turkey, where opium production is currently used for the international medicinal market. These are rather small-scale projects, but they do offer insights into how a much larger Afghan opium-based industry might operate. In India, where pharmaceutical opium is produced in poor areas such as Madhya Pradesh, Uttar Pradesh, and Rajasthan, farmers are given a license to grow opium, and the Indian Central Bureau of Narcotics purchases their entire crop at a fixed price. It is estimated that as many as 1 million Indian farmers are employed in the harvesting of around 35,000 hectares of opium poppy each year.[23] Two key questions have bedeviled the Indian licit opium scheme: are farmers paid enough to get them out of their abject poverty, which is as much the consequence as the cause of instability; and is diversion to the illegal market, in which prices are much higher, kept at an acceptable level? Indian farmers seem to profit little from licit opium production.

They make just enough to cope with poverty but not enough to defeat it. Although there is no clear data, as much as 20 percent of Indian licit opium production might be diverted to the illegal market. This is too much to call the scheme a complete success but is small enough to encourage Afghanistan to make a serious effort.[24]

Turkey's successful transition from a culture of widespread, unregulated poppy cultivation to a licensed, controlled system for the production of medicines is even more applicable to the current situation in Afghanistan.[25] In the 1960s, Turkey was one of the world's main opium producers, but after several years of tense negotiations, it switched from unregulated crop growing to licensed poppy cultivation for the production of medicines. The Turkish political dynamic was such that poppy farmers' interests were essential to the political stability of the country, as they are in Afghanistan. When Turkey deemed total eradication both technically and socially impractical, the U.S. and Turkish governments worked together to implement a poppy licensing system supported by the UN and a preferential trade agreement with the United States.

Following these examples, in the short term the real effectiveness of an Afghan poppy licensing system should be tested through pilot projects. Projects should be set up in different provinces where various poppy varieties could be cultivated, producing medicinal opium to be tested in laboratories. Although Turkey and India show the way, the Afghan situation remains unique because poppy cultivation is the cornerstone of the country's economy, with warlords, the Taliban, and criminal networks deeply involved. Although the scale of such a program would be unprecedented, this should not prevent the introduction of a controlled poppy-licensing system in Afghanistan.

Engaging Afghan Stakeholders

Proponents of this plan must convince key players of the political wisdom and practical feasibility of a poppy licensing scheme for Afghanistan. Using only a fraction of the current spending on counternarcotics, a new medicinal industry could be created to accommodate the economic and political interests of all stakeholders involved in the illegal industry. First, farmers working in a licit opium industry must be offered a competitive income, which is feasible thanks to the high markup in the market price of medicinal morphine. In a new legal economy, farmers would not need to spend money on repayment of opium-denominated loans and the lavish bribes of government officials. Credit offers farmers the opportunity to invest in other produce and technologies and allows for the development of other economic activities, including agro-industry. As such, opium licensing is also the right tool to foster diversification of the Afghan rural economy, important because a single-crop agricultural sector would hamper economic growth.

Former warlords and other regional leaders should be included in this poppy licensing system. Otherwise, they would merely obstruct its introduction. Following the September 2005 parliamentary elections, many warlords and commanders entered the world of politics, for some as a means of securing their economic privileges. Both former warlords and drug traffickers currently benefit directly from the illegal opium trade by reaping the profits of poppy farmers' labor. Only the traffickers, however, will lose out under a licensed system. Given the important role some former warlords play in rural areas and in the new Afghanistan at large, they will be involved with other regional leaders and religious scholars in setting up the licensing scheme.

The poppy licensing proposal would not simply be a tool to create licit income opportunities and boost impoverished rural communities. It would also empower these communities in a way that respects Afghan culture. Poppy licensing depends on control systems that prevent diversion to illicit markets. Field research conducted by Dr. Ali Wardak of Glamorgan University has revealed that existing systems of social control, which are deeply rooted in rural communities in Afghanistan, could be empowered to play a crucial role in organizing and controlling poppy licensing, as well as other rural development projects.[26] For centuries, traditional rural assemblies such as the *jirga* and the *shura* have functioned as the primary forum of consensus building and order enforcement in rural communities. Moreover, *shari'a* (Islamic law) allows for the cultivation of opium when it does not harm but rather benefits society, as is clearly the case of the opium for medicine project. Rural Afghanistan thus provides an excellent opportunity to integrate these informal social-governance structures with formal control. Such an integrated system could oversee and control the different stages of poppy licensing but could also be applied to other rural development or humanitarian aid projects.

These innovative proposals have been received both with interest and skepticism. For several years now, the Afghan government has tried to convince farmers not to grow opium poppy, a policy similar to that employed by the Taliban in July 2000.[27] To implement a scheme that distinguishes between illegal opium production and the licensed production of opium-based medicine, the Afghan government needs to clearly communicate the procedures and rules of licit poppy growing. Currently, they are worried that promoting poppy licensing will send the wrong message to farmers, given five years of trying to convince farmers to abandon poppy cultivation.

The poppies for peace proposal met with an initial welcome by the Afghan authorities. In March 2005, Afghan minister for counter narcotics Habibullah Qaderi welcomed further research on these innovative proposals because they could offer a new economic horizon for his country.[28] That same month, Karzai said at a joint press conference with U.S. secretary of state Condoleezza Rice that the proposal was "an interesting suggestion."[29] More recently, however, the Afghan government has suggested that it is perhaps "not the right time" to implement such a system, as it is still difficult for the government to control many provinces. Qaderi argued that "the poor situation in the country means that there will simply be no guarantee that opium will not be smuggled out of the country for the illicit narcotics trade abroad. Without an effective control mechanism, a lot of opium will still be refined into heroin for illicit markets in the West and elsewhere."[30] With recent research findings on integrated social control systems and the possibility to market Afghan morphine internationally, the Afghan government should reassess this proposal and allow a scientific pilot project to determine if local control mechanisms can limit diversion to the illegal market, paving the way for a poppy licensing system.

Aside from sharing some of the government's concerns, the international community has additional objections to poppy licensing. According to UN figures, there does not seem to be a global shortage of opium-based painkillers, such as morphine. This would undercut the moral argument for the licit production of pharmaceutical morphine. The UN figures are based, however, on projected demand calculations that are limited to the highly protected market of painkillers. Potential demand from developing countries that lack those essential medicines is not taken into account in these calculations. Most governments did not respond to the UN's questionnaire on their medical needs for painkillers.[31] Even Afghanistan itself has almost no opium-based medicines available, which means that production limited to the domestic market would already be a huge step. If developing countries would get access to affordable analgesics, a new, major market would be opened up for Afghan medical opiates, supported by a preferential trade agreement if necessary.

Afghanistan should be fully responsible for and in control of such a new system of licit opium production. Afghan authorities already have full control of the management of the UN's trust fund to fight drugs. Recent developments in Afghanistan have been favorable to a poppy licensing system. The new Afghan Counter Narcotics Law, which came into force in December 2005, contains explicit provisions for a licensing scheme.[32] Following this law, an Afghan Drug Regulation Committee was established in August 2006. This body is to regulate the licensing, sale, dispensation, import, and export of all drugs in Afghanistan. Qaderi commented that "this is another step forward. Regulation of export, import, sale, dispensation and licensing of drugs by this committee will be solely for scientific, pharmaceutical and licit industrial purposes."[33]

In the short term, however, Kabul clearly requires the political backing, technical support, and investment of the international community to set up a licensing system, find the best way to prevent diversion, and produce high-quality medicinal opium for the domestic and export markets. Afghans can obtain political support for this initiative by casting the Afghan drug crisis as part of the larger war on terrorism. Over the past few years, the Taliban and Al Qaeda have been gaining power and establishing their presence in Afghanistan, especially in the southern and eastern regions of the country. Through their poppy cultivation, ordinary farmers are at the mercy of warlords and insurgents, who grant them protection, agricultural necessities such as seeds and fertilizer, and other services that the weak formal government is not able to provide. This weakness offers terrorist groups a good environment for recruitment and hideouts. Not all Afghan warlords are terrorists, but there certainly is a direct relationship between the two groups. Opium has funded the activities of warlords for many years, and the consequent anarchy opened a window of opportunity for notorious terrorist groups to operate.

Escaping the Cycle of Violence

Afghanistan must turn the tables on the opium crisis, as reconstruction will be impossible as long as opium dependence remains. It is a structural development and security issue, not just a drug problem per se. Afghanistan should be granted full sovereignty and ownership to solve its predicament but should be able to count on the support of the international community as necessary.

The international community should follow suit and actively help set up a scientific pilot project and subsequent implementation of a poppy licensing scheme. In January, the European Parliament paved the way for a broader European consensus on the need to look into the proposal. It adopted a resolution urging participants of the Afghanistan donor conference earlier this year in London to take into consideration the proposal of licensed opium production.[34] This text earned the support of almost all of the political groups in the European Parliament, demonstrating that European politicians are starting to see the need to investigate innovative approaches that have a serious chance of pulling Afghanistan out of the quagmire of economic misery and political instability.

There is no time to waste, as Afghanistan could well be slipping back to chaos and civil strife. Tackling the drug economy is central to easing Afghanistan's ills, and the only remaining alternative is the poppies for peace proposal, using medicinal poppy cultivation as a bridge to sustainable development and lasting security in Afghanistan.

Notes

1. United Nations Office on Drugs and Crime (UNODC), "Afghanistan Opium Survey 2005," November 2005, http://www.unodc.org/pdf/afg/afg_survey_2005.pdf; UNODC, "Afghanistan Opium Survey 2006," September 2006, p. 1, http://www.unodc.org/pdf/execsummaryafg.pdf.
2. UNODC, "Afghanistan Opium Survey 2006," p. 1.
3. UNODC, *World Drug Report 2000* (Oxford: Oxford University Press, 2000), p. 24.
4. Scott Gates and David Lektzian, *Drugs, Governance and Civil Conflict* (Oslo: International Peace Research Institute, 2005), p. 1.
5. See Vanda Felbab-Brown, "Afghanistan: When Counternarcotics Undermines Counterterrorism," *The Washington Quarterly* 28, no. 4 (Autumn 2005): 59; Jorrit Kamminga, "Afghanistan: Linkages Between the Illegal Opium Economy, International Crime, and Terrorism" in *Feasibility Study on Opium Licensing in Afghanistan for the Production of Morphine and Other Essential Medicines*, ed. David Spivack (Kabul: MF Publishing, 2005), pp. 345–378.
6. "Lawless Iraq Is 'Key Drug Route,'" *BBC News*, May 12, 2005, http://news.bbc.co.uk/2/hi/middle_east/4541387.stm.
7. UNODC, "Afghanistan Opium Survey 2005," p. iii.
8. UNODC, "Afghanistan Opium Survey 2006," p. 1.
9. Ibid., p. 17.
10. Foreign and Commonwealth Office and the Department for International Development, Government of the United Kingdom, "The UK and Afghanistan," July 2005, http://www.dfid.gov.uk/pubs/files/uk-afghanistan.pdf.
11. "Karzai Warns Afghan Poppy Farmers of World Backlash," Agence France-Presse, November 29, 2005.
12. Pierre-Arnaud Chouvy, "Licensing Afghanistan's Opium: Solution or Fallacy?" *Asia Times*, February 1, 2006, http://www.pa-chouvy.org/Chouvy-Asia_Times-1FEB2006-Licensing_Afghanistans_Opium_Solution_or_Fallacy.html.
13. "Afghanistan," February 7, 2006, col. 728, http://www.publications.parliament.uk/pa/cm200506/cmhansrd/cm060207/debtext/60207-02.htm (House of Commons debates).
14. Rachel Morarjee, "Afghan Peasants Bear the Brunt of Curbs on Opium," *Financial Times*, May 10, 2006, http://www.ft.com/cms/s/f27cffa0-dfc0-11da-afe4-0000779e2340.html; Tom Coghlan, "Afghan Poppy Farmers Expect Record

Opium Crop and the Taliban Will Reap the Rewards," *Independent*, May 11, 2006, http://news.independent.co.uk/world/asia/article363606.ece; Christoph Ehrhardt, "Der Soldat als Opiumbauer," *Frankfurter Allgemeine Zeitung*, July 24, 2006, p. 3.

15. Senlis Council, "Helmand at War: The Changing Nature of the Insurgency in Southern Afghanistan and Its Effects on the Future of the Country," June 2006, http://www.senliscouncil.net/documents/Helmand_Report_June_2006.
16. Senlis Council, "Canada in Kandahar: No Peace to Keep: A Case Study of Military Coalitions in Southern Afghanistan," June 2006, p. 6, http://www.senliscouncil.net/modules/publications/013_publication/documents/Kandahar_Report_June_2006.
17. See "The EU's Relations With Afghanistan - Overview," May 2006, http://ec.europa.eu/comm/external_relations/afghanistan/intro/index.htm.
18. Aref Adamali, "Can the Afghan Carpet Sector Grow to Become a Global Leader," Centre for International Private Enterprise, http://www.cipeafghanistan.org/modules.php?op=modload&name=News&file=article&sid=111.
19. David Spivack, ed., *Feasibility Study on Opium Licensing in Afghanistan for the Production of Morphine and Other Essential Medicines* (Kabul: MF Publishing, 2005), pp. 345–378.
20. International Narcotics Control Board (INCB), "Critical Shortage of Drugs for Pain Relief, Says INCB," UNIS/NAR/899, May 26, 2005, http://www.incb.org/incb/press_release_2005-05-26_1.html.
21. Ibid.
22. "Pragmatism Over Opium Production in Afghanistan," *Lancet*, September 24–30, 2005, p. 1052.
23. David Mansfield, "An Analysis of Licit Opium Poppy Cultivation: India and Turkey," April 2001, p. 7, http://www.pa-chouvy.org/Mansfield2001AnalysisLicitOpiumPoppyCultivation.pdf.
24. U.S. General Accounting Office, "Drug Control: U.S. Heroin Control Efforts in Southwest Asia and the Former Soviet Union," May 1997, p. 5.
25. Jorrit Kamminga, "The Political History of Turkey's Opium Licensing System for the Production of Medicines: Lessons for Afghanistan," May 2006, http://www.senliscouncil.net/modules/publications/010bis_publication/documents/Political_History_Poppy_Licensing_Turkey_May_2006.
26. Ali Wardak, "Integrated Social Control in Afghanistan: Implications for the Licensed Cultivation of Poppy for the Production of Medicines," May 2006, http://www.senliscouncil.net/modules/publications/012_publication/documents/integrated_social_control_afghanistan.
27. UN Office for Drug Control and Crime Prevention, "Afghanistan Ends Opium Poppy Cultivation," *UNODCCP Update*, June 2001, p. 3, http://www.unodc.org/pdf/newsletter_2001-06-30_1.pdf.

28. Zubair Babarkarkhail, "Impact of Legalizing Poppy Cultivations Needs Study Says Minister," Pajhwok Afghan News, March 15, 2005.
29. "Afghan President Karzai Says the Idea of Legalizing Poppy to Produce Medicine Is an Interesting Suggestion," Pajhwok Afghan News, March 20, 2005.
30. Habibullah Qaderi, "Drug Policy Challenges in Afghanistan" (speech, 4th International Symposium on Global Drug Policy, Vienna, March 8, 2005), http://www.senliscouncil.net/modules/events/vienna_2005/qaderi; "Make Opium Legal, Report Tells Afghans," Reuters/Agence France-Press, September 26, 2005, http://www.iht.com/articles/2005/09/26/news/opium.php.
31. INCB, "Report of the International Narcotics Control Board for 2000," p. 2, http://www.incb.org/incb/en/annual_report_2000.html.
32. Islamic Republic of Afghanistan, *Counter Narcotics Law*, December 17, 2005, art. 7.
33. Afghan Ministry of Counter Narcotics, "Establishment of Afghan Drug Regulation Committee," press release, August 1, 2006, http://www.mcn.gov.af/eng/downloads/press_release/drug_committee.htm.
34. See "Afghanistan: Emma Bonino's Statement After the European Parliament Vote," Strasburg, January 18, 2006, http://www.emmabonino.it/press/world/3309.

Vanda Felbab-Brown

Afghanistan: When Counternarcotics Undermines Counterterrorism

Today's counternarcotics chic contains the idea of a fundamental synergy among curbing the international drug trade, fighting the war on terrorism, and promoting democracy. In recent years, widespread attention to these links has introduced hip new terms such as narcoterrorism, narcoguer-rilla, narcostate, and narcofundamentalism into the lexicon of U.S. officials, major international organizations, and the larger policy community. In Afghanistan, presumably consistent counterinsurgency, democratic stabilization, and counternarcotics measures have become the cornerstone of the international community's policies. A huge explosion of opium poppy cultivation since the fall of the Taliban has led President Hamid Karzai, the United States, and the United Kingdom—the lead nation responsible for counternarcotics activity in Afghanistan under the UN Assistance Mission in Afghanistan (UNAMA) framework—as well as major international organizations to declare that drugs now constitute the greatest threat to Afghanistan's democratic consolidation and economic development.[1] The prevailing strategy to prevent Afghanistan from becoming irretrievably addicted to its nar-

Vanda Felbab-Brown is a Ph.D. candidate in political science at the Massachusetts Institute of Technology and a fellow at Harvard University's Belfer Center for Science and International Affairs.

The Washington Quarterly • 28:4 pp. 55–72.

coeconomy has been to intensify counternarcotics efforts. Karzai has declared a war against poppies, describing the Afghan opium trade as a worse "cancer" than terrorism or the Soviet invasion of 1979.[2] In March 2005, the Pentagon even expanded the mission of U.S. military forces in Afghanistan to include support of counternarcotics operations, including "transportation, planning assistance, intelligence, [and] targeting packages," as well as in extremis support for Drug Enforcement Administration and Afghan officers who come under attack.[3]

Yet, paradoxically, counternarcotics efforts frequently complicate counterterrorism and counterinsurgency objectives and can also undermine democratization in fragile situations. Counternarcotics measures frequently threaten the security environment by undermining efforts at political stabilization and democratic consolidation without addressing the underlying economic causes. They compromise intelligence gathering, alienate rural populations, and allow local renegade elites successfully to agitate against the central government. Among the three most common counternarcotics strategies—eradication, interdiction, and alternative development—eradication poses potentially disastrous risks for Afghanistan's political stabilization and economic reconstruction while interdiction greatly complicates counterterrorism objectives. The obstacles to achieving successful alternative development are enormous. A fourth, softer strategy toward the drug dealers—amnesty—also entails serious negative repercussions.

The Opium Boom

The explosion of drug cultivation in Afghanistan has been ignited both by opportunity and necessity. The state's critical weakness and the existence of powerful local sponsors have provided the opportunity, while the devastation of the Afghan economy has left the impoverished Afghan people with no alternative to survive. Afghanistan's legal economy has been ruined, first in the 1980s when Soviet counterinsurgency policy attempted to deprive the mujahideen of resources and popular support by destroying rural agriculture and depopulating the countryside,[4] then by the civil war of the 1990s, and subsequently by the fundamental neglect of economic development and the brutalization of women under Taliban rule.

The Taliban profited immensely from drug production in territories under its control, as did the Northern Alliance in its regions. After an initial year of religious zealousness to try to eradicate the burgeoning poppy cultivation in 1994–1995, the Taliban decided that eradication was both financially unsound and politically unsustainable. The fundamentalist religious movement progressively shifted its attitude toward tolerating poppy cultivation, then to levying a 10–20 percent *zakat*, or tax, on cultivation and processing, and finally to actively encouraging poppy cultivation and even teaching farmers how to achieve greater yields.[5] Profits from the opium trade, estimated at $30–200 million a year, were roughly comparable to the Taliban's profits from illegal traffic of legal goods under the Afghan Transit Trade Agreement and constituted a major portion of the country's gross domestic product (GDP) and income.[6] In 2000–2001, when the Taliban finally declared poppy cultivation illegal to placate the international community, receive recognition as a legitimate government, boost opium prices, and possibly also consolidate its control over Afghanistan's drug trade, it had already stored enough heroin to maintain its money supply without new poppy cultivation for many years.

The devastating drug statistics coming out of Afghanistan since the fall of the Taliban are old hat. It has become common knowledge that Afghanistan supplies more than 75 percent of the heroin in the global market and more than 95 percent in the European market. Profits from the drug trade are the equivalent of more than 60 percent of Afghanistan's legal GDP.[7] Statistics for 2004 paint a bleak picture, the latest in a steadily worsening trend since 2001: last year, poppy seeds were the crop of choice for 131,000 hectares of land in Afghanistan. Opium poppy cultivation thus increased 64 percent from 2003 and had spread to all 32 provinces. Opium production was up by 17 percent, totaling 4,200 tons. These numbers are very high, but they are still far lower than the potential resin harvest from 131,000 hectares.[8] This "limited" production was the result of unfavorable weather conditions, not counternarcotics measures. Moreover, unlike in other drug-producing countries, poppy cultivation in Afghanistan is not limited to remote areas inaccessible to the government. It is everywhere.

In a country where 70 percent of the population lives below the poverty line, drugs represent not only a lucrative but also, crucially, a reliable source of livelihood. Although good weather and auspicious international market conditions can cause legal agricultural products such as saffron, specialty fruits, or even wheat to sell sometimes at higher prices than opium, other structural factors strongly favor the cultivation of illicit crops. First, the majority of microcredit available in Afghanistan is currently based almost solely on opium, which, being less susceptible to bad weather conditions and market price fluctuations, is a less risky investment. Local creditors advance money to peasants to buy seed for next year, as well as food and clothes to withstand the winter, in return for the peasants' agreement to grow a determined amount of opium.[9] Credit for other forms of economic activity is almost nonexistent. Second, legal crops involve large sunk and transaction costs. They require fertilizers and irrigation, both of which are expensive or largely absent in Afghanistan. Legal crops such as fruit also tend to spoil easily and thus lose their value if not delivered on time to local markets, unlike the lightweight and nonperishable opium. Furthermore, local traffickers occasionally pick up raw opium directly from farmers, relieving them of the need to undertake an expensive trip to regional markets on a poor road system.

The UN Office on Drugs and Crime estimates that 7 percent of the Afghan population profits directly from the drug trade.[10] Yet, this number fails to capture the true size, scope, and economic importance of the drug economy. It does not include the itinerant laborers hired during harvest times and their families; those who live off of imports such as durable consumer goods, fuel, and medicines that are purchased with drug profits; those who profit from the development of local production and sales underwritten by drug profits; or those who benefit from the development of local services such as teashops and resthouses for traffickers. Even as U.S. officials point to the real estate boom and business activity visible in many Afghan cities as a sign of progress, the reality is that such progress is in large part financed by profits from the drug industry.[11]

The Consequences of the Opium Boom

The opium poppy cultivation boom not only negatively affects U.S. and western European interests in reducing their own domestic drug consumption, but it also has had negative consequences for Afghanistan's security, politics, and economics. Regional warlords reap vast benefits from drug production, threatening Afghanistan's fragile security environment.[12] With profits in the tens of millions of dollars, local strongmen can easily finance their militias and buy their popularity by subsequently investing a portion of the profits in local development projects such as schools, sewage and irrigation systems, and clinics. Even after the partial demobilization of some of the most prominent warlords' militias, accumulated profits make it potentially simple for many warlords to reconstitute them. Adding to the state's difficulty in maintaining security is the problem of border patrol, given Afghanistan's rough terrain. Drug-smuggling routes used in the 1980s to move drugs in one direction and weapons in the other via Pakistan, Iran, and Central Asia are similarly used today.[13]

Burgeoning drug production also threatens Afghanistan politically by providing an avenue for criminal organizations and corrupt politicians to enter the political space, undermining the democratic process. These actors, who enjoy the financial resources and political capital generated by sponsoring the illicit economy, frequently experience great success in the political process and are able to secure official positions of power as well as wield influence from behind the scenes. Consequently, the legitimacy of the political process is subverted. The problem perpetuates itself as successful politicians bankrolled with drug money make it more difficult for other actors to resist participating in the illicit economy, leading to endemic corruption both at the local and national levels.

Finally, in the long term, large-scale drug production has severe negative economic impacts, contributing to inflation, encouraging real estate speculation and a rapid rise in real estate prices, and undermining currency stability.[14] Afghanistan is already experiencing widespread real estate speculation behind the construction and business activity visible in cities. In major drug-producing and -trafficking regions, such as Badakshan, poppy cultivation has driven up prices of consumer goods and dowries.[15] Drugs also displace legitimate production. In Badakshan, the opium boom raised the cost of labor to the degree that no wheat was harvested in 2003. During that year, although farmers could earn as much as $12 a day cultivating opium, the U.S. Agency for International Development only offered $3–$6 a day to its Afghan employees.[16] The local population is thus frequently uninterested or unable to participate in a different form of economic activity, complicating efforts at local development. Those who grow opium are able to purchase televisions, electric generators, motorcycles, and even cars and can afford medical care in Pakistan and large dowries for their daughters. Growing poppies is thus not simply about survival in the face of grinding poverty, but also upward mobility.

Although the damage that the opium boom inflicts on Afghanistan's security, politics, and economy is undeniable, the frequently mentioned connection between Al Qaeda (or some loose post–Al Qaeda network) and the drug trade in Afghanistan is in fact rather murky. Belligerent groups such as warlords, local terrorists, and insurgents generally profit in one of three ways: taxing production or processing, providing protection for traffickers and taxing them for this service, or engaging in money laundering. Taxing production and processing requires at least partial control of the territory engaging in cultivation, which Al Qaeda does not have in Afghanistan today. Similarly, direct trafficking and providing security for traffickers within the drug-producing country—fairly common revenue sources for belligerent groups in countries such as Peru and Colombia[17]—demand an intimate and up-to-date knowledge of territory and the positions of counternarcotics forces as well as an ability to move through the territory easily. Although some Al Qaeda members undoubtedly have knowledge of Afghanistan's territory, given U.S. anti–Al Qaeda efforts in Afghanistan, it is a much easier endeavor for non–Al Qaeda actors to provide such services and a much riskier investment for regional drug barons to hire Al Qaeda affiliates for traffic within Afghanistan.

Still, some analysts maintain that Al Qaeda is profiting from the drug trade by supplying gunmen to protect drug labs and convoys.[18] Although this assertion is plausible, Al Qaeda's ability to penetrate the Afghan drug trade depends on whether other actors are alternatives able to protect the same labs and convoys. The greater the number of local militia commanders available, the smaller the opportunity for Al Qaeda to inject itself into this role. Currently, many local actors in Afghanistan are willing to provide these services. Ironically, if the Afghan government and international forces manage to expel local warlords from the drug trade and disrupt the current trafficking routes, Al Qaeda, if not also neutralized, would have all the more opportunity to benefit from trafficking. The best available evidence seems to indicate that Al Qaeda has penetrated some transit segments of the drug routes outside of Afghanistan. A Baluchistan trafficker linked to Al Qaeda's financing, Haji Juma Khan, is believed to be employing a fleet of cargo ships to move Afghan heroin out of the Pakistani port of Karachi.[19] The arrest of Afghanistan's number one drug dealer, Haji Bashir Noorzai, in New York at the end of April 2005 was surrounded by reports that Noorzai had hired Al Qaeda operatives to transport heroin out of Afghanistan and Pakistan.[20]

It is also possible that Al Qaeda could profit from drug-related money laundering, which remains the weakest and most underemphasized issue in counternarcotics efforts. Combating money laundering is extraordinarily difficult because there are a large menu of laundering options, such as cash smuggling, currency exchange bureaus, front companies, purchase of real estate, securities, trusts, casinos, and wire transfers, and because it requires intensive international cooperation that is frequently lacking.[21] In the case of Al Qaeda, the problem is further complicated by the availability of informal funds transfer systems, such as *hawala*, that easily escape monitoring. Experience with drug money laundering in Latin America indicates that, at least in that drug market, drug traffickers would pay 4–8 percent and sometimes as much as 12 percent for laundering services.[22] Some counternarcotics experts believe that Al Qaeda and the Taliban make tens of millions of dollars on drug-related activities. It is therefore possible that, if Al Qaeda were involved with money laundering, it could make at least $400,000.[23] Because the FBI estimates that the September 11 attacks cost $300,000–500,000, such profits from drug-related money laundering would be significant.[24] On the other hand, U.S. intelligence officers have been quoted estimating that Al Qaeda's annual budget is in the tens of millions.[25] From this perspective, the $400,000 from drug-related money laundering would seem less noteworthy. Regardless, there is little publicly available data to determine whether Al Qaeda is involved in this activity.

In fact, the problem with many of the reports on Al Qaeda's involvement in the drug trade is their conjectural quality. The allegations always lump together Al Qaeda and the Taliban when referring to their involvement in the Afghan drug trade. Consequently, even if it were true that combined the two groups make tens of millions of dollars on the drug trade, it would still not be clear how much of it actually goes to Al Qaeda.

The Shortcomings of Counternarcotics Strategies

The U.S. counternarcotics policy in Afghanistan has evolved from not dealing with the drug situation to emphasizing the most counterproductive counternarcotics strategy: eradication. In mid-2002, the Pentagon decided that, to avoid diverting the already small numbers of U.S. troops in Afghanistan from their primary anti–Al Qaeda and anti-Taliban missions, U.S. forces would not participate in drug interdiction and eradication.[26] Under the UNAMA framework, counternarcotics efforts were delegated to the United Kingdom as the lead country while police and judicial reform, which also influence counternarcotics, were delegated to Germany and Italy, respectively. Since 2002, the British have tried several approaches, from a scheme to buy back illicit crops to a governor-led provincial eradication program, neither of which succeeded in making a dent in the burgeoning drug production and trade. Although large-scale, comprehensive alternative rural development was supposed to accompany eradication, it has been extraordinarily slow to begin.

In the summer of 2004, under growing criticism from the international community, nongovernmental organizations (NGOs), and Sen. John F. Kerry (D-Mass.) during the U.S. presidential election campaign, the Bush administration began reevaluating the counternarcotics policy in Afghanistan. U.S. officials spoke increasingly of the need to make speedy progress on large-scale eradication and faulted both Karzai and the British for the failure to eradicate more acres of poppy.[27] The United States has steadily increased pressure on Karzai to destroy the poppy fields. Moreover, in March 2005 the Pentagon issued new directives under which U.S. forces in Afghanistan will assist in drug interdiction operations.[28] However, both eradication and interdiction, the standard counternarcotics strategies, are extremely problematic in Afghanistan, as is a third possible strategy: offering amnesty to drug traffickers. As a fourth strategy that is necessary but difficult, alternative development efforts are woefully lacking.

Eradication: The Wrong War

Eradication, traditionally the U.S. government's preferred counternarcotics policy, seeks to disrupt the drug trade by destroying the illicit crops. It is predicated on the belief that, if peasants face the destruction of their crops, they will have greater incentive to abandon their illicit cultivation and grow legal products. The traffickers will not have any drugs to transport, and pernicious belligerent actors such as terrorists and warlords will not be able to make any money on the drug trade, thereby severely diminishing their financial resources, if not bankrupting them. Despite efforts by Washington and Kabul to persuade local Islamic clerics to issue a fatwa against drug production, eradication remains an unpopular counternarcotics strategy in Afghanistan. This is hardly surprising, given that eradication frequently deprives populations of their sole source of livelihood. The inability of peasants to repay their creditors as a result of eradication only drives them deeper into debt, pushing them to grow even more poppy in the subsequent year. This is exactly what happened in the few regions where drug eradication was carried out in Afghanistan in 2003 and 2004. If farmers fail to repay their debt, they frequently end up in a form of serf labor, growing poppy on their moneylender's land. Some are forced to flee to Pakistan,[29] where they may end up in the radical madrasas of the Deobandi movement, whose harsh interpretation of Islam and strong anti-U.S. stance became the primary ideological and religious influence on the Taliban. Pakistani and Afghan students indoctrinated in these schools during the 1980s and 1990s provided a large portion of the Taliban's fighters, and current students appear to be restocking the ranks of Taliban remnants today.

Eradication drives the local population into the hands of regional warlords, even if they now call themselves politicians or have secure government jobs, strengthening the centrifugal forces that historically have weakened Afghanistan as a state. Local warlords can capitalize on popular discontent with eradication by claiming something such as "the evil Karzai government, having sold out to the foreign infidels, is impoverishing the rural people and forcing them into semi-slavery." Predictably, the Afghan government eradication teams that actually attempted to carry out their orders, rather than simply accepting bribes, have frequently met with armed resistance from peasants, even in the restricted and relatively safe areas where they have been deployed. Although the new Pentagon policy of supporting counternarcotics operations is meant to avoid alienating the local population by not involving the U.S. military directly in eradication, it will put U.S. soldiers in the position of fighting against local peasants who violently resist counternarcotics operations. The favorable image of the U.S. military in Afghanistan will be destroyed if U.S. soldiers are forced to return fire at a mob of armed, angry villagers. Wider cooperation and intelligence provision will fall apart rapidly.

Aerial eradication, for example, with a fungus, would somewhat reduce the physical danger faced by eradication teams. Yet, spraying, which is always extremely unpopular among populations in drug-producing countries, would further alienate the Afghan people and invite local strongmen to start shooting at eradication planes. U.S. soldiers protecting the spraying planes would once again be placed in danger and enmeshed deeper in armed confrontations with local populations, delegitimizing the U.S. presence. Even if a private contractor such as Dyncorp, which has experience spraying in Colombia, carried out such an operation secretly and both the Kabul government and the international community denied any knowledge or authorization, the United States, which controls Afghanistan's air space, would inevitably receive the blame as a bully sentencing poor Afghan Muslims to starvation, and Karzai's government would face discredit as an impotent U.S. stooge.

The amnesty for the Taliban announced by the U.S. and Afghan governments in January 2005 will further complicate eradication efforts. The Taliban activists returning to their villages will remind the population of the "good times" before 2000 when the Taliban sponsored the illicit economy and poppies bloomed unharmed. The Taliban can thus exploit the popular frustration with eradication and agitate against the Karzai government and the United States. Moreover, any unequal enforcement of eradication, which could result from varying levels of security in different regions, will result in the perception of ethnic and tribal favoritism, augmenting ethnic divisions. The northern non-Pashtun provinces, for example, already have complained that they bear the brunt of eradication while their Pashtun counterparts were let off easy. Whether such claims are accurate does not matter to those ethnic political entrepreneurs that seek to exploit tribal and ethnic divisions and insecurities. Conversely, the relationship between ethnicity and counterdrug measures is acutely uncomfortable for Karzai, whose victory in the presidential elections depended on the support of his fellow Pashtuns. Any effective crackdown against poppy cultivation will have to take place in the Pashtun Helmand region, thus alienating his very support base.

Still, the criticism the United States levied against Karzai just before his May 2005 visit to Washington was unfounded. In a memo sent from the U.S. embassy in Kabul in advance of Karzai's visit and leaked to the press, embassy officials criticized Karzai for being "unwilling to assert strong leadership" in eradication and doing little to overcome the resistance of "provincial officials and village elders [who] had impeded destruction of significant poppy acreage." The memo also criticized Karzai for being unwilling to insist on eradication "even in his own province of Kandahar."[30] In fact, despite the political repercussions for his government, Karzai has been rather compliant with the U.S. demand to undertake eradication. To satisfy international pressure, however, he has unwisely been promising unrealistic outcomes, including the eradication of all poppy fields in two years.[31] The United States cannot be blind to the political realities in Afghanistan: in the absence of large-scale rural development, eradication is politically explosive. Strong-fisted measures to suppress the peasant resistance will further fuel unrest. Such actions will undermine Karzai's government as well as Afghanistan's process of stabilization and democratization.

Compensated eradication, as it has been applied in the past, is also not a viable solution. Recognizing the significant negative repercussions of eradication on the livelihood of the population and the resistance it generates, compensated eradication schemes seek to mitigate these problems by providing peasants with some monetary compensation for the losses incurred from the destruction of their illicit crops. First, even when actually delivered and not simply promised, such financial compensation has always been a small, one-time payment that requires peasants to forgo large, long-term profits. Moreover, much of the money dispensed by the British in their 2002–2003 compensated eradication scheme in Afghanistan ended up in the hands of regional strongmen, while many of the peasants who agreed to eradicate their plots never saw any money.[32] Yet, even if corruption were eliminated from the process, the traffickers could still retaliate by simply outbidding the government's compensation for next year's crops—the international community is unlikely to be willing to devote escalating sums of money to outbid local druglords to continue buying opium from the peasants for many years. In sum, eradication is rarely successful in significantly limiting drug production for a sustained period of time and is tremendously politically destabilizing and explosive.

Interdiction: Undermining Counterterrorism

Interdiction, lab busting, and the prosecution of traffickers carry fewer negative consequences than eradication, as they do not directly harm the local population. Nevertheless, interdiction and lab busting are problematic in Afghanistan. First, in the absence of larger economic development, interdiction, like eradication, is only marginally effective in reducing drug production. The adaptability of traffickers, coupled with the vast territory and difficult terrain in which interdiction teams must operate, make it very difficult to catch any substantial portion of drugs.

A complicating factor in Afghanistan is the counterterrorism/counterin-surgency objectives of the U.S. and Afghan governments. Both counterter-rorism and counterinsurgency efforts require good, local human intelligence. The local warlords are unlikely to provide such intelligence to those who are destroying their business. This was one reason why the U.S. military had been only a reluctant participant in counternarcotics operations in Afghanistan until 2004 and why, for several years after the fall of the Taliban, it failed to destroy many of the heroin labs and stashes it uncovered. For example, a prominent warlord and the chief of police in Jalalabad, Hazrat Ali, despite being a key drug trafficker, was on the U.S. military's payroll after the September 11 attacks to help fight Al Qaeda. Ali's cooperation facilitated U.S. troop operations in the area under his control. As Major James Hawver, a reservist in Jalalabad in 2002, commented, "He was sort of our benefactor. He let it be known that if anybody messed with us, he'd deal with them."[33] Although interdiction tends to be a much more sensible counternarcotics policy in the context of active insurgency and has worked well, for example, in Peru, it has been a problematic strategy in Afghanistan because of the nature of U.S. counterterrorism and counterinsurgency policy there. Unlike eradication, interdiction does not alienate the overall population and hence feed insurgency and terrorism by losing the hearts and minds of the people, but it alienates the local strongmen on whom the United States has come to rely for intelligence and support for anti–Al Qaeda and anti-Taliban operations. If the United States ended this reliance, it could undertake serious interdiction efforts.

Drug Amnesty: Destabilizing When Mixed with Eradication

Given the problematic, politically sensitive nature of catching the traffickers, many of whom are regional warlords and officials at different levels of government, and given the Afghan state's fundamental inability to capture and prosecute traffickers, offering them amnesty could begin to alleviate this dilemma. Because catching the trafficking warlords alienates them and compromises both intelligence gathering and political stability, perhaps the traffickers could be brought in from the cold by giving them conditional amnesty. The Karzai government has in fact been discussing pardoning those traffickers who come clean and invest their profits in local development.[34]

Yet, unfortunately even this approach has its problems. The regional warlords cum politicians, governors, and police chiefs as well as other traffickers have been investing their illicit money from drugs and other illegal smuggling in local development since the 1980s, generating political legitimacy in the process. It is no accident that Herat, a region through which much of the contraband headed for Iran and beyond passes, has been a thriving province. The money from the traffic helped this region's relative economic development while other parts of Afghanistan remained destitute. Providing amnesty would strengthen the warlords' power while allowing them to buy their way into the political system. Questions about the legitimacy of the political process and basic justice would emerge. Moreover, the Karzai government lacks the capacity to punish those who would violate such an agreement and secretly (or not so secretly) continue profiting from drugs. A widespread failure to punish violators would undermine the entire scheme as well as Karzai's future credibility to get tough with the traffickers.

Much more importantly, however, such amnesty would be a moral and political disaster if accompanied by eradication. The local strongmen making large profits from drugs would be pardoned while the poor peasants who can barely make ends meet would face prosecution. The result is a prescription for violence. Civil unrest in Bolivia and Peru during their eradication efforts in recent years may well be a preview for Afghanistan, but in Afghanistan, many more citizens are armed. Such amnesty could make sense if eradication were suspended until the government developed the capacity to put down renegade warlords and uprisings and until genuine, large-scale economic development alternatives, not futile schemes to grow pomegranates, became available to the rural population. If political pressure prevents such an approach and the eradication policy continues, Afghanistan's stability, as well as basic justice, would be jeopardized by an amnesty.

Alternative Development: A Necessary but Rarely Successful Strategy

Alternative development is meant to reduce drug production by offering economic alternatives to a rural population otherwise dependent on growing drugs to make ends meet. Comprehensive alternative development is a requirement for the success of any durable strategy to reduce the production of illicit crops and to diminish the size and scope of the benefits belligerent groups derive from illicit economies. Alternative development cannot mean only crop substitution, such as encouraging Afghan peasants to grow saffron or pomegranates. Even though these crops may be lucrative, price profitability is only one factor driving the cultivation of illicit crops. Other structural economic conditions, such as the state of infrastructure, market instability, and availability of credit, play crucial roles.[35] For alternative development to succeed, it must encompass building infrastructure, distributing new technologies such as fertilizers and better seeds, marketing assistance to help the rural population sell their products on domestic or international markets, and developing local microcredit, to name a few of the most elementary components. In other words, alternative development really is comprehensive rural development.

Yet, even policies that attempt to mitigate some of the structural drivers do not necessarily immediately result in a decrease in the drug trade. Improvements in infrastructure, for example, although crucial for any development, actually help traffickers whose transaction costs fall as they are able to transport drugs faster. Thus, Afghan drug traffickers heartily welcomed the rebuilding of the Ring Road, the main circular artery connecting Kabul, Kandahar, Herat, and Mazar-i-Sharif and the pride of U.S. reconstruction efforts in Afghanistan.

Although essential, alternative development is a long-term process that has rarely been successful in improving rural conditions to the point of substantially reducing a country's drug cultivation. A key problem with many alternative development schemes around the world has been their limited and very short-term nature. Thailand is one place where investments in alternative rural development over three decades resulted in a significant decrease of opiate cultivation, although traffic in opiates and synthetic drugs continue.[36] Afghanistan's current drug problem, however, is of far greater magnitude than that of Thailand, Peru, or Colombia. Apart from requiring substantial funding over many years, one crucial condition for the large-scale success of alternative development is a stable security situation. The government must disarm warlords and insurgents, either by defeating them or integrating them into the political process, and the state must be present in rural areas to provide both security and social services.

The Necessity of State Building

Unfortunately, in the context of Afghanistan's counterterrorism, stabilization, and democratization efforts, the narcotics problem today has no rapidly effective policy solution. After the fall of the Taliban, the United States deployed a minimum number of troops to Afghanistan for postconflict peacekeeping in order to preserve troops for the war against Iraq, undermining reconstruction and counternarcotics efforts. Postconflict Afghanistan had the lowest ratio of international peacekeeping troops to population as well as to the area of territory compared to other postconflict regions, despite the presence of many heavily armed warlords and a vast amount of small arms floating among the population.[37] Despite the success of Afghanistan's October 2004 presidential election, the central government is still weak and absent from large swaths of its territory. Had the United States deployed a much larger number of troops in Afghanistan, it would not have needed to rely on local warlords to help capture Al Qaeda and Taliban fighters to such a large extent. Washington could have helped Kabul subjugate the warlords early on, leaving both the Kabul government and the international community much better equipped to undertake comprehensive counternarcotics policies, including eradication.

Under today's circumstances, U.S. counternarcotics policy options are highly contingent on U.S. counterterrorism and stabilization efforts. As long as the United States continues to rely on warlords enmeshed in the drug trade to provide intelligence on Al Qaeda and Taliban members who choose not to take advantage of the amnesty offer, it should not urge eradication. The Afghan government should halt eradication until the entire country's security situation is stable. Interdiction should be left to Afghan counternarcotics units, even though their capabilities are limited. The new Afghan counternarcotics units' small numbers, frequently inadequate equipment, and lack of training make it inevitable that they will be able to interdict only a limited number of shipments and destroy only a limited number of heroin labs. Although government officials claim that narcotics are impeding the development of the Afghan state, that diagnosis actually confuses the symptom and the cure: state building must come before the narcotics epidemic can be controlled. Counternarcotics efforts should concentrate on strengthening the Afghan state's capacity, through its own military and police, to subdue any uprisings and renegade warlords, enforce prohibition of drug processing and trafficking, and promote judicial capacity to indict and prosecute traffickers. A cornerstone of the counternarcotics effort should be speeding up economic reconstruction efforts, especially rural development. Swift progress on introducing an alternative microcredit system through local banks, NGOs, or charities throughout Afghanistan would help mitigate some of the crucial drivers of poppy cultivation.

The United States should also insist that only drug-free politicians participate in the legitimate political process, at least at the national level. Even if this policy will be impossible to enforce in the short term, given the pervasiveness of drug-related corruption and the weakness of the Afghan state, such a policy, whether publicly announced or not, helps prevent the emergence of a culture of complete impunity for such drug-related criminal behavior. The policies described above cannot be expected to bring immediate visible improvement to the narcotics situation, but they do hold the possibility of long-term progress and do not threaten to destabilize the Karzai government.

When the United States concludes that it no longer needs the Afghan warlords for effective counterterrorism operations in Afghanistan, it should then support Afghan units in interdiction and lab busting. In fact, the new Pentagon mission directives of March 2005, coupled with the recent offer of amnesty for the Taliban, indicate that U.S. policy has already shifted in this direction. The Taliban's renewed insurgency activity, seeking at a minimum to frustrate the September 2005 parliamentary elections, may once again increase the importance of warlord-generated intelligence and would complicate drug interdiction, as local actors will be reluctant to provide such intelligence to those who threaten their drug business. Meanwhile, disarmament of warlords and their militias must proceed swiftly and must occur not only at the unit level with a focus on heavy weapons, but also by disarming individual militia members and confiscating small arms. Only after the state has removed the warlords and militias, gained effective control throughout Afghanistan's territory, and secured the ability to put down popular unrest or uprising by a renegade warlord should Afghan or international forces undertake large-scale eradication. Of course, even then, eradication will only be effective if reconstruction has provided enough economic alternatives for the population.

Finally, the Karzai government and the international community should begin exploring the possibility of legalizing Afghanistan's opium production for pharmaceutical purposes, namely the production of morphine, codeine, and thebaine. Although this policy has been tremendously successful in Turkey, the Afghan case would pose difficult obstacles. Diversion of licit opium into illegal traffic would loom paramount, especially under weak security conditions. Moreover, the International Narcotics Control Board that regulates the licit cultivation of opium requires good government control over production and the prevention of diversion as necessary preconditions. Kabul would also likely face resistance from Turkey, India, and Australia, whose market for licit opiates would be threatened by Afghanistan's participation. With improvements in its security situation, however, Afghanistan could attempt at least some pilot projects. The international community could subsidize the distribution of available technologies that make diversion of opium gum into illicit production very difficult. Yet, even if some illicit activity took place, partial diversion would still be better than the current 100 percent "diversion" for illicit uses.

Counternarcotics policymaking will have a profound effect on Afghanistan's future. Doctrinaire adherence to standard policies and strategies irrespective of local security and social conditions will likely heighten Afghanistan's drug crisis and contribute to the state's destabilization. Only patience, a careful calibration of traditional counternarcotics policies to the evolving local situation, and a steady commitment to alleviating Afghanistan's poverty can result in a sustainable, long-term reduction of the illicit economy and curbing of the drug trade.

Notes

1. Ashraf Ghani, "Where Democracy's Greatest Enemy Is Flower," *New York Times*, December 11, 2004, p. 19; Carlotta Gall, "Afghan Poppy Growing Reaches Record Levels, U.N. Says," *New York Times*, November 19, 2004, p. 3.
2. John Lancaster, "Karzai Vows to Combat Flourishing Afghan Opium Trade," *Boston Globe*, December 10, 2004.
3. Thom Shanker, "Pentagon Sees Antidrug Effort in Afghanistan," *New York Times*, March 25, 2005, p. 1.
4. Scott B. MacDonald, "Afghanistan," in *International Handbook on Drug Control*, eds. Scott B. MacDonald and Bruce Zagaris (Westport, Conn.: Greenwood Press, 1992), pp. 315–324.
5. Ahmed Rashid, *Taliban* (New Haven: Yale University Press, 2001), pp. 117–127.
6. "Merging Wars: Afghanistan, Drugs and Terrorism," *Drugs and Conflict Debate Paper*, no. 3 (November 2001), http://www.tni.org/reports/drugs/debate3.htm; "Heroin," *Jane's Intelligence Review*, June 1, 1998, p. 5; Barnett R. Rubin, "The Political Economy of War and Peace in Afghanistan," *World Development* 28, no. 10 (2000): 1789–1803.
7. The estimated overall profits from the opium economy in 2003 were $2.3 billion, while Afghanistan's estimated GDP for 2002 was estimated at $4.4 billion. UN Office on Drugs and Crime (UNODC) and the Government of Afghanistan, "Afghanistan Opium Survey 2003," October 2003, http://www.unodc.org:80/pdf/afg/afghanistan_opium_survey_2003.pdf; UNODC, "2004 World Drug Report: Vol. 2: Statistics," 2004, p. 206, http://www.unodc.org:80/pdf/WDR_2004/volume_2.pdf. In 2004 the export value of raw opium was $2.8 billion while Afghanistan's licit GDP in 2003 was an estimated $4.6 billion. Larry Goodson, "Afghanistan in 2004: Electoral Progress and Opium Boom," *Asian Survey* 45, no. 1 (January/February 2005): 93.
8. UNODC and the Government of Afghanistan, "Afghanistan Opium Survey 2004," November 2004, http://www.unodc.org/pdf/afg/afghanistan_opium_survey_2004.pdf.

9. David Mansfield "What Is Driving Opium Poppy Cultivation? Decision-Making Amongst Poppy Cultivators in Afghanistan in the 2003/4 Growing Season" (paper prepared for the UNODC/Office of National Drug Control Policy Second Technical Conference on Drug Control Research, July 19–21, 2004).
10. UNODC, "2004 World Drug Report: Vol. 2: Statistics," p. 206.
11. Barnett R. Rubin, "Road to Ruin: Afghanistan's Booming Opium Industry" (paper for the Center for American Progress and the Center on International Cooperation, October 7, 2004, http://www.cic.nyu.edu/pdf/RoadtoRuin.pdf).
12. See Samina Ahmed, "Warlords, Drugs, and Democracy," *World Today* 60, no. 5 (May 2004): 15–17.
13. Ikramul Haq, "Pak-Afghan Drug Trade in Historical Perspective," *Asian Survey* 36, no. 10 (October 1996): 945–963.
14. For economic analyses of the negative effects of the illicit drug economy on the overall economy, see Mauricio Reina, "Drug Trafficking and the National Economy," in *Violence in Colombia 1990–2000: Waging War and Negotiating Peace*, eds. Charles Berquist, Ricardo Peñaranda, and Gonzalo Sánchez G. (Wilmington, Del.: Scholarly Resources Imprint, 2001); Francisco E. Thoumi, *Illegal Drugs, Economy, and Society in the Andes* (Washington, D.C.: Woodrow Wilson Center Press, 2003).
15. Amy Waldman, "Afghan Route to Prosperity: Grow Poppies," *New York Times*, April 4, 2004, p. 5.
16. Jim Lobe, "Afghanistan: Concerns Grow Over Taliban Resurgence, Opium," *Global Information Network*, January 29, 2004, http://proquest.umi.com/pqdweb?did=533932931&sid=8&Fmt=3&clientId=5482&RQT=309&VName=PQD.
17. See, for example, Gabriela Tarazona-Sevillano with John B. Reuter, *Sendero Luminoso and the Threat of Narcoterrorism* (Washington, D.C.: CSIS, 1990); Angel Rabasa and Peter Chalk, *Colombian Labyrinth: The Synergy of Drugs and Insurgency and Its Implications for Regional Stability* (Santa Monica, Calif.: RAND, 2001).
18. Tim McGirk, "Terrorism's Harvest," *Time*, August 9, 2004, p. 41 (quoting Mirwais Yasini, head of the Afghan government's Counternarcotics Directorate).
19. Ibid.
20. Julia Preston, "Afghan Arrested in New York Said to Be a Heroin King," *New York Times*, April 26, 2005, p. 10.
21. See Peter Reuter and Edwin M. Truman, *Chasing Dirty Money* (Washington, D.C.: Institute for International Economics, 2004).
22. U.S. Department of Treasury, "2002 National Money Laundering Strategy," July 2002, p. 12, http://www.treas.gov/offices/enforcement/publications/ml2002.pdf.
23. McGirk, "Terrorism's Harvest."

24. U.S. Department of Treasury, "2003 National Money Laundering Strategy," 2003, p. 57, fn. 50, http://www.treas.gov/offices/enforcement/publications/ml2003.pdf.
25. Gregory L. Vistica and Douglas Farah, "Syria Seizes Six Arab Couriers, $23 Million," *Washington Post*, December 20, 2003, p. 16. For a more detailed analysis of anti–money laundering efforts and Al Qaeda, see Reuter and Truman, *Chasing Dirty Money*, pp. 143–144, 146–147.
26. Unnamed U.S. and British officials, interviews with author, summer and fall of 2004. See Eric Schmitt, "U.S. to Add Forces in Horn of Africa," *New York Times*, October 30, 2002, p. 16.
27. David S. Cloud and Carlotta Gall, "U.S. Memo Faults Afghan Leader on Heroin Fight," *New York Times*, May 22, 2005, p. 1.
28. Thom Shanker, "Pentagon Sees Antidrug Effort in Afghanistan," *New York Times*, March 25, 2005, p. 1.
29. Mansfield, "What Is Driving Opium Poppy Cultivation?"
30. Cloud and Gall, "U.S. Memo Faults Afghan Leader on Heroin Fight."
31. Nat Ives, "Karzai Plans to Destroy Poppy Fields in Two Years," *New York Times*, December 13, 2004, p. 9.
32. Unnamed U.S. and British officials, interviews with author, summer and fall of 2004. See Peter Oborne and Lucy Morgan Edwards, "A Victory for Drug-Pushers," *Spectator*, May 31, 2003, pp. 26–30; John F. Burns, "Afghan Warlords Squeeze Profits From the War on Drugs, Critics Say," *New York Times*, May 5, 2002, p. 22.
33. Quoted in Anne Barnard and Farah Stockman, "U.S. Weighs Role in Heroin War in Afghanistan," *Boston Globe*, October 20, 2004.
34. Stephen Graham, "Afghans Mull Amnesty for Drug Traffickers," *Boston Globe*, January 10, 2005.
35. Mansfield, "What Is Driving Opium Poppy Cultivation?"
36. Pierre-Arnaud Chouvy, "Drugs and War Destabilize Thai-Myanmar Border Region," *Jane's Intelligence Review*, April 1, 2002, http://www.pa-chouvy.org/JIR1.htm.
37. Michael Bhatia, Kevin Lanigan, and Philip Wilkinson, "Minimal Investments, Minimal Results: The Failure of Security Policy in Afghanistan," *AREU Briefing Paper*, June 2004, http://www.cmi.no/afghanistan/themes/docs/AREU-Brief-2004-June-security.pdf.

Part VI:
Pakistan

Craig Cohen and Derek Chollet

When $10 Billion Is Not Enough: Rethinking U.S. Strategy toward Pakistan

In the five years since Pakistani president General Pervez Musharraf announced his intention to cut ties with the Taliban and join the war on terrorism, U.S. policy toward Pakistan has been one of unstinting support. That approach has brought some genuine gains: more al Qaeda members have been captured and killed in Pakistan than anywhere else in the world since the September 11, 2001, terrorist attacks. Yet today, it is worth asking whether U.S. policy has reached its limits and if it is now being guided more by inertia than strategy. Washington's close alliance with Musharraf may now have run its course.

Many experts see Afghanistan's growing insurgency as a consequence of Pakistani weakness, if not outright complicity, with militants in the Pashtun border areas.[1] Criticism has centered on the September 2006 peace deal between Islamabad and local leaders in North and South Waziristan, one of the seven tribal regions on the rugged Afghan border

---

Craig Cohen is a fellow in the Post-Conflict Reconstruction Project and deputy chief of staff at CSIS and an adjunct professor at the Maxwell School of Syracuse University. Derek Chollet is a fellow in the CSIS International Security Program, a nonresident fellow at the Brookings Institution's Global Economy and Development Center, and an adjunct associate professor at Georgetown University. This article derives from a report due out in early 2007. Ayub Khawreen, Bradley Larson, and Mark Irvine contributed research assistance to this article.

The Washington Quarterly • 30:2 pp. 7–19.

that have historically fallen outside of government control. Pakistan's initial military efforts to root out Taliban and al Qaeda elements in North Waziristan largely failed. Army operations proved ineffective, and the country's heart was never in the fight.[2] Musharraf's decision to use tribal elders to rein in insurgents is less a strategy for victory than a means of removing his army from the battlefield and protecting them in their barracks.[3] Anyone who doubts that the threat to the Pakistani forces is real need only consider the November 2006 suicide attack that killed 41 recruits just days after the military's air strike on a madrassa in the Bajaur border area.

In the coming months, Musharraf's retreat is likely to run up against an increasing number of officials in the U.S. government and on Capitol Hill who view Afghanistan as a major front in the global counterinsurgency, who are dissatisfied with progress against the Taliban, and who imagine that the road to a sustainable government in Kabul passes through Islamabad. When asked in December 2006 about the presence of Taliban and al Qaeda fighters moving across the Pakistan border, then–U.S. national intelligence director John Negroponte said that "sooner or later, [Musharraf's government] will have to reckon with it."[4] That day may not be far off.

The U.S. approach to Pakistan is heavily influenced by personal relationships at the top. When President George W. Bush met with Musharraf at the White House in September 2006, he echoed many of the familiar themes he has voiced for the past five years on Pakistan. "When [Musharraf] looks me in the eye and says … there won't be a Taliban and won't be al Qaeda, I believe him, you know?" Bush said.[5] This personal affinity forged in the aftermath of the September 11 attacks has set the course for the past five years of the U.S.-Pakistani relationship.

How deep this trust runs will play out over the coming months as insurgent activity in Afghanistan likely increases with winter's thaw and Musharraf takes steps to ensure his election victory in late 2007 or early 2008. Bush may consider Musharraf to be his man in Pakistan, but partnerships based on coercion and inducement often give the weaker parties unexpected leverage. Musharraf has demonstrated his skill at convincing Washington that he maintains just enough control over extremist forces to be reliable, but not enough to prevent him from being vulnerable and requiring the type of bolstering that Washington is well suited to provide. Musharraf's memoir, *In the Line of Fire*, and the subsequent U.S. media tour successfully reinforced this dual message of threat and indispensability.[6]

The ultimate reason for the consistency of U.S. policy toward Pakistan, however, is not Musharraf's vision or trustworthiness but the perceived lack of alternatives.[7] The two "centrist" political parties and their exiled leaders, Benazir Bhutto and Nawaz Sharif, are considered by many Pakistanis and Pakistan experts to be hardly more democratic, honest, or capable than Musharraf's military rule.[8] The dominant view holds that the military is the only effective institution in Pakistan and will likely play the dominant role in politics for the foreseeable future.[9] Democracy advocates must contend with the notion that even if Musharraf decides to take off his uniform and to hold free and fair elections, the military will still be calling the shots after the votes have been counted.

For all the talk of the United States' global dominance and despite considerable U.S. support to the Pakistani military, Washington finds itself with relatively little leverage to influence events in Pakistan.[10] During the past five years, the United States has given Pakistan more than $10 billion in assistance, channeled primarily through the Pakistani military. What Pakistan gives in return may be only enough to keep the money coming.

After the September 11 attacks, many U.S. policymakers believed that Pakistan was one place where they were justified in saying, "You are either with us or against us." Nevertheless, despite the billions of dollars spent, the United States has not made the necessary commitment to solidify the relationship for the long term. This is not merely a function of the scale of assistance, but of its type. U.S. engagement with Pakistan is highly militarized and centralized, with very little reaching the vast majority of Pakistanis. More problematic still, U.S. assistance does not so much reflect a coherent strategy as it does a legacy of the initial, transactional quid pro quo established in the immediate aftermath of the September 11 attacks and a familiar menu of what the United States was already organized to provide. U.S. soft power in Pakistan, the ability to influence by attraction and persuasion, is far lower than it could be, considering the historic, economic, and personal bonds that unite the two countries.

Is it possible for the United States to convince Pakistanis that it is interested in a serious, long-term partnership rather than merely a short-term alliance of convenience? Doing so will require a better understanding of Pakistan and an assistance strategy more aligned with the needs of average Pakistanis. In January 2007, the U.S. House of Representatives passed a bill to fully implement the recommendations of the National Commission on Terrorist Attacks Upon the United States, more widely known as the 9/11 Commission. Included was a 90-day window for the Bush administration to develop a long-term strategy for Pakistan and the threat of an aid suspension if the president does not attest to Islamabad's commitment to rooting out the Taliban. Because those commissioners graded the administration's approach to Pakistan a C+ in 2006, this policy review is long overdue.

A closer look at the numbers for U.S. assistance to Pakistan since the September 11 attacks may spark a broader discussion of long-term objectives. Money is not everything, but it often sends a clearer signal of our priorities than official statements. Elections and transitions offer the opportunity to rethink U.S. interests and policy options. If Washington squanders the chance and allows its approach to Pakistan to be governed by little more than blind faith, both Musharraf and U.S. policy are sure to remain in the line of fire for the foreseeable future.

U.S. Engagement since 9/11

Between the end of the Cold War and the September 11 attacks, the United States distanced itself from Pakistan, closing off the financial spigots that had once flooded Islamabad with support aimed at driving the Soviets out of Afghanistan.[11] The freewheeling days of funneling $200,000 monthly stipends as well as weapons and supplies to anti-Soviet commanders through Pakistan's intelligence services were replaced with a web of sanctions intended to punish Pakistan for its nuclear program and later for a military coup. On account of Islamabad's then-undeclared nuclear program, in October 1990 the United States blocked the delivery of about 70 F-16 jets that Pakistan had purchased, which comprised the core of their conventional defense.[12] New weapons purchases became off-limits, and exchange programs with Pakistani military officers ground to a halt, causing U.S. policymakers to lose touch with a generation of the Pakistani military. What had once been one of the largest U.S. Agency for International Development (USAID) offices in the world, employing more than 1,000 staff around the country, shrank to almost nothing virtually overnight.

The urgency of responding to the September 11 attacks precipitated a major U.S. reengagement with Pakistan despite Washington's prolonged absence and prohibitive legislative restrictions. Once it became clear that Pakistan would condemn the attacks, turn against the Taliban, and help the United States, Washington's immediate objective became to secure logistical support for military operations in Afghanistan against al Qaeda and potentially the Taliban regime.[13]

This eventual support took six forms that now provide the strategic foundation for the bilateral relationship.[14] First, Pakistan allowed the United States to fly sorties from the south over Pakistani airspace, vital because of Iran's unwillingness to open its airspace to U.S. planes. Second, Islamabad granted U.S. troops access to a select number of its military bases, although it insisted that the bases should not be utilized for offensive operations. Third, tens of thousands of Pakistani troops provided force protection for these bases and U.S. ships in the Indian Ocean. Fourth, Pakistan provided logistical support to the U.S. war effort, including vast amounts of fuel for coalition aircraft and port access for the delivery of vital supplies. Fifth, the military deployed to its western border in a mostly failed effort to cut off retreat to al Qaeda and Taliban members fleeing Afghanistan. Sixth, Islamabad provided Washington with access to Pakistani intelligence assets in Afghanistan and Pakistan. The bulk of this cooperation continues today.

What is truly unique about this arrangement is that no formal agreement or user fees were negotiated, nor was a repayment mechanism created.[15] Yet, a quid pro quo had been established. Musharraf saw his government's effort as a concession for which he would pay a domestic price and therefore needed a demonstration of U.S. support in return.[16] Bush waived U.S. sanctions, reopened the U.S. assistance pipeline, and promised to forgive $2 billion of Pakistan's debt and encouraged other creditors to do the same.

The reality is that U.S. assistance since the September 11 attacks is not money intended to transform the nature of the Pakistani state or society or to strengthen Pakistan's internal stability. In effect, it is politically determined assistance, a "thank you" to Musharraf's regime for the critical role Pakistan has played in Operation Enduring Freedom. This is why the 9/11 Commission members concluded that U.S. assistance had not "moved sufficiently beyond security assistance to include significant funding for education efforts."[17] In this way, very little is unique about the current U.S.-Pakistani relationship. It is history repeating itself, resembling the 1980s, when the United States established a quid pro quo with General Muhammad Zia ul-Haq to help fight the Soviets. Any efforts by U.S. officials to alter its terms to focus on internal reforms would prompt Zia's reply, "Sir, what you are proposing is neither part of the quid nor the quo."[18]

The legacy of the initial post–September 11 arrangement persists today. The strategic direction for Pakistan was set early on by a narrow circle at the top of the Bush administration and has been largely focused on the war effort in Afghanistan rather than on Pakistan's internal situation—even though in many ways the two are related. The various departments and agencies have largely been left to operate within this preexisting framework. For those in Congress who argue that U.S. taxpayers should be getting more for their money, the Bush administration and Islamabad's reply is that the terms of the agreement have been set. The more the United States wants from Pakistan, the more it will have to give.[19]

The Balance Sheet

The most interesting questions to ask Pakistan experts inside and outside of the U.S. government are the simplest ones: how much money does the United States provide to Pakistan, and what is it meant to do? The answers almost always vary. The United States has provided Pakistan with more than $10 billion in military, economic, and development assistance over the past five-plus years. This number has likely been matched, if not exceeded, by classified monies that have gone toward intelligence and covert military action. One supposes the "millions of dollars" in bounties, or "prize money," that Musharraf's memoir alleges that the CIA paid to the Pakistani government for captured al Qaeda members would fall in this basket.[20]

Although the nonclassified assistance numbers are public, not all are easily accessible, even within the U.S. government. Like blind men groping at different parts of an elephant, the various departments and agencies of the U.S. government see limited pieces of the assistance budget. Those whom one would imagine to see the full picture at the embassy still may not have access to all of the defense money.[21] Perhaps more surprisingly, not everyone at the National Security Council or the Office of Management and Budget (OMB) or in Congress may have access to full accountings of what the U.S. government is spending in Pakistan, as it is disaggregated by sectors and accounts. This raises the question of how one goes about making strategic decisions about a country whose future is vital to U.S. interests without seeing the full scale of the assistance involved.

There are four main categories of assistance. The majority of the $10 billion, 57 percent, has gone toward Coalition Support Funds, money intended to reimburse U.S. partners for their assistance in the war on terrorism. Roughly 18 percent, or $1.8 billion, has gone toward security assistance. The Pakistanis have spent the majority of this money on purchases of major weapons systems. Another 16 percent has gone toward budget support as direct cash transfers to the government of Pakistan with few real accountability mechanisms built in. This leaves less than 10 percent for development and humanitarian assistance, including the U.S. response to the October 2005 earthquake. Education, which has been the showcase of USAID programming in Pakistan and which the 9/11 Commission report argues ought to be central to U.S. engagement in Pakistan because of its potential to play a moderating influence, comes in at only $64 million per year for more than 55 million school-aged children, or $1.16 per child per year.

The details of this assistance raise several concerns. Coalition Support Funds, which account for the majority of U.S. assistance to Pakistan, are given to 20 nations, but Pakistan is by far the largest recipient.[22] Officially, the money is reimbursement for food, fuel, clothing, ammunition, billeting, and medical expenses. The Pakistani government regularly provides receipts to U.S. Central Command, which shares oversight duties with the Pentagon's comptroller, the Department of State, and OMB. The real level of scrutiny is uncertain. U.S. military officials in Islamabad, for instance, have recommended changing the program to pay for specific objectives planned and executed rather than paying for whatever Pakistan bills.[23] The support funds are now being doled out at a rate of as much as $100 million per month, raising the question of whether the money is provided on the condition of counterterrorism performance or as political and military support more broadly constituted.[24]

The vast majority of security assistance money ($1.8 billion, or 18 percent of total assistance) has gone toward foreign military financing, although other parts go toward other types of "train and equip" or counternarcotics programs.[25] Although foreign military financing is often justified to Congress as playing a critical role in the war on terrorism, in reality the weapons systems are often prestige items to help Pakistan in the event of war with India.[26] When high-ranking Pakistani officials visit the U.S. secretary of defense, they are more likely to hand him a wish list of hardware than have a discussion about strategy.[27] Looking at the total approved U.S. weapons sales, including weapons purchased without the benefit of direct U.S. assistance, Pakistan has spent $8.4 billion between 2002 and 2006. Most of this has been spent on weapons such as F-16s and other aircraft, anti-ship Harpoon Block II missiles, and antimissile defense systems. Few of these weapons are likely to provide much help in rooting out al Qaeda or the Taliban.

Clearly, the weapons are intended to reward Pakistan, bring it more closely into the U.S. orbit, and satisfy its security concerns vis-à-vis India. If winning the war on terrorism is about relationships, the Bush administration has made material items the basis of these relationships.

Military training, on the other hand, which brings young Pakistani officers to the United States and which has been ramped up since the September 11 attacks, includes only 157 officers that were scheduled to be trained in 2006.[28] At a time when U.S. policy is almost completely reliant on the Pakistani military, there may be important facets of this institution the U.S. government does not know or cannot access or that may be anti-Western in their orientation.

Pakistan is one of four countries that receive budget support (16 percent of total U.S. foreign assistance) from the United States; Israel, Egypt, and Jordan are the others. The official purpose of a direct cash transfer to Pakistan is to help that country pay off its debt so it can spend more on its social sector. As Pakistan's debt burden has been eased since the September 11 attacks, its economy has realized five straight years of dramatic growth, almost 7 percent annually. Yet, there is little accountability in how Pakistan spends U.S. money. Whereas the Egyptians have conditions placed on their budget support, no specific numbers or benchmarks exist for Pakistan beyond vaguely worded "shared objectives."[29] Contrast this with the budget support provided to Pakistan by the World Bank, whose contribution is contingent on the Pakistani government meeting specific performance goals related to privatization and macroeconomic stability. When the government has failed to comply, this aid has been cut off. The seemingly unconditional nature of U.S. budget support, on the other hand, is a sign that economic goals have in many ways been subordinated to U.S. political and military goals.

Development assistance to Pakistan accounts for 9 percent of the total reported U.S. foreign assistance budget. Throughout much of 2006, Director of Foreign Assistance and USAID administrator Randall Tobias has been developing a process to generate greater transparency and consistency and to better align strategy and resources in the delivery of foreign aid. Pakistan was the first place he visited, and it has been designated a "fast track," or high-priority, country.[30] Despite hopes and fears within the foreign aid community that Tobias's framework would radically change the way business is carried out, early indications are that, for Pakistan at least, very little will actually change in the short term.[31] The USAID mission remains small, and restrictions on travel and local partners are severe. Although a new development initiative in the Afghan border regions has been launched within the past year, for the most part U.S. development assistance is not well targeted to the main drivers of conflict, instability and extremism in Pakistan, but instead is comprised of a generic mix of primary education and literacy, basic health, food aid, and democracy and governance assistance mainly focused on the upcoming elections.

Asking the Right Questions

This brief breakdown reveals a U.S. assistance budget heavily weighted toward short-term military cooperation with remarkably little emphasis on long-term domestic stability. Billions of U.S. dollars are provided without an overall perspective or any real sense of objective aside from support to Pakistan's military.

This absence of a long-term strategy is especially disconcerting considering how tenuous the premise of U.S. policy—Musharraf as the guarantor of stability in Pakistan—actually is. It has become something of a parlor game in Washington to discuss the likelihood of future crisis scenarios for Pakistan, most involving the demise of Musharraf.[32] Considering how dangerous a Pakistan meltdown could be for U.S. interests, the perceived lack of viable policy alternatives is truly alarming. Given the scale of U.S. assistance and Pakistan's importance to current and future U.S. national security interests, the Bush administration and the new Democratic-majority Congress should ask tough questions regarding U.S. policy in the region.

First and most critically, what are U.S. taxpayers getting for their $10 billion? Are they safer because of it? Are U.S. troops in Afghanistan better able to complete their mission? Are Pakistanis and their government more likely to turn away from extremist ideologies and orient themselves toward the West on account of our aid? Is U.S. money ineffective or even counterproductive, potentially sowing the seeds of a future crisis? To some extent, these judgments are political, colored by personal ideology and outlook. Some might argue that the United States should cut assistance to Pakistan, whereas others would argue that the United States should give more. Whatever the recommendation, a clear accounting by the Bush administration of what U.S. money is expected to achieve would provide a better understanding of what would constitute a successful or a failed policy.

Second, Washington policymakers should ponder a question that is almost always overlooked: what are the Pakistanis getting for our $10 billion? Are they safer? Is their government more capable of handling their toughest problems, for instance, relations between provinces and the Punjabi center or the country's growing energy needs? Do U.S. money and policies reinforce or subvert the rule of law? Are there more good jobs for Pakistanis and better-educated people to fill those jobs? If Pakistan needs Musharraf to have a "George Washington moment"—taking off his uniform and eventually walking away from power—has U.S. money encouraged it?

Pakistanis' views of the United States and their willingness to share our values are shaped not only by external events such as the war in Iraq and the Israeli-Palestinian conflict, but also by how we spend our money in Pakistan. Despite such generosity, most Pakistanis do not believe the United States is on their side.[33] When the U.S. government urges military action in the tribal areas and seeks to close madrassas or calls for curriculum reform, the perception in Pakistan is that the United States has a problem with Islam. Most Pakistanis do not perceive the Taliban as a threat to their national interests, but as a potential asset if the United States were to walk away from Afghanistan again, providing "strategic depth" to prevent an Indian-friendly regime on their Western border. Despite the talk of a long-term commitment to Pakistan and support for democracy and education, these words ring hollow outside the fortress-like U.S. embassy compound in Islamabad.

Third, U.S. policymakers should be asking who else is giving support to Pakistan and what influence their money is having. Given Islamabad's displeasure with the recent U.S.-Indian nuclear deal and its consideration of Beijing as an "all-weather friend," U.S. officials ought to look more closely at the full nature of China's military and economic support to Pakistan. Washington should also investigate how much money is being channeled to Pakistan from the Persian Gulf through Islamic charities and for what purposes. This is broader than merely disturbing terrorist financing; it goes to the heart of the battle of ideas being waged. What might the United States learn from the way these charities operate and deliver assistance? Even though Pakistan now constitutes the largest Fulbright program, bringing Pakistanis to the United States on educational grants, U.S. diplomacy requires a new narrative that has the potential to inspire rather than threaten the Muslim world.

Answering these difficult questions is vital to implementing a successful policy in Pakistan. Unfortunately, there seems to be little political will in Washington or in Islamabad to ask or answer them and risk altering agreements reached at the highest levels. The default setting is to stay the course, at least until the next crisis erupts. U.S. officials are constrained by the risk-averse nature of bureaucracies and by officials personally invested in the present course. Once set, no one ends up driving the strategy, and no one wants to admit heading in the wrong direction.

Moreover, structural constraints in the way in which money is allocated and dispersed in the U.S. budget makes it difficult to change course or to be flexible.[34] Money is appropriated and programmed with existing authorities and accounts, making it difficult to shift money according to the needs on the ground. U.S. bureaucracies are greatly reluctant to go back to Congress and ask for authorities to move money around on account of the perception that lawmakers will not look fondly on such requests (which is often true). Each department and agency is responsible for a different tool in the toolbox, none wants to give its tool up, and each lacks the ability to work as a component of an integrated strategy.

To break out of this policy stalemate, the United States needs a broader circle of decisionmakers debating what constitutes the U.S. national interest in Pakistan and what options Washington has there. More information should be put in the public domain. Congress should hold hearings to explore these questions. The Bush administration and Congress should instruct the intelligence community to produce a national intelligence estimate on Pakistan's stability and on U.S. influence in the country and should release a version of this report to the public. The Government Accountability Office should report on whether or not U.S. money being spent in Pakistan is achieving its goals. Is the priority to steer India and Pakistan away from the nuclear precipice, to keep nukes out of the hands of terrorists, to rebuild Afghanistan, to hunt down al Qaeda, or to support Pakistan's long-term stability and prosperity? Arguing that support to Musharraf accomplishes all of these goals obscures the key question of what Washington wants in the first place and only reaffirms U.S. dependency on a man who might be gone tomorrow.

The United States also must develop a better understanding of how Pakistan is changing. With more than one-half of Pakistan's population under the age of 15, today's certainties are unlikely to be tomorrow's. Pakistan experts may agree on the reliability and capability of Pakistan's military, but the U.S. government knows relatively little about the lower reaches of the military and intelligence services, let alone the business community and Islamist parties. Who is likely to be the next Musharraf? Will this new leader emerge from the military and adopt an "enlightened" form of Islam or something more akin to what has emerged in Palestine or Iran? Billions in military hardware and supplies are unlikely to diminish the deep cynicism toward the U.S. war on terrorism within Pakistan's security establishment and Pakistani society at large.

The current U.S. approach toward Pakistan is more about buying time than about adjusting means to goals. With the new Congress and the 2008 U.S. presidential election campaign already under way, Americans deserve a more serious public debate on what the United States is trying to do with Pakistan and how it is trying to do it. This requires leadership from the top at a time of competing priorities in Iraq, Iran, North Korea, and elsewhere, as well as flexibility in how to interpret the nature of the U.S. commitment to Pakistan. A successful U.S.-Pakistani relationship is critical to Afghanistan's reconstruction, regional stability, nuclear nonproliferation, U.S. engagement with the entire Muslim world, and Americans' safety at home. Plan A has forestalled disaster for five-plus years, but there is no Plan B, and the costs of crisis in Pakistan are too great to live without workable options.

Notes

1. Barnett Rubin, "Saving Afghanistan," *Foreign Affairs* 86, no. 1 (January/February 2007): 57–78; Carlotta Gall, "At Border, Signs of Pakistani Role in Taliban Surge," *New York Times*, January 21, 2007, p. A1.
2. Samina Ahmed, "Pakistan's Tribal Areas: Appeasing the Militants," *Crisis Group Asia Report*, no. 125 (December 11, 2006), http://www.crisisgroup.org/home/getfile.cfm?id=2672&tid=4568&type=pdf&l=1; Jan Cartwright, "Musharraf's Waziristan Deal: Shrewd Strategy or Tacit Surrender?" *CSIS South Asia Monitor*, no. 100 (November 1, 2006), http://www.csis.org/media/csis/pubs/sam100.pdf; Happymon Jacob, "U.S.-Pakistan Military Operations in Pak-Afghan Border" *Issue Brief* 1, no. 3 (March 2004), http://www.observerindia.com/publications/IssueBrief/ib040317.pdf.
3. Jack Reed, "Iraq Trip Report," http://reed.senate.gov/documents/Trip%20Reports/tripreport%20oct06%20final.pdf.
4. Walter Pincus, "Pakistan Will Have to Reckon With Tribal Leaders, Negroponte Says," *Washington Post*, December 15, 2006, p. A26.
5. Office of the Press Secretary, The White House, "President Bush and President Musharraf of Pakistan Participate in Press Availability," September 22, 2006, http://www.whitehouse.gov/news/releases/2006/09/20060922.html.
6. Pervez Musharraf, *In the Line of Fire: A Memoir* (New York: Free Press, 2006).
7. "Pakistan: Ally or Adversary?" *Atlantic Monthly* 298, no. 5 (December 2006): 44.
8. James Astill, "Parliamentary Puppetry: The Messy Business of Pakistani Politics," *Economist*, July 8–14, 2006, http://economist.com/surveys/displaystory.cfm?story_id=7107902.
9. Teresita C. Schaffer, *Pakistan's Future and U.S. Policy Options* (Washington, D.C.: CSIS Press, 2004).
10. Ibid.; "Out of the Firing Line" (CSIS table-top exercise for current and former U.S. government officials, Washington, D.C., November 2006).
11. Stephen Coll, *Ghost Wars: The Secret History of the CIA, Afghanistan, and bin Laden, From the Soviet Invasion to September 10, 2001* (New York: Penguin Press, 2004); George Crile, *Charlie Wilson's War* (New York: Atlantic Monthly Press, 2003); "Pakistan: America's Unstable Ally; An Interview With Ambassador Robert Oakley, Ambassador to Pakistan, 1988–1992," America Abroad Media, February 6, 2004, http://www.americaabroadmedia.org/media/On%20line%20extra%20materials/Pakistan-Oakley.pdf.

12. "Pakistan: America's Unstable Ally."
13. "The 9/11 Commission Report: Final Report of the National Commission on Terrorist Attacks Upon the United States," July 22, 2004, http://www.9-11commission.gov/report/index.htm.
14. Ibid.; Musharraf, *In the Line of Fire*; Christine Fair, *The Counterterror Coalitions: Cooperation With Pakistan and India* (Santa Monica, Calif.: RAND, 2004).
15. Fair, *Counterterror Coalitions*.
16. "9/11 Commission Report."
17. Thomas H. Kean et al., "Final Report on 9/11 Commission Recommendations," 9/11 Public Discourse Project, December 5, 2005, p. 4, http://www.9-11pdp.org/press/2005-12-05_report.pdf.
18. Former U.S. intelligence official, interview with author, Washington, D.C., June 2006.
19. U.S. State Department official, interview with author, Washington, D.C., April 2006.
20. Musharraf, *In the Line of Fire*, p. 237.
21. Mark Mazzetti, "Military Role in U.S. Embassies Creates Strains, Report Says," *New York Times*, December 20, 2006, p. A8.
22. Office of the Secretary of Defense, "Coalition Support Fund Tracker, FY2002–FY2005," February 2006.
23. Reed, "Iraq Trip Report."
24. Pentagon officials, interviews with author, Washington, D.C., November 2006.
25. Chris Fair and Peter Chalk, *Fortifying Pakistan: The Role of U.S. Internal Security Assistance* (Washington, D.C.: USIP Press Books, 2006).
26. "Proposed Sale of F-16 Aircraft and Weapons Systems to Pakistan," hearing before the Committee on International Relations, U.S. House of Representatives, July 20, 2006, http://commdocs.house.gov/committees/intlrel/hfa28787.000/hfa28787_0f.htm.
27. Pentagon officials, interviews with author, Washington, D.C., May 2006.
28. U.S. Department of State, "Foreign Military Training: Joint Report to Congress, Fiscal Years 2005 and 2006," September 2006, http://www.state.gov/t/pm/rls/rpt/fmtrpt/2006/74686.htm.
29. U.S. Treasury Department official, interview with author, Washington, D.C., February 2006.
30. USAID, Country-Level Foreign Assistance Extended Framework, "Proposed Fast Track Countries" (draft, May 2006).
31. State Department and USAID officials, interviews with author, Washington, D.C., December 2006.
32. For the best work on Pakistan's future, see Stephen Cohen, *The Idea of Paki-*

stan (Washington, D.C.: Brookings Institution Press, 2004).

33. 150 Pakistanis, interviews with author, various Pakistani cities, March 2006.

34. For a discussion of congressional-executive relations on foreign assistance, see Charles Flickner, "Removing Impediments to an Effective Partnership With Congress," in *Security by Other Means*, ed. Lael Brainard (Washington, D.C.: Brookings Institution Press/CSIS, 2007).

Ashley J. Tellis

U.S. Strategy: Assisting Pakistan's Transformation

Pakistan today is clearly both part of the problem and the solution to the threat of terrorism facing the United States. Although it did not set out to do so, the landmark report issued by the 9/11 Commission ended up highlighting Pakistan's deep involvement with international terrorism. For more than two decades, beginning with the Sikh insurgency in the Indian Punjab in the early 1980s, Islamabad consciously nurtured and supported terrorist groups as a means to secure its geopolitical goals vis-à-vis Afghanistan and India. Although in the immediate aftermath of the September 11 attacks Islamabad made the difficult decisions to stand aside as the United States destroyed the Taliban regime in Afghanistan and to assist Washington in hunting down the remnants of Al Qaeda, President Gen. Pervez Musharraf's regime has regrettably still not irrevocably eschewed supporting terrorism as a matter of state policy. Unfortunately, the 9/11 Commission's report glossed over this fact.

Although Musharraf has been rightly commended for his courageous early post-9/11 decisions in the global war against terrorism, Pakistan today deliberately remains reluctant to pursue the Taliban along its northwestern frontier and continues to support various terrorist groups operating in Kashmir. The many welcome changes in Pakistan's strategic

Ashley J. Tellis is a senior associate at the Carnegie Endowment for International Peace in Washington, D.C. He wishes to thank Teresita Schaffer and George Perkovich for their helpful comments.

The Washington Quarterly • 28:1 pp. 97–116.

direction under Musharraf since September 11 have therefore not extended to completely renouncing terrorism as an instrument of national policy. Islamabad continues to support terrorist groups in pursuit of geopolitical interests it perceives as critical, such as securing a friendly, even pliant regime in Afghanistan and wresting the state of Jammu and Kashmir away from India.

Although Pakistan's interest in these objectives is understandable, its support of terrorist groups is troublesome because even Islamabad cannot be certain that its control over the extremist forces it has unleashed will be robust in perpetuity. The terrorist groups nurtured by Islamabad today for its own strategic purposes may end up turning against the Pakistani state, as has already happened in some instances, with grave consequences for stability in a large, populous, nuclear-armed Muslim country. The violent, antediluvian Islamist ideology that animates many of the terrorist groups supported by Pakistan also places them in natural opposition to the United States and, as a consequence, could result in attacks on U.S. as well as Afghan or Indian interests.

Assisting the transformation of Pakistan to avert its continued threat to U.S. security in particular and to Western interests more generally, therefore, represents a difficult challenge for the United States. Pakistan has accumulated a complex set of strategic, economic, political, and societal problems throughout its 50 years of troubled statehood that are not only individually challenging but also mutually and viciously reinforcing.[1] Successive Pakistani leaders have shied away from promoting serious reform because the daunting nature of their country's crisis has inevitably implied that even partial amelioration would require extensive revolutionary change. They have therefore traditionally settled either for half-baked or sham efforts at reform, none of which survived their terms in office.

Thus far, Musharraf has not demonstrated that he is an exception to this rule. The structural reforms he has overseen have focused mainly on strengthening his own hold on power, and reforms related to policy improvements carry no guarantees of surviving his term in office. For all his pleas about "enlightened moderation,"[2] Musharraf has in fact done little to develop institutions that will promote a democratic temper or provide moderate political forces in Pakistan an opportunity to prosper. To the contrary, his political machinations have resulted in Islamist political parties rising to prominence in Pakistan's highest legislative bodies for the first time, while his strategies for preventing Islamist control of the state in the long term all hinge on continued military supremacy in Pakistani politics.

Most of the changes necessary to transform Pakistan into a success story have to be undertaken and led by Pakistanis themselves. Outsiders, including powerful allies such as the United States, can only play a supporting role. Successful transformation will require Pakistani leaders to make difficult choices, including subordinating immediate, often important institutional interests for larger national gains. Few, however, have historically appeared capable of meeting this challenge; and the current military leadership, despite being well intentioned, is unlikely to prove exceptional in this regard. Musharraf's refusal to implement an agreement previously reached with Pakistan's major political parties to retire as chief of army staff is the latest example of how short-term, sometimes personal, interests still trump larger concerns of public importance. In this case, Musharraf's actions will further retard the return to democratic rule and prevent a highly regarded reformist officer, Gen. Yousaf Khan, from ascending to the army's senior-most leadership position.

Assisting the transformation of Pakistan into a stable, nonthreatening state will also require important allies such as the United States to demonstrate a willingness to sacrifice key short-term interests to realize long-term benefits. Because such a transformation inevitably demands that Pakistan become a fully democratic regime in which the military functions as the guardian, not the master, of the state, the key question is whether Washington and other capitals have the foresight, skill, and political will actively to pursue policies that push Islamabad in this direction while still maintaining its cooperation in fighting the war on terrorism.

Anatomy of a Crisis

After the bloody partition of 1947, Pakistan found itself a deeply insecure state—territorially bifurcated, administratively handicapped, economically deprived, and soon at war with its larger neighbor India over Kashmir. For almost 10 years after its independence, Pakistan struggled to create a constitutional democracy. The universal adult suffrage associated with democratic governance, however, would have granted the more numerous Bengalis in East Pakistan the right to rule over the Mohajir- and Punjabi-dominated western wing of the state. Because this outcome was unacceptable to these groups, various constitutional drafts were rejected, and the opportunity to develop democratic institutions was irrevocably lost as the jostling ethnic and bureaucratic elites who quickly dominated Pakistan's political vacuum forged "rules of the game" that would undermine democracy for many decades to come.[3]

Further, the "viceregal" tradition—the habit of bureaucratic dominance that characterized governance in those British Indian states that would eventually become West Pakistan—the problematic role of Islam in the founding and legitimization of Pakistan, the competitive relationship between the provinces and the center, and the asymmetry of power between elected officials and unelected bureaucracies all combined to create unresolved sources of tension that survive to the present day. The failure to correct these fundamental problems during the critical formative years after independence radically weakened the foundations on which a democratic political order could be constructed. Therefore, it was not surprising that in 1958, barely two years after being promulgated, Pakistan's draft constitution was abrogated by its first military coup, an event that cemented the deformation of Pakistani politics.

The military's usurpation of political authority in Pakistan was meant initially as nothing more than a remedial act to strengthen the country's defenses temporarily against internal disorder caused by fractious politics, ideological schisms, and interprovincial disputes, as well as external threats posed by India. Before long, however, the Pakistani military, emboldened by U.S. assistance during the early Cold War and determined to recover Kashmir from India, renounced its previously apolitical role as the guardian of the state to become just another interest group vying to preserve its control over the state itself.[4] Each subsequent military intervention, justified by the internal and external security challenges of the day, further compounded this problem by exacerbating existing political divisions while creating new ones.[5]

The army controlled the nation's internal and external security policies, the prized share of the national budget, extensive political and economic patronage, and a vast network of commercial organizations run by retired military officers. Taken alone, this consolidation of power dealt a lethal blow to Pakistan's democracy; when combined with Pakistan's revanchist goal of wresting control of Kashmir from India (a superior and more capable power) by force, it also proved fatal to Pakistan's internal stability. Over time, as the country progressively transmuted into a garrison state with a war economy, it also became a breeding ground for radical groups, many cultivated by the military in its effort to resolve various domestic and foreign policy challenges. As Teresita Schaffer concluded succinctly, "The role of the military is a major obstacle impeding Pakistan's political viability."[6]

The crisis in Pakistan is extensive and systemic. Although strategic, economic, political, and societal obstacles exist and each has its specific causes, in their totality they indicate Pakistan's failure to resolve its internal and external security problems without resorting to military rule. Tackling internal instability requires revitalizing democratic politics, reorienting economic growth toward developmental objectives, ensuring interprovincial equity, and developing a national identity rooted neither in radical Islam nor in reflexive opposition to India. Tackling external security requires an accommodation with New Delhi that both preserves Pakistan's dignity and resolves the vexing dispute over Kashmir. Thus far, military rule in Pakistan has been unable to secure any of these objectives.

Most observers today appropriately conclude, therefore, that Pakistan will not be able to remedy its multifaceted failures in governance, economic management, and foreign and strategic policy unless its leaders restore civilian democratic rule, governed by a constitutional framework with appropriate checks and balances.[7] Any attempt at reform that attacks Islamabad's complex problems piecemeal will produce only temporary palliatives. Rather, resolution will require significant external assistance, a permanent commitment to reconstituting a democratic order free of military interference, and time.

What Can Be Done

Outsiders can provide assistance in limited though important ways, but Pakistanis themselves will have to institutionalize solutions to their country's problems. The key elements of an eventual, integrated solution fall into the four primary realms in which Pakistan's most difficult challenges exist: strategic, economic, political, and societal.

Strategic

At the strategic level, Pakistan remains in a permanent state of war with India, fearful of India's natural dominance yet determined to limit New Delhi's capacity to cause harm by exploiting its weaknesses. In recent decades, Pakistan has exploited these frailties by supporting various insurgencies within India on the expectation that New Delhi will not retaliate against Pakistan through military action for fear of sparking a nuclear holocaust.[8] This strategy has further strengthened Pakistan's determination to acquire the weapons of mass destruction (WMD) necessary to deter and defeat India at any level of escalation, even if that acquisition has come at the cost of lax oversight of its WMD programs.

Competition with New Delhi has also pushed Islamabad to prevent India from restoring its influence in Afghanistan. In this effort to preserve its "strategic depth," Pakistan has consciously tolerated the presence of Taliban remnants along its northwestern frontier as a hedging strategy in case Afghan president Hamid Karzai's government turns out to be overly friendly to Indian interests. Finally, largely as a result of its tumultuous history, Pakistan views its external allies today entirely as transitory instruments of convenience, with their utility dependent mainly on their ability to assist Islamabad in its enduring conflict with India. Therefore, the core challenge in the strategic realm is to mitigate the Pakistani military's perception of permanent, inevitable conflict with India.

The strength of this perception has led the Pakistani army to pursue a variety of risky and destabilizing strategic initiatives, including terrorism and wars, during the last 50 years. It has also resulted in the military's commandeering of domestic politics and its domination of the economy. The restoration of stable civilian rule in Islamabad would greatly help attenuate this problem; historically, civilian regimes in Pakistan have been far less obsessed with the Indian threat than have their military counterparts. On the few occasions when civilian governments in Islamabad have engaged in active security competition with India, they did so for the most part to placate the military and thus minimize the potential for military interference in their rule.

Beyond restoring civilian rule, specific actions are also necessary to address Pakistan's strategic challenges, including ending Pakistani state support of all terrorist groups, including those operating in Afghanistan and Kashmir; sustaining conflict management and possibly conflict resolution through diplomatic dialogue with India; instituting a rigorous program to control the proliferation of nuclear materials and know-how as well as enhancing the security of Pakistan's nuclear assets; and developing a cooperative U.S.-Pakistani relationship.

Economic

The economic challenges facing Pakistan are so complex and interrelated that no summary, let alone one spanning a few paragraphs, can provide a complete solution. What follows, therefore, is only partial and impressionistic. Pakistan's unending conflict with India has resulted in the creation and maintenance of a war economy with high military expenditures sustained at the cost of social, developmental, and human investments.[9] These expenditures, being a significant percentage of gross domestic product and central government expenditures, have resulted in low public and private savings, as well as depressed rates of growth; this trend was most evident during the 1990s. Low savings have necessitated high external borrowing to meet defense-heavy public expenditures, creating high debt-servicing costs that further impede savings and investment. The government's neglect of human investments such as public education and health care has resulted in low levels of social welfare, but more problematically has created opportunities for Islamist institutions to fill the gap. The military's connections with and reliance on rural elites for military manpower and cooperative social bases has also resulted in a traditional unwillingness to tax agriculture and institute land reforms that might increase the state's revenue.

In sum, Pakistan faces two major economic challenges. The first is to correct the macroeconomic problems caused by Pakistan's inefficient war economy, and the second is to create stable, rule-bound institutional arrangements that permit productive individual behaviors to sustain desired, long-term macroeconomic outcomes without repeated state intervention. The Musharraf regime has presided over a welcome correction of Pakistan's macroeconomic performance, with rising growth rates, a reduced fiscal deficit, lower inflation, and higher tax revenues. Three factors have helped advance these improvements: the discipline imposed by international financial institutions (IFIs), U.S. economic assistance associated with Operation Enduring Freedom, and the beginnings of structural reform in Pakistan.[10]

Long-term economic success will depend on the completion of structural change, including the creation of new institutional arrangements that alter microeconomic behaviors. These arrangements' ability to endure and thus produce lasting results will depend on their perceived legitimacy. Although agreements with IFIs and foreign governments that bind future Pakistani regimes may in the short term circumvent legitimacy issues, the long-term survival of any new institutional arrangements will depend on their acceptance by the body politic at large. Even as that process of securing political consent evolves, sustaining economic success will require the Pakistani government to contain defense expenditures; increase investments in agriculture, small- and medium-sized industries, and irrigation to raise the employment level, alleviate poverty, and avert rural socioeconomic collapse; increase spending on education, health, and social safety nets in order to improve human capital; and build institutions of accountability for good economic management outside of executive control.

Political

At the political level, the view of India as a permanent existential threat not only justifies the Pakistani military's own claims to relevance and primacy within Pakistani politics but has also resulted in the destruction of the normative, legal, and institutional foundations necessary to sustain a democratic regime. The abrogation of successive constitutions in Pakistan has destroyed the sanctity and effectiveness of the basic law necessary for stable governance. It has also completely undermined the judiciary, which has been compelled to legitimize each successive military usurpation through a "doctrine of necessity" that, in effect, permits the new leader to annul the constitution in the name of saving the country.

Further, when in power, military regimes have not worked either to establish effective conditions for the return to civilian rule or to develop institutions that might make military usurpation unnecessary in the future. Rather, they have focused on immunizing themselves against criticism and deflecting any popular challenges that might arise. More dangerously, in an effort to ensure their survival and mitigate perceptions of their illegitimacy, military regimes have repeatedly undermined centrist social forces and political parties in Pakistan by encouraging radical political groups opposed to democracy. They have also deliberately privileged party-less local governments over central and provincial institutions because the former typically cannot threaten core military interests relating to security policy, national budgets, and economic organization.

If Pakistan is to become a moderate Muslim state that exists in peace with itself, its neighbors, and the international community, its political process must be reformed. A stable, successful Pakistan will be a democratic regime governed by a constitution that incorporates effective checks and balances. A civilian government, freely and regularly elected, responsible to the constitution, and protected by the military as part of its constitutional responsibilities, will advance the marginalization of radical Islamist forces in Pakistan.

Only the establishment of democratic institutions and stable civilian rule offer some hope of overcoming the myriad challenges confronting Pakistan today, including resolving the security dilemmas with India that drive the military's support for Islamist terrorist groups; removing the economic distortions that privilege military expenditures over social investments and that create the preconditions for the rise of disaffected Islamists; and correcting the failures of command politics associated with military ascendancy, which prevents the national interest from being defined by open competition in a vibrant civil society.

The resuscitation of democracy in Pakistan offers no guarantee that it will successfully break out from its current state of morass. The absence of democracy, however, will almost certainly ensure the perpetuation of dangerous structural trends that will lead inevitably to state breakdown. Moreover, the failure of previous attempts to institute democratic reforms should not deter future efforts. Democratic civilian rulers held office in 1973–1977 and 1988–1999, but their fear of military interference kept them focused primarily on self-preservation rather than good governance. The missteps of these democratic moments in Pakistan's history should not be used as an argument against the restoration of democracy. Rather, they underscore the importance of military abstention from rule.

In order to restore democracy, Pakistan must take several important steps, including convening a new constitutional convention to discuss how the 1973 constitution, as the only document that accommodated proposals from all Pakistani political parties and received universal acceptance, may be revitalized as the "basic law" governing Pakistan's political life; restoring centrist political parties, through a truth and reconciliation panel if necessary; curtailing the role of the federal civil services in provincial administration and strengthening provincial governments; reforming the civil service, judiciary, and police to support civilian government and the rule of law; and amending Musharraf's 2000 Devolution Plan—which seeks to empower local governments—to permit party-based local elections, parliamentary review mechanisms, and fiscal decentralization.

Societal

At the societal level, repeated bouts of military rule, especially in recent decades, have effectively empowered radical Islamist elements, which have been perceived as useful instruments both to marginalize the moderate opposition domestically and to advance Islamabad's regional ambitions externally. Yet, the responsibility for this presence does not rest solely with the military. Indeed, radical Islamist elements have existed in Pakistan since partition, when founding father Mohammed Ali Jinnah's inflammatory "Islam in Danger" campaign exploited the power of Muslim militancy to assure Pakistan's creation.[11] Jinnah tried to disavow this approach once the new state was formed; in a speech before the Constituent Assembly in 1947, he told the Pakistani people, "You may belong to any religion or caste or creed—that has nothing to do with the business of the state.... We are starting with this fundamental principle that we are all citizens and citizens of one state."[12]

The evocative symbols and imagery he had exploited in the run-up to partition, however, had already done their damage.[13] Pietist groups in Pakistan challenged his vision immediately, arguing that, if the new state was to be secular, the new Muslim arrivals need not have migrated from India, which was secular already. Jinnah's inability to answer this critique satisfactorily created a space for Islamist groups to survive as permanent challengers to secularism in Pakistan. Although these groups were never dominant in national politics during the early decades, they were nonetheless prominent enough to be exploited periodically by civilian as well as military regimes in support of their own ends.

Whereas blame for the presence of radical Islamism in Pakistan is shared, the military is primarily responsible for its sharp growth in recent decades. Indeed, the two key episodes that marked the consolidation of radicalized Islam occurred under military rule. Gen. Zia-ul Haq (1977–1988) began enshrining Islam throughout the state in order to resolve legitimacy problems, undermine his civilian opposition, and raise committed foot soldiers for the anti-Soviet war in Afghanistan. More recently, Musharraf, in an attempt to destroy the mainstream political parties that threatened to undermine his authority during elections in 2002, brought an Islamist coalition to prominence at the national level for the first time in Pakistan's tumultuous political history.

What has corrupted the social fabric in Pakistan irrevocably has been the military's deliberate use, since the early 1990s, of radical Islamic groups to fuel the jihad in Kashmir and Afghanistan.[14] The military's conviction that the jihad in Kashmir is both just and necessary and that Pakistan needs a friendly regime opposed to India to its west resulted in the proliferation of armed Islamist surrogates. In theory, these groups would promote Pakistan's strategic interests on the country's eastern and western borders. In practice, they often embrace a worldview that leads them to treat not only India but also Israel; the United States; and, increasingly, secular elements of the Pakistani military itself as mortal threats. The dramatic spread of poverty in Pakistan during the last 20 years caused by economic mismanagement and the demands of a wartime economy, coupled with the weakening of democratic institutions that could peacefully channel the aspirations of the underclass, have only further strengthened the influence of these groups.

Thus, the transformation of Pakistan as a state requires not only strategic, economic, and political reform but also the revitalization of Pakistani society. Pakistan needs an active civil society that is Muslim in a cultural sense rather than an exclusivist ideological one. Achieving this goal will be difficult; five decades of deformations have left these societal problems deeply entrenched and recalcitrant and viciously connected with and reinforcing of Pakistan's failures in strategy, economics, and governance. Given the complex nature of the challenges, however, several issue areas will require direct and focused activity, including correcting gender inequalities, containing ideological mobilization, improving civil society, and selectively expanding state control. Several initiatives can be identified as the minimum actions necessary to achieve these ends: regulating, restructuring, and controlling the *madrassas* (the Islamic religious schools) as Musharraf initially intended; slowly beginning deweaponization in accordance with the army's post-1990 plans; investing in targeted health care and in the education of women, especially in rural areas; working with nongovernmental organizations (NGOs) to invest in programs to strengthen political parties, student organizations, press and media organizations, and governmental institutions; and initiating rural and infrastructure development programs for the Federally Administered Tribal Areas, the frontier provinces that historically were loosely controlled by Islamabad and currently remain hotbeds of Al Qaeda and Taliban presence.

In sum, these strategic, economic, political, and societal solutions only touch on the actions required to assist Pakistan's transformation into a modern state. When considered in their totality, these solutions appear to share some common characteristics. For example, they are complex and expensive in terms of resources and political will, and they must be initiated and implemented primarily by Pakistanis, despite outsiders' ability to play helpful subsidiary roles. The solutions vary, however, in terms of their "intrinsic effectiveness," defined as their relative importance in assisting Pakistan's transformation into a healthy and modern Muslim state, and the time frames required for successful implementation.

The Role of the United States

The wide breadth of obstacles threatening to impede the Pakistani state's transformation to moderation, stability, and democracy demand that Washington concentrate on only a small subset of issues when deciding how most effectively to offer U.S. assistance. The 9/11 Commission's recommendations on how to wean Pakistan away from its involvement with terrorism offer one set of guidelines, but they may prove insufficient. "Sustaining the current scale of aid" and embarking on "a comprehensive effort that extends from military aid to support for better education"[15] are essential actions, but they cannot be substitutes for transforming the structures of rule in Islamabad. The report's conclusion "that Musharraf's government represents the best hope for stability in Pakistan"[16] is deeply problematic. Although true in the immediate future, any U.S. policy based on this premise would have the long-term effect of reinforcing the power of the Pakistani military and intelligence services—each has cultivated terrorism—and would come at the expense of Pakistan's already battered civilian political institutions.

Alternative measures should be selected where the United States possesses the comparative advantage to make a difference or U.S. interests are particularly salient. There will obviously be many more matters that engage American concern and where various kinds of U.S. private and governmental, as well as international, assistance may be relevant. Washington should nevertheless concentrate its energies principally on those key problems that meet the tests of comparative advantage or relative salience, namely, safeguarding Pakistan's nuclear estate and restoring democracy in Pakistan as part of a larger grand bargain with Islamabad that stabilizes the U.S.-Pakistani relationship over the long term.

Safeguarding Pakistan's Nuclear Estate

The first and most important issue on which the United States should focus is preventing the diffusion of Pakistan's nuclear technology and the loss of control over Pakistan's nuclear weapons. This problem affects U.S. security directly and is an area in which U.S. assistance can make an important difference.

In the short term, the United States should secure a full accounting of the A. Q. Khan network activities regarding nuclear proliferation from the Pakistani government, including details about what was transferred and to whom. It also should ensure that Pakistan implements the appropriate technical, organizational, and procedural safeguards to prevent a recurrence of illicit proliferation. The Bush administration began discussions with Islamabad on both of these issues, but U.S. and international concerns are far from being fully assuaged.

Over the medium term, or about the next four years, the United States should help Pakistan improve the physical protection and the oversight of its critical materials at each of its strategic sites. This effort entails providing assistance to develop simulations and exercises; transferring appropriate materials from military handbooks on nuclear weapons security; providing technology for more sophisticated vaults, access doors, portal control equipment, surveillance gear, and advanced instrumentation for materials accounting; helping Pakistan's Strategic Plans Division develop effective personnel reliability programs; and helping develop procedures to reduce the likelihood of sensitive information leaks.[17] Given the relatively large size of Pakistan's nuclear estate, even if the United States were to offer this aid presently, it will take time before it can be fully absorbed and implemented. The Bush administration conducted preliminary discussions with Pakistan on these matters, but Islamabad's suspicions about U.S. intentions and its fears about compromising the security of its nuclear assets imply that U.S. technical assistance may not be fully utilized for some time. In any event, Washington should continue and even accelerate these endeavors.

In addition to improving passive protection, the United States should also help Pakistan eliminate the threat of unauthorized use of its nuclear weapons. Confronting this challenge contributes both to increasing regional security and mitigating another possible danger to the United States. Despite significant public fears globally, the likelihood of unauthorized use stemming from theft or rogue launches is relatively low in peacetime because Islamabad's nuclear devices are stored in component form, rather than as complete, ready-to-use weapons, in relatively secure facilities. Under conditions of crisis, however, when these components are integrated into complete weapons and then dispersed into the field, the threat of loss, capture, or unauthorized use increases.

To the maximum degree possible, U.S. security interests demand reducing the prospect of these threats materializing, consistent with Pakistan's own requirements for stable deterrence. The only solution that satisfies both these goals is incorporating technical controls, which in turn implies that the United States should consider providing Pakistan with early-generation "permissive action links" (PALs), which ensure that the weapons could never be used without authorization if they were for any reason lost or compromised. This issue will require amending current U.S. commitments to international regimes and possibly to its domestic laws, but such exceptions are necessary given that ironclad technical controls on Islamabad's nuclear weapons will advance interests on both sides as well as increase regional security.

Over the long term, and as Pakistani confidence in the United States grows with respect to the security of its nuclear stockpile, Washington should work with Islamabad to develop plans for cooperative action in case of a nuclear emergency. Such plans should cover a variety of contingencies, including attempts to steal fissile material or nuclear weapons; a successful theft of sensitive items; or the discovery of dramatic weaknesses in material accounting, control, and protection systems at particular facilities. As a matter of prudence, the United States should also plan for dealing with such contingencies unilaterally.

Restoring Democracy in Pakistan

The potential for continued deterioration in Pakistan threatens to affect U.S. security even more deleteriously than it has previously. Today, Pakistan is populated by a variety of armed Islamist groups that possess both the desire and the capability to mount catastrophic attacks on U.S. interests. These terrorist groups will continue to be sustained by the Pakistani military so long as they are viewed as effective tools in Islamabad's ongoing conflict with India. Although containing these terrorists constitutes the short-term solution, getting the Pakistani army out of the business of terrorism remains pivotal for the long term. This cannot be ensured unless Pakistan develops strong institutions of democratic rule coupled with a liberal political ethos. This is undoubtedly a daunting challenge. Overwhelmed by the multitude of demands surrounding Pakistan's democratization, every U.S. government has been scared into conservatism. In each instance, successive U.S. administrations have preferred to deal with the Pakistani military regime of the day to resolve the most pressing immediate problems where Islamabad's assistance may be of value, all while hoping that a meltdown in Pakistan, if it came to that, would not occur on their watch.

After the September 11 attacks, the continued radicalization of Islamic groups in Pakistan and elsewhere has brought this approach of calculated neglect to the limits of its success. Washington should focus today on convincing Musharraf to relinquish his position as chief of army staff by some specified early date if he intends to renege, as it now appears, on his previous promise to demit office in December 2004 and on encouraging him to remain active in Pakistani political life as a civilian politician who holds office as part of a normalized political process with regular elections. Musharraf's own transition to some alternative political persona must be part of a larger evolution leading to the restoration of full civilian rule. This restoration, which should be Washington's main objective concerning Pakistan's domestic reform over the next four years, should aim to persuade Pakistan's army and its principal political parties to accept and prepare for a constitutional convention that reestablishes the 1973 constitution, modified if necessary, as the fundamental law of the land.

Defining stable, new rules of the game is only the first, albeit vital, step in the process of Pakistan's transformation. Success ultimately requires the empowerment of civil society in the form of political parties, NGOs, the media, and other associations.[18] The United States can and, indeed, has already begun to help by expanding and realigning its official assistance to aid the development of these institutions. Washington should also pressure Pakistan to complete the registration of *madrassas* and reform their curricula, even though it should refrain from financially assisting these institutions. In general, U.S. economic assistance should focus away from debt forgiveness, so that Pakistan bears some responsibility for its previous decisions and discovers the concept of opportunity costs, and toward investments in building social and human capital, especially in rural areas. Increased human and physical investments such as schools, roads, and primary health care in the Federally Administered Tribal Areas of Pakistan, in collaboration with allies and with the private sector, are also desirable.

Constructing a Grand Bargain with Pakistan

A stable U.S.-Pakistani relationship would serve the long-term interests of both countries as well as larger U.S. objectives in South Asia, which include minimizing the risks of another Indo-Pakistani war and transforming the U.S.-Indian relationship in order to preserve a stable, lasting balance of power in Asia. Although Pakistan is currently central to the global war on terrorism, Washington will have difficulty building a long-term relationship with Islamabad if it does not address the latter's core concerns about security, particularly its external security. Indeed, fostering democracy in Pakistan requires that Washington make democracy promotion a priority in its relationship with the Pakistani military leadership, but the Pakistani army is likely to resist all such initiatives unless they are embedded in a larger U.S. commitment to Pakistan's security.

Yet, helping Pakistan manage its problems of external security will remain a challenging and nettlesome endeavor for the United States. The chief difficulty here remains the clash between U.S. and Pakistani priorities, specifically Pakistan's policies toward Kashmir and its relations with India. The United States would obviously prefer Pakistan to use only peaceful means in its struggle over Kashmir and for India and Pakistan to work together toward a peaceful settlement. Islamabad, however, believes that, if it does not foment terrorism in Kashmir, New Delhi will ignore Pakistan and attempt to resolve the dispute by means of an internal agreement with the state's disaffected population. Furthermore, the experience of the Soviet Union in Afghanistan in the 1980s appears to have convinced the Pakistani military that low-intensity conflict can drive India from Kashmir or, at the very least, bring New Delhi to the table with the promise of significant concessions.

If U.S. policy acquiesces to this Pakistani strategy, it would undermine the moral foundations of the ongoing global war on terrorism; impede Washington's effort to develop a strategic partnership with India; and help precipitate another major Indo-Pakistani political crisis and, perhaps, even war. If, conversely, the United States aggressively assists India in its struggle against Pakistani-supported terrorism in Kashmir, Islamabad might be less cooperative in Operation Enduring Freedom. It would certainly view Washington as unresponsive to its security concerns and ungrateful for all the assistance it has provided thus far in the war on terrorism.

The zero-sum quality of these opposing pressures makes managing U.S.-Indo-Pakistani relations a very difficult challenge. The best that can be hoped for is that the contradictory pressures may be mitigated, but even mitigation, which is all that can be accomplished in the short term, would require a complex and sophisticated strategy. First, the United States would have to continue to pressure Pakistan to end terrorist infiltration against India permanently, thus giving New Delhi an incentive to remain at the negotiating table. Then, as the recently initiated dialogue process unfolds, the United States should encourage both sides to expand trade, people-to-people contacts, transportation links, and cultural exchanges, hopefully to create new gains for both parties. Finally, Washington should press India to improve the political and economic conditions in Jammu and Kashmir, restrain the abuses of its security forces operating there, and conduct a serious dialogue with representatives of its disaffected population in order to assuage Pakistani sentiments and minimize the temptation for Islamabad to take provocative action.

This approach, however, which represents current U.S. policy, will provide only temporary relief. The fundamental problem arises over goals and motivations: Pakistan seeks negotiations with India principally to alter the status quo in Kashmir, whereas India accepts negotiations with Pakistan primarily to ratify it. This conundrum is irresolvable because of the differences in relative capability between the two sides. Pakistan is the state that feels most strongly about changing the status quo, yet it has no peaceful way of compelling India to surrender control over the contested territory. India, on the other hand, already possesses the prized territory and is strong enough to withstand any Pakistani efforts to wrest it away. Until one side or the other changes its grand strategic objective, therefore, the Indo-Pakistani dispute over Kashmir will continue to elude resolution.[19]

The United States has neither the incentives nor the capability to compel India to alter its goals in Kashmir. Because Pakistan's means of attaining its goals have come to threaten both its own security and that of the United States, however, Washington must exert influence on Islamabad. During the next four years, therefore, the U.S. administration will not necessarily have to change Pakistan's goals in Kashmir, but it will have to lean on Pakistan to change the means it has used since at least 1994, the most dangerous being the unleashing of Islamic terrorist groups. Washington can reinforce its message in multiple ways: first, by enlarging and sustaining its economic aid program as long as Pakistan meets its commitments on terrorism—both in Kashmir and Afghanistan—proliferation, and democracy; second, by increasing the quality of U.S. military cooperation with Pakistan, primarily through expanding military education and exercises as well as providing spare parts for equipment already in Pakistan's inventory; and, third, by exhibiting a willingness to use U.S. and IFI aid, U.S. domestic laws, and other political instruments of influence as leverage to induce Pakistan to control terrorism, curb proliferation, and undertake meaningful political reform.

Washington has moved in this direction, but with two significant distinctions. Although it initiated a large economic and military assistance program for Pakistan, it did not impose any conditionality on the delivery of aid. Given the history of U.S.-Pakistani relations, formal conditionality might have been counterproductive, but relinquishing even tacit conditionality denies the United States the best instrument of influence it has to wean Pakistan away from its involvement with terrorism. Furthermore, the Bush administration's ultimatum to Islamabad shortly after September 11 to renounce terrorism has only selectively been implemented.[20] Washington has held Islamabad closely to its promise to eradicate Al Qaeda but has been more forgiving of Pakistan's ambivalence toward eliminating the Taliban or permanently ceasing its support for Kashmiri terrorism against India. The dangers of Taliban reconstitution and its threat to U.S. reconstruction efforts in Afghanistan, as well as the consequences of resurgent Kashmiri terrorism for a renewed Indo-Pakistani conflict that threatens Operation Enduring Freedom, however, compel the United States to consider recalibrating its current policy toward Pakistan.

If the United States is to sustain a stable, long-term relationship with Pakistan despite these grave challenges without alienating India, it must encourage Islamabad to seek a permanent resolution of the Kashmir dispute on the full understanding that a plebiscite will never be held in the contested state and that substantial territorial change or radically altered frameworks of sovereignty will certainly not be part of any bargain between the two South Asian rivals. If Pakistan is willing to accept such a solution in principle, Washington should respond by demonstrating willingness to legitimize Pakistan's nuclear weapons and by offering peaceful nuclear cooperation within the limits of current policy; providing Islamabad with missile defense; becoming a "normal" supplier of conventional military hardware to Pakistan on commercial, but not concessional, terms; and pledging long-term economic assistance to Pakistan on the scale provided to Egypt after the Sadat-Begin agreement.

Such a grand bargain represents a willingness to provide a long-term U.S. commitment to Pakistani security in exchange for Islamabad's decision to end its permanent state of war with India.[21] The success of such an arrangement depends in large part on whether Pakistan has successfully begun its internal transformation toward democracy, economic stability, and moderate politics. If Islamabad has, the risks of a long-term U.S.-Pakistani partnership are minimized for the United States and for the dramatically transformed U.S.-India relationship because a democratic Pakistan is unlikely to concentrate on challenging India militarily and, by implication, would not force the United States to choose between supporting India or Pakistan as in the past. Even in the best of times, however, successfully concluding such a grand bargain is likely to be very difficult because it requires the United States to cajole Pakistan toward outcomes that the most powerful constituency within the Pakistani state—the military—would find fundamentally distasteful. The United States arguably has the leverage, at least in theory, to move Pakistan in this direction, but its reliance on Musharraf's cooperation to complete Operation Enduring Freedom successfully limits its ability to exercise this leverage practically.

As Dennis Kux has demonstrated in his history of U.S.-Pakistani relations, the record suggests that near-term pressures of necessity have traditionally trumped what may be vital in the long run.[22] Because Washington needs the Islamabad military regime's assistance to fight the war on terrorism, it will be tempting for the administration to avoid focusing its energy on restoring democracy in Pakistan and instead acquiesce to the continuation of military rule.

The United States—indeed, future Pakistani civilian leaders as well—should avoid this temptation to continue to put off the structural transformation agenda interminably and simply settle for partial, near-term, ameliorative reforms. Several previous Pakistani military and caretaker regimes did engage in important, though partial, reforms that unfortunately did not survive because the fundamental problems relating to democratic governance were not settled. Unless Washington and Islamabad learn this lesson of history, Pakistan will continue to be an expanding source of long-term security threats.

Notes

1. This record has been usefully synthesized in Sundeep Waslekar et al., *The Future of Pakistan* (Bombay: International Centre for Peace Initiatives, 2002).
2. Pervez Musharraf, "A Plea for Enlightened Moderation," *Washington Post*, June 1, 2004.
3. For more details, see Zulfikar Khalid Maluka, *The Myth of Constitutionalism in Pakistan* (Karachi: Oxford University Press, 1995), pp. 118–169.
4. The factors leading up to this process have been detailed in Ayesha Jalal, *The State of Martial Rule: The Origins of Pakistan's Political Economy of Defence* (New York: Cambridge University Press, 1990).
5. Leo Rose and D. Hugh Evans, "Pakistan's Enduring Experiment," *Journal of Democracy* 8, no. 1 (January 1997): 87.
6. Teresita C. Schaffer, "U.S. Influence on Pakistan: Can Partners Have Divergent Priorities?" *The Washington Quarterly* 26, no. 1 (Winter 2002–2003): 177.
7. Aquil Shah, "Democracy on Hold in Pakistan," *Journal of Democracy* 13, no. 1 (January 2002): 74–75.
8. For details about this strategy, see Ashley J. Tellis, *Stability in South Asia* (Santa Monica, Calif.: RAND, 1997), pp. 5–33.
9. This problem has been systematically detailed in Ahmad Faruqui, *Rethinking the National Security of Pakistan: The Price of Strategic Myopia* (Burlington, Vt.: Ashgate, 2003).
10. S. Akbar Zaidi, *Pakistan's Economic and Social Development: Domestic, Regional and Global Perspectives* (New Delhi: Observer Research Foundation, 2004).
11. For more on the politics behind this mobilization, see H. V. Hodson, *The Great Divide: Britain-India-Pakistan* (New York: Atheneum, 1971); Anita Inder Singh, *The Origins of the Partition of India, 1936–1947* (New York: Oxford University Press, 1987).
12. Mohammed Ali Jinnah, "Presidential Address to the Constituent Assembly of Pakistan at Karachi," August 11, 1947, http://pakistanspace.tripod.com/archives/47jin11.htm (accessed October 5, 2004).
13. Ishtiaq Ahmed, "The Fundamentalist Dimension in the Pakistan Movement," *Friday Times*, November 22–28, 2002, http://www.sasnet.lu.se/ishtiaqtext.html (accessed October 4, 2004).

14. For an excellent review, see International Crisis Group, "Pakistan: Madrassas, Extremism, and the Military," *Asia Report*, no. 36 (July 29, 2002); International Crisis Group, "Pakistan: The Mullahs and the Military," *Asia Report*, no. 49 (March 20, 2003).
15. National Commission on Terrorist Attacks Upon the United States, *The 9/11 Commission Report* (Washington, D.C.: Government Printing Office, 2004), p. 369.
16. Ibid.
17. For a good discussion of these issues, see David Albright, "Securing Pakistan's Nuclear Weapons Complex" (paper for the Stanley Foundation for the 42nd Strategy for Peace Conference, Strategies for Regional Security [South Asia Working Group], Warrenton, Va., October 25–27, 2001).
18. This point in strongly emphasized in Teresita C. Shaffer, *Pakistan's Future and U.S. Policy Options* (Washington, D.C.: CSIS, March 2004).
19. This issue is discussed further in Husain Haqqani and Ashley J. Tellis, *India and Pakistan: Is Peace Real This Time?* (Washington, D.C.: Carnegie Endowment for International Peace, 2004).
20. For more on this issue, see Walter Andersen, "South Asia: A Selective War on Terrorism?" in *Strategic Asia 2004-05: Confronting Terrorism in the Pursuit of Power*, eds. Ashley J. Tellis and Michael Wills (Seattle: National Bureau of Asian Research, 2004), pp. 227–259.
21. On the centrality of peace with India for the success of Pakistan's transformation, see Alyssa Ayres, "Musharraf's Pakistan: A Nation of the Edge," *Current History* 103 (April 2004): 151–157.
22. See Dennis Kux, *The United States and Pakistan, 1947–2000: Disenchanted Allies* (Washington, D.C.: Woodrow Wilson Center Press, 2001). See also Robert J. McMahon, *The Cold War on the Periphery: The United States, India, and Pakistan* (New York: Columbia University Press, 1994).

C. Raja Mohan

What If Pakistan Fails? India Isn't Worried ... Yet

The issue of failed states has risen to the forefront of international relations in the last few years, with Pakistan widely considered as a potential case. The Indian establishment has closely followed U.S. debate over the prospect of Pakistan weakening and disintegrating. Although many Indians relish this thought, as it would weaken its historical adversary, few decisionmakers in New Delhi are convinced that the likelihood of this prospect lies just around the corner. India is currently in no rush to prepare for such a contingency.

Some in New Delhi suspect that attempts to diagnose Pakistan with failed-state syndrome merely serve to perpetuate the long-standing alliance between Washington and Islamabad. Pakistani rulers have been adept at manipulating Washington's fears of political uncertainty in their nation. At every stage, Washington tends to argue that the current regime in Islamabad is indeed indispensable and often advises New Delhi to ease up on immediate disputes with its western neighbor. New Delhi recognizes Washington's enduring political dependence on Islamabad, especially on Pakistan's military, in order to pursue its political interests in south and southwest Asia. Washington's decision, for whatever reason, to discretely handle the Abdul Qadeer Khan affair—the so-called father of the Paki-

C. Raja Mohan is professor of South Asian studies at Jawaharlal Nehru University in New Delhi.

The Washington Quarterly • 28:1 pp. 117–128.

stani bomb whose extensive network of nuclear proliferation was unveiled earlier this year—confirms New Delhi's assessment that Washington will allow Islamabad to get away with anything. Washington declared Khan an individual offender and allowed the Pakistani government to pardon Khan rather than consider him part of a system in Pakistan that has deliberately promoted the spread of weapons of mass destruction.

Although the Bush administration since the September 11 attacks and the initiation of the global war against terrorism has pressured Pakistan to end its support of extremists and terrorists, especially eliminating Al Qaeda and remnants of the Taliban in Afghanistan, India believes that Washington has been either unable or unwilling fully to press Pakistan to end its support for terrorists in Jammu and Kashmir. India attributes U.S. reluctance to challenge Pakistan on its Kashmir policy to Washington's prioritization of the situation in Afghanistan. This ambiguity in U.S. policy toward the sources of terrorism in Pakistan, however, tends to leave India somewhat skeptical about Pakistan's fragility and the broader debates on failed states and their role in sustaining international terrorism.

New Delhi also harbors some apprehension that the focus on Pakistan as a potential failed state and its implications for nuclear proliferation could end up shining a spotlight targeting the nuclear programs of India and Pakistan. New Delhi is aware that nonproliferation specialists in Washington do not make much of a distinction between the two countries' nuclear and missile programs. The prospect of nuclear war between India and Pakistan combined with the countries' refusals to join the Nuclear Non-Proliferation Treaty regime has led India and Pakistan to be frequently grouped together on nuclear issues. Thus, from the Indian perspective, U.S. remedies for nuclear proliferation challenges arising from potential state failure in Pakistan could have the undesirable side effect of raising calls for similar actions against Indian strategic programs.

Is Pakistan Failing?

Indian skepticism toward applying state-failure theory to Pakistan is rooted in the complex evolution of the triangular relationship among the United States, India, and Pakistan. Notwithstanding the historical baggage that surrounds India's assessments of Pakistan, the Indian view that the Pakistani state is nowhere near collapsing has some merit. One of the problems with the theory of state failure lies in the fundamental difficulty of distinguishing between the range of problems that arise during the state-building process in postcolonial societies and the potential for actual state failure. A postcolonial nation's inability to address general developmental goals it set for itself nearly five decades ago does not necessarily mean that it is approaching collapse.

State failure of the kind in Somalia, for example, is nowhere near likely on the subcontinent. Across South Asia, civil societies, standing apart from the state, remain fairly strong. Despite the current political turbulence, social cohesion endures thanks to the inherited structures of an old civilization. Many states in South Asia, including Pakistan, have not fully measured up to popular expectations or presumed state responsibility in meeting the aspirations of the people. South Asia may have slipped into the unenviable position at the bottom of the list for a number of world social indicators. This does not necessarily imply, however, that failure is inevitable in all South Asian states.

The collapse of the state might certainly be a possibility in Nepal, where the Maoist insurgency has gained control of a large swath of territory outside the Kathmandu Valley, which hosts the capital and the ruling elite, and threatens to overrun the old order. In Bangladesh as well, state failure seems a long-term possibility. There, an unbridled confrontation divides Dhaka between the two leading political parties, driven not only by irreconcilable personal animosity between their leaders but also numerous disputes, including one over the history of the state's creation.

These types of conflicts, however, are not characteristic of the Pakistani situation. No serious and organized popular challenge to state authority exists in Pakistan, nor do people question the basis for the organization of the Pakistani state and its ideology. The attempted car bombings against President Gen. Pervez Musharraf by Islamic extremist groups at the end of 2003 also do not suggest any impending failure of the Pakistani state. Although these groups might be motivated by ideology, they scarcely enjoy popular support. Political assassination, in any case, has long been a tradition in South Asia. Although it has often weakened states temporarily, it has rarely led to the collapse of state structures in the subcontinent.

A primary feature of failing states is a fatal weakening of the central authority. Although India appreciates the many problems that Pakistan faces today, Indian leaders do not believe that the Pakistani state is in its terminal stages. On the contrary, many in India point to the extraordinary strength of Pakistan's army, which lies at the core of the Pakistani nation-state. The army is capable of disciplining any particular section of society at any given moment. The expansion of its profile in national politics since Musharraf's coup in 1999 has faced little resistance from the established political parties. Musharraf's ability to exile the leader of the largest political party in Pakistan—Benazir Bhutto of the People's Party of Pakistan—and to destroy the base of support of the next most popular political leader—Nawaz Sharif of the Muslim League—speaks volumes about the political dominance of the army and the rapid erosion of the two major political parties' credibility.

The Pakistani courts have justified the army's repeated manipulation of the constitution as a necessity. Musharraf, unlike his predecessors who had ruled without any need for political justification, requires some measure of political and constitutional legitimization for his rule. A relatively free and vibrant press in Pakistan continuously questions Musharraf's legitimacy and attacks many of his domestic policies. Although political parties have been marginalized, Musharraf has to buy or persuade at least part of the political class to go along with him. Yet, this has by no means reduced the overwhelming power that the army exercises in Pakistan today. In fact, India believes that the army is in a position to crack down fully on the sources of terrorism and religious extremism in Pakistan. Whether it chooses to do so is an entirely different question.

A second measure of a failed state is a bitter and enduring contest among warring factions. Pakistan has survived many types of internal conflicts, including sectarian and ethnic disputes. Although one of these conflicts led to the secession of Bangladesh from Pakistan in 1971, there appears to be no real danger of this recurring today. Few other provinces in Pakistan today have the kind of ethnic homogeneity or unity of purpose that East Pakistan had more than 30 years ago. Although Baluch and Pushtun nationalism in the provinces of Baluchistan and the North West Frontier provinces, respectively, are often perceived as potentially threatening, the capacity of the state either to discipline or co-opt them remains fairly strong. Although sectarian clashes between Shi'a and Sunni Muslims have become a localized menace in recent years, they have not acquired much intensity or a pervasive hold over the entire population.

Another commonly accepted distinguishing feature of a failed state is the inability to exercise border control. The porous, uncontrolled border that Pakistan shares with Afghanistan has allowed members and leaders of Al Qaeda to move at will across its difficult terrain and could be seen as an indication of impending state failure in Pakistan. The uncontrolled western frontier, however, is part of Pakistan's geographic inheritance. Since the British Raj cut through kindred tribal communities to draw the artificial Durand Line in 1893, separating Afghanistan from British India, state practice has been to leave the tribal populations to their own devices while ensuring their support for the purpose of maintaining access to the outlying regions of the empire.

Although this vision of defensible frontiers served the empire well, it laid the foundation for a problem when Pakistan was created in 1947, after the British partitioned the subcontinent. In continuing the British policy, Islamabad virtually ceded its responsibilities over territories on its side of the border along the Durand Line, which remained the border between Pakistan and Afghanistan, to local sovereignty. The wars in Afghanistan from 1979 to the present have further complicated the situation. Pakistan's western frontiers became the front line in the final years of the Cold War. Pakistan's support of a variety of insurgent groups trying to oust the Soviet army-backed Afghan regime had the full backing of the West, as well as many Arab states. Large-scale migration from Afghanistan to Pakistan across the war-torn Durand Line made things even worse. Pakistan's policy of creating a friendly regime in Kabul after the withdrawal of the Soviet troops in the late 1980s exacerbated the post-Soviet civil war in Afghanistan. As a result, the regions across the Durand Line became a haven for international terrorism beyond the control of any state.

In the last few months, under pressure from the United States, Pakistan has demonstrated the political will to depart from its tradition of noninterference in the tribal affairs of its frontier regions by conducting unpopular military operations inside Waziristan, on the border with Afghanistan, for the first time since 1893. Musharraf has hinted at massive plans to extend the reach of the state and its activities into many previously untouched parts of the federally administered tribal areas along the Afghanistan border. Although these operations cause resentment within the general population and the armed forces, Islamabad does seem to have the ability to absorb the political consequences.

Finally, from the Indian perspective, the relationship between failed states and terrorism, often posited in U.S. international relations literature, has little relevance to the Pakistani case. The principal argument in the literature is that a failing state allows its sovereign territory to become a haven for international terrorism. The rise of religious extremism and terrorism on Pakistani soil, however, has had little to do with the weakening of the state in the last few decades. Rather, it was the result of deliberate decisions by the Pakistani army to instrumentalize political Islam and employ terrorism as a conscious tool in foreign and national security policies since the late 1970s.

Although Gen. Zia-ul Haq, who led Pakistan after a military coup in 1977 until his death in a plane crash in 1988, was personally religious, he chose to begin the process by promoting religion for his own political legitimacy in a predominantly moderate Pakistani society. Not until after the Soviet invasion of Afghanistan in December 1979 did the Pakistani state, supported by the strategy and tactics adopted by the United States, begin to employ religious extremism and terrorism as tools of its foreign policy. The United States found it politically ingenious to nurture and mobilize the mujahideen, or holy warriors, from within Pakistan as well as elsewhere in the Islamic world to challenge the occupation of Afghanistan by the "godless" Communists. This crusade strategy turned out to be enormously successful in bleeding the Soviet bear in

Afghanistan and ultimately driving it out. Once the Americans turned their back on Afghanistan, however, Pakistan continued with the strategy of using the deadly cocktail of religious extremism and terrorism to pursue its long-standing objectives in Afghanistan as well as in Jammu and Kashmir. In Afghanistan, Pakistan had long sought a friendly if not pliable regime while Kashmir offered the final retribution to India's vivisection of Pakistan in 1971 with the creation of Bangladesh.

Therefore, the weakening of the state did not produce Pakistan's sources of terrorism. Rather, supporting these groups was part of a conscious national security strategy. Although these forces have arguably now acquired a life of their own, threatening the future of the Pakistani state, nothing currently suggests that the Pakistani army is badly positioned to confront and defeat these forces. To an extent, Musharraf, under pressure from the United States, has already undertaken this task, at least on the western frontiers with Afghanistan. On the eastern frontiers, Musharraf has often said that a resolution of the Kashmir issue would allow him to rein in the extremist forces. Thus, the persistence of destabilizing forces in Pakistan reflects Islamabad's self-defined fundamental interests for its regional policy, not the inability of a failing state to control sources of extremism and terrorism.

The Current State of Indo-Pakistani Relations

Another significant contemporary legacy of the U.S. war in Afghanistan against the Soviet Union was the intense militarization of Indo-Pakistani relations and eventual nuclearization of the subcontinent. U.S. arms sales and assistance to Pakistan in the 1980s, amounting to nearly $6 billion, induced a competitive military buildup in India. Although the acquisition of conventional arms by India and Pakistan slowed in the 1990s thanks to economic difficulties in each country, they had crossed the nuclear threshold and begun to introduce missiles into their arsenals. During the 1980s, the United States largely ignored the nuclear and missile programs underway in Pakistan because it was dependent on Pakistani support to pursue its Cold War objectives in Afghanistan. India responded with its own programs, and by the 1990s, both countries had become overtly nuclear. The Indo-Pakistani conflict, with its new nuclear dimension, witnessed a series of military crises in 1987, 1990, and 1999 and more intensively at the end of 2001 and in the summer of 2002. Given the real danger of military tensions escalating to a nuclear level, the international community deepened its engagement with India and Pakistan and demanded an end to Pakistan's support of cross-border terrorism as well as substantive negotiations between New Delhi and Islamabad to resolve the Kashmir dispute.

The greatest harm to come from the war in Afghanistan in the 1980s was the legitimization of antimodern, extremist, and intolerant forces in the region. U.S. and Pakistani state support for militant and fundamentalist Islamic groups in the course of defeating the Soviet Union reinforced the rise of religious radicalism in a region that until the 1980s had largely kept religion at bay in the conduct of state affairs. Even Pakistan, an avowedly Islamic state, had been moderate in its religious orientation. As Zia co-opted religious forces to lend legitimacy to his military dictatorship and promoted religious radicals across the border to defeat the Soviet army, however, Pakistan saw the rise of extremism and sectarianism. Pakistan's shift inevitably had an impact on Muslims in the rest of the subcontinent and elsewhere in the world. In the late 1980s and 1990s, the rise of Islamic radicalism also exacerbated growing Hindu fundamentalism in India. Together, Pakistan's radicalization and the rise of Hindu fundamentalism intensified Hindu-Muslim tensions across the subcontinent and more fundamentally gave a boost to anti-Enlightenment ideas in the region. Majoritarianism, sectarianism, obscurantism, opposition to the traditional regional notions of tolerance, and a rejection of the Western idea of separating state from religion became increasingly powerful.

In recent years, a number of factors have created a new set of conditions facilitating the management of Indo-Pakistani relations. Since the September 11 attacks, the international community has become less tolerant of the use of religion and terrorism as instruments of state policy. U.S. pressure on Pakistan has not led to a complete destruction of the sources of terrorism in that country, but it has certainly pushed Islamabad in a direction fundamentally different from the previous two decades. India has welcomed, albeit skeptically, Musharraf's new emphasis on transforming Pakistan into a moderate Islamic state. The Bush administration has also pursued a more balanced policy toward the subcontinent, seeking to improve relations with India and Pakistan simultaneously. Furthermore, the active involvement of the international community in the military crises of South Asia has resulted in greater awareness in New Delhi and Islamabad of the principal consequence of their nuclear weapons: the globalization of South Asian security.

In sum, the current situation is one in which the prospects of a successful Indo-Pakistani engagement have significantly improved. Tensions between India and Pakistan rose dramatically immediately after September 11, but the new international context provided a different basis for Indo-Pakistani engagement. Whereas all Indo-Pakistani peace attempts before the September 11 attacks had failed, efforts since the beginning of 2004 have begun to gain traction. A full-blown Indo-Pakistani peace process is now in the works. The entire range of bilateral issues, including Jammu and Kashmir, is now on the table. Significantly, since January 2004, Pakistan has kept cross-border violence to a level that India is willing to tolerate for now. Although no one can predict the ultimate success of this process, its durability seems greater than in the past.

The current Indian dialogue with Pakistan is built around three elements: Indian willingness to explore an early and final settlement of the long-standing question of Jammu and Kashmir; Pakistani willingness to stop using terrorism as an instrument of state policy; and, along with a discussion of the Kashmir question, movement by both sides toward the normalization of bilateral relations. The possibility of state failure in Pakistan has not yet been a significant consideration. Could it acquire more weight in the Indian calculus in the coming years?

Planning for the Future

An assessment that Pakistani state failure is not imminent should not blind India to Pakistan's multifaceted problems. Pakistan's rapidly growing population (already greater than Russia's); the army's excessive intrusion into domestic affairs; the presence of nuclear weapons; the rise in poverty levels; the social and strategic consequences of using religious extremism as a tool of foreign policy since 1979, coupled with the inability of the state to deliver a variety of necessary services including primary education; the persistence of premodern formations such as feudalism; the rise of forces that are not merely anti-Western but also antimodern; and the growing strength of Islamic parties do figure in Indian discourse on Pakistan but are not a significant cause for concern at this stage.

Like Washington, New Delhi has put most of its faith in Musharraf and the Pakistani army. Although Musharraf has sought to reduce the influence of Islamism that has overtaken sections of the army, neither his complete success nor the continuation of his policies under his successors is certain. As India embarks on a prolonged engagement with Pakistan, the prospect of fundamental changes in Pakistan, including the weakening of the present state, the rise of an extremist-aligned general in the armed forces, or the emergence of debilitating divisions within the armed forces, are not far-fetched possibilities. Although India is not currently anticipating political surprises in Pakistan, New Delhi should nonetheless be prepared for their occurrence. To that end, India should consider five elements in its contingency strategy to account for potential radical changes in Pakistani state and society.

First, forestalling state failure in Pakistan should be an important Indian objective. The current Indian commitment to engage Pakistan seriously and explore solutions to the long-standing conflict over Kashmir pursues this objective to an extent. Unlike past interactions with Pakistan, the current Indian policy seeks to open up large-scale people-to-people contact and integrate Pakistan into the regional economy through free trade and projects such as natural gas pipelines and transport corridors. Pakistan is currently conditioning such economic integration and expansive cultural contact to a resolution of the Kashmir question. If India can find a way to resolve the Kashmir question and simultaneously normalize the bilateral relationship, it could neutralize the political wind that has gathered behind the sources of religious extremism and terrorism in Pakistan. Hostile relations with India have been one of the principal reasons for the growth of destabilizing forces in Pakistan. The decompression of Indo-Pakistani tensions, followed by wide-ranging bilateral cooperation, could dramatically alter the political environment in Pakistan and create space for the rise of moderate and modernizing forces.

Second, although resolution of the conflict over Kashmir and economic integration could transform both the internal and external orientation of Pakistan, India cannot be sanguine that its current policy of engagement will move forward without any further twists and turns. India needs safeguards against potential negative developments in its western neighbor. In particular, India needs to reach out to the full spectrum of political voices in Pakistan. Although Musharraf and the army hold the key to the current peace process, India cannot afford to exclude the many other political forces, weak as they are at the moment, from its engagement. Such forces might be critical to resisting extremist elements and creating alternative political futures for Pakistan.

Third, given the extraordinary dangers that would arise from Pakistan becoming a failed nuclear state, India needs to accelerate its current program for missile defense and develop capabilities for counterproliferation that allow its forces to operate in a nuclear environment. India's unexpected support for the Bush administration's missile defense initiative in May 2001 surprised many in Washington. Yet, one element of the intuitive logic behind the Indian decision has been the search for ways to mitigate the potential threat from Pakistani nuclear weapons and missiles. Although the effectiveness of missile defenses will continue to be questioned and counterproliferation capabilities are difficult to procure, advances on these fronts could help induce some restraint in a future radical regime in Pakistan.

Fourth, developing the conventional military force capabilities to defeat a potential future rogue regime in Pakistan is an option. It would, however, be difficult and controversial. In the past, India has never enjoyed the kind of conventional military superiority over Pakistan required to enable the use of force to achieve political ends. India would need massive financial resources, not readily available at the moment, to rapidly modernize and upgrade its conventional military forces to acquire an effective edge over Pakistan. Sustained and high economic growth rates in the coming decades could, however, produce the necessary resources to modernize India's armed forces. At the political level, the very attempt to develop such a force could trigger an arms race with Pakistan and undermine the current peace process. Even if India were to develop such capabilities, their use against Pakistan would encounter many difficulties, including the risk of nuclear escalation and the political costs of conventional action.

India has not been squeamish about the use of force in its neighborhood. As the legatee of the British Raj in maintaining political order in South Asia, India has repeatedly used force in the subcontinent since its independence in 1947. Many current themes of the U.S. strategic debate, such as regime change, humanitarian intervention, and state preservation, have all been part of India's regional history. In 1950, New Delhi helped Nepal rid itself of the oppressive rule of the Ranas and restore the Nepalese monarchy to its rightful place in Kathmandu. In the late 1950s, India aided Burma in its war against insurgent forces. In 1971, India provided military assistance to Sri Lanka to counter a threat from extreme leftist forces. In the late 1980s, India intervened in Sri Lanka to end the threat of secession from the Liberation Tigers of Tamil Eelam. Also in the late 1980s, India intervened in Maldives to defeat a coup against the legitimate government in Male. More famously, India's humanitarian intervention in East Pakistan in 1971 led to the creation of Bangladesh. These experiences in using force in the region, however, pale in comparison to a potential intervention in a nuclear-armed Pakistan. Moreover, India's costly, unpopular, and unsuccessful action in Sri Lanka has induced a great deal of caution in New Delhi against future military interventions in the region.

Fifth, and finally, the development of any of the above options or of a combination of them would have to involve considerable cooperation with the international community, especially the United States and China. India will need significant international support for a political resolution of the Kashmir question or the containment and defeat of a future radical regime in Pakistan. Yet, acquiring international support from other great powers runs counter to the conventional wisdom in

New Delhi. India has traditionally promoted a policy of keeping other powers out of South Asia. This Indian variation of the Monroe Doctrine, involving spheres of influence, has not been entirely successful in the past, but it has been an article of faith for many in the Indian strategic community. India has, however, modified this policy at the margins in recent years, for example, by allowing Norway to mediate in Sri Lanka between the government and the Tamil rebels since 2000. It also has consulted with the United States and the United Kingdom on finding ways to help the Nepalese monarchy deal with the threat of Maoist insurgency.

Given the scale of the effort required to deal with potential state failure in Pakistan, India should develop the concept of "security multilateralism" on the subcontinent. Although New Delhi will always have to take principal responsibility in preserving subcontinental order, it should welcome the help of other responsible forces in dealing with the emerging challenges of state failure in the region. India is unlikely to accept the role of the United Nations in preserving regional stability, given its own negative experience with the organization in dealing with the Kashmir dispute with Pakistan. Cooperation with other great powers, then, acquires some importance. Thus, a prudent Indian approach aimed at reducing the political and economic costs of intervention against Pakistan would require substantial cooperation with the United States and China.

Will such cooperation be forthcoming from two of Pakistan's most important allies? Suggestions for such cooperation among India, the United States, and China on regional security would have been dismissed as outlandish until recently. Political consultations among the three powers on Pakistan might have become a feasible option today given India's rapidly expanding relations with both the United States and China. State failure in Pakistan and its consequences would give Washington and Beijing much to worry about regarding their own long-term interests in the region. Accordingly, New Delhi should engage both nations in bilateral discussions on the future stability of Pakistan. Until now, the United States and China, given the high stakes in their relationships with Islamabad, have been reluctant to be perceived as engaging

New Delhi on the question of Pakistan's stability. Yet, a serious dialogue among the three countries on the future of Pakistan has become an urgent necessity. On their own, none of them can prevent state failure in nuclear-armed Pakistan or manage its consequences.

State failure in Pakistan might not be likely, but the potential that an irresponsible regime might emerge in Islamabad cannot be completely ruled out. Given the presence of nuclear weapons, the consequences of such an outcome—remote as it may seem in New Delhi—could indeed be disastrous. Therefore, India will have to develop some contingency planning to address such a situation. Over the long term, political cooperation among India, the United States, and China holds the key to preventing state failure in Pakistan and has the potential to facilitate Pakistan's evolution toward political moderation and economic modernization and lay the foundation for regional stability and economic integration in the subcontinent.

Husain Haqqani

The Role of Islam in Pakistan's Future

Although listed among the U.S. allies in the war on terrorism, Pakistan cannot easily be characterized as either friend or foe. Indeed, Pakistan has become a major center of radical Islamist ideas and groups, largely because of its past policies toward India and Afghanistan. Pakistan supported Islamist militants fighting Indian rule in the disputed territory of Jammu and Kashmir and backed the Taliban in its pursuit of a client regime in Afghanistan. Since the September 11 attacks, however, the selective cooperation of Pakistan's president and military ruler, Gen. Pervez Musharraf, in sharing intelligence with the United States and apprehending Al Qaeda members has led to the assumption that Pakistan might be ready to give up its long-standing ties with radical Islam.

Nevertheless, Pakistan's status as an Islamic ideological state is rooted deeply in history and is linked closely both with the praetorian ambitions of the Pakistani military and the Pakistani elite's worldview. For the foreseeable future, Islam will remain a significant factor in Pakistan's politics. Musharraf and his likely successors from the ranks of the military will continue to seek U.S. economic and military assistance with promises of reform, but the power of such promises is tempered by the strong links between Pakistan's military-intelligence apparatus and extremist Islamists.

Husain Haqqani is a visiting scholar at the Carnegie Endowment for International Peace in Washington, D.C.

The Washington Quarterly • 28:1 pp. 85–96.

Pakistan's future direction is crucial to the U.S.-led war on terrorism, not least because of Pakistan's declared nuclear weapons capability. The historic alliance between Islamists and Pakistan's military has the potential to frustrate antiterrorist operations, radicalize key segments of the Islamic world, and bring India and Pakistan to the brink of war yet again. Unless Pakistan's all-powerful military can be persuaded to cede power gradually to secular civilians and allow the secular politics of competing economic and regional interests to prevail over religious sentiment, the country's vulnerability to radical Islamic politics will not wane. With the backing of the U.S. government, the Pakistani military would probably be able to maintain a façade of stability over the next several years but, bolstered by U.S. support, would also want to maintain preeminence and is likely to make concessions to Islamists to legitimize its control of the country's polity. The United States is supporting Pakistan's military so that Pakistan backs away from Islamist radicalism, albeit gradually. In the process, however, the military's political ambitions are being encouraged, compromising change and preserving the influence of radical Islamists. Democratic reform that allows secular politicians to compete for power freely is more likely to reduce this influence.

Weakness of the Pakistani State

The disproportionate focus of the Pakistani state since its independence in 1947 on ideology, military capability, and external alliances has weakened Pakistan internally. The country's institutions, ranging from schools and universities to the judiciary, are in a state of general decline. The economy's stuttering growth is dependent largely on the level of concessional flows of external resources. Pakistan's gross domestic product (GDP) stands at about $75 billion in absolute terms and $295 billion in purchasing power parity, making Pakistan's economy the smallest of any country that has tested nuclear weapons thus far. Pakistan suffers from massive urban unemployment, rural underemployment, illiteracy, and low per capita income. One-third of the population lives below the poverty line, and another 21 percent subsists just above it.

Soon after independence, 16 percent of Pakistan's population was literate, compared with 18 percent of India's significantly larger population. By 2003, India had managed to attain a literacy rate of 65 percent, but Pakistan's stood at only about 35 percent. Today, Pakistan allocates less than 2 percent of its GDP for education and ranks close to the bottom among 87 developing countries in the amount allotted to primary schools. Its low literacy rate and inadequate investment in education has led to a decline in Pakistan's technological base, which in turn hampers the country's economic modernization. With an annual population growth rate of 2.7 percent, the state of public health care and other social services in Pakistan is also in decline. Meanwhile, Pakistan spends almost 5 percent of its GDP on defense and is still unable to match the conventional forces of India, which outspends Pakistan 3 to 1 while allocating less than 2.5 percent of its GDP to military spending.

Pakistan's military dominance can be traced back to the early years of its statehood. The partition of British India's assets in 1947 left Pakistan with one-third of the British Indian army and only 17 percent of its revenues. Thus, the military started out as the dominant institution in the new state, and this dominance has continued over the years. Since Gen. Ayub Khan assumed power in 1958, ruling through martial law, the military has directly or indirectly dominated Pakistani politics, set Pakistan's ideological and national security agenda, and repeatedly intervened to direct the course of domestic politics. On four occasions, despite the constant rewriting of its constitution ostensibly to pave the way for sustained democracy, generals seized power directly, claiming that civilian politicians were incapable of running the country. Even during periods of civilian government, the generals have exercised political influence through the intelligence apparatus, notably the Interservices Intelligence (ISI) organization. The ISI plays a behind-the-scenes role in exaggerating political divisions to justify military intervention. Partly due to the role of the military and partly because of their own weakness, Pakistan's political factions have often found it difficult to cooperate with one another or to submit to the rule of law. As a result, Pakistan is far from developing a consistent system form of government, with persisting political polarization along three major, intersecting fault lines: between civilians and the military, among different ethnic and provincial groups, and between Islamists and secularists.

The first crack in contemporary Pakistan's body politic continues to be this perennial dispute over who should wield political power. Musharraf has described Pakistan as "a very difficult country to govern"[1] in view of its myriad internal and external difficulties. Musharraf's view reflects the thinking of the Pakistani military and is possibly self-serving. The military does not allow politics to take its course, periodically accusing elected leaders of compromising national security or of corruption. Repeated military intervention has deprived Pakistan of political leaders with experience governing, leading to serious lapses under civilian rule. Because the military periodically co-opts or fires civilian politicians, established and accepted rules for political conduct have failed to evolve. Issues such as the role of religion in matters of state, the division of power between various branches of government, and the authority of the provinces are not settled by constitutional means or through a vote. The military does not let civilians rule, but its own rule lacks legitimacy in the eyes of the general public, creating an atmosphere of permanent friction. Thus, instead of governing, Pakistan's rulers, including Musharraf, have been reduced to managing ethnic, religious, and provincial tensions.

The second major source of conflict in Pakistan is based on these ethnic and provincial differences. Although the majority of Pakistan's ethnically disparate population has traditionally identified with secular politicians, that majority has not always determined the direction of Pakistan's policies, even when its opinion is expressed in a free and fair election. Highly centralized and unrepresentative governance has created grievances among different ethnic groups, and the state has yet to create any institutional mechanisms for dealing with such discontent. The constitutional provisions relating to provincial autonomy, which could placate each province by allowing self-government, have often been bypassed in practice. Intraprovincial differences, such as those between the Baluchis and the Pashtuns in Baluchistan, between the Punjabis and Saraiki in Punjab, between the Pashtuns and Hindko speakers in the North West Frontier Province, and between the Sindhis and Mohajirs in Sindh, have also festered without political resolution.

The third relates to the ideological division over the role of Islam in national life. Having started out as a pressure group outside the Pakistani parliament, Pakistan's religious parties have now become a well-armed and well-financed force that wield considerable influence within different branches of government. Religious groups have benefited from the patronage of the military and civil bureaucracy, which has viewed them as useful tools in perpetuating the military's control over foreign and domestic policy. Because the Islamist worldview is incompatible with the vision of a modern Pakistan, the violent vigilantism of some Islamists has become a serious threat to Pakistani civil society and has also promoted sectarian terrorism. Operating outside the framework of the rule of law, the Islamists have the potential to disrupt the conduct of foreign policy, especially in view of their support for anti-India militants in Kashmir and the Taliban in Afghanistan.

Islam and the Rise of Militancy

Radical Islamic groups, which portray themselves as the guardians of Pakistan's ideology, have had a special status conferred on them by the military and civil bureaucracy that normally governs Pakistan. The Islamists claim that they are the protectors of Pakistan's nuclear deterrent capability, as well as the champion of the national cause of securing Kashmir for Pakistan. Secular politicians who seek greater autonomy for Pakistan's different regions or demand that religion be kept out of the business of the state have come under attack from the Islamists for deviating from Pakistan's ideology.

Establishing Islam as the state ideology was a device aimed at defining a Pakistani identity during the country's formative years. Indeed, Pakistan's leaders started playing on religious sentiment as a means of strengthening the country's national identity shortly after Pakistan's inception. Emerging from the partition of British India in 1947 as the result of a relatively short independence movement, Pakistan faced several challenges to its survival, beginning with India's perceived reluctance to accept Pakistan's creation. Pakistan's secular elite used Islam as a national rallying cry against perceived and real threats from predominantly Hindu India. They assumed that the country's clerics and Islamists were too weak and too dependent on the state to confront the power structure. Therefore, unsure of their fledgling nation's future, the politicians, civil servants, and military officers who led Pakistan in its formative years decided to exacerbate the antagonism between Hindus and Muslims that had led to partition as a means of defining a distinctive identity for Pakistan, with "Islamic Pakistan" resisting "Hindu India." Notwithstanding periodic peace processes, hostility between India and Pakistan continues, and in Pakistan it serves as an important element of national identification.

This political commitment to an "ideological state" gradually evolved into a strategic commitment to exporting jihadist ideology for regional influence. During the Bangladesh crisis in 1971, the Pakistani military used Islamist rhetoric and the help of Islamist groups to exclude elected secular leaders supported by the majority Bengali-speaking population from power in East Pakistan prior to its secession. The Bengalis' rebellion, with India's assistance, and their brutal suppression by the Pakistani military followed an election that would have given power to Bengali politicians in a united Pakistan. After the 1971 war, Pakistan was bifurcated with the birth of an independent Bangladesh, exacerbating Pakistan's insecurity.

Whereas India and Bangladesh have each evolved as secular democracies focused on economic development, Pakistan continues to be ruled by a civil-military oligarchy that sees itself as defining and also protecting the state's identity, mainly through a mix of religious and militarist nationalism. Hence, in western Pakistan, the effort to create national cohesion between Pakistan's disparate ethnic and linguistic groups through religion assumed greater significance, and its manifestations became more militant. Religious groups, armed or unarmed, gradually became more powerful as a result of this alliance between the mosque and the military. Radical and violent manifestations of Islamist ideology, which sometimes appear to threaten Pakistan's stability even today, can be seen in some ways as a state project gone awry.

Pakistan's rulers have traditionally attempted to "manage" militant Islamism, trying to calibrate it so that it serves the state's nation-building function without destabilizing internal politics or relations with Western countries. Pakistan's emphasis on its Islamic identity increased significantly as the civilian semiauthoritarian government of Zulfikar Ali Bhutto (1971–1977) channeled Pakistan's Islamic aspirations toward foreign policy. Pakistan played a key role in developing the Organization of Islamic Conference and opened up to special relations with Islamic groups and countries.

Gen. Zia-ul Haq's military regime (1977–1988) took matters a step further domestically, basing Pakistan's legal and educational system on Islamic law, formalizing the preexisting state ideology into an official policy of Islamization. Through his Islamization efforts, Zia made Pakistan an important ideological and organizational center of the global Islamist movement, including its leading role in the anti-Soviet campaign in Afghanistan in the 1980s by allowing Afghanistan's mujahideen to operate from bases in Pakistan, inflicting a heavy toll on the Red Army.

The success of the jihadist experiment against the Soviets encouraged Pakistan's strategic planners to expand the jihad against India and into post-Soviet Central Asia. Pakistan's sponsorship of the Taliban in Afghanistan, together with the presence in its territory of Islamist militants from all over the world, derived from Islamabad's desire to emerge as the center of a global Islamic resurgence. Ironically, religious fervor did not motivate all Pakistani leaders who supported this strategy; in most cases, they simply embraced Islam as a politico-military strategic doctrine that would enhance Pakistan's prestige and position in the world. The focus on building an ideological state, however, has subsequently caused Pakistan to lag behind in almost all areas that define a functional modern state.

In the last few years, the situation has deteriorated even further. The Islamists are not content with having a secondary role in national affairs and have acquired a momentum of their own. Years of religious rhetoric have influenced a younger generation of military officers. The ISI, in particular, includes a large number of officials who have assimilated the Islamist beliefs they were rhetorically called on to support in the course of jihad in Kashmir and Afghanistan. Because Musharraf and the Pakistani military still see secular politicians, rather than the Islamists, as their rivals for political power, they have continued to use Islamists for political purposes. Last year, Musharraf's administration sought the backing of the Islamists for a set of constitutional amendments increasing the president's power and in return recognized an Islamist as the leader of the parliamentary opposition. Major figures of the secular opposition have been exiled or jailed on corruption or sedition charges, positioning the Islamists as Pakistan's major opposition group. This has enabled Islamists to exercise greater influence than would have been possible in an open, democratic political system, given the poor electoral performance of Islamic groups in Pakistan's intermittent elections since gaining independence.

Some Things Never Change: Musharraf's Pakistan Today

Pakistan's Islamists made their strongest showing in a general election during parliamentary voting in October 2002, securing 11 percent of the popular vote and 20 percent of the seats in the lower house of parliament. The Musharraf regime's decision to bar two former prime ministers, Nawaz Sharif and Benazir Bhutto, and several of their followers from the election helped the Islamists achieve these electoral results. The two leading secular parties, Sharif's Pakistan Muslim League (PML) and Bhutto's Pakistan People's Party (PPP), had to contend with corruption proceedings relating to their tenures in office as well as the Musharraf government's intense propaganda supporting these allegations. The candidates of the alliance of Islamic parties—the United Action Council (*Mutahhida Majlis Amal* [MMA])—did not face disqualification, and Islamic party leaders campaigned freely. Anti-U.S. sentiment in the areas bordering Afghanistan particularly benefited the MMA, which made electoral gains without dramatically increasing the share of votes traditionally won by Islamic parties. Secular parties suffered due to redistricting as well as the disqualification of some non-Islamist candidates. PML and PPP leaders were forced into exile, but MMA leaders could campaign freely. This ensured full turnout of Islamist voters at the polls while some supporters of the major parties did not show up to vote.

The Musharraf government now recognizes the MMA as the main opposition in parliament, even though Bhutto's PPP has the single-largest bloc of opposition parliamentarians, 81, to the MMA's 63. Critics argue that Musharraf is deliberately projecting the MMA as his primary opposition to create the illusion that radical Islamist groups are gaining power through democratic means, thus minimizing the prospect that the international community, especially the United States, will press for democratic reform in Pakistan, especially while Musharraf offers support in the war against Al Qaeda.

Musharraf has also made repeated pronouncements to reassure the world of his intention to alter Pakistan's policy direction radically since the September 11 attacks, moving it away from its Islamist and jihadist past. Musharraf's administration continues to project the war on terrorism as a U.S. war being waged with Pakistani help, even after attempts on his life and that of his handpicked prime minister, Shaukat Aziz. Islamabad continues to make a distinction between foreign fighters, such as those from Al Qaeda, whom Pakistani forces have been pursuing, and homegrown terrorists who were originally trained to fight Indian troops in Kashmir. Musharraf is, in fact, even reversing Zia's course of Islamization but only marginally. The government now encourages women's participation in public life, and cultural events involving song and dance are openly allowed, even encouraged. State-owned media has become more culturally liberal, and private radio and television stations with unrestricted entertainment content have been permitted. Controversial Islamic laws, however, such as those relating to blasphemy and *Hudood* (Islamic limits), have not been withdrawn.

Still, although Musharraf speaks of a vision of "enlightened moderation" for Pakistan, contradictions in his domestic, regional, and international policies are apparent. The greatest commitment he has demonstrated thus far is his view that he is indispensable to Pakistan and that Pakistan is safer under the stewardship of the military rather than under civilian democratic rule. This duality in speaking of enlightened moderation while keeping alive the perception that he is faced with Islamist opposition justifies military intervention and governance and reflects the structural problem in Pakistan's politics, a situation created by the weakness of civilian institutions and the armed forces' dominance of decisionmaking.

Islam has therefore become the central issue in Pakistani politics because of conscious and consistent state policy aimed at excluding secular politicians from power while maintaining a centralized state controlled by the military and civil bureaucracy, not just as the inadvertent outcome of decisions made after the Soviet intervention in Afghanistan, as has been widely assumed. Pakistan's self-characterization as an Islamic ideological state is thus unlikely to change in the near term. The country's population remains fractured by ethnic and linguistic differences, with Islam being used as the common bond in an attempt to achieve unity.

U.S. Policy Response (or Lack Thereof)

On several occasions, Pakistan has been seen as a state on the brink of failure, temporarily restored with U.S. military and economic assistance only to return to the brink again. Pakistan, suffering from chronically weak state institutions, continues to face a deep identity crisis and a rising threat from independent, radical Islamists. The government's fears about its viability and security have led Islamabad to seek an alliance with the United States while pursuing a nuclear deterrent and subconventional military capability, that is, Islamist terrorism, against India. The U.S. response to the September 11 attacks left Pakistan with little choice but to turn more drastically toward the United States. Confronted with an ultimatum to choose between being with the United States or against it, Pakistan's generals opted to revive the alliance. At every stage since, however, Pakistan has proven to be a U.S. ally of convenience, not of conviction, seeking specific rewards for specific actions.

Pakistan has historically been willing to adjust its priorities to fit within the parameters of immediate U.S. global concerns. The purpose has been to ensure the flow of military and economic aid from the United States, which Pakistan considers necessary for its struggle for survival and its competition with India. The military, which has dominated the Pakistani state since the mid-1950s, has embraced a tripartite policy that emphasizes Islam as a national unifier, rivalry with India as the principal objective of the state's foreign policy, and an alliance with the United States as a means to defray the costs of Pakistan's massive military expenditures. Ironically, these policy precepts have served to encourage extremist Islamism, which in the last few years has been the source of threats both to U.S. interests and global security.

The United States even recognized the troubling potential of Islamist politics in the very first years of U.S. engagement with Pakistan. In a policy statement issued on July 1, 1951, the U.S. Department of State declared that, "[a]part from Communism, the other main threat to American interests in Pakistan was from 'reactionary groups of landholders and uneducated religious leaders' who were opposed to the 'present Western-minded government' and 'favor a return to primitive Islamic principles.'"[2] However, over the last four decades—until September 11—the U.S. government did little to discourage Islamabad's embrace of obscurantist Islam as its state ideology, empowering Pakistan's religious leaders beyond their support among the populace and tying the Islamists to Pakistan's military-civil bureaucracy and intelligence apparatus.

Washington has never been able to develop a policy that exclusively focuses on dealing with Islamabad and its dysfunction. Instead, Pakistan has generally been placed into broader U.S. policy objectives: containment of communism in the 1950s and 1960s, restrictions on Soviet expansion in Afghanistan during the 1980s, nuclear nonproliferation during the 1990s, and the war on terrorism since September 11. Washington's quid pro quo approach in dealing with Pakistan has often helped confront the issue at hand while creating another security problem down the road. Gen. Ayub Khan had found U.S. eagerness to contain communism during the 1950s useful to extract the right price for Pakistan's participation in anti-Communist treaties. U.S. Cold War support subsequently enabled the Pakistani military to use force in the Bangladesh crisis of 1971, leading to Pakistan's bifurcation.

History repeated itself when the Soviet Union's occupation of Afghanistan in 1979 made Pakistan a front-line state in resisting Communist expansion. Just as General Khan had previously, Zia bargained for more aid in return for allowing Pakistan to be the staging ground for an anti-Soviet insurgency during the 1980s. Zia also used the cover of the Afghan jihad to acquire nuclear weapons capabilities for Pakistan, circumventing U.S. legislation aimed at nonproliferation. With help from the United States, Zia also modernized Pakistan's military and prepared for a broader jihad to expand Pakistan's influence in the region, building a cadre of Islamist guerrillas and giving rise to Pakistan's ambitions to create a client regime in Afghanistan, which in turn resulted in the Taliban's ascendancy and ability to provide sanctuary for Al Qaeda. Washington's preoccupation with the success of the anti-Soviet struggle enabled Pakistan to defeat two U.S. objectives (nuclear nonproliferation and security in the Middle East and South Asia) while attaining one (the end of the Soviet occupation of Afghanistan) and empowered an entirely new threat of radical Islamic terrorism.

In some ways, Islamabad's relationship with Washington has become a contributing factor to the Pakistani crisis by allowing Pakistan's leaders to believe that they can continue to promote risky domestic, regional, and pan-Islamic policies. The availability of U.S. assistance, offered to secure Pakistani cooperation in U.S. grand strategy, has exacerbated Pakistan's dysfunction and its structural flaws.

The Solution: A Man or a System?

Currently, U.S. hopes in Pakistan are pinned to Musharraf's commitment to U.S. interests. Assassination attempts on Musharraf, from which he has narrowly escaped, have raised the question of whether U.S. policy interests would be adequately served beyond Musharraf's indefinite tenure. Although it may be difficult for U.S. and Pakistani policymakers to force an end to Pakistan's status as an Islamic ideological state, changes in the nature of the Pakistani state can gradually wean the country away from Islamic extremism. Musharraf can't. Over the years, military rule has fomented religious militancy in Pakistan. Under military leadership, Pakistan has defined its national objective as wresting Kashmir from India and, in recent years, establishing a client regime in Afghanistan. Unless Islamabad's objectives are redefined to focus on economic prosperity and popular participation in governance, which the military remains institutionally reluctant to do, the state will continue to turn to Islam as a national unifier.

If Pakistan proceeded along the path of normal political and economic development, it would not need the exaggerated political and strategic role for Islam that has characterized much of its history. The United States, for its own interests, cannot afford the current rise in Islamic militancy in a large Muslim country that has nuclear weapons capabilities, a large standing army, and a huge intelligence service capable of conducting covert operations to destabilize neighboring governments in the Persian Gulf, South Asia, and Central Asia.

The influence of Islamists in Pakistan can perhaps be best contained through democracy. In elections, a majority of Pakistanis has repeatedly demonstrated that the populace does not share the Islamist vision for the country. Despite the MMA's unprecedented electoral performance in 2002, the alliance garnered only 11 percent of the total votes cast. The Islamist vote as a percentage of total registered voters has been more or less stagnant since the 1970s. The strength of the Islamists, however, lies in their ability to mobilize financial and human resources. Islamists run schools, operate charities, and publish newspapers; moreover, they are able to put their organized cadres on the streets. Thus, in the absence of democratic decisionmaking, the Islamists can dominate the political discourse. Pakistan's secular civil society is either apolitical or insufficiently organized, and secular political parties have consistently been dismembered by successive military governments.

Strengthening civil society and building secular political parties as a countervailing force in Pakistan can contain the demands for Islamization made by the religious parties and radical Islamist groups. Whenever an elected political leader has rejected Islamists' demands, fears of a backlash have failed to materialize. Between 1972 and 1977, Zulfikar Ali Bhutto was able to successfully expand the role of women in the public arena despite Islamist opposition, and in 1997, Prime Minister Sharif faced only a limited reaction when he reversed the decision to observe Friday as a weekly religious holiday. Conversely, the Islamists have won their major policy victories thanks to regimes seeking their support to garner political legitimacy or to achieve strategic objectives.

Unlike the situation in Muslim countries such as Egypt and Turkey, the Pakistani state and particularly the military have encouraged political and radical Islam, which otherwise has a relatively narrow base of support. Democratic consensus on limiting or reversing Islamization would gradually roll back the Islamist influence in Pakistani public life. The Islamists would maintain their role as a minority pressure group representing a particular point of view, but they would stop wielding their current disproportionate influence over the country's overall direction.

The United States can help contain the Islamists' influence by demanding reform of Pakistan's governance. Washington should not condone the Pakistani military's support for Islamic militants, its use of the intelligence apparatus for controlling domestic politics, and its refusal to cede power to a constitutional democratic government. In its role as an aid donor, Washington has become one of Islamabad's most important benefactors. A large part of U.S. economic assistance since the September 11 attacks, however, has been used to pay down Pakistan's foreign debt. Because Washington has attached few conditions to U.S. aid, the spending patterns of Pakistan's government have not changed significantly. The country's military spending continues to increase, and spending for social services is well below the level required to improve living conditions for ordinary Pakistanis. Consequently, the United States should use its aid as a lever to influence Pakistan's domestic policies. Even though Musharraf's cooperation in hunting down Al Qaeda terrorists is a positive development, Washington must not ignore Pakistan's state sponsorship of Islamist militants, its pursuit of nuclear weapons and missiles at the expense of education and health care, and its refusal to democratize. Each of these issues is directly linked to the future of Islamic radicalism in Pakistan.

Notes

1. "Win-Win Situation for Pakistan, Says Musharraf," November 27, 2001, http://www.sindh.gov.pk/press_release/win_situation.htm (accessed October 6, 2004) (press release by the Government of Sindh).
2. As cited in Ayesha Jalal, *The State of Martial Rule* (Cambridge and New York: Cambridge University Press, 1990), p. 127.